Kristin Seidel

Assessment of Social and Auditory Intelligence
New Perspectives and Approaches

PABST SCIENCE PUBLISHERS
Lengerich, Berlin, Bremen, Miami,
Riga, Viernheim, Wien, Zagreb

Bibliografische Information der Deutschen Nationalbibliothek
Die Deutsche Nationalbibliothek verzeichnet diese Publikation in der Deutschen
Nationalbibliografie; detaillierte bibliografische Daten sind im Internet über
<http://dnb.ddb.de> abrufbar.

DR. KRISTIN SEIDEL
Abt. Luft- und Raumfahrtpsychologie, Deutsches Zentrum für Luft- und Raumfahrt
e.V., Sportallee 54 a, 22335 Hamburg, E-Mail: kristin.seidel@dlr.de

© 2008 Pabst Science Publishers, D-49525 Lengerich

Druck: KM Druck, D-64823 Groß-Umstadt
ISBN 978-3-89967-522-1

Acknowledgements

This book is a shortened and slightly revised version of my dissertation thesis. I am thankful for the help of many people who contributed to both the thesis and the resulting book at hand. I would like to express my gratitude to the Department of Aviation and Space Psychology (German Aerospace Center) for providing the financial support that allowed me to publish this book and for their general support. My friend and advisor Heinz-Martin Süß deserves special thanks for the excellent time I was allowed to spend with him working together and sharing thoughts and ideas. I would like to thank Susanne Weis for her collaboration, in particular for the help she provided in making my start easy in the project "Cognitive Facets of Social Intelligence" at the University of Magdeburg. I am grateful for the excellent work the students and interns Jenny Papenbrock, Janet Feigenspan, Ulrike Richter, Saskia Sage, Alexandra Brett, Kerstin Bremer, Anika Fischer, and Eva Wohner carried out, which contributed a great deal to the success of the research project. I am especially grateful for the help of Daniel Caywood-Barker, Lazar Stankov, Lee Sechrest, Fay McGinley, Michele Walsh, Barbara Brumbach, Kara Johnson and Kuang Chen who contributed a lot to this work in different ways: providing material, edits, scientific suggestions and literature, and helping to improve my English. It would fill pages to mention all the people who contributed to the recordings of the scenarios and to the development of the language-based social and auditory intelligence tasks. Therefore, I restrict myself to saying thanks to all the friends and acquaintances who spent an extraordinary amount of time to make the construction of the tests possible. I cannot express the gratitude I feel for my family: Dankwart and Krimhild Seidel, Marc-Björn and Verena Seidel, Raphael and Romina Seidel, Helmar and Ruth Seidel, for encouraging me, providing practical help and keeping me in prayer. Likewise, I would like to thank my close friends and people from the church all around the world for their support. I am blessed by my fiancé Ruben Conzelmann, who has made such a difference in my life. I thank him for his love and encouragement. Last but not least Jesus Christ deserves my gratitude for providing everything I needed while working on this book. His love and grace changed my life.

The fundamental work in order to make this book possible was carried out within the context of the DFG–project "Cognitive Facets of Social Intelligence" (grant SU 196/3-1) and supported by the German National Merit Foundation (Studienstiftung des Deutschen Volkes).

Table of Contents

List of Tables

List of Figures

List of Boxes

List of Abbreviations

a	Auditory
AcI	Academic Intelligence
ACT	American College Testing
AIT	Auditory Inspection Time ; AIT-P: pitch; AIT-L: loudness
AuI	Auditory Intelligence
AuIT	Auditory Intelligence Test
EQ-I	Emotional Quotient Inventory
BIBB	Bundesinstitut für Berufsbildung (German Institute of Job Education)
BIS	Berlin Intelligence Structure
BIS/BAS	Behavioral Inhibition System/Activation System and corresponding scales
CI	Confidence Interval
CARAT	Communication of Affect Receiving Ability Test
CFA	Confirmatory Factor Analysis
CFI	Comparative Fit Index
CHC	Cattell-Horn-Carroll
CTT	Classical Test Theory
CV	Construct Validity
CVC	Consonant-vowel-consonant
DANVA	Diagnostic Analysis of Nonverbal Accuracy
DAT	Differential Aptitude Test
EARS	Emotional Accuracy Research Scale
EFA	Exploratory Factor Analysis
EI	Emotional Intelligence
ETS	Educational Testing Service
f	Video-based (film)
F_0	Fundamental frequency
FACS	Facial Action Coding System
FEEST	Facial Expressions of Emotion–Stimuli and Tests
FPI	Freiburger Persönlichkeitsinventar (Freiburg Personality Inventory)
g	General Academic Intelligence
Ga	Auditory processing
gc/gf	Crystallized intelligence/fluid intelligence
GCA	General cognitive ability
Glr	Long-term retrieval
GMA	General mental ability

GPA	Grade point average
Gq	Quantitative knowledge
Grw	Reading and writing
Gs	Processing speed
Gt	Decision/reaction time/speed
Gv	Visual processing
GVEESS	Geneva Vocal Emotion Expression Stimulus Set
GWSIT	George Washington Social Intelligence Test
HES	Hogan Empathy Scale
I/O	Industrial/Organizational
ICI	Interpersonal Competence Inventory
IFI	Incremental Fit Index
IIP-C	Inventory of Interpersonal Problems-Circumplex
IPT	Interpersonal Perception Task
IQ	Intelligence Quotient
IRI	Interpersonal Reactivity Index
IRT	Item Response Theory
IT	Inspection Time (Information processing speed)
JACBART	Japanese and Caucasian Brief Affect Recognition Test
KR	Kuder Richardson
MAP	Musical Aptitude Profile
MEIS	Multifactor Emotional Intelligence Scale
MERT	Multimodal Emotion Recognition Test
MSCEIT	Mayer-Salovey-Caruso Emotional Intelligence Test
MTMM	Multi-Trait Multi-Method
NEO-FFI	NEO Five Factor Inventory
NNFI	Non-normed Fit Index
PCA	Principal components analysis
PDA/PDE	Perceived Decoding Ability scale/Perceived Encoding Ability scale
PI	Practical Intelligence
p	Pictorial
pk	Personality
PMA	Primary Mental Abilities
PMMA	Primary Measures of Musical Audiation
PONS	Profile of Nonverbal Sensitivity
Prob.	Probability value
QMEE	Questionnaire Measure of Emotional Empathy
RMSEA	Root Mean Square Error of Approximation

RT	Reaction time
S1/S2	Study 1/Study 2
SAT	Scholastic Aptitude Test
SCNF	Social Competence Nomination Form
SEIS	Schutte Emotional Inteligence Scale
SEM	Structural Equation Modeling
SI	Social Intelligence
SIM	Social Intelligence Test - Magdeburg
SM	Social memory
SOI	Structure-of-Intellect
SP	Social perception
SPUD	Speech under distraction
SRMR	Standardized Root Mean Square Residual
SSA	Similarity Structure Analysis
SSI	Social Skills Inventory
STAI	State-Trait Anxiety Inventory
STEM/STEU	Situational Test of Emotion Management/Emotion Understanding
STM	Short-term storage
SU	Social understanding
TBAC	Test of Basic Auditory Capabilities
T-data	Test data
TEMINT	Test of Emotional Intelligence
TIM	Test of Implied Meaning
TK	Tacit Knowledge
TKIM/TKML	Tacit Knowledge Inventory for Managers/ Military Leaders
ToM	Theory of Mind
VISION	Videobased Identification of Social Intelligence- Online
Vocal-I	Index of Vocal Emotion Recognition Test
w	Written
WAIS-R	Wechsler Adult Intelligence Scale-Revised
WJ-III	Woodcock–Johnson Test Battery III
WM	Working Memory Capacity

1 Introduction

1.1 Theoretical and Practical Relevance

Intellectual abilities have always fascinated people. Whole branches of industry deal with the question of which talents and gifts a person has and how they can be used effectively. Despite the variety of suggested ability constructs, research has concentrated on classical academic intelligence, namely reasoning, memory, speed and creativity measured visually with verbal, numerical and figural-spatial material. Although academic intelligence is an important predictor of educational and professional success, it is limited in predicting successful functioning in everyday life (Brody, 1992; Stankov, 1999). In order to cover the spectrum of human cognitive abilities more broadly, several authors began to integrate other intelligences and abilities in their models and tests (see Dulewicz & Higgs, 2000). Gardner (1983) added to classical academic intelligence by including musical-, kinesthetic-, and intra- and interpersonal intelligence. Guilford (1967) integrated social intelligence as well as auditory abilities in his Structure-of-Intellect Model (SOI model). Further approaches widening the intelligence construct include practical intelligence (Sternberg & Wagner, 1986); emotional intelligence (Goleman, 1995); success intelligence (Sternberg, 1997a, 2005); operative intelligence (Dörner, 1986); learning ability (Guthke, 1972); cultural intelligence (Early & Ang, 2003; Sternberg & Grigorenko, 2006); and, recently, sexual intelligence, psychosomatic intelligence, spiritual intelligence, network intelligence and intuitive intelligence (see e.g. Furnham, 2005). According to Weber and Westmeyer (2001), the many new intelligence constructs proposed in the last few years may make the construct of intelligence non-functional. The authors point to the important fact that in differential and diagnostic psychology there is a relative carelessness concerning the introduction of new constructs that lack empirical evidence. However, there is still no consensus about the conditions that have to be met in order to propose a valid construct. Construct validity (CV) concerns the extent to which a measure reflects accurately the variability among objects as they are arrayed along the underlying (latent) continuum to which the construct refers (Sechrest, 2005). Since an underlying variable cannot be directly observed, there are no hard and absolute criteria telling us that CV is established. Nevertheless, indications for construct validity do exist, for example when a potential audience believes that the construct has been defined in a satisfactory way, that the measure captures what is implied by the definition and that scores on the measure are related to broader phenomena implied by the idea of the construct (see Cronbach & Meehl, 1955; Sechrest, 2005). Many of the just mentioned attempts to widen the intelligence construct neither make use of the just specified and additional (see chapter 1.2) indications that indicate CV nor do they examine them and proved their fulfillment. However, there are theoretical as well as practical reasons not to extend the general criticism of the so-called "inflation of intelligences" to constructs like social and auditory intelligence. In this book I will use a framework to examine the CV of both constructs.

According to Cronbach and Meehl (1955), to be judged as valid, a construct has to demonstrate its place in the nomological net of related and empirically established constructs. In order to consider a domain of intelligence as truly separate from general intelligence there must be theoretical justification and empirical support. I will argue that social intelligence and auditory intelligence meet these criteria. Social intelligence (SI) can be understood via many sensory avenues, including auditory functions among others (e.g., vision). Auditory intelligence (AuI) can be understood as a sensory avenue that can be expressed via other intelligences, including social intelligence (e.g., also general intelligence). See Figure 1-1 for a visual conceptualization of social intelligence, auditory intelligence, and how they fit within the broader context of general intelligence.

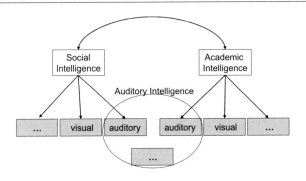

Figure 1-1: Conceptualization of Intelligence

In contrast to other new constructs (e.g., emotional intelligence), social intelligence has quite a long research tradition since it was first introduced by Dewey (1909, cited in Landy, 2006), not long after research in academic intelligence began. Recognition of the importance of social abilities has increased enormously during the last few years and they are now identified as among the most success-relevant characteristics in different jobs (e.g., Bundesinstitut für Berufsbildung, 1998; Frey & Balzer, 2003; Huffcutt, Conway, & Roth, 2001; Nigsch, 1999; Porath & Bateman, 2006; Rosenstiel, 2001; Schmidt, 2002; Schuler & Funke, 1995; Seyfried, 1995), as well as in private life (e.g. Kanning, 2002). Because of increasingly complex tasks and their higher demands, modern jobs often require more certifications, greater responsibilities and more teamwork skills in the context of globalisation. According to a study carried out by the German Institute of Job Education (Bundesinstitut für Berufsbildung, BIBB), social competences were rated as highly important in about three quarters of 4000 job offers (BIBB, 1998). Social competences are required in nearly every situation that concerns interactions with other people. Such situations include introducing new people to a group, educating children, and avoiding misconceptions during email reading or talking to people on the phone. Both basic and complex social abilities are important. Remembering what another person said in a conversation about a friend's problems is an example of a basic social ability. Asserting one's own position while respecting others' opinions is an example of a complex social ability. Both basic and complex social abilities require cognitive abilities. Such cognitive abilities include perception (e.g. perceiving a certain mood when meeting new people), memory (e.g. remembering the faces of school children in a class), understanding (e.g. understanding the feelings, thoughts and relationships of a certain person) and creativity (thinking about possible ways to resolve a socially difficult problem, e.g. an inheritance dispute). The diversity of social abilities and their applications indicates that social intelligence is likely to be a multidimensional construct consisting of dimensions such as perception, memory, understanding, and creativity. In addition, both vision and audition appear to be important for the expression and reception of social intelligence.

The most direct and obvious means of communication between people is spoken language. People impart social information not only through the content but also in the way things are said. The voice helps to reveal if someone is lying or telling the truth, if speakers feel sympathy or antipathy for each other, and if the implicit message corresponds to its content (e.g. Giles, Mulac, Bradac, & Johnson, 1987; Kramer, 1963; Shintel, Nusbaum, & Ok, 2006). Effective interpersonal relationships and social performance require that individuals accurately decode nonverbal expressions of emotions in other people. However, the ability to decode prosodic emotional cues in voices has not received much attention in literature when compared to the investigation of emotion recognition in faces (Baum & Nowicki, 1998; Scherer, 1986). Auditory communication has major importance for work settings like telephone counselling and other situations in which the interaction concentrates on the auditory channel and the person's emotional state has to be recognized (Wallbott, 2003). Auditory abilities play an important role in basic tasks (discrimination, memory and reasoning), for example, within conversations (especially on the phone) or while listening to the radio. The existence of a performance bottleneck, e.g., while driving an emergency vehicle or piloting a plane, places additional demands on the auditory channel (see Kallinen & Ravaja, 2004). Auditory abilities are also especially relevant for the acquisition of foreign languages. Better auditory discrimination and memory abilities should lead to a better pronunciation (minimization of accent), ensure a quicker and more accurate acquisition, and enable a person to adjust quickly in a foreign country (Albrecht, 2005; Bundesministerium für Bildung und Forschung, 2006). Besides their practical relevance, auditory abilities have a rather long research tradition, particularly within the domain of musical abilities (see Carroll, 1993). It is therefore surprising that existing ability and intelligence tests present stimulus material almost exclusively visually (Carroll, 1993; Horn & Stankov, 1982; Shuter-Dyson & Gabriel, 1981).

Despite their apparent importance, the question of whether social and auditory intelligence are useful constructs remains unanswered. Attempts to separate social intelligence from academic intelligence, especially from verbal academic intelligence, have been problematic and mainly unsuccessful (e.g. Brown & Anthony, 1990; Ford & Tisak, 1983; Hoepfner & O'Sullivan, 1986; Keating, 1978; Probst, 1975; Tenopyr, 1967; Thorndike & Stein, 1937; Walker & Foley, 1973). As early as 1958, Wechsler called into question whether social intelligence differs from "general intelligence applied to social situations" (p. 57). The domain of auditory intellectual abilities is even less developed than the domain of social intelligence. Clear definitions of auditory abilities and of how these can be separated from general intellectual abilities (e.g., verbal comprehension) are hard to find in the academic intelligence literature. Carroll (1993), who based his conceptions on studies implemented by Stankov and Horn (1980; Horn & Stankov, 1982), and research in music psychology (see chapter 2.5.4) are an exception.

For several reasons, reliable results and convincing evidence for both constructs are still missing. Social intelligence instruments were often developed without being based on a theoretical model, methods were often inappropriate (e.g. performance subconstructs were examined with questionnaires), tasks were oriented mainly towards classical academic intelligence tasks (see Asendorpf, 1996), and the social context of the situation was neglected. Instruments that attempt to cover the whole spectrum of the purportedly multidimensional SI construct are rare and outdated (e.g. Moss, Hunt, Omwake, & Woodward, 1955; O'Sullivan & Guilford, 1966, 1976). Using realistic material for test development was difficult because it was expensive and there was a lack of appropriate technique. But although today reasearchers do not have to deal with technique and quality problems any more, the very commendable studies assessing SI with Multi-Trait Multi-Method (MTMM) designs (e.g. Wong, Day, Maxwell, & Meara, 1995) still rely on the aforementioned test batteries. Auditory intelligence research has been sparse, and a broad and at the same time thorough measure of the construct does not exist. Test batteries are only available for limited domains, e.g. auditory perception (Surprenant & Watson, 2001; Watson, Johnson, Lehman, Kelly, & Jensen, 1982) or have not been fully developed and published (Horn & Stankov, 1982; Stankov & Horn, 1980). An exception is the Woodcock-

Johnson III battery (Woodcock, McGrew, & Mather, 2001), which also includes a plethora of auditory tests. What they actually measure and how they can be classified theoretically needs further research (see also chapter 2.5.2). Results obtained in musical psychology have rarely been integrated into academic auditory intelligence research (for exceptions see chapter 2.5). One of the primary factors limiting previous work on intelligence constructs was the expense and limitations of early computer software. The early software could not handle the extensive calculations and statistical models necessary to address complex causal models adequately.

Redressing these shortcomings in research on social and auditory intellectual abilities will be the next important step to advance the field of research on intelligence. These can be overcome with (1) a clear construct definition of social and auditory intelligence, (2) an underlying theoretical model, (3) a suitable design, (4) a representative selection and development of tasks, and (5) the use of modern techniques for media presentation. The current set of studies addresses all five areas.

1.2 Purpose of This Book

This book has three primary objectives. The first objective is to examine aspects of validity in auditory and social intelligence. The second objective is to contribute to the clarification of the position of auditory and social intelligence within the nomological network of human intellectual abilities. With the third objective, the relationship between social auditory and general auditory intellectual abilities should be clarified.

According to Süß (1996, 2001), several conditions must be met in order to argue for an ability construct. These conditions are:

1) an empirical foundation with test data (T-data; Cattell, 1957),
2) the construct should be measured by performance-based tasks,
3) the ability should require only basic knowledge,
4) the ability should have a high degree of generality (that is, can be operationalized across different tasks),
5) the construct should demonstrate construct validity that is evident through partial autonomy in the nomological network of established models and constructs,
6) the construct should be stable across time, and, finally,
7) the construct should show evidence of incremental criterion validity when compared to established constructs.

In this book, this framework will be used to investigate whether social and auditory intelligence are coherent and useful constructs (see 5). In order to examine the validity of measures of both constructs, an empirical foundation is laid using test data (see 1). Performance-based tests (see 2) are developed requiring only basic knowledge (see 3). The measures include different types of tasks and assess different groups of people (see 4). The domains of the purportedly multidimensional SI construct should emerge regardless of the kind of material (e.g. auditory or visual) used in a test. Similarly, following the facets of academic intelligence, auditory abilities are hypothesized to split into discriminative, memory and reasoning abilities and make up at least two content domains: a tonal (nonverbal) domain and a speech (verbal) domain. Subsequent steps examine the separability of social intelligence and auditory intelligence from academic intelligence. Shortcomings of past investigations (lack of theory-based studies, unsystematic method application, ignoring social context) are addressed. The final steps include combining the social and auditory constructs and examining the overlap and distinctiveness of social auditory intelligence and general auditory intelligence, controlling for the variance of academic Intelligence. It is important to mention that construct validation depends on the measure we use as an indicator for the construct and on the conditions of the use of the measure (see Sechrest, 2005; Süß, 2006). Therefore, instruments have to be developed carefully and the investigations should be planned and implemented with as little disturbing influences as possible. Conditions 6) and 7) are not addressed in this book but should be examined in subsequent studies.

This book was carried out within the broader context of the goals and aims of a collaborative research group. Conceptual development and implementation of tests of social intelligence were carried out by Susanne Weis, Heinz-Martin Süß and me. The auditory intelligence work was carried out together with Jenny Papenbrock and Heinz-Martin Süß. Therefore, I use the first person plural to present our common views and ideas.

1.3   About Terms and Concepts

Literature on intelligence research differentiates among terms and concepts related to intelligence, ability, aptitude, or skill, and these terms are often used interchangeably. Spearman (1927) states: "In truth, intelligence has become a mere vocal sound, a word with so many meanings that finally has none" (p. 14). This overall confusion highlights the importance of bringing order into the chaos of terms and concepts within intelligence research. However, it is not within the scope of this work to address the totality of definition problems in intelligence research. Therefore, I pick up the thread of Snow who did a great deal of work in defining "aptitude" and related terms, and beginning with his definitions, describe how I will use terms within the context of this book.

Snow (1996) regards intelligence as an organization of aptitudes for learning and problem solving. Intelligence is required in situations with novel or complex information that is also meaningful information, particularly when the information available in a situation is partial or incomplete. Cognitive abilities, in his view, are more specialized than intelligence. Intelligence and abilities are subsets of the category labeled "aptitudes." The original meaning of aptitude was aptness, appropriateness, and suitability for performance in a (learning) situation. Snow (1986) relates aptitude to any measurable person characteristic that is needed as preparation for future achievement. In his view, aptitude is not limited to intelligence but includes personality and motivational differences, styles, attitudes, and beliefs. Though stable, aptitude can be modified by education and learning.

There has been an aversive reaction within the academic community toward the term "intelligence" in the last few years (see Schmidt, 2002). Predetermined abilities are not very popular in a world in which self-actualisation, self-control, and self-influence gain increasing importance. Therefore, the idea that an intelligence may determine success in training, profession, and life in general is not welcome. In the United States, and with industrial/organizational (I/O) psychologists in general, it is more acceptable to speak of cognitive abilities, general cognitive ability (GCA) or general mental ability (GMA) rather than using the term "intelligence" (Schmidt, 2002). With this controversy comes the even more controversial view that there are group differences in intelligence (see VanRooy & Viswesvaran, 2004). Jensen (2000) describes the possibility of introducing group norms. However, group norms predominating over individual rights does not solve the problem and would not necessarily diminish the adverse impact of psychological intelligence testing. A change of wording (e.g., intelligence versus cognitive ability) does not change the problem, which was also recognized by Horn (2006) writing about Spearman who changed the label of the term "intelligence" to "g" to avoid the problematic connotations. However, the g-labeling did not free Spearman from the definitional and conceptual difficulties associated with "general intelligence". Is there one (academic) intelligence or should the concept of intelligence be extended beyond the scope of academic intelligence? Is intelligence mainly predetermined or do we consider intelligence open to modifications? As soon as we take a clear perspective on our view of that what we mean by "intelligence", it does not really matter whether we call it general mental ability or academic intelligence. In this book, I will use the term "intelligence" as specified below.

Another distinction concerns the differentiation between the terms "competence" and intelligence. The following conceptual distinctions are mainly based on a detailed literature review (Süß, Weis, & Seidel, 2005). We regard "competence" as the potential to show the required behavior in a specified situation. Competence is seen as domain- and situation-specific and can be modified through learning processes. The term "competence" can cover a spectrum of features varying in broadness, subsuming only one variable (e.g. conflict management) or several interacting variables in highly specific social situations (dealing with a low-self-esteem leader whose company merges with another one and who is involved in a family conflict) (see Süß et al., 2005). On the contrary, intelligence can be seen as a precondition to acquire competences and describes cognitive abilities that can be used to deal with very different tasks and problems (Carroll, 1993). Compared to competence, we see intelligence as more stable and genetically determined to a higher degree (see Süß et al., 2005).

Similarly, the terms "skills" and "abilities" often are not used systematically and sometimes are even used as synonyms. As outlined above, abilities are less open to modifications and learning processes and comparatively more predetermined. Skills concern the concrete practice of complex behavior sequences and the acquisition of cognitive operations for concrete problems. Cognitive and behavioral skills are situation specific and are almost entirely automatic. Skills are acquired in several steps. Within this process they are automated successively, requiring high cognitive resources and being associated with more faults and less speed in the first cognitive stage and growing quicker and less faulty in the course of proceduralization (Ackerman, 1987).

For the purposes of this book, I take the position that intelligence has its genetic predispositions, is rather stable, and is restricted to the cognitive domain. This position corresponds to the results we observed in the literature review (see e.g., Ackerman, 1987; Carroll, 1993; Greif, 1987; Schneider, Roberts & Heggestad, 2002). In addition to genetic influences on intelligence, there are proxies for environmental enrichment influencing its expression (e.g., parents' education and family background). I conceptualize intelligence as narrower than the concept of aptitudes because aptitudes include noncognitive abilities like attitudes and motivation. Second, I consider intelligence to be different from the concept of (general) abilities that may also include arts, sports, music, teaching, and leadership. Abilities can be specific and tailored whereas intelligence is a more basic and general concept. However, intelligence in my view can subsume several explicitly *cognitive* abilities also treated as intelligence subconstructs. Many more specific cognitive abilities (or intelligence subconstructs) -but fewer broad and general intelligences- seem to exist. See Figure 1-2 for the relationship between aptitude, intelligence and cognitive abilities.

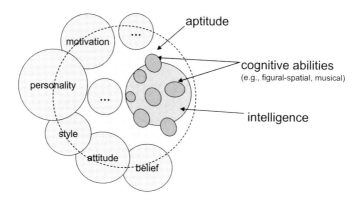

Figure 1-2: Relationship between Aptitude, Intelligence and Cognitive Abilities

The third major position I take is that social and auditory intelligence are located at the most fundamental level of understanding. These intelligences can be seen as preconditions for developing more specific social and auditory competences that are open for modifications. In addition, I regard social and auditory intelligences as generalizable across different situations that require cognitive effort and, therefore, these intelligences have to be distinguished from cognitive and behavioral skills. In spite of these rather clear distinctions, it is obvious that transitions are imprecise and sometimes it will be not as easy to differentiate amongst intelligence, abilities etc.

Some notes are necessary regarding the position I take on incremental validity in the context of condition for valid constructs (see chapter 1.2). In comparison to the already mentioned problems we have in establishing construct validity, there is not a single criterion validity. The data produced by a specified academic intelligence test that was applied to a certain group of subjects may predict success in academic studies but does not have to be related to dealing with patients in a hospital. A measure that is taken to predict "success," the definition of which is also important, in a specified proficiency should always be related to the demands that are placed on that proficiency. In other words, the predictor and the criterion must be symmetrical (see Wittmann, 1988). I acknowledge the empirical results that although leaving a large portion of 75% variance unexplained, found academic intelligence to be unmatched in predicting training and proficiency success (see e.g. Schmidt & Hunter, 1998; Schmidt, Ones & Hunter, 1992; Jensen, 1986; Olea & Ree, 1994; Van Rooy, Dilchert, Viswesvaran & Ones, 2006). However, there may be further predictors that will be even more successful in predicting other (or more specific) criteria (e.g. a social intelligence test predicting social behavior in dealing with patients) with different methods (e.g. different from supervisory ratings that have been widely applied, see Schmidt, 2002). Therefore, additional instruments introduced in this book should not be regarded as in competition with academic intelligence tests and their already well-established results but rather as complementary in providing possibilities to cover an intelligence domain in order to make predictions for criteria that differ from those summarized and analyzed by the just mentioned authors. In the same way, I regard social and auditory intelligence as complementary, not competitive, constructs to academic intelligence. However, both constructs have to show incremental validity against academic intelligence in predicting adequate symmetric criteria. Social and auditory intelligence will be defined in further detail in chapter 2.2 and 2.5.

2 Theoretical Background

This chapter starts with a short insight into the already established academic intelligence construct. It continues with a literature review including the theoretical conceptions, the empirical findings, and the relationships to other constructs for both social intelligence and auditory intelligence, and their combination (social/emotional auditory abilities). I present my own perspective at the end of each section. The chapter concludes with objectives for the development of measures for social intelligence and auditory intelligence I derive from the conclusions of past research.

2.1 Academic Intelligence

Intelligence has long been defined in several ways. The following definitions reflect the variability: mentally effective coping with changing environments (Anastasi, 1986); dealing with actual situations (Binet & Simon, 1905, cited in Amelang, 1996); mental self-government (Sternberg, 1986); an ensemble of abilities that is common to successful people in one culture (Wechsler, 1964); compound ability to act wisely, to think sensible and to deal effectively with the environment (Hofstätter, 1957); adaption to new tasks (Stern, 1911) or situations (Rohracher, 1965); and thinking in an abstract or concrete way within language, numerical, or figural-spatial relations (Groffmann, 1964). Differences in the definitions of intelligence are based on models or theories that differ according to the number of dimensions/factors they distinguish and according to the levels of hierarchy they include in their models. Carroll (1993) remarks that "the long-discussed problem of defining intelligence is transformed into one of defining the various factorial constructs that underlie it and specifying their structure," (p. 627).

2.1.1 Overview of Intelligence Approaches

There are several possibilities for classifying conceptualizations of intelligence into different kinds of approaches (e.g., Amelang, 1996; Davidson & Downing, 2000; Kail & Pellegrino, 1988). I chose the classification of Davidson and Downing (2000), who distinguish between four different approaches, namely biological, psychometric, contextual, and complex system approaches. The biological approach is based on the neural efficiency hypothesis and assumes that intelligent people have brains that operate more quickly and accurately than those of people who are less intelligent (e.g. Hendrickson, 1982; Deary & Stough, 1996; Haier, Siegel, Nuechterlein, Hazlet, Wu, Paek, Browning & Buchsbaum, 1988; Reed &

Jensen, 1991). Representatives of this approach use evoked potentials, inspection time tasks, cerebral glucose metabolic rates and nerve conduction velocity in their work. This view is also known under the label "mental speed hypothesis" (e.g., Vernon, 1983; Kail & Salthouse, 1994; Neubauer & Bucik, 1996). In contextual approaches, it is assumed that the meanings and instantiations of intelligence are culture and context dependent (e.g. Berry & Irvine, 1986; Berry, Irvine & Hunt, 1987; Ceci & Roazzi, 1994; Das, 1994). Representatives argue that intelligent behavior in one culture is sometimes rather idiotic in another culture and that different conclusions about the nature of intelligence are drawn depending on the context intelligence is assessed in. According to psychometric approaches, the structure of intelligence can be discovered by analyzing the interrelationship of ability test scores (e.g. Carroll, 1993; Cattell, 1943; Spearman, 1927; Thurstone, 1938). This approach makes use of statistical techniques (e.g. factor analysis) applied to data from a large number of people. Complex system approaches assume intelligence to be dynamic and changeable depending on the predominant conditions (Sternberg, 1985, 1997b; Gardner, 1983, 1998; Ceci, 1996). These approaches combine the biological, psychometric and contextual approaches and lead to a broader view that is more successful in reflecting the complexity of intelligence and enlarging it beyond a static and narrow conception (Davidson & Downing, 2000). As an example, Gardner (1983) extends the conception of conventional academic intelligence and includes musical, bodily-kinesthetic, intra- and interpersonal and naturalist intelligence in his model (see also chapter 2.2.2 and 2.5.2). Gardner also attaches great importance to the context in which intelligence is measured. It can be viewed as positive that he includes tasks that are performed in real-world settings and avoids paper-pencil measures; however, Gardner's work is not confirmed through empirical findings. Empirical foundation is a general problem with contemporary approaches since it is not yet clear how they can be validated completely. Until now, only parts have been tested empirically.

This book is based on the empirically testable psychometric approach of intelligence research. However, it extends the psychometric approach in the direction of contemporary models in assuming intelligence components (e.g. social intelligence and auditory abilities) that are only minimally addressed in well-established models of intelligence. An important aim of this book is to include the context in the measurement and to use new media instead of relying only on paper-pencil measures. In the present work, intelligence is seen as a composite of different component abilities, and is regarded as a complex, latent (hypothetical) and open construct that can be differentiated and enlarged.

2.1.2   Intelligence Theories in the Psychometric Tradition

Sternberg and Powell (1982) describe the development of psychometric intelligence theories in an evolutionary model. They suggest that theories of intelligence undergo an evolutionary process that leads to a deeper level of construct understanding. Three stages represent successive degrees of complexity. These stages are (1) monistic vs. pluralistic theories, (2) hierarchical vs. non-hierarchical theories, and (3) integrative theories. The first stage differentiates monistic theories of intelligence from pluralistic theories. In monistic theories (i.e., Spearman, 1914), a single instantiation of the given unit of analysis dominated thinking about intelligence. Spearman (1914) assumes a general factor (g) that permeates performance in all varieties of tests. In pluralistic theories, many independent instantiations of a given unit influence thinking about intelligence. As an example, Thomson (1939) sees general intelligence as a composition of many independent structural bonds including reflexes, habits and learned associations.

The second stage differentiates between hierarchical and non-hierarchical theories. In hierarchical theories, instantiations of successively lower orders are nested within instantiations of successively higher orders. For example, Cattell divides a superordinate "g-factor" into two higher order factors, crystallized and fluid ability, which in turn subsume several lower order factors. Carroll's (1993) Three-Stratum model is another example of a hierarchical second stage model (see below and chapter 2.5). Thurstone's (1938) theory of primary mental abilities (PMA) can be classified into the category of nonhierarchical theories. Thurstone regards intelligence as the sum of relatively independent constructs (PMA) extracted by means of factor analysis. He could find and justify seven abilities. Perceptual speed, word fluency, and memory are seen as rather specific abilities whereas verbal, spacial, numeric and reasoning ability are regarded as more general abilities.

In the third stage, the competing views of hierarchical and non-hierarchical theories (stage 2) are merged. Representative of this stage is Guttman's Radex theory (1954, 1958). In addition, Guilford's Structure of Intellect model (1967, see section 2.1.4) can be classified within this stage. A radia extension of complexity unites two distinct notions in a single theory, namely different kinds of tests and degrees. Guttman's radex is the basis for the so-called facet theories. Integrative models that combine facet theoretical and hierarchical approaches into a superordinate theory can be regarded as an advancement of the third stage (e.g. Jäger's Berlin Intelligence Structure model, BIS, 1982, 1984, see section 2.1.5). This work is based on an integrative theory and makes use of both facet and hierarchical models. Therefore, representative hierarchical and facet models and their backgrounds will be described in the following sections.

2.1.3 Hierarchical Models of Intelligence

About Hierarchical Models

Most current psychometric models propose a hierarchical structure of intelligence since empirical results have not yielded verification for non-hierarchical models (e.g. Thurstone), monistic models (Spearman), or pluralistic (Thomson) models (Davidson & Downing, 2000). Hierarchical models place one or more factors at the top and delegate specific factors to lower hierarchical levels. Higher level (second order) factors are expected to explain the correlations of lower level (first order) factors. The higher a factor is in the hierarchy, the farther it is removed from people's actual performance on psychometric tests (Davidson & Downing, 2000).

Advantages of Hierarchical Models

Hierarchical theories comprehensively depict general as well as more specialized abilities and their interrelationships, and this research has empirical support (see Carroll, 1993; Davidson & Downing, 2000; Sternberg & Powell, 1982). In addition to having stimulated extensive research, hierarchical approaches have, in contrast to other types of models (contemporary and context models, some types of radex models, see Ackerman, 1989 and this chapter), the advantage of being empirically testable. However, the nature of the factors extracted or found in a given study is influenced by the intelligence tests that are applied and by the choice of factor analytic techniques used. This is especially true with regard to a general academic intelligence factor (g), which often lacks comparability across studies.

Applications of Hierarchical Models

The two most widely acknowledged hierarchical models are the Three-stratum theory (Carroll, 1993) and the Theory of crystallized (gc) and fluid (gf) intelligence (e.g. Horn & Cattell, 1966). With respect to the latter, gf is defined as innate reasoning ability using culture reduced material, gc as knowledge due to formal education and acculturation. In the view of Cattell (1971) gf is the precondition to acquire gc, which is also described as invested intelligence. Indicators of gf were mainly figural tasks (considered as culture-independent measures). Gc was assessed with numerical and verbal tasks (culture-dependent measures). On a second hierarchical level, the broad cognitive factors of perception (auditory and visual), memory (short- and long-term), speed, and knowledge were added in an extension of the theory (see e.g. Horn, 1994; Horn & Noll, 1997). The latest empirical findings do not support the gf-gc model but instead argue for three factors: perceptual, verbal, and image rotation (see Johnson & Bouchard, 2005).

The Three-Stratum theory of Intelligence (Carroll, 1993) is based on the reanalysis of more than 460 available datasets reported in the psychometric literature applying statistical procedures thoroughly and consistently. Carroll (1993) distinguishes three levels that differ in generality, or stratums (The model is illustrated in the context of auditory intelligence, see Figure 2-9). On the top, the third stratum, Carroll describes a general intelligence factor "g" that underlies all aspects of intellectual abilities. The second stratum is comprised of eight subconstructs, namely (1) fluid and (2) crystallized intelligence, (3) general memory and learning, (4) broad visual perception, (5) broad auditory perception, (6) broad retrieval ability, (7) broad cognitive speediness and (8) processing speed. These subconstructs are listed in descending order according to the degree to which they are influenced by the third stratum g-factor. On the first stratum, altogether 68 primary order factors are further specifications of the secondary order factors on the second stratum and are dominated by the respective second order factor. They represent specialized skills reflecting the acquisition of particular strategies or specific types of knowledge. According to Carroll, the three strata are open for extensions, for example concerning additional (intermediate) strata. The Three-Stratum model is supported by the research of Bickley, Keith, and Wolfe (1995) who performed a hierarchical confirmatory factor analysis on tests scores obtained in a study with more than 6000 participants. Although the Three-Stratum structure was supported, a competitive model with an additional intermediate stratum between the third and the second stratum provided an even better fit. Factors on the intermediate level were interpreted as gf and gc.

The Three-Stratum theory (Carroll, 1993) and the theory of gf and gc (Horn & Cattell, 1966) were recently integrated into a common Cattell-Horn-Carroll (CHC) theory (see McGrew & Evans, 2004). CHC theory maintains Carroll's Three-Stratum structure with a g-factor at the top (stratum III), broad cognitive abilities (stratum II), and narrow cognitive abilities (stratum I). The broad cognitive abilities include nine second order factors very similar to the Carroll factors: fluid intelligence (Gf) and crystallized intelligence (Gc), visual processing (Gv), auditory processing (Ga), long-term retrieval (Glr), processing speed (Gs), decision/reaction time/speed (Gt), reading and writing (Grw), and quantitative knowledge (Gq). The nine factors subsume about 70 narrow cognitive abilities. They are seen as positively intercorrelated but independent through structural evidence (best-weighted linear combination of any set of the eight factors does not account for the reliable covariance among the elements of the ninth factor). However, Horn and Carroll do not agree with regard to a general "g-factor". According to Horn (2006), most of the empirical analyses do not support "g-theory" (p. 43). Different curves of development with age confirm this assumption, since gc and Glr increase with age whereas Gf, short-term storage (STM), and Gt decline with age. The CHC theory underlies the Woodcock–Johnson test battery III (WJ-III) as one of the best known tests in the USA, and influenced others, for example the revised Binet-Simon tests and the WAIS-III. In empirical analyses (see Lohman, 2003; McGrew & Murphy, 1995; Woodcock, 1998), selected factors could be confirmed. Instead of studies reporting support of the whole CHC factor structure with one test, confirmatory factor analysis revealed four higher order factors (Woodcock, 1998): STM, stores of knowledge, thinking abilities and automatic processing speed. Thinking abilities are regarded as the core "classical intelligence" applied in novel and difficult tasks and requiring reasoning. I will refer to this theory again in the context of auditory intellectual abilities (see chapter 2.5.2).

2.1.4 Facet Models of Intelligence

About Facet Theory

According to Guttman (cited by Gratch, 1973; see also Borg, 1976), facet theory is a "hypothesis of a correspondence between a definitorial system for a universe of observations and an aspect for the empirical structure of those observations together with a rationale for such a hypothesis." Facet theory can be regarded as a general research methodology in the social sciences containing instructions for the implementation of studies and a composition of principles often called "metatheory" (Canter, 1985; Holz-Ebeling, 1991). Facet theory assumes that human behavior is a function of situations and person characteristics. The major aim of facet theory is to define the relevant facets that describe a specified research domain completely and economically for a certain field of research. A facet can be described as a set (C) involved in a Cartesian product of a finite number of sets (A and B). C contains the combined elements of A and B (Guttman, 1954, 1958). The combination of different types of facets and their elements are the foundation of a facet design. The design is specified through a "mapping sentence," which links facets of a definitional domain "person" and "stimulus" with a complex variable range "reaction" (or result). Qualitative and quantitative categories are distinct and supplement each other in addition to characterizing the facet in further detail. The use of general already existing and commonly accepted ranges is preferred rather than creating new mapping sentences for every kind of study. According to Guttman (1965), among the most important facets are the communication modes. Guttman distinguishes between the five senses sight, sound, touch, smell and taste. Each mode of communication may define a different kind of intelligence. After the specification of a facet into its main characteristics, it should be possible to describe every observation in terms of the basic characteristics. Within such a system, prognostic statements regarding the empirical similarities between the observations are possible (Holz-Ebeling, 1991). With the formalization of the assumptions of a facet design, it is also specified under which conditions it is valid. Any theory could benefit from being enunciated in facet-theoretical terms and tested using the facet approach to data analysis (Canter, 1985).

Advantages of Facet Models

A plethora of advantages and corresponding methodological applications exist concerning the application of facet models. To begin with, facet models allow a systematic description of a field of research that make a transfer into an empirical operationalization easier (Holz-Ebeling, 1991). Facet theory leads to multifactorial measurement designs that have an important impact on the content and construct validity of a measure. With regard to content validity, at the stage of test development, facet theory allows the theoretical understanding of the construct serving as a basis for the item development. A rational for item construction ensures the representativeness and completeness of the item universe for the construct to be measured. If test items correspond to the facets, positive correlations between test items are expected, whereas, if there is no correspondence, there should be no positive manifold. Items that share more similarities concerning their conceptual definitions should be more similar empirically (principle of contiguity) (Brown, 1985). The combination of scores according to the facets leads to a relatively large number of ability measures with a relatively low number of scores and therefore provides efficient tools for psychological assessment (Süß & Beauducel, 2005). Concerning construct validity, the application of facet theory helps to guarantee internal and external validity of the construct. Tests that share two facets require the same cognitive operation and apply the same content. In addition, they are assumed to correlate higher than tests sharing only one facet (e.g. same content but different cognitive operation). The lowest correlation is expected between tests having no facets in common. As a very general approach, facet theory can be related to construct validation (e.g. Ridgway, 1980) similar to the Multi-Trait Multi-Method approach (MTMM, see Campbell & Fiske, 1959). The MTMM approach describes a validational process that makes use of a matrix presenting all of the intercorrelations resulting when each of several traits is measured by each of several methods. Measures of the same trait should correlate higher with each other than they do with measures of different traits involving separate methods. Moreover, these validity values should be higher than the correlations among different traits measured by the same method. However, these criteria are seldom met. The MTMM approach can be regarded as a special form of a facet approach in which the contiguities of the construct facet should be more pronounced than the contiguities of the other facets (methods).

Facet theory is very flexible, can cope with virtually any content area, and has been applied successfully in a wide context of ability research: in working memory capacity, (Oberauer, Süß, Schulze, Wilhelm, & Wittmann, 2000; Oberauer, Süß, Wilhelm, & Wittmann, 2003; Süß, Oberauer, Wittmann, Wilhelm, & Schulze, 2002), in intelligence (Beauducel, Brocke, & Liepmann, 2001; Guttman & Levy, 1991; Snow, Kyllonen, & Marshalek, 1984), and in a facet approach that integrates working memory, intelligence and knowledge (Kyllonen, 1994). Two applications of facet theory in the domain of intelligence research that are theoretically relevant in the context of this book are described in the following section.

Applications in Academic Intelligence

a) Radex Model (Guttman, 1958)

Guttman (1958) developed hypotheses regarding the correlations between tests according to their common characteristics. He first introduced the "level of complexity" as a facet of tests. This facet is regarded as a continuum: the more components a test includes, the more complex it is. More complex tests, therefore, include the components of simpler tests plus additional components. The more components tests have in common, the higher their correlation should be. The order of correlations is called a simplex. In similarity structure analysis (SSA), correlations are represented as distances between points. Points that are close together indicate high correlations, points that are far from one another indicate low correlations. Tests of similar complexity though should form a circular array, a circumplex, in SSA. Tests of the same content but different in complexity should be located on a straight line array in SSA (simplex). The combination of simplex and circumplex forms a radex –a disc or sphere in two- or three-dimensional SSA– divided into verbal, numerical and figural content areas. In contrast to Guttman, who expected complex tasks to be located at the periphery of the radex, empirical analysis showed that complex tests were located at the center of the radex (Marshalek, Lohman, & Snow, 1983; Schlesinger & Guttman, 1969; Snow et al., 1984). Marshalek et al. (1983) assumed that the shorter the average distance of a test from all other tests in the universe, the closer a test would be located to the center of the radex. Tests measuring rather general abilities thus would be located in the center whereas tests that represent more specific abilities would be more peripheral (see Figure 2-1). As SSA differs from traditional factor analysis, an evaluation of the radex model is rather difficult. Results obtained with SSA could not be compared with structural models of intelligence based on factor analysis. Consequently, the model and its empirical results received only minor criticism but were also not sufficiently integrated in the process of theorizing in intelligence. Adler and Guttman (1982) replicated Guttman's radex structure of intelligence tests, having 200 school children work on 13 intelligence tests that were defined within a framework containing four facets: rule type (inference, application, practice), modalities of expression (verbal, figural, numerical), language of communication (paper-pencil; manual), and dimensionality of object portrayed (two, three). SSA revealed the hypothesized facets.

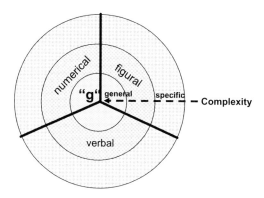

Figure 2-1: Radex Model of Intelligence (Marshalek et al.,1983)

Note. The level of generality is indicated by the resolution of the pattern. High resolution indicates a high level of generality; low resolution indicates a low level of generality.

b) The Structure-of-Intellect Model (Guilford, 1967)

Guilford (1967) postulated an information-processing model that should describe and sort but also explain intellectual functioning. Guilford cross-classified mental abilities into three facets: Operations (mental processes), content (kind of information) and products (form of information). In terms of the information-processing approach, the contents represent stimuli, the operations represent processes and the products represent responses (Süß & Beauducel, 2005). The three facets were arranged in a cube representing the Cartesian product of all elements of all facets, the Structure of Intellect model (SOI model). The operation facet contains the following elements: evaluation, convergent production, divergent production, memory and cognition. The content facet consists of the five elements: visual, auditory, symbolic, semantic and behavioral. The products contain the elements, namely units, classes, relations, systems, transformations and implications. Each of the postulated 150 basic abilities (5 contents x 5 operations x 6 products) is identified by its unique conjunction of one element of each of the three facets. In 1988, Guilford added another 30 abilities to his model when he decided to split up the memory operation into memory recording (immediate recall) and memory retention (recall after a period of time). However, the statistical procedures Guilford used were rather problematic (inadequate factor rotation, no availability of fit indices, use of random hypotheses), hence the empirical status of the model is not clear. Guilford did not expect a general intelligence factor but several second and third order factors emerging according to the facet elements the tests have in common. Even though Guilford claimed to have identified more than half of the 85 second-order abilities, empirical investigation indicated that the identification of the higher order factors, especially the product factors, was problematic. Nevertheless, the SOI model provides a large map of potential factors and stimulated the identification of new factors (e.g. social intelligence, see chapter 2.2) and the development of new tests (Süß & Beauducel, 2005).

2.1.5 Integrative Models of Intelligence

One of the most important integrative theories, especially in the domain of German language, is the Berlin model of Intelligence Structure (BIS; Jäger, 1982). The BIS model combines a facet structure with a hierarchical component and adopts the advantages of both types of models. The purpose of the BIS development was to explain the differences between most of the competing models (Jäger, 1967). Jäger ascribed the differences between these models to different tasks (generality), different subjects (universality), and different techniques of data analysis (Pfister & Beauducel, 1993). Therefore, in a first empirical-inductive stage, Jäger used about 2000 intelligence tasks he found up to the year 1973 in the literature in order to develop his integrative model. 191 tasks that contained marking variables for principal components of competitive structure models of intelligence were selected according to the maintenance of diversity and were then administered to an age homogeneous (16-21 years) German-speaking sample of 545 high school students in Berlin. Data were analyzed and interpreted by means of factor and cluster analysis. Stability was tested with a retest study after four years with 347 of the previously tested high school students. Exploratory factor analysis revealed four unambiguous operational factors: processing capacity (equivalent to reasoning), processing speed, memory, and creativity. Jäger (1984, p. 30) defines the operations as presented in Box 2-1.

Box 2-1: Operations of Academic Intelligence According to the BIS (Jäger, 1984)

PROCESSING SPEED (S)
Processing speed refers to the ability to perform simple tasks quickly and accurately.

MEMORY (M)
Memory refers to the ability to recognize and recall lists and configurations of items a few minutes after learning them.

CREATIVITY (C)
Creativity refers to the ability to produce fluently many different ideas.

PROCESSING CAPACITY (= REASONING, R)
Processing capacity corresponds to reasoning factors in other models. It refers to the ability to process complex information including inductive and deductive reasoning, construction, judging and planning.

Jäger and colleagues predicted that there would be seven primary order factors. However, when they ran the initial model, they did not find the typical content factors -verbal, numerical and spatial-figural- as originally predicted. Jäger and his colleagues assumed that they were hidden by the operation factors because the highly educated sample could have overlearnt the use of words and numbers. In a second quasi-experimental stage, Jäger and his colleagues used a special aggregation technique (Jäger, 1982, 1984). Following a suggestion of Humphreys (1962), tests heterogeneous with respect to operations but homogeneous concerning their content were aggregated to so-called parcels. Verbal, numerical and figural parcels were formed. Only those 48 tasks that were pure with regard to their content were used for further analysis. Four tasks were available for each of the 12 cells (4 operations x 3 contents) and consequently four parcels could be formed for each content domain. The facet model was replicated very clearly. The hypothesis that the content variance was masked by the operation variance could be confirmed. Jäger (1984, p. 31) defines the content domains as follows (see Box 2-2).

Box 2-2: Contents of Academic Intelligence According to the BIS (Jäger, 1984)

VERBAL (V): Ability to deal with language.

NUMERICAL (N): Ability to deal with numbers.

SPATIAL-FIGURAL (F): Ability to deal with figures and space.

Parceling technique was also applied in order to reveal a general intelligence factor (academic intelligence, AcI). Parcels heterogeneous with regard to their content as well as their operation were formed and analyzed. AcI was identified which explains the correlations between content and operation factors. One should note that empirical investigations have shown that parceling did not produce a result where there is no empirical basis in the correlation matrix (Jäger & Tesch-Römer, 1988; Süß & Beauducel, 2005) and therefore the data was not conducive to manipulation. Figure 2-2 represents the structure of the BIS model.

To summarize, the BIS has a hierachical structure with a general intelligence factor on the top. It can also be described as a facet model with seven principal components at the same level arranged in two facets, contents and operations. The twelve cells should be regarded as multifactorial conditioned performances rather than as primary ability factors as in Guilfords SOI model. The facets and classes of the BIS model do not have to be independent from one another (Jäger, 1982, 1984). Until now, only two facets have been specified but the model is open to the integration of new facets (Jäger, Süß, & Beauducel,

1997). The completion of the model can concern additional operations and contents, facets and performances. The BIS has been replicated several times and with different methods (e.g. Beauducel & Kersting, 2002; Bucik & Neubauer, 1996; Jäger et al., 1997; Jäger & Tesch-Römer, 1988; Süß et al., 2002).

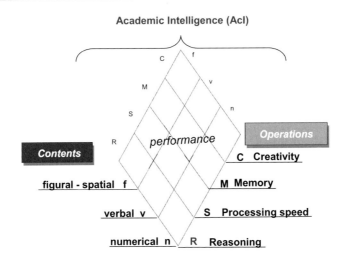

Figure 2-2: Berlin Model of Intelligence Structure (Jäger, 1984)
Note. The model is adapted according to Jäger (1984, p. 26)

2.1.6 Conclusions from Academic Intelligence Research

Integrative models combining the advantages of both hierarchical and facet models are expected to be empirically most valid. They provide an approach that can be empirically validated. Therefore, the BIS model is chosen within this book as a foundation and reference model in order to contrast academic, social and auditory intelligence. The BIS model has been validated extensively and is well-established in theoretical context and practical application. However, neither social nor auditory intellectual abilities, which are included in some widely accepted intelligence models (e.g. Carroll, 1993, broad auditory perception; Guilford, 1967, social intelligence), are taken into account within the BIS model. Attempts (see Jäger et al., 1997) to add a social content domain were never implemented. In the following chapters, research with regard to definitions, conceptions, models and measurement of social and auditory intelligence is reviewed. Both constructs are related to constructs within their nomological network with a focus on academic intelligence.

2.2 Social Intelligence

Hendricks (1969, cited in Probst, 1982) already wondered whether academic intelligence is a sufficient precondition to solve social problems. In his view, "A quite different kind of intelligence is most needed for that purpose, namely a kind increasingly recognized as social intelligence." (p. 201). Sternberg, Forsythe, Hedlund, Horvath, Wagner, Williams, Snook, & Grigorenko (2000) argue that these differences are obvious in our daily lives: "We see people who succeed in school and fail in work or who fail in school but succeed in work. We meet people with high scores on intelligence tests who seem inept in their social interactions. And we meet people with low test scores who can get along effectively with practically anyone." (p. 32). Whereas this chapter explicitly focuses on social intelligence, the next two chapters (2.3 and 2.4) explore the position of social intelligence within other currently popular concepts of social competences, including emotional and practical intelligence, as well as empathy and wisdom.

Among laypersons as well as in work and clinical contexts, the concept of social competences is more common than social intelligence. It is not easy to maintain an overview about the many concepts that are similar to or overlap with social intelligence and competence. In English-speaking countries, words such as empathy, clinical intuition, person perception, social perception, social understanding, social sensitivity, social judgment, accuracy in judging, social skill and predictive skill were used as conceptions for social intelligence (Probst, 1998). It is often unclear as to exactly what people mean when they speak in terms of these concepts (see chapter 1.3). Confusion even increases when popular-science books such as the recently published social intelligence book of Goleman (2006) help to shape public opinion. This book focuses on social intelligence as an intellectual ability domain that can be classified within a broader conceptualization of social competences (see also chapter 2.3). Similarly to academic intelligence, in social intelligence several approaches exist, leading to different models and measurement strategies. The psychometric approach (how socially intelligent is a certain person) can be differentiated from an approach that focuses on general cognitive structures and processes (how do the processes and structures determining social intelligence develop over the life course and how do they influence social interactions). This work deals with the psychometric approach. Definitions, models and instruments are presented and discussed in the following sections.

2.2.1 Definitions and Conceptualizations of Social Intelligence

Social intelligence (SI) was first introduced by Dewey (1909, cited in Landy, 2006), who defines social intelligence as "the power of observing and comprehending social situations" (p. 43). E. L. Thorndike (1920), however, was the first person who included SI in a model of human intellectual abilities. Thorndike distinguished between abstract intelligence (ability to understand and manage ideas), mechanical intelligence (ability to understand and manage concrete objects), and SI. He defined SI as "the ability to understand and manage men and women, boys and girls -- to act wisely in human relations" (p. 228). In his definition, Thorndike refers to two aspects of SI, cognitive (e.g., to understand) and behavioral (e.g., to act wisely). Table 2-1 provides an overview of additional well-known definitions of SI. In the far right column, the component the definition focuses on is listed. Besides concentration on cognitive and/or behavioral SI, knowledge is a possible defining component.

The existing definitions seem to reveal three major characteristics of SI: it depends on (1) cognitive preconditions (basic ability) and/or (2) knowledge that can be transferred into (3) socially intelligent behavior. Moreover, some of the definitions are based on or include knowledge (or the former experience of people within social situations). Thorndike's definition of social intelligence in the SI literature is considered to be one of the broadest, which served, and still serves, as a basis for many former and topical studies. With regard to the distinctions concerning the term "intelligence" I made in chapter 1.3, only the cognitive part of the definitions are candidates for the status of "intelligence." Social behavior and social knowledge in particular cannot be evaluated separately from the social context. If a certain behavior is evaluated as socially intelligent, it will depend on the culture we live in, on the values and norms and the social reference group within the specified culture. In Japan, for example it is socially intelligent to slurp one's soup because it shows appreciation for its quality, whereas in Germany this would be regarded as impolite and rather inappropriate behavior. As another example, whether behavior is regarded as socially intelligent seems to depend on the people's occupation. For example, a socially intelligent manager is one who deals effectively with people and who can handle complex relationships. Nurses, however, are regarded as socially intelligent if they support their patients and establish a positive and warm atmosphere (Probst, 1982). Correspondingly, social knowledge is also cultural- and situation-specific knowledge and depends on the behavior rules, the "dos and don'ts" of a certain culture and/or situation. Therefore, it is rather remarkable that only one of the mentioned definitions (Wong et al., 1995) explicitly takes the social context into view. However, regarding operationalizations not referring to the social context, validity problems should arise because the effectiveness and acceptance of social behavior cannot be evaluated apart from taking the social context into account.

Table 2-1: Definitions of Social Intelligence

Author	Definition	Component
Thorndike (1920)	s.o.	cognitive and behavioral
Vernon (1933, p. 44)	"ability to get along with people in general, social technique or ease in society, knowledge of social matters, susceptibility to stimuli from other members of a group, as well as insight into the temporary moods or underlying personality traits of strangers"	cognitive and behavioral
Moss & Hunt (1927, p. 108)	"ability to get along with others"	behavioral
Wedeck (1947, p. 133)	"ability to judge people, with respect to feelings, moods, and motivation of individuals"	cognitive
Cantor & Kihlstrom (1987, p. 71)	Social intelligence "can be construed as declarative and procedural expertise for working on the tasks of social life in which social goals are especially salient."	knowledge
O'Sullivan, Guilford, & deMille (1965, p. 6)	"ability to judge people with respect to feelings, motives, thoughts, intentions, attitudes, etc."	cognitive
Kang, Day, & Meara (2005, p. 99)	"availability, accessibility, and richness of social and emotional knowledge (e.g., Kang & Shaver, 2004) and the ability to entertain multiple pespectives and hypotheses about unusual social/emotional behavior or behavior in unfamiliar social/emotional situations"	knowledge and cognitive
Kaiser (1998, p. 231)	"ability to deal with tasks that emerge throughout social life, considering both the own interests, aims and orientations as well as the interests of the community."	behavioral
Ford (1982, p. 323)	"attainment of social goals in specified social environments, using appropriate means and resulting in positive developmental outcomes"	behavioral

The reason for concentrating our work on social cognitive intelligence rather than on behavior or knowledge will be explained in the folllowing. Social cognitive intelligence is seen as a necessary but not sufficient precondition for socially intelligent behavior. Whether a certain behavior is regarded as socially intelligent depends on the social context and the current social situation. Social knowledge should also mainly result from the experience a person gains while behaving in social situations. Knowledge can also be acquired by learning theoretically how to behave (e.g., in school), or how to adapt to the specific culture of a company. However, the main learning occurs as a consequence of behavior. In order to explore the construct "social intelligence" systematically, it makes sense to start with the cognitive social intelligence as a potential for future social behavior and accumulated social knowledge. In our view, the cognitive potential for socially intelligent behavior and the resulting knowledge has to be clear before starting research about the conditions required to turn that potential into social action and gain knowledge. This straight focus on social cognitive intelligence is particularly important as former studies often confused the underlying cognitive abilities with the actual behavior resulting from these abilities. As a next step, after having specified the research domain, an adequate model has to be found.

2.2.2 Models and Classification Systems of Social Intelligence

Guilford's Structure of Intellect (SOI) model

Most factor analytic intelligence models do not include social intelligence (e.g. Kit of factor-referenced cognitive tests, Ekstrom, French, & Harman, 1976; CHC theory, see McGrew & Evans, 2004; Spearman, 1927; PMA, Thurstone, 1938, 1947; Humphreys, 1962; Vernon, 1950). However, there are some exceptions. Within Guilford's (1967, see also chapter 2.1.4) SOI model, the domain of social intelligence is covered the most thoroughly. Interestingly, Guilford considered his model to be an expansion of Thorndike's classification of intelligence. The symbolic and semantic content domains correspond to Guilford's abstract intelligence, the figural domain to practical intelligence, and the behavioral content domain to social intelligence (see Figure 2-3). In contrast to Thorndike, however, who regarded SI as a unity Guilford regarded SI as a multidimensional construct and suggested many ways to be socially intelligent. Social intelligence is composed of 5 (operations) x 6 (products) = 30 different subconstructs.

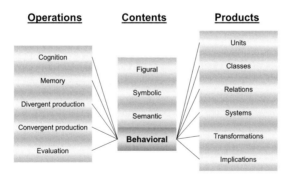

Figure 2-3: Social Intelligence in Guilford's Structure of Intellect (SOI) Model

Measurement instruments were devised for six SI subconstructs (O'Sullivan et al., 1965; Hoepfner & O'Sullivan, 1969) and six divergent production abilities (Hendricks, Guilford, & Hoepfner, 1969) and cover 12 of the 30 cognitive abilities that were proposed by Guilford (1967). Six cognitive abilities that were assumed for social intelligence have been confirmed in a factor analysis with 229 high school students including 23 experimental tests of social intelligence and 24 tests of other well-established intellectual factors (O'Sullivan et al., 1965). However, besides the lack of confirmation of the complete model, Guilford's analyses were criticized with respect to the factor analytic technique he applied (Prokrustes rotation, which specifies the solution that is strived for in advance and approaches it as far as possible) (see Kail & Pellegrino, 1988). In later revisions, Guilford also accepted higher order factors and approached the hierarchical models without accepting them completely.

Gardners "Frames of Mind"

Howard Gardner (1983, 1998) viewed intelligence as the capacity to solve problems or to fashion products that are valued in one or more cultural setting (Gardner & Hatch, 1989). His contemporary intelligence theory (see also chapter 2.1) should be an account of human cognition in its fullness. According to Gardner, human beings are organisms possessing a basic set of intelligences, everyone having a unique blend. Gardner initially formulated a list of seven intelligences that rarely operated independently and tended to complement each other during skill development and problem solving: linguistic intelligence, logical-mathematical intelligence, bodily-kinesthetic intelligence, spatial intelligence, interpersonal intelligence, intrapersonal intelligence, and musical intelligence. Later on, he added naturalistic intelligence to his model and reflected on existential, spiritual, and moral intelligence. According to Gardner, interpersonal intelligence is concerned with the capacity to understand the intentions, motivations and desires of other people. It allows people to work effectively with others. Educators, salespeople, religious and political leaders and counselors all are assumed to need a well-developed interpersonal intelligence. Gardner's methods to prove his model were psychological rather than traditional psychometric. For the identification of an intelligence, he used the following criteria: isolation by brain damage; anchoring in phylogeny, history and ontogeny; suitability for symbolic coding; discernable core-functions; confirmation through experiment and psychometry and exceptional cases with extremely high or low levels of ability. His approach stems from personal experience and literature research rather than empirical confirmation (Gardner, 2002).

Sternberg's Triarchic Theory of Intelligence

Another rather eclectic theory is Sternberg's Triarchic Theory of Intelligence (Sternberg, 1985). In his view, intelligence consists of analytical, creative and practical cognitive abilities. Social intelligence is included in the practical domain. According to Sternberg, the measurement of all types of intelligences depends on the context in which it is assessed. Sternberg regards all intelligences to be independent from each other.

Concluding Remarks to Social Intelligence (SI) Models

Thorndike, Guilford and Gardner conceptualized social intelligence as independent from and at a comparable level to academic intelligence. Although social intelligence is represented in some of the broader (facet and contemporary) models of intelligence, a generally accepted independent model of social intelligence does not exist. Therefore, most of the studies were not based on any SI model, and consequently the expected subconstructs were examined without an explicit theoretical reference. It is also surprising that in most of the SI conceptions auditory material is not included. In the summary of Probst (1982, p. 204/205), auditory material is not even mentioned; only written, pictorial, and videobased material as well as behavioral methods are considered.

Classification Systems of Social Intelligence (SI) Subconstructs

Despite the problems concerning definitions and models of SI, there seems to be some consensus about the multidimensionality of SI (e.g. Cantor & Kihlstrom, 1987; Ford & Tisak, 1983; Jones & Day, 1997; Lee, Wong, Day, Maxwell, & Thorpe, 2000; Lee, Day, Meara, & Maxwell, 2002; Marlowe, 1986; Mayer & Salovey, 1993; O'Sullivan & Guilford, 1975; Schneider et al., 2002; Wong et al., 1995). Thus, there are several ways to be socially intelligent, leading to some dimensions that have been repeatedly mentioned. In an extensive literature review, Orlik (1978) identified five major components of SI: perception of others' internal states and moods, ability to deal with people, knowledge about social norms and rules, insight and sensitivity in complex social situations, and use of social techniques to manipulate others (Orlik, 1978). Kosmitzki and John (1993) added perspective taking, social adaptation and social memory to that list (Walker & Foley, 1973; Moss et al., 1955; Berg, 1986). Kosmitzki and John (1993) suggest a classification into the SI domains capacity, motivation and social-cognitive. Schneider et al. (2002) differentiated between social knowledge, social memory, social insight (or understanding) and social appropriateness as parts of the purportedly multidimensional SI construct. With the exception of social appropriateness and social knowledge, the mentioned dimensions are cognitive. The specific role of social knowledge was already described. Social appropriateness contains an evaluation of aims on which behavior is based. In some studies (e.g. Wong et al., 1995) social flexibility and social perception were suggested as additional social intelligence dimensions.

Preliminary Model of Social Intelligence (SI)

With regard to theoretical and operational definitions in the literature, four cognitive SI dimensions can be assumed: social perception, social memory, social understanding, and social creativity (or flexibility). These dimensions are integrated into a preliminary SI model, described in Süß et al. (2005, Weis & Süß, 2005). In addition, a social knowledge domain is assumed. Since social knowledge is acquired throughout learning, it differs from other operations that rather focus on the *potential* of a person to perceive, to remember and to understand. The potential as well as the acquired and imparted social knowledge have an impact on actual social behavior. Just as academic intelligence is only a precondition to demonstrate (academically) intelligent behavior, social cognitive intelligence is a necessary but not sufficient condition to show socially intelligent behavior. Besides motivation and personality characteristics, situational demands, values and norms as well as moods, interest, aims and experience influence whether and how the potential is transferred into action. Figure 2-4 illustrates the dimensions described in the following.

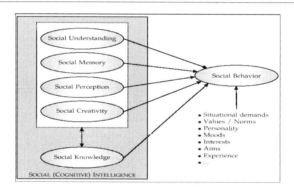

Figure 2-4: Preliminary Model of Social Intelligence

We define *social perception* as the ability to quickly perceive social information. Analogous to perceptual speed in academic intelligence, we handle this ability as social perceptual speed (see Carroll, 1987). This dimension was also proposed by Wong et al. (1995).

Social memory is seen as the ability to intentionally remember and either recognize or recall social episodic and semantic information of a given social situation that differs in complexity (Weis, Seidel, & Süß, 2006). Moss et al. (1955) define and operationalize social memory as the ability to remember people's names and faces. Kosmitzki and John (1993) found that the ability "social memory" as it is defined in Moss et al. (1955) is of little relevance to people's conceptions of social intelligence.

Social flexibility or creativity is the ability for a flexible production of ideas that can be used for interpretation, solution or management of social situations (e.g. entertaining different hypotheses of what is going on at a party, considering different options for how to behave in novel social situations, for example when meeting the parents of the boyfriend for the first time). Jones and Day (1997) defined social flexibility as the flexible application of social knowledge in order to solve novel problems. They separated it from declarative and procedural social knowledge.

Social understanding can be regarded as the central dimension and is defined as the ability to identify social information in a given situation and to understand and judge it correctly. Social information varies according to its complexity, its implications for the given situation and the underlying characteristics (Weis et al., 2006). This dimension was also suggested and found by Wong et al. (1995) as well as Lee et al. (2000). In our view, it is important to regard existing definitions of the core dimension social understanding carefully because they differ in meaning and broadness. Figure 2-5 classifies the most important definitions of the social understanding dimension.

perception	understanding	more complex social abilities
Recognition of the mental states (Moss, Hunt, Omwake, & Woodward, 1955) Decode nonverbal communications (Barnes & Sternberg, 1989; Sternberg & Smith, 1985)	Understand people (Thorndike, 1920; Kosmitzki & John, 1993) Insight into moods, personality traits of strangers (Vernon, 1933) Judge feelings, moods and motivations (Wedeck, 1947) Comprehend behavior in the social context (Wong et al., 1995) Define a given situation in terms of the behavior imputed to others present (Chapin, 1942) Judge people with respect to feelings, motives, thoughts, intentions, attitudes etc. (O'Sullivan, 1965)	Role taking / perspective taking ability (Kosmitzki & John,1993) Social problem solving (Moss et al., 1955)

Figure 2-5: Definitions of Social Understanding

The first category deals with recognition of, decoding of and sensitivity to social information (e.g. recognition of a certain emotion in a voice during a conversation). In our view, this category is difficult to separate from social perception (for a definition see above). In the second category, complexity increases because more than one element has to be taken into account. For example, a certain person is presented in a social context. Moods, motives, thoughts, intentions, attitudes and personality traits are possible contents of tasks that have to be identified, interpreted or judged. The third category can be differentiated from the second insofar as it deals with really complex social abilities, which require not only perception but also understanding and flexibility (e.g. social problem solving, role-taking ability). Flavell, Botkin, Fry, Wright, and Jarvis (1968) describe five conditions that have to be met to be able to showing role-taking behavior: (1) recognition of the existence of perspective; (2) recognition of the need for an analysis of the perspective of the other and recognition that such an analysis is useful in obtaining one's goal; (3) the ability to carry out this analysis or predict with accuracy the relevant role attributes of the other; (4) the maintenance of cognitions yielded by the analysis in the face of conflicting cognition representing one's own point of view; (5) the application of these cognitions to the end at hand. It is obvious that even the preconditions are quite complex and include parts of the other SI subconstructs already mentioned. Role-taking ability is therefore assumed to be a compound ability requiring social understanding but at the same time clearly exceeding it. Regarding meaning and content, it is difficult to separate the third category from social flexibility.

With respect to the social understanding subconstruct, we decided to focus on the middle category and to exclude recognition and identification abilities (first category), since they overlap with social perception. Social understanding compared to pure perception and discrimination is seen as more complex. Although intuitive understanding and heuristic information processing are not intended to be critical for the task solution, they may be partly used in order to come to a judgment about a person or situation. Therefore, the clear separation between the operational SI domains cannot be enhanced but only limited by the use of appropriate test material and instructions (see Probst, 1982). We also exclude role/perspective-taking ability and social problem solving (third category) as these domains are only vaguely defined and can also be treated as compound abilities (see Hough & Ones, 2001; Ones, Viswesvaran, & Dilchert, 2005). In order to measure social understanding properly, enough context information has to be provided to make the judgment of a persons' feelings, thoughts and relationships possible. Consequently, for test construction it is important to bear in mind that the presentation of the relevant persons has to be long enough to allow identification and interpretation of the relevant stimuli. It also implies providing background information, allowing assessment in different situations with different people.

Social understanding has also been mentioned in a different research perspective, the Theory of Mind (ToM). According to this theory, a relationship between external states (expressions, gestures, signals, etc.) and internal states of mind is established. The capacity to predict behavior, namely to recognize emotions, intentions, and thoughts of other individuals in various settings, arises as a consequence of this relationship. Well-known mind-reading accuracy tasks are, e.g., (1) personality traits ratings, the ability to make judgments about (2) the mental state (both affective and nonaffective), (3) behavior, and (4) roles, identities or status (Davis & Kraus, 1997). In addition, (5) metaperception (i.e., the ability to know what others think about oneself) is included in this concept. For further information see chapter 2.4.1.

Social knowledge takes on a special role. It can only be measured in a manner dependent upon cultural conditions and influences (Weber & Westmeyer, 2001). For the implementation of social knowledge at the same level as the other SI dimensions, an exhaustive classification of social situations and culture-dependent norms and values has to be basis for the construct. That contradicts the cognitive nature of the remaining SI dimensions. Nevertheless, social knowledge is assumed to influence the other cognitive SI dimensions and vice versa. On the one hand, someone who is able to perceive socially relevant stimuli quickly, who can remember them and judge the feelings, thoughts and relationships of different people is able to gain social knowledge more quickly and accurately than a person whose socially cognitive abilities are developed to a lesser extent. On the other hand, a person with a wider social knowledge (e.g. how to deal with administrative services, how to deal with a school class, how to deal with superiors, how to behave at a gala dinner) will interpret the behavior of others differently than a person without that knowledge. According to Cantor and Kihlstrom (1987; see also Kihlstrom & Cantor, 2000), social knowledge consists of declarative and procedural parts. Declarative knowledge again consists of semantic and episodic memory, which emphasizes the relationship between social memory and knowledge. Bye and Jussim (1993) differentiate between three types of social knowledge: (1) fact knowledge about human interactions (appropriateness in social life), (2) procedural knowledge (how to [re-]act in social life, knowledge about role-behavior and prototypical behavior), and (3) self-knowledge (knowledge about one's own history, one's abilities and limitations). Despite this great variety of different types of social knowledge, until now operational definitions only operationalized social knowledge as knowledge of etiquette and tacit knowledge. Etiquette knowledge could be subclassified neither beyond declarative nor beyond procedural knowledge. Tacit knowledge could be clearly separated from memory (Lee, Day, Meara, & Maxwell, 2002; see also chapter 2.3.2 and 2.4.3. A social knowledge factor could be identified in the MTMM studies of Wong et al. (1995, measuring social knowledge through a test of etiquette), Jones and Day (1997) and Lee et al. (2000, 2002). For further information, see chapter 2.2.4.

2.2.3 Measurement of Social Intelligence

"Convenient tests of social intelligence are hard to devise.... Social intelligence shows itself abundantly in the nursery, on the playground, in barracks and factories and salesroom (*sic*), but it eludes the formal standardized conditions of the testing laboratory. It requires human beings to respond to, time to adapt its responses, and face, voice, gesture, and mien as tools" (Thorndike, 1920, p. 231). Thorndike foresaw the problems the measurement of social intelligence would be confronted with. Nevertheless, there were several attempts to measure social intelligence in different ways, with performance measures, behavior-oriented measures, knowledge tests and self- and peer reports. Instruments should be designed depending on the particular definition of the SI (sub-) constructs and the purpose of measurement (see section 2.2.1). Performance measures are recommended in order to measure the potential of a person to react in a socially intelligent manner. To obtain an index of the actual social behavior of a person, behavior-oriented instruments should be taken into account. In self- and other-report measures the person him- or herself or a peer judges the person's social intelligence. Social knowledge should be evaluated with a knowledge test. In the following, different types of instruments are classified within five tables: broad performance test-batteries (Table 2-2), performance instruments for trait measurement (Table 2-3), behavior-based instruments (Table 2-4), self-/other report (Table 2-5), and knowledge tests (Table 2-6). Within each table the author and test, underlying definition and/or model (if existent) and its postulated dimensions as well as some important results concerning convergent and divergent validity are presented. With respect to performance tests, researchers used different materials that can be classified into four categories: written and spoken language, pictures, and videos. The type of material is also presented in one column of the table presenting performance measures (see Dimensions/Material). The instruments are related to the dimensions that were defined in Süß et al. (2005; see also Weis & Süß, 2005). As already mentioned, the terms social intelligence and competence often were not applied systematically. Therefore, in the table, instruments that are sought to measure social competence are included, if they are similar to "SI measures." The tables do not claim to be complete. The source of the validity results is the corresponding test manual if no other reference is mentioned. Note: Social/emotional auditory measures that were developed in the tradition of emotion research can be found in chapter 2.6.5.

Table 2-2: Social Intelligence Performance-based Test Batteries

Test name	Definition/ Model	Dimensions/ Material	Scales (mentioned in the test)	Studies/Results
Six and Four Factor Test of Social Intelligence (O'Sullivan & Guilford, 1966, 1976) "ability to understand the inner feelings or affect states of other persons" (Hoepfner & O'Sullivan, 1968, p. 340)	SOI Model, content: behavioral - *cognition*: ability to judge people (p. 4) - *convergent production*: "doing the right thing at the right time" (p. 5) - *divergent production*: coping with the behavior of other people - *memory*: ability to remember the social characteristics of people - *evaluation*: ability to judge the appropriateness of behavior.	Dimensions: understanding, flexibility Material: pictorial, verbal, auditory	Tests were realized for 6 cognitive and 6 divergent production abilities (of 30 predicted factors). Examples of tasks: - classes: expression grouping - systems: missing pictures; missing cartoons - transformations: picture exchange; social translation - implications: cartoon prediction	Reliability: - internal consistency of all subtests: (.32 - .85) - internal consistency of auditory tests: inflection (Alpha=.26, items k=27); sound meaning (Alpha=.36, items k=27); reflections: (Alpha=.43, items k=18) Convergent validity: - separable factors: cognitive and divergent production, no common SI factor - factor structure regarding "behavioral cognition" and "divergent production" could be replicated with 306 and 252 high school students, respectively (PCA) Divergent validity: - independence from Academic Intelligence (Probst, 1982) - substantial correlations with AcI, particularly verbal (Riggio, Messamer, & Thockmorton, 1991; Shanley, Walker, & Foley, 1971) - no correlations with SI self-report measure (Social Skills Inventory, SSI, Riggio, 1989)
George Washington Social Intelligence Test (GWSIT; Moss, Hunt, Omwake, & Woodward, 1955)	Ability to get along with others (p. 108) (behavioral)	Dimensions: social flexibility (1); social memory (2); social knowledge (3); social understanding (4; 5; 6) Material: pictorial, verbal	Tests: (1) Judgment in social situations (2) Memory for names and faces (3) Observation of human behavior (4 + 5) Recognition of the mental states behind words / facial expression (6) Social information (7) Sense of humor Later on, tests 5 and 6 were excluded and test 7 was added.	Reliability: - satisfying reliability around .80 Convergent validity: - no convergent validity proof, no relationships to other SI measures (Walker & Foley, 1973) Divergent validity: - aggregate GWSIT score correlated r = .54 with aggregate score on GWMAT an early IQ scale (Hunt, 1928; see also Broom, 1928, r=.60) - no separate AcI and SI factors (Thorndike,1936) - test variance is mainly explained through verbal AcI measures (Orlik, 1978, p. 346) → AcI-SI correlations up to .70 - correlations with introversion around .53 (Guilford, 1934)

Conclusions from Performance-based Test Batteries

Table 2-2 presents two broad performance-based SI test batteries that are rather old but nevertheless exemplary. I am going to direct attention to some particularities of these approaches. Concerning the Six and Four Factor Test of Social Intelligence (O'Sullivan & Guilford, 1966, 1976), the authors assumed that "expressive behavior, more particularly facial expressions, vocal inflections, postures, and gestures, are the cues from which intentional states are inferred" (p. 6). The investigators recognized the value of assessing the decoding ability in real-life contexts with real people. Economic constraints forced them to rely on photographs, cartoons, drawings, and tape recordings that were not available in high quality. Nevertheless, Guilford and his colleagues were successful in devising measures of two rather different SI domains: understanding the behavior of other people (cognition of behavioral content), and coping with the behavior of other people (divergent production of behavioral content). The success of the tests is attributed to the rather low portion of words (Hoepfner & O'Sullivan, 1968). Therefore, people with low verbal IQ have a chance to show their social intellectual abilities. However, the studies of O'Sullivan et al. (1965) and Hendricks (1969, cited by Probst, 1982) went only part of the way towards establishing the construct validity of social intelligence. Additional research within the other suggested SI domains as well as evidence for the tests to predict external criteria of SI are needed.

Although the authors of the George Washington Social Intelligence Test (GWSIT; Moss et al., 1955) clearly address the behavioral aspect of SI in their definition (ability to get along with people, ability to deal with people, Hunt, 1928; Moss & Hunt, 1927), their subtests focus on the cognitive aspect. In the subtests of the GWSIT, subjects have to choose among four alternatives to judge social situations, remember several faces and the accompanying names and choosing them from among a range of photographs and names after some time, and judge statements about human behavior as right or wrong. The test clearly follows the tradition of AcI testing in focusing on verbal material. According to Anastasi (1954) "it is doubtful, for instance, whether, the George Washington Test measures abilities not covered by tests of abstract verbal intelligence with which it correlates highly." (p. 503)

Table 2-3: Social Intelligence Performance Measures

Test name	Definition/ Model	Dimensions/ Material	Scales (mentioned in the test)	Results/Studies
Couples Test & Supervisors Task (Barnes & Sternberg, 1989; Sternberg & Smith, 1985)	Measures nonverbal decoding ability (SI=accurate decoding of social information)	Dimensions: understanding Material: pictorial	Pictures of heterosexual couples have to be judged (is it a false or a true couple?)	*Reliability: a) confidence rating; b) proportion correct* (1) Couples: a) .49/.34, b) .81/.87 (40 Items, N=24/24 Items, N=40) (2) Supervisors: a) .92 /.47, b) .84 (40 Items, N=24/24 Items, N=40) - median scale intercorrelations: .33 Convergent validity: - significantly related to social competence self-report inventories Discriminant validity: - discrimination from AcI not significant
Chapin Social Insight test (Chapin, 1967; Gough, 1968)	Recognition of psych. dynamics underlying a particular behavior, the stimulus, compromise or innovation necessary to resolve the situation or to carry it through to a constructive conclusion (across situations)	Dimensions: understanding Material: verbal	- 25 Items which describe a social situation - subjects have to select an appropriate explanation/ solution for a problem out of 4 alternatives	Reliability: - low reliability (Alpha: .64 - .78, N=100) and validity coefficients Convergent validity: - no convergent validity (Keating, 1978) - no consistent factor structure (was criticized to measure reading comprehension rather than SI) Divergent validity: - correlations with AcI: .20 -.40 (especially verbal); Md= .36 (Gough, 1965) - low reliability (.42; Weis & Süß, 2005) - zero Md correlation with California Psychological Inventory (Gough, 1965); MMPI: Md=.19 Incremental validity: - no incremental prediction of social behavior and perception (measured with peer-reports) in addition to AcI
Interpersonal Perception Task (IPT-15, Costanzo & Archer, 1993)	Measures perception of verbal and nonverbal behavior and its interpretation	Dimensions: understanding Material: video	- 15 real situations are shown - one out of two options has to be chosen as the right interpretation of the situation - target scoring	Reliability: Retest (5 Wochen): .73 (N = 52) Internal consistency (KR-20): .38 (N = 530) Construct validity: - correlation with peer-rating (N=18 College students) concerning interpersonal sensitivity r = .65

Table 2-3: Social Intelligence Performance Tests continued

Test name	Definition/ Model	Dimensions/ Material	Scales (mentioned in the test)	Results/Studies
Test of Implied Meaning (Sundberg, 1966)	Implicit meanings	Dimensions: understanding Material: auditory	Recognition of implicit messages (40 statements displayed auditory). Statements are spoken half by a male, half by a female. Excerpts similar to those frequently made by patients in clinical interviews were read to express a particular meaning. Subjects have to choose the correct meaning from a list of four alternatives. Example: 1 don't have a headache! Subjects have to decide if it means a) simple fact, b) "And I mean it!", c) "But I know someone who does." d) I want your sympathy!" Each statement is presented twice in succession, between items there is an interval of 12 seconds.	Reliability: - Retest reliability: .89 (N=85, several weeks, see manual) and .83 - .87 Hood (1962, cited after Sundberg, 1966) Convergent validity: - no relation to ratings of interpersonal sensitivity (40 male trainees) - .61 with communicating rating scale among counsellors (N=12) - significant correlation (.67; N=20) with "Socialization" (California Psychological Inventory) and intellectual efficiency (.72) Discriminant validity: - significant relation to the Ohio psychological test (no values presented) - .40 with verbal aptitude test - .26 with modern language aptitude test (MLAT, N=40) Criterion validity: Experienced therapists were significantly better than undergraduates. Group differences: - significant sex differences in favor of women
Videosimulation (Schuler, Diemand, & Moser, 1993)	Social competency, especially customers orientation and ability to work in a team	Dimensions: behavioral and cognitive Material: video, verbal	Seven different tests that arise from the possible combinations of stimuli (video or verbal situation description) and reaction (written, oral, role-play)	Convergent validity: - correlation between the two dimensions: r=.32 - two factors: social behavior competence and social judgment competence Discriminant validity - correlations with verbal Acl (possible reason: open answers)
Videobased Identification of Social Intelligence-Online (VISION, Runde & Etzel, 2003)	Social competence (private and work life); advanced into ISIS- Interactive System for Identification of Social competences	Dimensions: understanding Material: video/audio	Five facets of interpersonal and management competences: social perception, conflict and criticism ability, management of relationships, team competence, management competence Conflict situations are based on the following situation taxonomy contents (job, family, friends, public life); structure (dyad, group); quality (competitive, cooperative)	Psychometry: Cronbach's Alpha (scales): .69 -.78 (students, N=198); ISIS: .58 - .75 Convergent validity: -correlation with Interpersonal Competence Questionnaire (ICQ, Riemann & Allgöwer, 1993): r=.30 (relationship), r=.20 (management) (Bastians & Runde, 2002) -correlation with assessment center global score: r=.35 Discriminant validity: - IST-70: no significant correlations - personality (NEO-FFI): openness: r=.44, no other correlations Criterion validity: success in assessment center: .65 and .54

Conclusions With Regard to Performance Measures

The results of the presented studies do not lead to a clear statement about the validity of SI measured with performance tests. Verbal and also some pictorial performance measures were not clearly separable from AcI (e.g. Couples Test, Barnes & Sternberg, 1989; Sternberg & Smith, 1985; GWSIT, Moss et al., 1955, Thorndike, 1936; Orlik, 1978; Riggio et al., 1991, Shanley et al., 1971; Chapin Social Insight Test, Chapin, 1967; Gough, 1968; Weis & Süß, 2005). The use of nonverbal SI indicators suggests that a social cognitive ability domain separable from AcI exists (Six and Four Factor Test, O'Sullivan & Guilford, 1967; Hoepfner & O'Sullivan, 1968; Probst, 1982). However, these results were not confirmed in every study, which may be due to the similarity of cognitive requirements in tasks of both social and academic intelligence. In particular, social verbal tasks seem to fulfil characteristics of abstract reasoning tasks, since they deal with novel and complex stimuli that do not correspond to our expectations and consequently result in separation problems. However, the correlations between verbal AcI measures and SI instruments are not necessarily the result of bad scale construction. There is indeed an overlap between language ability and the ability to deal with social situations. Both abilities are acquired in social situations and are not only mediated through nonverbal but mainly through verbal communication (see also Kaiser, 1998). Thorndike (1920) already mentioned that a genuine situation with real people is essential. In order to keep a situation as realistic as possible, direct observation of people in social situations would be best. However, this method is susceptible to mistakes, not standardized or replicable, and costly. Alternatively, social situations can be approached as closely as possible by including dynamic auditory and video-based material instead of using static pictures and written language.

Issues of Scoring

In a performance test, scoring should be as objective as possible. This seems to be easier with regard to social perception and social memory tasks than for social understanding tasks (SU, i.e., interpreting and judging another person's feelings, thoughts and relationships). The latter dimension does not have a veridicaly determined correct answer (see also Roberts, Zeidner, & Matthews, 2001) since the items of SU tasks measuring, for example, social understanding approach the complexity of real-life situations. Rules cannot be applied as easily as in more simple, static and structured problems. Therefore, alternative scoring procedures have to be taken into account, namely (1) target scoring, (2) consensus scoring, and (3) expert scoring. These procedures are described in the following.

In target scoring, the target (creator) of the item stimuli determines the correct answer (e.g., a person's voice was recorded, and the person him- or herself decides about the emotion that is expressed). The problem with target scoring is the reliability of the target person's answer and the well-known social cognition effects, for example the actor-observer bias.

Consensus scoring reflects the opinion of the majority, in most cases the opinion of the group of test takers (laypersons). Usually, proportion scoring is applied. That means if the group chooses alternative A in 30% and alternative B in 50% of cases, all test takers who chose alternative A will get a value of .30 and all who selected option B will receive .50. According to MacCann, Matthews, Zeidner, and Roberts (2003), proportion scoring results in artificially inflating internal consistency estimates. In addition, distributions of total test scores cannot be both normally distributed and internally consistent. In a reliable test, subsets from the same group reflecting the group's opinion (who form a majority) choose the most popular option on most items. That results in skewed distributions on the item level being accentuated at the total score level. The resulting distribution of test scores will be highly negatively skewed and most scores will form a highly peaked cluster at the top end of the distribution (MacCann, Roberts, Matthews, & Zeidner, 2004b). Another problem is that people with an exceptionally high ability in a certain task different from the majority answer would get a lower score than they deserve.

Expert scoring occurs when experts determine the correct answer. However, criteria for being an expert are usually not defined. Zeidner, Matthews, and Roberts (2001; see also Roberts et al.; 2001) propose that there may be multiple domains of expertise besides academic knowledge (e.g., understanding and managing people's relationships and goals, where experts might be coaches). Empirical results revealed that test takers with similar characteristics to the experts showed better results compared to others. Roberts et al. (2001) could show that white males scored more highly using expert scoring when the experts were white males in an emotional intelligence test (MEIS, see chapter 2.3.1). In the view of Legree, Psotka, Tremble, and Bourne (2005), in some instances, an expert is no more than a reliable indicator of the group; thus one could use the groups (consensus) mean and save time and money in test development and validation. The authors report a correlation of .72 between expert and consensus scoring. However, even if this procedure works in some cases, it may not apply to every expert and may not apply when the target has extra information that is not available to the outside observer (own feelings, thoughts, knowledge). In this case, in the opinion of Mayer and Geher (1996), the target can be considered to be a special case of the expert whose knowledge extends beyond what the group knows and is not reducible to the group consensus.

It appears that target scoring has the fewest negative implications. One could argue that other scoring methods should be applied to support the findings obtained with target scoring. However, results on the agreement between the two scoring procedures can be summarized ranging between 0% and 60% (see Ekman, Friesen, & Ellsworth, 1972; Levenson & Ruef, 192; Ickes et al., 1990; Mayer & Geher, 1996) and thus in most cases do not exceed chance level. Possible reasons for the unexpected low relations may be the lack of modern technique (older studies), unreliability of the target person's information (e.g., because of social desirability or a lack of self-awareness), and because of highly complex and/or specific stimuli/situations. The lack of a positive relationship between the group consensus and the target's reports in the Mayer and Geher (1996) study may also be attributed to the restriction to written material. I assume that using written material instead of dynamic video-based and/or auditory material does not provide as much information about the person and the corresponding situation. (Internal) processes of the target person thus are not transferred into cues that are visible to or able to be heard by the group. That makes an agreement between group and target harder.

There are only a few instruments that make use of target scoring, since the effort is much higher compared to consensus scoring. The IPT-15 is an example of a test that makes use of target scoring. Each scene has one (of two or three) correct answer, for example one of two interacting players indeed won the basketball game the two persons are talking about in the presented video scene (see Archer, Costanzo, & Akert, 2001). Other measures that apply target scoring are the Test of Implied Meaning (TIM, Sundberg, 1966) and the Emotional Accuracy Research Scale (EARS, not listed in the table). The EARS requires the participant's accurate identification of others' emotions. Participants were asked to describe three situations that most strongly reflected their mood. They had to provide information about the situation (e.g., what led to the situation, what happened) and had to complete a 78-item mood scale. Researchers using target scoring must ensure that the target person's information is valid and reliable and influenced only minimally by variables such as social desirability, self-monitoring ability, and self-awareness.

Social Auditory Intelligence Measures

Auditory tests of social intelligence are not only rare but, with regard to SI research tradition, also limited to social understanding (see TIM, Sundberg, 1966; subtests of the 4/6 Factor Test). The other existing measures present video and auditory material together and mainly stem from practical application based needs in the field of I/O psychology. There seems to be a lack of measures testing social auditory abilities more broadly (e.g. perception, understanding, memory, flexibility). In chapter 2.6, additional measures that are derived from emotion research tradition will be presented. At this point, I concentrate on some interesting details about the subtests of the 4/6 Factor Test and the TIM.

In O'Sullivan's and Guilford's tests (1965), auditory abilities are measured with three subtests (For further details beyond the information provided here, see O'Sullivan & Guilford, 1965.). In the subtest "inflections" (behavioral units), one of four drawn facial expressions has to be chosen that expresses the same feeling as a tape-recorded vocal inflection. For test construction, six neutral phrases were selected (yes, mother, I did it, well, really, that's good). Three actors produced a variety of inflections for each of the six phrases. Five inflections of each phrase were selected (5 x 6 = 30 items). Half of the inflections and pictures are male, half female. Concerning the subtest "sound meaning" (behavioral classes), three classes of emotive sounds were formed, produced by a man and a woman (non–actors). For each emotive sound the appropriate class has to be chosen. For example, three sounds: heavy breathing, startled laugh, whimper, were produced; the appropriate class to select would be "fear". Within the subtest "reflections" (behavioral implications), subjects have to choose one out of four alternative interpretations that correctly reflects the feeling of a tape-recorded statement. The material (statements) for the test stems from published reports of therapy cases. An example: Which alternative statement expresses the attitude or feeling underlying the given statement? - "I'm just wondering how I'll act – I mean how things will turn out." Alternatives: a) She's looking forward to it., b) She's worried about it., c) She's interested in how things will work out. With respect to psychometrics, the auditory tests "inflections" and "sound meaning" have the lowest reliabilities within the battery (see also Table 2-2). O'Sullivan and Guilford expected reasons in little agreement among subjects with a single auditory stimulus (e.g. Kramer, 1963), but there was good agreement. Test intercorrelations were between .14 and .25 ("reflections" with "inflections": r=.18; "reflections" with "sound meaning": r=.25; "sound meaning" with "inflections": r=.14) Despite reliability problems, all three tests loaded most highly on the expected factor (units, classes, implications): .22-.38. "reflections" also showed a high loading (.35) on "semantic relations". Common variance is assumed to be due to the verbal part of the factor and subtest. According to O'Sullivan and Guilford (1965, p. 24), "inflections" assesses mainly the ability to understand facial expressions. The difficulty of the test lies in the drawings (match appropriate drawings to sound sequences). The test sound meaning did not show any significant loading on any factor. Partially, this result can be explained with the low reliability of the subtest. In addition, verbal variance was not sufficiently controlled. Also, note that O'Sullivan and Guilford (1965) did not use any auditory reference test in the validation of their test battery. They only included standard academic intelligence measures like verbal comprehension vocabulary, verbal and word classification, verbal analogies, Differential Aptitude Test (DAT), mutilated words, hidden figures, picture arrangement, etc.).

The TIM suffers from technical limitations, as a tape is used. During test taking, the test takers had to be very quiet, and there should have been differences in understanding

41

dependent on where subjects sat (close to the tape recorder or far away). The TIM has the advantage of target scoring. The content of the 40 statements was taken from patient's interviews. Stricker and Rock (1990) made some minor changes in the questionnaire of the TIM but everything else remained untouched (email correspondence with Larry Stricker, January 9th, 2007).

Table 2-4: Behavior-oriented Social Intelligence Measures

Test name	Definition/ Model	Scales (mentioned in test)	Approach	Results/Studies
Interview (Ford & Tisak, 1983)	Keating's (1978) model SI= behavioral effectiveness of social per- formance	Criteria: (1) react appropriately to questions of the interviewer (2) show appropriate nonverbal behavior (3) …	Interview	Reliability: Interrater Reliability: 65% agreement Cronbach's Alpha: Hogan's Empathy Scale (.46 & .47), social goal attainment (.48 & .43), self-report (.76), other report (>=.90) Convergent validity: Intercorrelation SI measures: .33 - .36 Discriminant validity: - cross-domain correlation: .21 - .26 - no relation neither to self- and peer report social ability inventories nor to Academic Intelligence measures → indicators of SI and AcI loaded on different factors Criterion validity: SI tests were of higher validity in predicting a behavioral criterion than AcI tests (N=620, 9th and 12th grades)
Frederiksen, Carlson & Ward, 1984	---	Task: - take on the role of a doctor who interviewed his patient - ratings on warmth, control and organization	Interview / Role - play	Discriminant validity: - no positive significant correlations between interview scores (SI) and reasoning (-.08 - .14), verbal abilities (-.24 -.01), science achievement (-.41 -.03), cognitive flexibility (-.12 -.16), ideational fluency (-.01 - .15), and medical knowledge (-.09 -.16); 91 students
Behavioral Role play Test (Mc Fall & Marston, 1970)	---	Social situations are briefly described. Afterwards the role-play starts wherein the subject answers like he or she would in real-life. Everything is recorded by tape and then evaluated. Subjects are interviewed about the feelings accompanying their behavior.	Interview / Role - play	Reliability: -interrater-reliability: .73 - .93 Validity coefficients not available
Interpersonal Competence Inventory (ICI, Stricker & Rock, 1990)	Interpersonal Competence= effectiveness in dealing with other people	- videoscenes display an interview between superior and employee - reply section: Subjects have to answer within the scenes instead of the boss; - criteria: originality and effectiveness - test also included a judgment section: Description of the situation as indicator of academic intelligence.	Interview / Role - play	Reliability: - internal consistency of ICI-scores: .81 (effectiveness of answers); .92 (originality of answers); .74 (accuracy of judgment) Convergent validity: - no convergent validity with nonverbal social skills (e.g. CARAT, TIM) and SI self-report instruments Discriminant validity: - significant correlations with verbal AcI, no separability - correlations with vocabulary test: .41 - .50 (Stricker & Rock, 1990) - role-taking ability increases with age - no relations to verbal fluency and verbal intelligence
Role-taking test (Feffer, 1959; Feffer & Suchotliff,1966)	ability to change perspective	- measure of balanced decentering - subject has to invent stories about certain pictures and tell the stories from the view of every person that is shown in the pictures.	Role - play	

Conclusions With Regard to Behavior-oriented Measures

Within studies that included behavior-oriented measures, SI could often be separated from AcI (e.g. Feffer, 1959; Ford & Tisak, 1983; Frederiksen et al., 1984). On the one hand, more realistic measures that implement the actual social behavior seem to be more useful tools for the measurement of SI. On the other hand, the differences in the method applied (paper-pencil tests for the measurement of AcI vs. role-plays and interview settings for SI measurement) could be responsible for separate factors. Verbal skills of a person may also have an influence on rating the answers. However, the results were not uniform (e.g. Stricker & Rock, 1990). It can be concluded that behavior-based measures of SI tend towards being separable from AcI. Interestingly, researchers relying on behavioral measures of SI and considering SI as behavioral -rather than cognitive- attribute the problems of separating SI from AcI to the cognitive operationalization of SI (see Ford, 1982, 1994; Keating, 1978; O'Sullivan et al., 1965; Walker & Foley, 1973).

Since the acquisition of social cognitive skills (e.g. role-taking behavior, person perception and moral reasoning) does not ensure socially intelligent behavior (Ford & Tisak, 1983), ideally, social behavior should be measured in real-world settings that require behavioral responses to real people (O'Sullivan et al., 1965). If this is not possible and testing relies on nonverbal behaviors (e.g. drawings, gestures, vocalizations), individual differences in drawing, acting, or public-speaking ability interfering with the measurement of actual social intelligence per se have to be controlled (O'Sullivan & Guilford, 1966, 1976).

I take the perspective that success in separating SI operationalized as behavior, from AcI is not surprising as different levels (cognitive preconditions vs. behavioral implementation) are contrasted. The use of behavior-orientated measures in comparison to AcI would make more sense if academically intelligent behavior was contrasted to socially intelligent behavior. We encounter similar problems when dealing with self-report measures (see the following section).

Table 2-5: Social Intelligence Self-/Peer-report Measures

Test name	Definition/ Model	Scales (mentioned in the test)	Results/Studies
Social Skills Inventory (SSI, Riggio, 1989)	Measurement of basic social skill components that underlie social competence	Contents (social and emotional) cross skills (sensitivity, expressivity and control) → 6 dimensions (90 Items): Social Sensitivity (SS) Social Expressivity (SE) Social Control (SC) Emotional Sensitivity (ES) Emotional Expressivity (EE) Emotional Control (EC)	Reliability: Alpha: .62 - .87 (different samples) Retest: .81 - .96 (N=40, two weeks) Convergent validity: - no coherent correlations with SI performance measures - substantial correlations with self-reports of social behavior as well as social contacts - total SSI-ACT: 64; Total SSI - PONS: .12 (EE & ES: .18; 19) Discriminant validity: - no coherent correlations with Acl - substantial correlations with personality variables Group differences: women perform better
Marlowe (1986) Used several self-report instruments (e.g. PDA, Zuckerman & Larrance, 1979)	SI=ability to understand feelings, thoughts and behaviors of persons, including oneself, in interpersonal situations and to act appropriately upon that understanding	Model (Marlowe, 1985) -Social interest -Social self-efficacy -Empathy -Social behavioral skills (performance)	Convergent validity: - Postulated dimensions could not be justified (N=188, mean age: 43.4 years; 83.5 female) - five separate factors emerged (prosocial attitude, social skills, empathic skills, emotionality, social anxiety) → multidimensionality of SI Discriminant validity: - no significant correlations with Acl (that can be attributed to the fact that Acl was measured via objective tests whereas SI was assessed via self-reports)
Brown & Anthony (1990)		Social skills (evaluation via Social acceptance and effectivity) & Personality for both self- and other rating	Reliability: - average intercorrelation among social variables: r=.34 Discriminant validity - in a factor analytic study (1) Acl could be separated from (2) Peer-ratings of social behavior and personality and (3) self ratings- of social behavior and personality (method effects) - average correlation Acl-SI: .15
Prototypical Acts on SI (Amelang, Schwarz & Wegemund, 1989)	Self- and peer rating of social intelligent behavior	-Social Intelligence (SI)-perception, behavior knowledge, memory	Reliability: - Cronbachs Alpha = .91 - middle act intercorrelation: .13 Convergent validity: 40 (peer- and self-ratings) Divergent validity: only minor correlations with Academic Intelligence (CBI 1 /CBI 3) (N=119) (-.01 - .03)

Table 2-5: Social Intelligence Self-/Peer-report Measures, continued (part 2)

Test name	Definition/ Model	Scales (mentioned in the test)	Results/Studies
Perceived decoding / encoding ability scale (PDA, PEA, Zuckerman & Larrance, 1979)	Measurement of the extent to which a person believes to have decoding ability (interpretation of nonverbal cues)	32 items	Reliability: - internal consistency: .85 Convergent validity: - correlation with PONS (N=88): .13 (full version, see Riggio & Riggio, 2001); .26-.28 (brief version) - No correlations with vocal cues of affect
Social Competence Nomination Form (SCNF, Ford, 1982), To be used for multiple source feedback	Social competence is the attainment of relevant social goals in specified social contexts, using appropriate means and resulting in positive developmental outcomes.	Social competence has to be judged according to performance in six hypothetical social situations (e.g. peer counselor situation, double-date situation, etc.). For each situation subjects are asked to nominate six people (three female and male each) in their grade / group whom they thought would be particularly good at handling that situation. Then, subjects were asked the question, "How do you think you would do in the role of the ...?" (self-judgment on a 5-point scale; very well-poor).	Reliability: - internal consistency: about .70 - .95 (self-ratings are internally more consistent than peer nominations and teacher ratings) -interrater reliability: .85 - .95 Validity: - core social competence factor unique to the social domain, 11-15% of variance explained (but may also represent a self-report method factor) - empathy was consistently and highly related to social competence in different schools, both sexes, and age groups
Hogan's Empathy Scale (Hogan, 1969)	Empathy: the intellectual or imaginative apprehension of another's condition without actually experiencing that person's feelings (p. 308)	Non-affective Comprehensions of others and role-taking as social understanding components	Reliability: Kuder-Richardson (KR): .71; Retest: .84 (2 months) 64 item questionnaire Convergent validity: - 4 factor structure: Social self-confidence, even temperedness, sensitivity, non-conformity (Johnson, Cheek, & Smither, 1983)

Table 2-5: Social Intelligence Self-/Peer-report Measures, continued (part 3)

Test name	Definition/ Model	Scales (mentioned in the test)	Results/Studies
Social competence questionnaire (Schneider, Ackerman, & Kanfer, 1996)	Developed out of laypersons' descriptions of typical socially competent behavior	Extraversion, warmth, social influence, forming an interpersonal circumplex: social insight, -openness, -appropriateness, -maladjustment 72 items	Reliability: - Alpha of scales: .50 (maladjustment) - .87 (extraversion) Discriminant validity: - many significant correlations with personality composites - no correlations with measures of numerical and verbal reasoning (GPA, ACT) - social insight showed the greatest discriminant validity with respect to personality and academic intelligence
Rating Test of Empathy (Dymonds, 1949, 1950)	Empathy is defined as the imaginative transposing of one-self into the think-ing, feeling, and act-ing of another. (Dy-monds, 1950, p. 343)	Cross-questionnaire, Self-rating. Peer-rating and rating in the perspective of the peer (how would peer rate own person, and himself) on the traits: 1. superior-inferior 2. friendly-unfriendly 3. leader-follower 4. shy-self-assured 5. sympathetic-unsympathetic 6. secure-insecure	Reliability: - Split half: .82 - Retest reliability: .60 - Lindgren & Robinson, 1953: .69 - .73 Validity: - no relationship with academic intelligence (Wechsler) - no relationship with personality (MMPI) - The test seem to measure rather cultural norms than empathy (Lindgren & Robinson, 1953) - Orlik (1978): results not promising

Conclusions With Regard to Self-/Peer-report Measures

SI measured via self-report was separable from AcI (Amelang et al., 1989; Brown & Anthony, 1990; Marlowe, 1986; Riggio, 1989). However, when presented with personality variables, correlations were significant (e.g. Riggio, 1989). That leads to the assumption that SI self-report instruments are rather indicators of personality than of social intelligence. When presented together with peer reports and performance measures, clear method factors emerge (Brown & Anthony, 1990). On the one hand, SI self-report measures seem to have nothing in common with either academic intelligence or social intelligence performance measures (e.g. Barnes & Sternberg, 1989; Riggio, 1989). On the other hand, Furnham and Chamorro-Premuzic (2004) reported a moderate correlation (r = .30) between self-rated and measured IQ. A recent meta-analysis shows that information on intellectual performance (grades, class ranks, and test scores like the SAT) collected via self-reports should be interpreted with caution (Kuncel, Credé, & Thomas, 2005). Beyond the inability of examinees to self-report or self-estimate their (emotional) intelligence, the ease with which responses on such measures can be distorted may be one of the reasons for a dissociation between the responses and actual ability. Visweswaran and Ones (1999) state that respondents can fake self-report measures when they are instructed to. In addition, participants fake without explicit instruction (McFarland, 2003). It appears that the method, self-report or performance-based, is not the problem, but rather what is asked about. People know whether they are good liars, but not how accurate they are in detecting deception. Commenting on theoretical considerations and empirical findings that have been obtained again and again, Kihlstrom and Cantor (2000) state "the measurement of individual differences in social intelligence by means of self-report scales is a major departure from the tradition of intelligence testing [...]" (p. 364). Similarly, Bronfenbrenner, Harding, and Gallwey (1958) consider the conventional paper-pencil technique to be inappropriate in appraising the judge's ability to recognize whether other people actually behave in a certain manner (e.g., influential or submissive). Instead, we appraise the judge's sensitivity of whether or not other people regard him as behaving in a particular fashion. However, it is not that self-report measures do not include variance from the variable of interest; rather, they include so much in addition (Sechrest, 2005).

Table 2-6: Social Intelligence Knowledge Tests

Test name	Definition/ Model	Dimensions/ Material	Scales (mentioned in test)	Results/Studies
Tacit Knowledge Inventory for Managers (TKIM, Wagner & Sternberg, 1991)	Implicit knowledge in specific situations	Dimension: knowledge Material: verbal	Behavior patterns to deal with work situations, afflicted with problems have to be rated according to their effectiveness. Example for subscale: knowledge about the management of others	Reliability: - Cronbachs Alpha: .74 (84 students); .80 (631 Military); - Retest (3 weeks, N=84): .78 Divergent validity N=45 participants on a leadership development program (age M=44; 41 males) - correlation with computer simulations (Earth II, Energy International): -.61 - correlation with IQ: -.14 Criterion validity: -... with salary: r= .46 (N=54 manager) -... with management experience (nr. years: r -.30, N=64)
Social Etiquette Test (Wong, Day, Maxwell, & Meara, 1995)	Social knowledge= knowing rules of etiquette; Developed on the basis of several books of etiquette	Dimension: knowledge Material: verbal, pictorial	Pictorial: Participants have to identify etiquette mistakes pictured in drawings that show interacting people according to the standards of good etiquette. Verbal: Subjects get a short situation description. Then they have to answer a question by selecting the most appropriate option out of 4 alternatives. Both are 12 item MC tests.	Reliability: (N=240 undergraduates) - verbal subtest: .30 - pictorial subtest: .57 Convergent Validity: - intercorrelation of the two subtests: .24 - The verbal subtest correlated with the Judgments in social situations subtest of the GWSIT (soc. Insight) (.18) - The pictorial subtest correlated with, social perception nonverbal (Expression Grouping Test of the Four Factor Test of SI) (.20) and social insight nonverbal (Cartoon Prediction of the Four Factor Test of SI) (.16) Divergent Validity: - The pictorial subtest correlated with verbal AcI (.17). - Zero correlations between the verbal knowledge test and AcI.

Conclusions With Regard to Knowledge Tests

The available knowledge tests are rather specific (manager knowledge, etiquette knowledge). However, we regard social knowledge as having an important relationship to SI that influences how we perceive other people (our experiences form our view and expectations of others), whom we remember (e.g. voices and faces that are similar to someone in our family), and how we understand other people (e.g., extracting roles and normative behavior from the interpretation and assessment of the person's social behavior). There seems to be a lack of knowledge tests that investigate "everyday" knowledge (e.g. the typical behavior of a doctor, the role of a father/mother, teacher, etc.).

General Conclusions

The inability to discriminate between SI and AcI, as well as difficulties in selecting external criteria against which the SI tests could be validated, resulted in declining interest in the SI construct as a distinct intellectual entity (Kihlstrom & Cantor, 2000). However, interest in the construct revived when researchers tried to get a better comprehension of the construct applying MTMM designs. By means of MTMM approaches, method-related variance can be controlled (see also chapter 2.1.4). This seems to be especially important with regard to the high correlation between verbal SI measures and AcI. New techniques in data analysis yielded new possibilities. Instead of measuring only narrow and specific aspects of social intelligence, researchers tried to cover the SI construct more broadly. In the following section, well–known MTMM studies are presented.

2.2.4 MTMM Studies of Social Intelligence

The MTMM approaches presented included different kinds of measures –verbal and nonverbal performance measures, self- and other report data, and knowledge tests. New techniques of analysis (e.g., structural equation modelling) were used to separate trait- and method-related variance.

Study 1& 2: Wong, Day, Maxwell, & Meara, 1995

Wong et al. (1995) included academic intelligence, social cognitive perception and a social behavioral measure as traits in their MTMM study, they carried out with 134 female undergraduate psychology students (mean age: 19.8 years). Socially intelligent behavior was measured through a video-recorded encounter of a male and a female. The behavior was rated according to the effectiveness of the heterosexual interaction. Wong et al. operationalized social cognitive perception through "Recognition of the mental state behind words", a verbal subtest of the GWSIT (Moss et al., 1955, see chapter 2.2.3), and through the nonverbal expression grouping subtest of the Four Factor Test of Social Intelligence (O'Sullivan & Guilford, 1976). A model with four uncorrelated method factors (verbal, nonverbal, self-report, other-report) and three correlated trait factors (AcI, social perception, effective social behavior) emerged. Social perception showed a substantial overlap with academic intelligence (.67) that exceeded the correlation between the social cognitive and behavioral intelligence measures (.54).

In their second study, Wong et al. (1995) intended to measure social knowledge, social perception, and social insight with both verbal and nonverbal measures. Twohundred and twenty-seven psychology undergraduate students (59% female, mean age: 19.9 years) participated. Social knowledge was operationalized through a verbal test (task: identification of the best solution for a social problem) and through a nonverbal measure that required identification of etiquette mistakes in drawings. The Social Translation Test of the Four Factor Test of Social Intelligence served as a verbal measure of social perception. The Expression Grouping Test of the Four Factor test was used as a nonverbal measure of this facet. Social insight (verbal measure) was assessed with the Judgment of Social Situations subtest of the GWSIT (Moss et al., 1955) and the Cartoon Prediction subtest (nonverbal measure) of O'Sullivan and Guilford (1976). Social knowledge and social insight could be identified as separate factors, which are positively related to AcI. Social perception was not separable from social insight. Wong et al. (1995) conclude that, despite much criticism (e.g. O'Sullivan & Guilford, 1976; Walker & Foley, 1973), verbal measures of SI are not necessarily problematic (because verbal method factors did not form coherent factors with large loadings). One criticism is that Wong et al. (1995) used a selected sample of high-achieving college students in their study. Whether the results are generalizable to subjects with lower education and lower IQ is not yet clear. Further criticism concerns the lack of a theoretical model as a basis for the study. Consequently, their choice of SI subconstructs, social insight, flexibility and knowledge seems rather arbitrary.

Study 3: Jones & Day, 1997

Jones and Day applied the construct of gf and gc to social intelligence. Gf was operationalized as verbal and nonverbal social cognitive flexibility and gc as verbal and nonverbal social knowledge. In the social cognitive flexibility tasks, participants had to list all possible interpretations of social ambiguous situations presented video-based (nonverbal) or written (verbal). Social knowledge was operationalized with the Expression Grouping Subtest (O'Sullivan & Guilford, 1976) as a nonverbal measure. The Social Translation Test (O'Sullivan and Guilford, 1976) served as a verbal measure. A study with 169 high school participants (mean age 17.5 years, about 60% female) yielded a separable social cognitive flexibility factor that was positively related to AcI. Social knowledge could not be distinguished from AcI.

Study 4: Lee, Wong, Day, Maxwell, & Thorpe, 2000

Lee et al. (2000) used measures for both social and academic crystallized and fluid intelligence, and could identify all four trait factors. Social inference was sought to represent social fluid intelligence. Social knowledge served as a representative for social crystallized intelligence. Social inference and social knowledge correlated with .63; the two AcI factors correlated with .85. SI and AcI factors correlated between .24 and .40. The verbal and pictorial factor were not clearly separable (r= .92) but were uncorrelated with the self-/other-report measures. The study was implemented with 169 undergraduate psychology student participants (50% female and male) with a mean age of 19.76 years (18 – 22).

Study 5: Lee, Day, Meara, & Maxwell, 2002

Lee et al. (2002) used open-ended questions in social knowledge and social flexibility tasks and applied them in a sample of 246 psychology students (mean age: 19.65; 52% females). The authors took the view of Cantor and Kihlstrom (1987) who proclaimed open-ended questions as being more indicative of real-life social problems than tasks with only one correct answer. They used the Role Category Questionnaire (Lee et al., 2002) as a verbal measure. The questionnaire presents certain kinds of social roles that participants should use to describe persons fitting into a specified role in detail. Within the nonverbal measure, photographs from well-known persons are presented. The presented persons have to be described in depth. The number of different characteristics was taken as a performance score. Social cognitive flexibility was measured with the tasks Jones and Day (1997) applied (list all possible interpretations of social ambiguous situations, video-based and written). The postulated social intelligence trait factors emerged and were separable but correlated with creativity.

Study 6: Weis, 2002; Weis & Süß, 2007

Weis (2002) examined three cognitive SI domains, namely social knowledge, memory and understanding, relying on written, pictorial and video-based material. The Chapin Social Insight Test (Chapin, 1967; Gough, 1968), the Social Translation Test of the Four Factor Test of Social Intelligence (O'Sullivan & Guilford, 1976), and the Emotions in Relationships Subtest of the MSCEIT V.2 (Mayer, Salovey, Caruso, & Sitenarios, 2003) were used to measure written (verbal) social understanding. Pictorial understanding was measured with the Faces Test (MSCEIT V.2; Mayer et al., 2003) and with the Couples task (Barnes & Sternberg, 1989). The Interpersonal Perception Task-15 (IPT-15, Costanzo & Archer, 1993) was applied to assess video-based social understanding. The TKIM was used as a verbal indicator for social knowledge. Weis (2002) developed new social memory tasks, "Remembering couples" (pictorial), "Staff files" (written/verbal) and "Video scenes" (video-based). The Berlin Intelligence Structure Test served as a measure of AcI (BIS; Jäger, 1982, 1984). In addition, the 118 high school students (12th and 13th grade) and psychology students with a mean age of 19.7 years (SD = 3.22; range: 17 - 33 years) and a proportion of 67.2% women worked on several SI self-report measures (PDA/PDE, Zuckerman & Larrance, 1979; SSI, Riggio, 1989; Prototypical Acts on SI, Amelang et al., 1989, see chapter 2.2.3) and the extraversion, openness and agreeableness scales of the NEO-FFI (Borkenau & Ostendorf, 1993), which served as an indicator of personality. The findings revealed the three postulated SI domains separable from AcI. Although academic intelligence memory correlated with all SI domains, multiple regression analysis and confirmatory factor analysis indicated structural independence of SI factors. Compared to verbal tasks, nonverbal tasks showed less overlap with AcI. SI performance measures demonstrated only minor correlation with SI self-report measures; SI self-report measures were correlated with the personality scales.

Conclusions Concerning MTMM Studies

The studies just described confirm the hypothesis of SI being a multidimensional construct. Which subconstructs SI actually contains is still unclear. In addition, social intelligence measured via self-and other-report and performance measures did not load on the same trait factor. As mentioned by Cronbach (1960, see also Sackett, Zedeck, & Fogli, 1988) self-and other-report measures seem to measure the typical performance, whereas performance measures seem to be indicators of maximal performance. In Lee et al.'s study (2000, see above), SI and AcI were not correlated. In a SEM model allowing intercorrelation between the two factors, the AcI–SI relation was estimated to be .37 (< .05). However, a model that did without this path was not significantly worse and for parsimonious reasons would have been preferred. According to Carroll (1993) and Lee et al. (2000), the findings query whether SI can be considered to be an intelligence. However, what do we expect? As soon as we get correlations between SI and AcI, the constructs seem to be not separable. If AcI and SI are not correlated, SI is not considered to be an intelligence. Should the positive correlation with another intelligence be a criterion to be handled as an intelligence? If so, how high should it be to treat it as an intelligence? In my opinion it is very important to specify the expectations and criteria that are required to handle a construct as an intelligence (see chapter 1.2).

It is interesting, that most of the studies in the domain of SI have been carried out with young people. Of 44 studies published before 1983, 40 used students as subjects (primary school students, high school students, undergraduate students, graduate students) (Landy, 2006).

The graduate and undergraduate students were psychology majors. Only five studies (four of them applied the Guilford and O'Sullivan tests, 1965) were conducted with high school students. These studies revealed an AcI-independent SI factor. Landy (2006) criticizes rightly that these selections of participants are not representative. Moreover, most of the studies were implemented in rather individualistic cultures like the USA and Europe. Research of social and emotional intelligence would profit from including studies of Eastern and Arabic cultures (Landy, 2006).

Literature research showed that until 2004 no further studies in the domain of "social intelligence" were published. Possible reasons may be the already mentioned problems and the emergence of emotional intelligence as a (more) popular construct. Thus, scientific discussion and research these days concentrates rather on emotional intelligence and the broad and diffusely specified construct of social competences (see chapter 2.3).

2.3 Social Intelligence in the Context of Social Competences

Social intelligence can be seen as part of the larger construct of social competences. Besides social intelligence emotional intelligence, parts of practical intelligence and social competence can be subsumed under "social competences." Related constructs are social cognition, wisdom, self-regulative and control abilities. In this chapter, the SI construct will be classified within the nomological network of those constructs. Similar terms and constructs are differentiated, related and classified into a broader model of social competences (Süß et al., 2005).

2.3.1 Emotional Intelligence

Whereas social intelligence has a relatively long research tradition, emotional intelligence (EI) is a rather new ability construct suggested by Salovey and Mayer in the 1990s. Regarding it thoroughly, it was very similar to the old SI construct but ran under a new name and became popular as one of the most relevant factors of life success in theory, work environment and daily life (Goleman, 1995). Although Goleman's assumptions about the relevance of emotional intelligence for life success were not founded empirically, his book inspired other researchers to concentrate their research on the exploration of the "new" construct EI, which today is widely seen as an interaction between emotion and cognition.

In the last few years, research in the EI domain has expanded. Several volumes were published or are in press (e.g. Geher, 2004; Matthews, Zeidner, & Roberts, in press;

Schulze, Freund & Roberts, 2006; Schulze & Roberts, 2005), a vast number of studies have been carried out and several instruments (mainly self-reports) have been developed. Several of the published studies and instruments do not differ considerably from the older SI construct (Weber & Westmeyer, 1997). According to Weber and Westmeyer (1999), the popularity of the EI construct compared to AcI has three reasons: First, EI described by Goleman (1995) can be practiced and is not genetically predetermined. Thus, everyone can have it, if they want. Second, in contrast to academic intelligence, emotional intelligence is associated with "goodness" and "virtue" and thus combines the good with the correspondence to the intelligent. Finally, in EI there is no discrepancy between heart/feeling/passion and reason/intelligence. Both are reconcilable. Surprisingly, there have been almost no empirical considerations that relate EI to the older SI (e.g. Kang et al., 2005). When EI first emerged, it was defined as a subset of SI (Salovey & Mayer, 1990). In 1993, Mayer and Salovey regarded EI skills as grouped together with SI. In the subsequent literature, EI extended beyond the scope of SI (Mayer & Salovey, 1997), then SI disappeared from theoretical (and empirical) accounts of EI and was almost completely neglected in EI literature until 2004. EI constructs often were defined in such a broad manner that in some cases SI was even regarded as a part of EI (Barchard, 2003). Up to this point it appeared to be necessary to prove its scope. Those considerations took place almost without any empirical investigations. Our attempts to render the overlap and distinctiveness between social and emotional intelligence more precisely (Süß et al., 2005; Weis & Süß, 2005), have been taken up (e.g. Austin & Sakolofske, 2006) so that now, rare empirical results exist (Amelang & Steinmayr; 2006).

Models of Emotional Intelligence

Whereas a common model of SI has not existed before now, in EI research tradition different models came up. The models can be classified into two distinct groups – trait (or mixed) and ability models of emotional intelligence (Mayer, Salovey, & Caruso, 2000b) that vary considerably depending on the scope of conceptualizations and the instruments used. Table 2-7 summarizes important differences between mixed models and ability models of EI.

Table 2-7: Ability Models and Mixed Models of Emotional Intelligence

	Ability models	**Mixed models**
Definition	Mayer et al. (1999, 2000a) define Emotional intelligence as a collection of emotional abilities that can be divided into four branches that are arranged from more basic to higher-level skills (see Figure 2-6).	collection of (partially already well-known) abilities and non-ability traits (Neubauer & Freudenthaler, 2005, p. 31).
Construct (Petrides & Furnham, 2000, 2001)	Ability EI	Trait EI is often regarded as a diverse group of personality variables and others that should predict success in professional and everyday life.
Example of a model	Four-Branch Ability-Model (Mayer & Salovey, 1997, see Figure 2-6)	BarOn model (BarOn, 1997) (see below)
Type of performance (Cronbach, 1960; Sackett et al., 1988)	maximal	typical
Type of measurement	performance test	self-report
Examples of instruments	• Mayer-Salovey-Caruso Emotional Intelligence Test (MSCEIT, Mayer et al., 2000b) • Test of Emotional Intelligence (TEMINT, Schmidt-Atzert & Bühner, 2002) • Situational Test of Emotion Management (STEM) and the Situational Test of Emotion Understanding (STEU) (MacCann, 2006)	• BarOn Emotional Quotient Inventory (Bar-On, 1997, 1999) • Schutte Emotional Intelligence Test (SEIS, Schutte, Malouff, Hall, Haggerty, Cooper, Golden, & Dornheim, 1998) • Trait Meta Mood Scale (TMMS; Salovey, Mayer, Goldman, Turvey & Palfai, 1995)

Among existing conceptualizations of trait EI, the BarOn model (BarOn, 1997) is the broadest, and the only one, empirical findings exist for. BarOn defines emotional intelligence as an array of noncognitive abilities, competencies, and skills that influence one's ability to succeed in coping with environmental demands and pressures (p. 14) and regards it as "the key" to individual differences in life success. BarOn (1997, 2000) conceptualized four broad dimensions –intra- and interpersonal skills, adaptability and stress management– containing 13 subscales. Another five subscales form a facilitator scale of EI, known as general mood. In 2003, Pérez already identified more than 50 EI self-report measures (Pérez, Petrides, & Furnham, 2005) that were developed in order to assess "trait EI." Empirical results have shown again and again that ability and trait EI differ considerably (e.g. Warwick & Nettelbeck, 2004): self-report instruments of EI correlate strongly with personality variables, whereas performance measures of EI are related to cognitive variables. EI self-report measures are very similar to measures of self-reported social intelligence (see chapter 2.2.3). I compared the BarOn EQ-i and the Schutte Emotional Inteligence Scale (SEIS) with the social intelligence self-report measures Social Skills Inventory (SSI) and Perceived Decoding Ability Scale (PDA) (see chapter 2.2.3). A comparison of the items of the BarOn EQ-I and the SSI revealed a correspondence of about 50%. Often item wordings are almost identical, such as the BarOn EQ-I item "People think I am sociable," which corresponds to the SSI item "I love to socialize." The similarities between the SEIS and the PDA are even more apparent: 78% of the PDA items are covered through similar items of the SEIS, with item wordings being nearly identical in both tests (e.g. item 32 of the SEIS: "I can tell how people are feeling by listening to the tone of their voice" corresponds to PDA item 25: "I usually cannot tell how people feel from their tone of voice"). In a first preliminary study, the SEIS and the PDA correlated with r=.63 (p<.001; N=30; Seidel, Weis, & Süß, 2004). For a more detailed description of the comparison, see Weis et al. (2006). Strong overlap concerning definitions, scales and items can be found, particularly in the domains of emotion perception and expression, in understanding oneself and others, in emotional control or adaptation to social situations, and interpersonal interaction. There is uniqueness of social intelligence self-reports regarding sensitivity to interpersonal interactions and the application to social behavior (Weis et al., 2006).

In summary, EI models and the corresponding classification can be regarded as a major advantage for the new EI construct since the distinction has not been made in social intelligence research. Thereby, a general problem emerges more clearly: Does it make sense to talk about an emotional intelligence since it has been proven repeatedly that (self-report) indicators of "trait EI" can be treated as indicators of personality (see below and also Roberts, Zeidner, & Matthews, in press)? Scherer (in press) does not suggest the conceptual differentiation between trait and ability EI but instead lumps both together and calls it emotional competence. With regard to the specifications that have been made in chapter 1 and 2.2, I will concentrate my description of ability EI and provide more detailed information concerning definitions, models, instruments and results of research. Since the label "intelligence" does not appear appropriate for "a personality trait (EI)" I will only refer to "trait EI" as far as it is directly important to understand the studies we carried out. For further information about mixed models of EI, see the listed references.

Ability Models of Emotional Intelligence (Ability EI)

Currently, the most accepted EI ability model is the "Four-Branch Ability-Model" (Mayer & Salovey, 1997, see Figure 2-6). It seeks to incorporate a number of well-established constructs from emotion research and tries to synthesize the two psychological constructs of intelligence and emotions in the EI construct. The model focuses on emotions and their interactions with thoughts (Mayer & Salovey, 1997). The modified "Four Branch Ability Model" (Mayer & Salovey, 1997) is based on the original ability model developed in 1990 (Salovey & Mayer, 1990) and strictly restricts EI to mental abilities and delimits it from personality traits. Each branch of the model consists of four abilities. The ability domains are here briefly described, mentioning their overlap with social intelligence.

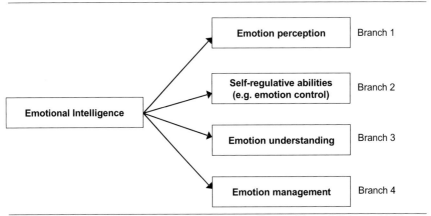

Figure 2-6: Four-Branch Ability Model of Emotional Intelligence (Mayer & Salovey, 1997)

Perception, Appraisal and Expression of Emotion (Branch 1) describe the ability to recognize/perceive one's own and other people's emotions, to discriminate among them and to express them accurately. These basic input processes are necessary for the further processing of emotional information in order to solve problems (Mayer, Salovey, Caruso, & Sitenarios, 2001). This ability can be assigned to parts of social perception as a domain of social intelligence.

Emotional Facilitation of Thinking (Branch 2) is the ability to use emotions in order to enhance reasoning, for example, the use of happiness that facilitates creativity and inductive reasoning. This ability does not refer to social intelligence.

Understanding and Analyzing Emotions (Branch 3) involves cognitive processing of emotions and includes the abilities to name emotions, to get insight into their emergence and to understand the changes of emotions. This ability is quite similar to social understanding.

Reflective Regulation of Emotions (Branch 4) is the ability to manage emotions in oneself and in others. This ability consists of the most advanced skills (staying open to different kinds of pleasant and unpleasant feelings, monitoring of emotions as well as coping with them by moderating unpleasant emotions and enhancing pleasant ones). This EI component shows a partial overlap with SI constructs in the domain of social understanding. Mayer, Salovey, and Caruso (2000a) regard emotional intelligence as broader than social intelligence, because EI includes personal (private) emotions that are important for personal growth. In their view, EI is more focused than SI, because it concentrates on the emotional part of problems rather than on (more complex?) social aspects.

Although currently the best available, Mayer et al.'s (2000b) four branch model raises several difficulties. There exist no explicit criteria for deciding which qualities belong to EI (e.g. emotional expressiveness, empathy, perspective-taking, etc. are excluded). The model ignores contextual information. The model excludes unconscious processes, assuming EI to be a crystallized ability, which is seen as declarative rather than procedural. Implicitly, it is assumed that the abilities of the corresponding Mayer-Salovey-Caruso Emotional Intelligence Test (MSCEIT) covered by the four branches are equal for all different emotions. However, each emotion is supported by its own distinct neuropsychological system (e.g. Panksepp, 1998). We also know that the preferred channel of emotion perception varies according to the type of emotion (e.g. negative emotions are better recognized auditorily).

Measurement of Ability Emotional Intelligence

In 1999, Mayer at al. (1999) developed the Multifactor Emotional Intelligence Scale (MEIS) consisting of 12 performance tasks intended to measure the abilities covered by the four branches (Salovey & Mayer, 1997). In order to score the test corresponding to a psychometric intelligence test, they used consensus and expert scoring (see chapter 2.2.3). Studies by Mayer et al. (1999); Roberts, Zeidner, and Matthews (2001); and Ciarrochi, Chan, and Caputi (2000) support the assumption of a general EI factor and validity of Branch I and IV (perception and management of emotion). Validity of the remaining branches is unclear. Moreover, some of the ability measures are problematic because of low reliabilities (Ciarrochi et al., 2000). Correlations between expert and consensus scoring are low and not satisfying. The correlations with criteria differ according to the scoring modus that was applied. That points to the question of whether the same ability is measured using different scoring modi. As a reaction to these problems, the Mayer-Salovey-Caruso Emotional Intelligence Test (MSCEIT, Mayer et al., 2000b) was developed. The authors used consensus scoring (based on a sample of more than 2000 people) and expert scoring (based on 21 members of the International Society of Research in Emotion, Mayer et al., 2003). Mayer et al. (2003) report higher reliabilities and a correlation of r=.91 between expert and consensus scoring (see also Mayer, Salovey, & Caruso, 2002; r=.93 - .99). Despite this high correspondence between two scoring modi, the MSCEIT is criticized since, according to their definition, objective perception tasks should need neither expert nor consensus scoring. Rather, they should use theoretical systems to score emotions that already have a long tradition in emotion research (see e.g. Ekman, 2004; Scherer, Banse, & Wallbott, 2001). Scherer (in press) adds that, through the scoring procedure measures, response agreement with population means is collected, since in the absence of clear criteria, even expert scoring is likely to reflect social agreement. Some further problems emerge with the MSCEIT: The test contains only static (verbal and pictorial) material rather than dynamic (video and audio) material. According to Brody (2004, p. 234), MSCEIT items reflect knowledge of how to regulate emotions rather than, corresponding to AcI tasks, also dealing with problem-solving (fluid) items. An additional personal criticism concerns the items presenting pictures of landscapes. Subjects are instructed to name the corresponding feelings that are expressed. I query whether a certain landscape picture evokes the same feeling in everyone.

Other performance-based EI instruments are, for example, the Test of Emotional Intelligence (TEMINT, Schmidt-Atzert & Bühner, 2002), the Situational Test of Emotion Management (STEM, MacCann, 2006) and the Situational Test of Emotion Understanding (STEU, MacCann, 2006). With regard to the TEMINT, short descriptions of real social/emotional situations of a target person are presented. Test takers have to judge the feelings of a target person. The answers are scored according to the deviation from the target person's answer. However, for me it seems almost impossible to interpret the emotions, because no context information is provided. According to Schmidt-Atzert and Bühner (2002), the TEMINT is useful to predict school grades. Compared to the MSCEIT, it covers the domains of perception and understanding of emotions. However, whether school grades are the appropriate criterion for an EI test is questionable. The STEU intends to assess the understanding of emotions occurring in different situations and is target-scored, allowing verification of the correct answer. The STEM measures emotion management in work-life and personal-life contexts for the emotions sadness, fear, and anger. Situations represent one of eight general content areas (e.g., health concerns, isolation and unfairness).

In the emotion research tradition, the Ekman-60 faces test (see also Facial Expressions of Emotion–Stimuli and Tests; FEEST; Young, Perrett, Calder, Sprengelmeyer, & Ekman, 2002) was developed, which is a power measure of EI. Sixty facial expressions are presented in a random order on a computer screen, and participants have to indicate via mouse click whether the emotion expressed is happiness, sadness, anger, fear, disgust or surprise. Each image remains on the screen for a maximum of five seconds. The test is a good example of performance-based EI measures; however, it is limited to the pictorial perception domain.

Overlap of Ability Emotional Intelligence with Social Intelligence

In spite of its shortcomings the MSCEIT (Mayer et al., 2002) at present is the only commonly accepted broad performance measure of emotional intelligence. Concerning the overlap between SI tests and the MSCEIT subtests (as an EI measure) we can conclude that, for the subtests "Pictures" (Branch 1) and "Sensations" (Branch 2), no equivalent tests in the domain of SI are available. In the "Pictures" test, participants have to indicate the extent to which certain images or landscapes express various emotions. In the "Sensations" subtest, subjects have to compare different emotions to different sensations, such as color or temperature. All other subtests of the MSCEIT vary in their degree of overlap with SI tests. Most similarities can be found with the subtests "Emotion Management" and "Emotions in Relationships," which show overlap with the Chapin Social Insight Test (Chapin, 1967, Gough, 1968, see chapter 2.2.3) and with the Tacit Knowledge Inventory for Managers (TKIM, Wagner & Sternberg, 1991, see chapter 2.2.3). The tests already mentioned are similar in that a social situation or problem has to be evaluated according to different possible reactions. The aim is to find the best solution for the situation or problem. The "Faces" subtest measures the ability to perceive emotions in faces. This ability is also very important to be successful in the IPT-15 (Costanzo & Archer, 1993) and in the "Couples task" (Barnes & Sternberg, 1989). The IPT-15 is a video-based test of social understanding (see chapter 2.2.3), which requires, for example, judgment of the relationship between people, recognition of deception, etc. In the Couples task, the kind of relationship between a man and a woman presented in a picture has to be evaluated (are they a couple or two strangers?). Most of the SI tasks requiring the same abilities as the newer EI tasks stem from the test battery of Guilford and O'Sullivan (1966; 1976). The "Pictures" and "Sensations" tests that do not have a correspondence in EI tests, do not refer to social interactions in social situations. Rather, they focus on emotions that evolve from nature or images. Conclusively, all MSCEIT tests have a correspondence in older SI tests except those that do not deal with people and thus are not important for socially intelligent behavior.

Kang et al. (2006) postulate SI and EI to overlap and to be multidimensional, depending on one another. In their opinion, SI and ability EI differ from AcI. They suggest transferring gf/gc theory of academic intelligence to SI/EI. Both SI and EI contain acquired declarative and procedural knowledge as well as fluid parts (p. 110). Crystallized social and emotional intelligence, according to Kang et al. (2006), can be specified as follows. Social knowledge is regarded as etiquette knowledge depending on culture. Emotional knowledge is seen as established perception ability. They distinguish social/emotional knowledge about oneself and others and they consider the flexible use of knowledge in order to find solutions to new problems as a fluid social and emotional ability. An additional attempt that examined the overlap and distinctiveness between SI and ability EI is described in Davies, Stankov, and

Roberts (1998). Davies et al. (1998) used the IPT-15 (Costanzo & Archer, 1993, see chapter 2.2.3), a social perception performance test relying on videos (indicators of SI), and the Emotion perception in faces (indicator of EI; Mayer, DiPaolo & Salovey, 1990). SI and EI correlated with r=-.09 (N=131) and showed bipolar loadings on one factor. Barchard (2003) applied the Four Factor Test of Social Intelligence (O'Sullivan & Guilford, 1976) in order to indicate SI and the MSCEIT 1.1 (cited by Barchard, 2003) as an EI measure. However, she does not report any correlations between both instruments.

Relationship Between Ability Emotional Intelligence and Academic Intelligence

This book does not aim to investigate whether EI is a useful construct. However, because of the similarities of EI and SI and the replacement of SI by EI, studies that were conducted in EI research can provide important results concerning the SI–AcI relation. Therefore, some notes about ability EI and AcI follow.

Austin and Saklofske (2006) report a study that relates EI measures to information processing speed (see also Austin, 2004, 2005). Amongst other measures, 97 participants worked on three information processing speed tasks (IT-tasks). The first dealt with discrimination between happy and neutral faces. In the second task, test takers had to differentiate between sad and neutral faces and in the third two stimuli without emotions were used (neutral condition). Another ability EI task involved recognition of faces without time limitation. As a main finding, the emotional IT tasks correlated significantly with the faces tasks (time unlimited), whereas the neutral IT tasks did not correlate with the time unlimited faces test. The faces test (EI ability) did not show correlations with crystallized intelligence tests, nor with a personality scale. Factor analysis revealed an overall processing speed factor that explained variance in all IT tasks. Additional variance of the emotional IT tasks can be explained through an emotion processing factor. The results indicate that there is indeed an emotional perception ability that is different from AcI, though emotion perception tasks also share systematic variance with the neutral perception task. This finding is especially important related to results obtained regarding social perception ability. The few studies in social intelligence dealing with perceptual abilities, had difficulties justifying social perception as a separate factor (see Wong et al., 1995).

MacCann, Matthews, Zeidner, and Roberts (2004a) investigated whether EI can be seen as a standard intelligence and used the Situational Test of Emotion Management (STEM) and the Situational Test of Emotion Understanding (STEU). Three marker variables of fluid and crystallized intelligence served as measures of AcI. Personality was represented through a personality questionnaire based on the NEO-PI-R (advanced version of the NEO-FFI, Ostendorf & Angleitner, 2004). Some other criterion values were collected. The results with

178 students (76.4% female) indicate that EI is separable from fluid and crystallized AcI. The correlations between ability EI and AcI are higher than the EI-personality correlations. MacCann, Matthews, Zeidner, and Roberts (2004a) draw the conclusion that performance-based EI can be regarded as a standard intelligence that constitutes new content areas within existing intelligences such as Gf and Gc. However, results are contradictory. Schulte, Ree, and Carretta (2004) investigated the construct validity of EI (measured with the MSCEIT) considering the relations to the Big Five (measured with the NEO-FFI) and to "g" (measured with the Wonderlic personnel test of intelligence). The "g" measure and EI correlated with r= 0.45. A regression analysis with the three predictors g, agreeableness, and gender could explain about 65% of the EI variance (corrected R= 0.81). Conclusively, the authors call EI as a separate construct into question.

Until now, there is no agreement among researchers whether EI can be regarded as a separate construct. Several authors support the view of Mayer and Salovey (1997), who proclaim that (ability) EI meets the conceptual, correlational, and developmental criteria of an intelligence. These authors regard the EI construct to be clearly distinguishable from personality traits but positively correlated with measures of AcI (Austin et al., 2004; Austin & Saklofske, 2006; Derksen, Kramer & Katzko, 2002; Mayer et al., 1999, 2000a, 2000b, 2001; Roberts et al., 2001). Austin and Saklofske (2006) expect EI to rise with age and experience with social interaction and overlap more with culture-dependent and acquired (crystallized) than with fluid abilities. Surprisingly, Austin et al. (2004), without providing reasons, regard EI as more likely to be an intelligence than SI since there are biological hints (e.g. with brain lesions) in EI research that point in the direction of an intelligence (z.B. Bar On, Tranel, Denburg, & Bechara, 2003). However, according to our knowledge, there have never been studies that examined SI in a similar way. Moreover, as already indicated, I wonder whether moderate correlations with AcI are really the right criteria to show that EI comprises an intelligence domain distinct from AcI. Obviously, EI research deals with the same problems SI research did. The result obtained for SI in this book should also yield interesting implications for EI research, taking into account the similarities between ability EI and SI discussed above.

Combined Studies of Trait and Ability Emotional Intelligence Related to Academic Intelligence

Engelberg and Sjöberg (2005) focused on emotion perception as a part of emotional intelligence. Their analysis was based on 282 respondents. EI was operationalized by both performance and self-report measures. Findings revealed that emotion perception (i.e., accuracy in the judgment of others' acute and habitual feeling states) was related to a comparably higher accuracy in the assessment of mood experienced by others. Results further suggest that successful social adjustment is related to a more accurate perception of variations in others' mood, which strengthens the hypothesis that emotion perception is essential for adaptation on a social level.

Some authors found relationships of EI self-report and EI ability measures. Austin (2004) found a significant correlation between the EI self-report subscale "Appraisal" (modified version of the SEIS) and EI ability measures (recognition of emotions on faces in IT tasks, see above) in a study with 92 students and volunteers (71.2% female; mean age: 32 years). Another study with 95 students (Austin, 2005) included the Raven Progressive Matrices along with the IT-tasks and the Ekman Faces test. Structural Equation modeling revealed two correlated factors: (1) a speed factor with high loadings of the nonemotional IT task and the Raven test, and (2) an emotion factor with high loadings of the emotional IT tasks and the Ekman Faces test. Self-reported EI was again significantly and positively correlated with the EI performance score. In addition, Brackett and Mayer (2003) report correlations between EI self-reports and ability measures between .12 (EQ-I and MSCEIT) and .18 (SEIS and MSCEIT) when controlled for personality variables.

Critical Conclusion on the Emotional Intelligence Construct

The hope arose that EI could explain even more than the 20–25% of variance on criteria such as training and proficiency success (see Schmidt & Hunter, 1998) predicted by IQ tests. However, in a meta-analytic study of VanRooy and Viswesvaran (2004) based on 59 independent empirical studies with aggregated sample sizes up to N=9522, EI has a value of only .23 in the prediction of job performance. EI correlated with all personality dimensions (Big Five) significantly (.23 - .34) and exceeded those between EI and job performance. When AcI and personality were accounted for, GMA provided substantial incremental validity above EI (.31) whereas EI provided no validity above GMA (.01) in predicting job performance (VanRooy & Viswesvaran, 2004). Bachard (2003) found that multiple measures of EI (trait and ability) did not show incremental validity over AcI and personality in the prediction of academic success. These results have been confirmed by several other authors (Amelang & Steinmayr, 2006; Austin et al., 2004; Schulte, Ree, & Carretta, 2004; Dawda & Hart, 2000; Derksen, Kramer, & Katzko, 2002; Newsome, Day & Catano, 2000; Petrides & Furnham, 2001; Parker, Summerfeldt, Hogan, & Majeski, 2004). On the one hand, this seems to confirm results obtained by Schmidt and Hunter (1998, see also chapter 1.3). On the other hand, it may stem from the inappropriate use and integration of criteria (i.e., aggregating results for different jobs) and their collection (e.g., sympathy-biased supervisory ratings) or inappropriate measures (indicators) of EI. No matter what is the actual reason for this result, EI has yet to prove its scope against AcI, as well as against the older construct of SI. Empirical results argue in favor of dealing with personality when talking about trait EI rather than approaching the status of an intelligence (see Weber & Westmeyer, 1999). Summarizing the current status of EI, Murphy (2006) remarks that EI is often poorly defined and measured, that the relationship of EI to other constructs (e.g. AcI, SI, personality) is not adequately understood, and that claims about the predictive power of EI for success in school etc. are not supported. Prospective research with regard to EI and its relationship of AcI and SI should begin with the development of a new appropriate EI test that extends the scope of the MSCEIT and may attain the status of a standard reference instrument. Expenses can be saved by doing without subtests that deal with emotions regarding stones and landscapes. With an appropriate ability EI instrument that concentrates on EI-specific components, it should also be possible to examine the relationship to SI with more reliability and validity. More detailed studies are needed to examine exactly, which EI components are predictive when controlled for other variables (see also Zeidner, Matthews, & Roberts, 2001).

2.3.2 Practical Intelligence

Definition and Construct

One can differentiate between two approaches to measure practical intelligence (PI). The first assesses practical abilities and skills (see Fleishman, 1967), while the second focuses on tacit knowledge (see Sternberg & Wagner, 1986; Wagner, 1994). Fleishman (1967) included practical-technical and technical-constructive abilities and skills as well as psychomotor coordination in the scope of the construct. Sternberg and Wagner (1986) modified the traditional construct, and define PI as the ability to successfully handle ill-defined problems and daily life tasks without clear answers. Neisser (1976) also talks about "intelligent performance in natural settings" and distinguishes this form of intelligence from AcI. Whereas the traditional construct did not have anything in common with SI or even explicitly excluded it (Mariacher & Neubauer, 2005; Sperber, 1995), PI according to Sternberg and Wagner (1986) seems to be related to SI. Dealing with the environment in general includes contact with a social environment to an important degree (Kaiser, 1998). PI in the view of Sternberg and Wagner is similar to the construct of problem solving (Dörner, 1987) treating practical, ill-defined and unformulated problems that are embedded in daily life and thus different from AcI (formulated by others, well-defined, disembedded from ordinary experience, see Hedlund, Forsythe, Horvath, Williams, Snook, & Sternberg, 2003). Their (often multiple possible) solutions mainly require additional information and are achieved with multiple methods. According to Wagner and Sternberg, PI is operationalized as practical know-how, or the ability to acquire "tacit knowledge" (TK). People with TK often are not able to explain their way of working on a certain task or problem. TK is acquired through personal experience and imitation of others and has a practical value for the individual (Hedlund et al., 2003). By means of the degree of TK, experts can be differentiated from laypersons.

Sternberg and Wagner (1986) suggested three parts of TK abilities: (1) knowledge about oneself (abilities, shortcomings, self-motivation strategies), (2) knowledge of how to solve tasks (how to work effectively), (3) knowledge of how to deal with others (managing different people, superiors, co-workers and subordinates).

Relationship to Social Competence

Sternberg and Wagner (1986) carried out studies on conceptions of laypersons concerning PI and social competence as well as their relationship. The prototypical everyday intelligent person is characterized by practical problem solving ability, social competence, character and interest in learning and culture (Sternberg, Conway, Ketron, & Bernstein, 1981). The prototypical socially competent individual is described by prosocial skills (responding to the need of others), social-instrumental skills (knowing how to get things done), social ease (enjoying social activities and involvement) and self-efficacy (having a good self-concept). Sternberg and Wagner (1986) regard social competence as a part of PI. Ford (1986) has a quite similar view and suggests that PI involves the pursuit of transactional goals that entail things outside the body (e.g. establishing a friendship with a playmate). In Ford's view, many of the transactional goals valued by individuals and their societies are social in nature (treating people fairly, having good relations with friends and family). Wagner (1994) sees the major difference between (academic) work in school and (practical) work performed outside the classroom in that the former is done independently whereas the majority of practical work is done in cooperation with others.

Measurement of Practical Intelligence

Instruments that measure PI in the sense of Sternberg and Wagner (1986) are rare. Some German-language tests and tasks concentrate on the ability to find practical solutions to problems that are not at all social (e.g. tasks described in Sperber, 1995; PAI30 test of daily intelligence, Mariacher & Neubauer, 2005). PI tests that focus on tacit knowledge can be classified according to their degree of realism. The ETS Basic Skills Test (1977, cited by Wagner, 1994) is a test with a rather low degree of realism and is mainly oriented on instruments measuring AcI. The tasks for example require reading a paragraph and describing the main theme afterwards, interpreting maps, and interpreting written guarantees for products. One of the most famous instruments is the "Tacit Knowledge Inventory for Managers" (TKIM; Wagner & Sternberg, 1991), which can be regarded as moderately realistic according to our classification since it makes use of realistic situations one might encounter in a job situation. Wagner and Sternberg (1991) postulate three dimensions that describe different tasks: (1) Managing self, (2) Managing tasks, and (3) Managing Others. Whereas the first two dimensions include knowledge about the motivational and organisational aspects of the own behavior as well as knowledge about the performance of tasks at work, the third dimension overlaps clearly with social intelligence. "Managing others" deals with knowledge about other people (e. g., successful contact with superiors, colleagues and co-workers). Knowledge about other people influences how someone interprets the behavior of a certain person (see chapter 2.2.1). The TKIM consists of 7–19 problem-solving scenarios that list 6–16 potential actions that have to be rated on a seven- or nine-point scale for either quality or importance. The test is mainly scored using expert ratings. Similar to the TKIM, the Tacit Knowledge for Military Leaders inventory (TKML) was developed to assess the knowledge leaders possess (Hedlund et al., 2003). The in-basket test (Frederiksen, Saunders & Wand, 1957, cited by Wagner, 1994) is a highly realistic measurement that places examinees at an executive's desk and asks them to handle items contained in an in-basket. Performance is evaluated against criteria (e.g. taking responsibility).

Empirical Results

The less realistic the test, the higher was the correlation with "classical IQ" in empirical studies (Wagner, 1986). However, differences in IQ correlations could also be due to differences in the methods applied (AcI paper-pencil test – PI paper-pencil test vs. AcI paper-pencil test – PI behavioral measure). Performance on practical tasks does not decline with age, as with crystallized ability (whereas fluid intelligence declines). Wagner and Sternberg (1985; Wagner, 1987) assessed TK in business managers, undergraduates, and graduates with the TKIM. TK differentiated the samples that were tested: undergraduates received the lowest scores, graduates' scores were significantly higher, and professionals performed the best. Professionals' scores were also predictive for indices of career performance (e.g. additional 32% of variance in performance in the problem solving scenarios Earth II and Energy International). Scores on TK measures rarely correlate with IQ measures (e.g. with verbal reasoning of the Differential Aptitude Test, $r = .16$, $N=22$ and $r=.12$, $N=60$). TK predicts real-world performance independently of IQ and personality (Wagner, 2000, obtained a correlation between citation count and tacit knowledge of .44 ($p<.001$) with psychologists). However, as Gottfredson (2003) mentions, a problem with criterion-related correlations arises for TK because of the limitation to the significant coefficients. For 22 reported correlations the n-weighted average is .26, the average for the 35 unreported correlations is only .08. For the entire 57 studies with well-known sample sizes, the weighted average is only .15 (Gottfredson, 2003). Dilchert and Ones (2004) estimated the incremental validity of PI beyond AcI to be .02 and .03 for the prediction of job performance and academic success, respectively.

Critical Discussion

Sternberg's conception of PI is rather broad and similar to the unspecific and all-inclusive conceptions of trait EI (e.g. BarOn, 1999). Because of the scope of the construct, there are some differentiation problems from his success intelligence (Sternberg, 2005), as well as from SI emerge, reminding us of the problem of intelligence inflation (Weber & Westmeyer, 2001, see also chapter 1.1). Another difficulty consists in the view of SI as a part of PI. Even though it is obvious that PI, according to Wagner and Sternberg as well as Ford, is quite similar to SI (with the combining part being TK), it seems to be presumptuous to include SI research occurring since 1920 in the "own conception" without a closer reflection. It is not yet settled how the purportedly multidimensional SI construct is actually related and integrated into PI. In my opinion, it is doubtful whether PI defined as TK is a separate construct beyond SI. It seems reasonable to include TK into SI. The specific PI that differs obviously from both AcI and SI is consequently better defined according to Mariacher and Neubauer (2005) or Sperber (1995). TK can be regarded as a superordinate mechanism that plays an important role in PI, SI, and EI. In Gottfredson's (2003) view, the TK construct points to a form of experience and knowledge that lends itself to the development of wisdom (see chapter 2.4.3). These theoretical considerations are supported by a closer examination of empirical results: Gottfredson (2003) states that Sternberg et al. have made an implausible claim that TK would reflect a general factor of intelligence that equals or exeeds g in generality and everyday utility. Their research presenting only meager data in a small number of small samples of higher-educated people (highly restricted samples), and working with many examples and anecdotes of mostly ill-educated people, does not justify a separate construct of tacit knowledge PI. Schmidt and Hunter (1993) also criticize the idea of tacit knowledge as something new and argue that the construct can be considered as an already existent and well-developed form of job knowledge rather than intelligence. Moreover, TKIM scales do not show sufficient reliability (average reliability of scales is alpha=.48). Austin et al. (2004) suggest to hold off on the question of whether PI can be treated as an intelligence because empirical studies are rare and show inconsistent results. Jensen (1993) remarks that "tacit knowledge seems to be an exceedingly mysterious variable, theoretically and empirically. We are told that it behaves like a personality factor (predicting "adjustment" in college), and that it also predicts scholastic performance. But then we are told that it is virtually uncorrelated with personality or with IQ or g, with almost anything else we know something about [...]." (p. 9)

2.3.3 Social Competence

Social competence is poorly defined and scientifically not well integrated into models and theories. Nevertheless, it is a widely used construct, in both our daily life and the work environment. Often, it is even regarded as more important than intellectual abilities. Consequently, many different opinions about the construct and its components exist.

Definitions and Models of Social Competence

The prevailing conceptions of social competence depend on the corresponding psychological discipline. Clinical psychologists emphasize assertion of one's own interests as socially competent behavior (e.g. Hintsch & Pfingsten, 2007). Within the field of developmental psychology, a socially competent person is able to adapt well to the norms and values of a society and the environment (Waters & Sroufe, 1983). According to Runde (2001, see also Kanning, 2002), these conflicting goals have to be balanced within an interaction situation. This compromise between adaptation and assertion reflects the view within Industrial/Organizational Psychology (see Kanning, 2003; Prechtl, 2005). Runde, Bastians, Kluge and Wübbelmann (2001) define social competences as "the knowledge and implementation of behavior in social interaction" (p. 3). Euler (2004) considers social competence as necessary in communication with other people. Social communication, in his opinion, is always specific for a certain situation. A successful social communication requires the person to behave appropriately. Euler (2004) regards this competence as a disposition for continuous behavior in specific types of situations. He postulates three dimensions of behavior: (1) recognition, (2) evaluation, and (3) skills/abilities. The communication with other people serves as a basis to apply social competences. Communication takes place on four levels: (1) object/domain, (2) relationship, (3) self-expression, and (4) purpose. By means of verbal and nonverbal expressions in a conversation all four types of information are given. The communication process is therefore dynamic. The possibility of misconceptions arises within the communicative behavior. The only way to measure socially competent behavior is by means of behavioral measures (situation exercises, observation of social behavior, etc.). According to Bechtoldt (2003), socially competent people are able to analyze human interactions and act purposefully. They have to have both perceptive and behavioral abilities, in order to be able to consider the interests of their interaction partners at the same time. That reflects once more the difficulty of measuring social competence properly, because several dimensions or variables have to be included into this concept.

Definitions and models of social competence can be classified as being potential-based, behavior-oriented, or mixed. Models that are known as behavior-oriented can be described as being dependent upon the context, while models that focus on the potential /preconditions of a person are independent from the context. The latter models assume that the characteristics that enable competent behavior exist independently from the given situation. In Table 2-8, three representative models are presented including their basic assumptions and differences.

Table 2-8: Models of Social Competence

	Greif (1987)	Kanning (2002)	Schneider et al. (1996)
Definitions of social competence	Successful realization of aims and plans in social interaction situations. Social competence corresponds to socially competent behavior.	Total knowledge, skills and abilities of a person, which support socially competent behavior (≈ context specific behavior that serves an aim that is socially accepted).	Socially effective, instrumental behavior (directed towards social aims) and its cognitive, affective and behavioral antecedents.
Characterstic dimensions	• Social perception • Interpretation of social indicators	• Social perception • Behavior control • Assertion ability • Social orientation • Communication ability	• Social intelligence • Social skills • Personality variabl. • Social self-regulation
Focusing potential vs. result	result-oriented	mixed model	potential-oriented
Dependence upon the social context	yes	yes	no
Evaluation standard	efficiency	efficiency and social acceptance	efficiency

Note. Table according to Süß et al., 2005, p. 356

In the view of Greif (1987), the acting person evaluates and perceives the relevant situation parameters starting with a specified aim. The evaluation results in a certain behavior that leads to a modification of the environment. The result is compared with the original aim. The process described in a behavior-oriented closed-loop system continues as long as the result corresponds to the aim. Kanning (2002) starts from a different perspective: He describes social competence as a mixed model and postulates a structure model containing four dimensions (see Table 2-8). In addition, two process models are assumed: (1) the model of elaborated genesis and (2) the model of automatic genesis of socially competent behavior. Both models are similar to the considerations suggested by Greif and can be differentiated according to the mode of information processing of the relevant situation parameters. Whereas in the model of eleborated genesis the relevant situation parameters are analyzed consciously, they are processed heuristically in the model of automatic genesis, Schneider et al. (1996) regard social competence as the person's potential, which does not depend on the context. In this book, social competence is expected to subsume parts of social, emotional and practical intelligence as well as moderator variables. The construct includes performance-based constructs such as SI as well as personality, interest, attitude and behavior variables such as self-monitoring, agreeableness, social commitment and altruism.

Measurement of Social Competence

The broadness of the social competence construct makes its measurement difficult, especially when the study is limited to only one indicator of social competence. Moreover, the lack of an explicit theory has a negative impact on systematic research (Kanning, 2002). Therefore, instruments are clearly orientated on practical needs (context of work environment) or are designed rather arbitrarily. Since social competence can be regarded as a conglomeration of SI, EI, PI, and additional personality and other variables, it is not possible to measure "one" social competence. Rather it should be specified which social competence aspect is measured (e.g. social intelligence). Alternatively, more than one or two instruments should be used. One could also state that the construct "social competence" is not specific enough to be able to operationalize it sensibly.

Studies in the Domain of Social Competence

Bechtoldt (2003) discovered that social competence is positively related to the suppression of negative emotions instead of coping with them. Integrative conflict management which can be regarded as the prototype of socially competent behavior, was positively related to positive affectivity and self-efficacy. In her study, 124 working people of different domains worked on the ISIS 2.0 (Interactive System for the Identification of Social competences, Runde et al., 1999, see chapter 2.2.3). Self-report instruments were used to assess the self-concept and affectivity variables. Interpersonal conflict situations with colleagues, employees and superiors were recorded as well as the solutions used to cope with the problems. At the end of each of the four weeks, examination occurred. Bechtoldt (2003) concluded that performance-based social competence includes the ability to regulate one's own behavior but not the ability to regulate one's own emotions. She describes social competence as a performance characteristic, which should not be measured with self-report questionnaires (p. 263).

Several authors found a positive relationship of social skills and academic achievement: Feshbach and Feshbach (1987) reported strong relationships for girls between empathic skills at the age of 8-9 and reading and spelling at age 10-11. According to a study of Green, Forehand, Beck, and Vosk (1980), children with high academic achievement were more accepted, less rejected, and less disliked by peers. Their teachers saw them as less deviant, and they more frequently engaged in positive interactions with peers than children with low academic achievement.

2.3.4 Social Competences: An Integration Attempt

Figure 2-7 illustrates our view of the overlap between SI, EI, and PI and their relationship to social competence. Obviously, we see these constructs as sharing common variance but also as having their unique parts. SI is completely included in the concept of social competence.

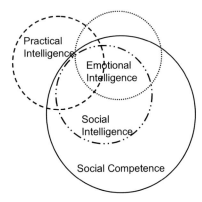

Figure 2-7: Relationship Between Social Competence and Social, Emotional and Practical Intelligence

We developed an integrative model of socially competent behavior that serves as a classification schema for social competences and as a tool to demonstrate their relationship (see Figure 2-8). Our model distinguishes between person characteristics, target-oriented actions (goal directed behavior) and evaluation standards. Each person has certain preconditions with respect to SI, EI, and PI (see Sternberg & Wagner, 1986) as well as specific values on moderating variables like altruism, self-monitoring or agreeableness. Potential and moderating variables together form the social competence of a person. The potential variables are action-independent and can be described as underlying variables that are expected to influence socially intelligent and competent behavior. However, having the cognitive preconditions to behave socially intelligently does not automatically imply a transfer of this ability into action. "A person might understand a social situation […] and be incapable of doing anything about it. To know is not to do." (p. 5; O'Sullivan et al., 1965). In our view, moderator variables influence the pursuance of socially intelligent and socially competent behavior. We assume these abilities to be independent of the given context, thus emerging in a variety of contexts. Abilities are expected to have a direct influence on behavior. Whether a certain behavior is considered as socially intelligent or competent is determined by the social context (social situation the person is in, see also Kaiser, 1998, p. 229). In one situation it may be competent to help another person, while in another situation it may be more adequate to be assertive. Wearing an evening dress is appropriate at a ball but not in a job application situation. Whether a certain behavior is competent or not is determined by the evaluation standard. Social behavior always pursues a certain aim, which does not have to be explicit or conscious. The effectiveness of a certain behavior depends on the degree to which the aim (e.g. promoting equity, caring and helping behavior, establishment of relationships, social responsibility, individuality, resource acquisition, safety, for more examples see Ford, 1994) is achieved. A behavior can be regarded as socially effective if the particular evaluation standard is attained. In addition, the social acceptance of the behavior has to be considered. Social acceptance depends on the culture (see example of Germany versus Japan in soup sipping, chapter 2.2.1). Behavior can be rated as socially competent if the means of goal attainment and the goal itself correspond to the group-specific (moral) norms and values (Süß et al., 2005). Knowledge that refers to social circumstances also depends on culture.

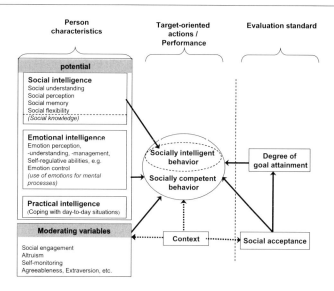

Figure 2-8: Integrative Model of Social Competences (Süß, Weis, & Seidel, 2005)

2.4 Related Constructs and Research Domains of Social Competences

In the view of laypersons, concepts such as empathy and wisdom are parts of the everyday life comprehension of SI (see e.g. Kaiser, 1998) beyond cognitive abilities (understanding others), behavior-related aspects (dealing with other people), and knowledge. Moreover, there are conceptions coming from different fields of science, namely, social cognition in social psychology and Theory of Mind (ToM) in neuropsychology. This chapter deals with the overlap and distinctiveness between these concepts and the SI construct. It would extend the scope of this book to relate the broad scope of associated constructs to SI (e.g. personality variables such as agreeableness and extraversion). Therefore, I selected those which are most often confused with SI and of which the position in the nomological network is least clear.

2.4.1 Social Cognition and the Theory of Mind

When talking about social intelligence, often the question of how SI can be differentiated from social cognition comes up. Social cognition deals with how people select, interpret and remember social information in order to make decisions and judgments (Aronson, Wilson, & Akert, 2004) and is also defined as the ability to interpret and predict others' behavior in terms of their beliefs and intentions and to interact in complex social environments and relationships (Baron-Cohen, Ring, Bullmore, Wheelwright, Ashwin, & Williams, 2000). Both definitions are similar to the subconstructs we conceptualized as being parts of SI, namely perception, memory and understanding. Further support for the similarity of both constructs is provided by Adolphs (2003) as well as Grady and Keightley (2002), who subsume the ability to understand and respond to the emotional content and environmental cues as well as the ability to remember emotional information under the construct of social cognition. Correspondent with our definition of social intelligence, social cognition seems to include perception, memory and understanding of relevant social information that is used in order to make decisions and judgments (see Aronson et al., 2004) and to interact in complex social environments and relationships (Baron-Cohen et al., 2000). Since social cognition seems to include social behavior, it is similar to SI definitions that contain a behavioral as well as a cognitive component (see definitions of SI, chapter 2.2.1). Almost no empirical studies relating social cognition to social intelligence exist. An exception is a study by Ford (1982) who examined the relation between social cognition and social competence applying nine social cognition measures and four social competence measures. Social competence was measured by means of the Social Competence Nomination Form (SCNF, Levenson & Gottman, 1978) including self, peer, teacher, and interviewer ratings. Social cognition measures contain tests such as means-end thinking (i.e., subjects have to find possible solutions in unfinished stories dealing with a protagonist in critical social situations) and awareness of consequences (i.e., subjects face a temptation conflict in which they have to describe the thoughts of the protagonist and the outcome of the situation). Both unpublished tasks are described in Platt and Spivack (cited by Ford, 1982). In addition, Hogan's empathy scale was applied (see also chapter 2.2.3). Findings of Ford's (1982) study show that social cognition is related to socially competent behavior (measured by the SNCF rating scale). Ford (1982) interpreted the result to indicate that socially competent adults are more cognitively resourceful in having more ways to address interpersonal problems and to construct plans and strategies for their solution. Empathy was strongly related to social competence measures, and higher social competence was associated with a larger and more elaborate social network. In addition, social competence tasks could be clearly separated from AcI. Although I appreciate this rare work of Ford (1982), there are some critical aspects which have to be considered in the interpretation of the results. First, Ford (1982) defines social competence as "the attainment of relevant social goals in specified social contexts, using appropriate means and resulting in positive developmental outcomes." (p. 323). However, whether an outcome is positive depends on the social context and of the evaluation processes of each individual involved in the social situation. The outcome may be positive for one person but negative for the other. Second, whereas in other studies Hogan's empathy scale was used to assess SI and social competence (see chapter 2.2.3), Ford (1982) uses it to measure social cognition. Third, some of the social cognition measures applied in Ford's study could also serve as social cognitive flexibility measures.

One particular aspect of "social cognition" is the Theory of Mind (ToM, see e.g., Adolphs, 2001). ToM should explain the ability to attribute mental states to oneself or another person (Premack & Woodruff, 1978) or infer other persons' mental states and emotions (Baron-Cohen, Wheelwright, Hill, Raste, & Plumb, 2001). We use this ability to make sense of or to predict another person's behavior (Baron-Cohen et al., 2001). ToM is also known as "mentalising" (Morton, Frith & Leslie, 1991), "mind reading" (Whiten, 1991), and "social intelligence" (Baron-Cohen, Jolliffe, Mortimore, & Robertson, 1997), and overlaps with the term "empathy". ToM represents an evolved psychological capacity most highly developed in humans. It probably emerged as an adaptive response to increasingly complex primate social interaction (Brüne & Brüne-Cohrs, 2006). Understanding a speaker's intention is a precondition for learning new words. A child begins to distinguish between own and others' mental states (e.g., "I think") at the age of four (Brüne & Brüne-Cohrs, 2006). The authors conclude that the development of ToM is paralleled by language acquisition. Their view is confirmed by Sperber and Wilson (2002), who regard the ToM as a prerequisite for the pragmatic use of human language. Greig et al. (2004) and Brüne and Bodenstein (2005) provide empirical findings showing that a violation of the rules of pragmatic use of language is linked to patients' impaired ToM in schizophrenia.

ToM is mainly applied in the clinical context for the diagnosis of cognitive dysfunction and the comparison between clinical and normal groups with regard to understanding and interpreting other people's behavior (see e.g. Baron-Cohen et al., 2001). ToM tests can be classified into (1) standard tests (e.g., (dis)prove that others can hold false beliefs different from one's own (correct) knowledge), (2) tests including the understanding of higher order false belief tasks, metaphor, irony, and faux pas (Brüne & Brüne-Cohrs, 2006) and (3) tests for adults with psychopathological conditions, containing short stories with double bluff, mistakes, persuasions, cartoons, or other visually presented material (see Brüne & Brüne-Cohrs, 2006). ToM tests are rarely available for the diagnosis of mild deficits in adults. The "Reading the Mind in the Eyes" test (Baron-Cohen et al., 1997) is an exception and can be considered as an "advanced ToM test." It taps one's ability to put himself/herself into the mind of another person and "tune in" to their mental state by using 25 photographs of the eye-region of the face in different actors. The test taker is asked to choose which of two words (in the revised version four words) best describes the feelings and thoughts of the person. Another popular ToM test is the "Faux-Pas Recognition Test" (Stone, Baron-Cohen, & Knight, 1998; Gregory, Lough, Stone, Erzinclioglu, Martin, Baron-Cohen, & Hodges, 2002), which presents written scenarios to test takers. The subjects have to answer questions concerning awkward behaviors as well as thoughts and feelings of the person in question. The following example gives an impression of the task.

Text:
Vicky was at a party at her friend Oliver's house. She was talking to Oliver when another woman came up to them. She was one of Oliver's neighbors. The woman said, "Hello," then turned to Vicky and said, "I don't think we've met. I'm Maria, what's your name?" "I'm Vicky." "Would anyone like something to drink?" Oliver asked.

Test takers have to answer questions like "Did anyone say something they shouldn't have said or something awkward?" If yes, ask: "Who said something they shouldn't have said or something awkward?", "Why shouldn't he/she have said it or why was it awkward?", "Why do you think he/she said it?", "Did Oliver know that Vicky and Maria did not know each other?", "How do you think Vicky felt?" The task also contains control questions to ensure proper understanding (e.g., "In the story, where was Vicky?", "Did Vicky and Maria know each other?") (Stone et al., 1998; Gregory et al., 2002).

To summarize and conclude, the instruments that are used to assess social cognition and ToM are quite similar to social and emotional understanding tasks involving additional knowledge and flexibility components (see also emotional expression of faces and word described in Keightley, Winocur, Burianova, Hongwanishkul, & Grady, 2006). In all research traditions, differential and diagnostic psychology (social intelligence), social psychology (social cognition), and (clinical) neuropsychology (ToM), the same construct seems to be subject of investigation. However, the term social *cognition* consisting of cognitions, emotions (see Adolphs, 2003; Grady & Keightley, 2002), and behaviors is in my opinion rather inappropriate. It is not specified what social cognition actually is and how it is related to other constructs. I agree with Adolphs (2001), who claimed that the components and boundaries of social cognition are for the most part ill-defined. Reasons for this lack are probably a different research approach in social- and neuropsychology, which lacks the profound methodology common in differential psychology, combined with interests in processes rather than in structures. In spite of the fact that parts of social cognition appear to be equal to what we define as SI (i.e., underlying components that determine the degree to which socially competent behavior can be shown), the research traditions differ considering the starting point. The social cognition research tradition focuses on general laws/general phenomena (e.g., the actor-observer difference, schemata and heuristics to facilitate judgments), whereas SI in differential psychology concentrates on individual structures and traits. Tests of social cognition and ToM tests also lack systematic development and an underlying theoretical model, and are subject to methodological shortcomings. Although some major methodological deficits were corrected in earlier versions of the ToM tests (see e.g. two options to choose, Baron-Cohen) the concentration on static stimuli does not do justice to the dynamic nature of the real world (Baron-Cohen et al., 2001).

2.4.2 Empathy

It is not surprising that SI and EI often get confused with empathy, because both constructs claim to contain parts of the empathy construct. Morover, within both EI and SI research traditions, empathy instruments were used to measure either EI or SI. In many trait conceptions of EI, empathy is an integral part (e.g. Goleman, 1995, 1998; Bar-On, 1997; Petrides & Furnham, 2003). Some empathy measures were applied as SI measures (e.g. Hogan Empathy Scale, 1969, see chapter 2.2.3), and some SI measures were used for research about empathy (e.g. the Chapin Social Insight Test, reported in Davis, 1996). In spite of these conception problems, people intuitively seem to assume that there is a specific empathy construct that differs from already defined SI and EI conceptions. Maybe therefore, in the literature, the question about the difference between empathy and various other constructs (e.g. emotional and social intelligence) is rarely addressed and far from reaching a consensus among researchers.

Definitions and Constituents of the Empathy Construct

There has been considerable confusion regarding the definition and measurement of empathy (Riggio, Tucker, & Coffaro, 1989). Knowledge concerning the essential constituents in experiences of empathy is scarce (Håkansson & Montgomery, 2003). In the following, I only summarize some of the existing definitions and include my comments about their relationship to SI and other related constructs in parentheses. Dymond (1950, S. 343) defines empathy as the imaginative transposing of oneself into the thinking, feeling and acting of another. In his view, insight is the relationship between self-perception and perception of the self by other (*similar to social perception and understanding*). In the perspective of Davis (1983), empathy refers to the reactions of one individual to the observed experiences of another (*social perception and correspondent social behavior*). According to Marlowe (1986), the ability to cognitively and affectively understand others can be regarded as an empathic ability (*social understanding and its transposition into social behavior*). According to Feshbach and Feshbach (1982), empathy includes three essential components: (1) the ability to use relevant information in order to perceive, recognize and label emotions; (2) perspective and role-taking as the ability to assume and experience another person's viewpoint; and (3) emotional responsiveness as the ability to share another person's feelings. These components overlap with regard to EI (see 1) and SI (see 2), which are cognitive. Specific to empathy seems to be the actual empathic behavior (see 3). Bohart and Greenberg (1997) summarize that most definitions of empathy include the idea of "trying to sense, perceive, share or conceptualize how another person is experiencing the world" (p. 419).

One can distinguish between two research traditions, cognitive empathy (includes perspective-taking) and emotional empathy (i.e. vicarious experience of another person's emotional state). Cognitive empathy is measured mainly through the Hogan Empathy Scale (HES, Hogan, 1969), whereas emotional empathy is measured by means of the Mehrabian and Epstein Questionnaire measure of emotional empathy (QMEE, Mehrabian & Epstein, 1972), both being self-report measures. Davis (1980), however, includes both traditions in his conception of empathy and even adds two additional components. Davis describes empathy as a multidimensional construct and views it as the phenomenon that connects two otherwise isolated individuals to each other: the empathizer, who empathizes with another person, the target (Davis, 1996). He discriminates between perspective-taking as the ability to adopt the point of view of others (cognitive empathy) and empathic concern as other-oriented feelings of sympathy and concern for unfortunate others (affective empathy), fantasy (i.e., tendencies to transpose oneself to fictitious characters), and personal distress (i.e., self-oriented feelings of personal anxiety and unease in tense interpersonal settings). Those four dimensions should be measured through the Interpersonal Reactivity Index (IRI), a 28-item self-report measure. Understanding as a result of perspective-taking should be considered an aspect of empathy (Davis, 1996). In Davis' studies, perspective-taking was related to interpersonal functioning (i.e., implies higher extraversion and self esteem, lower social dysfunction). There was no relationship with AcI (SAT, WAIS). Concerning the scales "fantasy" and "empathic concern," there was no relationship with interpersonal functioning.

Perceived similarity facilitates empathic response (Hoffman, 2000; Krebs, 1975), and empathy seems to increase with age (Björkvist, Österman, & Kaukiainen, 2000). A lack of empathy is also associated with the so-called machiavellianism. A machiavellian person makes use of social competence to manipulate people to reach his or her own aims. The ability to perceive feelings of other people has only strategic aims and does not serve the establishment of relationships. Machiavellian persons establish relationships without social closeness since such relationships could obstruct the assertion of their own aims. These people are not tied to social norms and values (Christie & Geis, 1970). Empathy exerts an influence on social relationships and outcomes through its impact on the frequency of specific relationship behaviors and the perception those behaviors create in social partners (Davis, 1996). Empathy is the affective response that stems from the accurate apprehension or comprehension of another person's emotional states. It often turns into sympathy or personal distress.

Uniqueness of Empathy? - Its Relationship to Social Intelligence and Emotional Intelligence in the Nomological Network

Regarding the suggested constituent parts of empathy, we have to query, what constitutes the specific empathic part that is not yet included in other constructs? In a study of Riggio et al. (1989), 171 undergraduates worked on the Social Skills Inventory (SSI), various empathy scales, an essay empathy task (i.e. they had to write about social failure and success), and on an emotional perception performance measure (Pictures of Facial Affect; Ekman & Friesen, 1975). Correlations between SSI and the empathy scales were positive and significant. Riggio et al. (1989) conclude that there is a tremendous overlap between social skills and empathy. Björkvist et al. (2000) believe that the socially intelligent individual is capable of producing socially intelligent behavior according to the goal he or she desires. This goal may be hostile or peaceful.

Empathy, according to most of the above mentioned definitions, is seen as putting oneself into someone's feelings, thoughts and actions (similar to SU), but more than that, to *feel* for that person. Concerning the relationship to SI, a person high in SU should have better preconditions for empathy than a person low in SU. This hypothesis is supported by Kaukiainen, Björkqvist, Lagerspetz, Österman, Salmivalli, Rothberg, and Ahlbom (1999), who regard the cognitive part of the empathy definition as nearly equivalent to the SI component social understanding. SI constitutes cognitive preconditions, whereas empathy can be regarded as a behavior. SI could be either positive (e.g., show empathic behavior, peaceful conflict resolution) or negative (ignoring the other person, asserting one's own goals) concerning the relevant aims in the situation. Empathy, however, can be considered as completely positive (on condition that it is not exaggerated).

The relationship between empathy and EI is quite similar when emotions are directed towards other people: an emotionally intelligent person (perceiving and understanding the emotions of others) should be more likely to show empathy than a person who does not have this ability. However, an emotionally intelligent person does not necessarily show empathy. That person can also use the ability for his or her own sake. I think that the specific part of the empathy conception is a feeling for other people that is rather behavioral than a cognitive precondition. All cognitive aspects mentioned in the context of empathy can be described through SI and EI. In my view, empathizing can be regarded as one component of socially intelligent behavior (provided that it is used for a certain aim).

2.4.3   Wisdom

"For wisdom, which is the worker of all things, taught me: for in her is an understanding spirit holy, one only, manifold, subtil, lively, clear, undefiled, plain, not subject to hurt, loving the thing that is good quick, which cannot be letted, ready to do good. Kind to man, steadfast, sure, free from care, having all power, overseeing all things, and going through all understanding, pure, and most subtil, spirits. For wisdom is more moving than any motion: she passed and went through all things by reason of her pureness." (Wisdom 7, 22-23, Douay-Rheims, American Ed., 1899). Refering to this citation, it appears that wisdom has to do with (1) a sense of understanding, (2) that it has good consequences (happiness, pleasantness, peace, honor, glory) (3) and that it results in socially positive behavior. Similar components are listed in the Merriam Webster Online Dictionary. In theory and research, implicit and explicit theoretical approaches to explore the construct of wisdom have to be distinguished. Implicit approaches try to find out how laypersons describe wise people, whereas explicit approaches focus on experts' views of wisdom. According to results of implicit approaches, Holliday and Chandler (1986) characterize a wise person as having extraordinary understanding of life problems, communicative abilities, interpersonal competences and social "unobtrusiveness." In Sternberg's view (1990), a wise person tries to avoid schemata of thinking and behavior but is able to understand automatic (schematic) thinking and behavior in others. A wise person tries to get an understanding of automatic assumptions of other people and their behavior (use of assumptions). With regard to results that stem from explicit-theoretical approaches, Baltes and Smith (1990) describe wise people as experts for life questions, including questions about living together (pragmatics of intelligence, Cantor & Kihlstrom, 1987, p. 2f). Baltes and Staudinger (1993, see also Baltes, Smith & Staudinger, 1992) propose five components of wisdom: (1) rich factual knowledge, (general and specific about life conditions), (2) rich procedural knowledge (general and specific about strategies of judgment and advice concerning matters of life), (3) life-span contextualism (knowledge about the contexts of life and their temporal relationships), (4) relativism (knowledge about differences in values, goals and priorities) and (5) uncertainty (knowledge about relative indeterminacy and unpredictability of life and ways to manage). An expert's answer should reflect more of these components whereas a novice's answer should reflect fewer of these components. Data support this assumption.

Wisdom in the Context of the Related Constructs Social, Emotional and Practical Intelligence

In Sternberg's view, wisdom has its core in tacit knowledge (TK), which is associated with practical intelligence (PI, see chapter 2.3.2). Sternberg (2000) defines wisdom as the application of TK as mediated by values toward the goal of achieving a common good through a balance among multiple, often competing, interests (inter-, intra-, and extrapersonal) and responses to environmental contexts (adaptation and shaping to existing environmental contexts, selection of new environmental contexts). In contrast to wisdom, in PI any sets of interests (individual or collective) should be maximized (Sternberg, 2000). According to Sternberg (2000), wisdom is at least partially domain specific, because TK is acquired within a given (set of) context(s). The ability to be wise may transfer, but the actual content of wise advice may vary. A wise person will know the limitations of his or her TK. Intelligence seems to be a precondition, necessary but not sufficient to be wise, and wisdom seems to be more related to crystallized than to fluid intelligence. Similar to empathy, all cognitive preconditions, PI, SI and EI can lead to good or bad aims, whereas wisdom always seeks the common good and fair judgment and balance interests. Sowarka (1989, p. 95) expresses the similarity of wisdom and SI through the notion that in his opinion, SI tests can measure common aspects of wisdom. Wisdom requires major EI components (understanding, judging and regulating emotions) but goes far beyond EI.

Conclusion

Conclusively, wisdom is based on preconditions such as PI (tacit knowledge), SI (understanding of other people), and EI (judgment and regulation of emotions) but goes beyond these constructs. Whereas PI, SI and EI can be regarded as preconditions of socially intelligent behavior, wisdom is part of that behavior; it can only become obvious in expressed behavior (consultations, judgments). This uncovers another difference: whereas the cognitive constructs (i.e., SI, PI, and EI) should be assessed with performance measures and have one completely correct solution, in wisdom there is no correct solution but different ways that will have different consequences.

2.5 Auditory Abilities as a Domain of Intelligence

Besides SI and its relationship to familiar conceptions, the construct of auditory intelligence (AuI) should be explored within this book and be related to AcI. Despite their importance (see chapter 1.1) and although many studies dealt with auditory abilities, they were almost never integrated in models or tests of intelligence (i. e., facet and hierarchical theories that exist in the domain of musical abilities). That does not do justice to the significance auditory abilities have. According to Atkin, Bray, Davison, Herzberger, Humphreys, and Selzer (1977), the expression of abilities in auditory tasks may be an even better indicator of "human intelligence" than expression through visual tasks. The next chapter provides theoretical knowledge about auditory abilities with regard to definitions, concepts, models and theories of auditory and the closely related musical abilities. Auditory and musical abilities will be classified in the nomological network with a focus on their relationship to AcI. Approaches will be described dealing with the past work that was conducted in order to measure auditory abilities. This chapter finishes with my own conception of auditory intellectual abilities and my suggestion for an approach to measure them.

2.5.1 Auditory Abilities: Definitions and Conceptions

Stankov (1994, p. 157) defines auditory abilities in the broadest sense as cognitive abilities that depend on sound as input and on the functioning of our hearing apparatus, encompassing simple sensory processes and abilities required for the solution of complex problems (verbally or musically). Carroll (1993) provides a very similar view in regarding auditory ability more specifically as depending mainly on the characteristics of the auditory stimulus itself and the individual's capacity to apprehend, recognize, discriminate, or even ignore those characteristics, independent of the individual's knowledge of structures (e.g. in language or in music) that determine the overall pattern of an extended auditory signal. He discriminates these abilities from those that are not strictly auditory abilities, e.g. speech comprehension or musical apprehension. Speech comprehension, according to Carroll, can only be regarded as an auditory ability when the signal is distorted or attenuated so that interference with normal speech comprehension occurs. Speech comprehension usually depends on knowledge of a language, only secondarily on auditory ability. Similarly, music appreciation ability can be regarded as an auditory receptive ability only as long as it depends on the individual's capacity to perceive and discriminate those features that make an appreciation possible. Buttsworth, Fogarty and Rorke (1993) subsume listening skills, including intonation, pitch discrimination etc., under the concept of aural abilities. Results indicate that musical aptitude is a "general ability to make discriminations and judgments with respect to all attributes of musical sounds" (Carroll, 1993, p. 373), at the same time comprised of different abilities in this domain depending on particular attributes of musical sounds or types of musical material. However, the differentiation between music and sound is, especially in the context of modern music, difficult. Bruhn, Oerter and Rösing (1993) suggest including sounds in music if the person who listens directs the attention to the sound. Stoffer and Oerter (2005) supplement this necessary but not sufficient condition by proclaiming that the sound also has to follow familiar conventions (e.g. a periodic structure that is similar to rhythm). An early distinction between musical and tonal psychology (Kurth, 1931) describes *tonal psychology* as referring to single impressions (tone, interval, chord, rhythmic pattern etc.) whereas *music psychology* regards the whole.

2.5.2 Auditory Abilities Within Established Models of Intelligence

Within well-known structure models of intelligence, only Guilford (1967, content domain: auditory), Gardner (1983, musical intelligence), Horn-Cattell-Noll (see e.g. Horn & Noll, 1997), and Carroll (1993, broad auditory perception ability) include auditory abilities, as well as the integrative CHC theory (see chapter 2.1.3; McGrew & Evans, 2004).

Within Guilford's facet model (1967, for a figure and description see chapter 2.2.2), auditory abilities can be classified in the symbolic input. Symbolic (S) input according to Guilford means that information is provided in single symbols that do not make sense in a single unit (e.g., letters, numbers, tones, and single words). Comparable to social abilities (see chapter 2.2), AuI is composed of 5 (operations) x 6 (products) = 30 different abilities using tonal symbols as a content domain. According to Gardner (1983) (see also chapter 2.2.2), musical intelligence involves skill in the performance, composition, and appreciation of musical patterns. It encompasses the capacity to recognize and compose musical pitches, tones, and rhythms, with pitch and rhythm being central aspects of musical intelligence. He regards musical intelligence running in a pattern almost structurally parallel to linguistic intelligence. Both authors, Guilford and Gardner, with their inclusion of musical/auditory abilities but also social/interpersonal abilities (see chapter 2.2.2), significantly contributed to a broader view of intelligence research.

Horn and Noll (1997) included a broad auditory function on a second level. The auditory factor together with the visual factor is seen as a perceptual ability. The authors of the Woodcock-Johnson test III (Woodcock, McGrew, & Mather, 2001) assume a clear association between reading achievement and the ability to analyze and interpret sounds in words. Auditory processing in their view is also closely related to short-term memory (STM). According to Schrank (2006), poor performance in STM is often associated with problems in auditory processing, since STM relies on the process of acoustic-articulatory coding. McGrew (1994) defines Ga as "a combination of Incomplete Words and Sound Blending tests that measures the ability to analyze and synthesize auditory-linguistic stimuli" (p. 1156) (see below for a description).

One of the broadest categorization models of intelligence is Carroll's (1993) Three-Stratum Model, which was already mentioned in chapter 2.1.3. Based on the reanalysis of 38 available datasets, Carroll (1993) proclaimed a broad auditory perception factor indicated by discrimination or perception of auditory sounds or speech. The broad auditory perception factor is classified with fluid and crystallized intelligence, general memory, learning and visual perception on the second stratum of his model (see also Figure 2-9). Carroll found the auditory factor to consist of twelve primary level abilities on the first stratum: (1) hearing and speech threshold; (2) speech sound discrimination; general sound discrimination, namely; (3) sound frequency and sound (4) intensity discrimination; (5) duration discrimination and (6) musical discrimination and judgment; (7) resistance to auditory stimulus distortion (SPUD); (8) temporal tracking; (9) maintaining and judging rhythm; (10) memory for sound patterns; (11) absolute pitch; and (12) sound localization. Within hearing and speech threshold (factor 1), Carroll found that auditory tests including speech exceed pure auditory threshold tasks. This finding corresponds to the results of Surprenant and Watson (2001), whose speech tasks explained variance in performance that was different from variance explained by pure tone tasks. Although Carroll clearly separated musical abilities from auditory abilities (see definition), he included musical discrimination and judgment (factor 6) as an auditory factor. However, the relevant tonal tests provide nearly any musical context and depend to a great deal on tests of elementary discriminations among tonal materials. Rhythm ability (factor 9) surely has to do with the ability to discriminate time relationships. Carroll (1993) therefore raises the question whether maintaining a beat is truly an auditory ability or should rather be considered as a temporal ability. SPUD seems to be different from processes that are required in the visual domain (visual closure). Temporal tracking found in a dataset of Stankov and Horn (1980) has potential as a separate individual differences factor, as it is not restricted to auditory content. Carroll also includes the factors of absolute pitch (11) and of sound localization (12). Since absolute pitch is relatively rare, a separate factor could not be identified in the studies Carroll reanalysed. Sound localization ability was identified in the study of Aftanas and Royce (1969) and until now was replicated in only one study (Dun, 2000). As is mentioned in the name of the factor (broad auditory *perception*), most of the factors seem to deal with discrimination and perception of auditory stimuli (factors 1-5, 7, as well as parts of 6, 8 and 11). The remaining factors can be classified as requiring memory abilities (10, parts of 9); reasoning (judgment) abilities (parts of 6 and 9); or special abilities, like temporal abilities (parts of 8 and 9), localization abilities (12) and expert abilities (11). A closer look at Carroll's Three-Stratum Model (1993), finds that all abilities except the auditory are covered by the abilities described in the Berlin Model of Intelligence Structure (BIS, Jäger, 1984, see chapter 2.1.5).

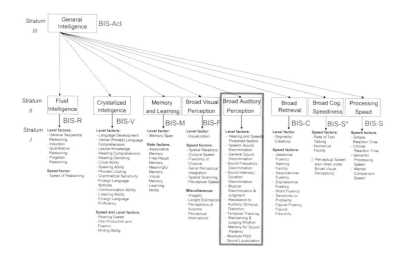

Figure 2-9: Abilities of the Three-Stratum Theory (Carroll, 1993) Covered by the BIS

Note: Auditory abilities are highlighted with a frame; BIS-R=reasoning; BIS-M=memory; BIS-F=figural; BIS-C=creativity; BIS-S=processing speed; BIS-Acl=Academic intelligence

In chapter 2.1.3, I mentioned that an auditory processing factor is included in CHC theory (see McGrew & Evans, 2004). This factor includes some of the primary abilities Carroll suggested in his reanalysis (1993), which stem from the studies carried out by Stankov and Horn (1980). The Ga factor in the corresponding Woodcock-Johnson Test battery (WJ III) is defined correspondinly to the definition mentioned earlier in this chapter (combination of the tests Incomplete Words and Sound Blending; ability to analyze and synthesize auditory-linguistic stimuli; McGrew, 1994). The auditory subtests (see chapter 2.5.3) represent the factors "Maintaining and judging rhythm" (in spoken language), "SPUD", and "Listening verbal comprehension".

According to my review, an established intelligence test measuring auditory abilities extensively and appropriately does not exist. However, there were two comparatively broad attempts to measure auditory abilities or parts of auditory abilities: the Test of Basic Auditory Capabilities (TBAC, Watson, Johnson, Lehman, Kelly, & Jensen, 1982, revised by Surprenant & Watson, 2001), and the auditory test battery described in Stankov and Horn (1980, Horn & Stankov, 1982). Moreover, auditory intellectual abilities are covered in the WJ III (see Woodcock, McGrew, & Mather, 2001). Their assessment will be described in the next chapter 2.5.3.

2.5.3 Auditory Ability Tests

Approach of Watson et al. (1982, Surprenant & Watson, 2001)

Watson et al. (1982) developed an extensive Test of Basic Auditory Capabilities (TBAC). The test concentrates on auditory discrimination abilities and comprises seven discrimination subtests (pitch discrimination, single-tone intensity discrimination, single-tone duration discrimination, pulse/train discrimination, embedded test-tone loudness, temporal order for tones, temporal order for syllables) and one nonsense syllable identification test. There are eight levels of difficulty for the seven discrimination tests. In the eighth test, subjects hear nonsense syllables in cafeteria noise and are asked to identify the sound by choosing one of three written alternatives. Christopherson and Humes (1992) report a general reliability value of .76 for the TBAC. The revised version (Surprenant & Watson, 2001) contains additional subtests of speech processing abilities. Surprenant and Watson (2001) report an overall alpha of .78 (including TBAC and supplemental speech tests), .75 for the TBAC alone and .64 for the supplemental speech tests alone. For the revised version, a factor analysis with 93 subjects (principal components analysis, Varimax, extraction criterion: eigenvalue > 1) revealed a three factor structure that was able to explain 54% of the total variance. The factors were interpreted as (1) nonspeech discrimination (including most of the TBAC measures), (2) speech identification (including supplementary speech tests and the syllable identification test), and (3) temporal order discrimination (including the two temporal order tests, Surprenant & Watson, 2001). The temporal order tests resemble the temporal tracking ability identified by Stankov and Horn (1980) and reported in Carroll's reanalysis (see this section). The results indicate that speech and nonspeech tests administered in this study share very little common variance. Surprenant and Watson (2001) performed a factor analysis on the data with 45 participants and included measures of AcI (Scholastic Aptitude Test, SAT, Educational Testing Service, and grade point average, GPA) in addition to the TBAC and the three supplemental speech tests. A four-factor solution resulted out of this study: AcI indicators (SAT, GPA) as well as temporal-order variables of the TBAC (Tones and Syllables) loaded on the first factor. The second factor subsumed tests of hearing threshold. The third factor consisted of nonspeech TBAC tests and the fourth factor was made of speech tests. This study is a further hint of the partial independence of speech and nonspeech auditory abilities. Speech processing measures correlated only weakly with measures of spectral and temporal auditory resolving power. However, the expressiveness of the results is doubtful, as the sample size was rather small (45 students). The first six TBAC subtests based on tones were strongly interrelated (mean .48, range: .35 - .65) (Watson & Miller, 1993). Principal components factor analysis revealed one factor, accounting for 57.2% of the variance (N=94 undergraduates). Watson (1991) reports correlations with the SAT ranging between .30 and .42 applying six of the TBAC tests. Later on, the tests "modulation detection for sinusoidally amplitude modulated tones (SAM) and for ripple-noise bursts, gap detection and gap discrimination, identification of noise-masked familiar environmental sounds (such as doors closing, electric saws, cars starting, doors barking, etc.) were added (Kidd, Watson, & Gygi, 2000; total of 19 tasks administered to 340 subjects). Results show a relative independence of speech processing tasks with words, nonsense CVCs (consonant-vowel-consonants) and sentences concerning other auditory abilities (Watson & Kidd, 2005). Results of their study indicate again that speech (and familiar non-speech sounds) is special and different from tones and other auditory stimuli.

Approach of Stankov and Horn (1980; Horn & Stankov, 1982; Stankov, 1980)

Since the end of the 1970s, there was not much interest in auditory abilities. Horn (1968) first had the idea of a broad auditory ability factor. He realized that an auditory factor corresponding to the primary visual abilities second order factor was missing. Since then, Stankov and Horn (Stankov, 1983; Stankov & Horn, 1980; Stankov & Spilsbury, 1978) searched for hints of a primary mental ability concerning auditory measures. They based their test construction on marker tests in the visual domain. Corresponding to tasks within the visual domain, auditory tasks should make use of basic stimuli as pure tones, chords and voices. Intensity and pitch were used as the main fundaments for the construction of auditory tests analogous to the fundaments of line and shape in visual tests. Stankov (1971) describes those fundaments as contents that should be distinguished from the cognitive operation that is required (discrimination, memory and reasoning). The auditory tasks they developed should demand the same cognitive operations as visual tasks but apply auditory material. For their tonal tasks, Stankov and Horn used piano tones and pure tones. Moreover, Stankov and Horn (1980) included tasks of music and language (speech) perception ability. They selected and developed tasks according to findings in the domain of music abilities (Drake, 1939; Karlin, 1941; McLeish, 1950; Seashore, Lewis, & Saetveit, 1960; Shuter, 1968; Wing, 1948) as well as results in the domain of speech perception and listening comprehension (Fleishman, Roberts, & Freidman, 1958; Hanley, 1956; Karlin, 1941; Solomon, Webster, & Cirtis, 1960; Spearritt, 1962; Sticht, 1972; White, 1954). In one of their main studies, 241 adult males participated and worked on more than 50 different auditory tests consisting of speech and musical material. Including 44 tests, factor analysis revealed a second order general auditory factor (Ga) which can be located next to a broad visual ability factor and seven primary auditory ability factors. The factors were interpreted as (1) tonal memory, (2) speech perception under distraction (SPUD), (3) verbal comprehension, (4) immediate memory, (5) cognition of relationships, (6) discrimination among sound patterns, and (7) maintaining/judging rhythm as primary auditory abilities (Stankov, 1983; Stankov & Horn, 1980; Stankov & Spilsbury, 1978). In addition, they discovered an ability called "temporal tracking," which is regarded as important for the understanding of language with extreme high or low tempo. Temporal tracking is expected to be related to working memory

(Stankov, 1983). The label "temporal tracking" emphasizes the sequential nature of many working memory aspects (temporal) and the specific mental manipulation (mental tracking). Temporal tracking was also found in the already reported study conducted by Surprenant and Watson (2001, temporal order factors). Four of five tests of loudness discrimination were excluded because of low reliability. That is probably the reason the expected loudness discrimination factor did not emerge. The primary abilities are quite different but can be sorted in categories of being more likely related to discrimination/perceptual abilities (factors 2, 6), to memory (factors 1, 4, parts of 7) or reasoning abilities (factors 3, 5, parts of 7).

Correlations between the seven primary factors are generally positive, whereby listening verbal comprehension, temporal tracking, auditory cognition of relationships, and discrimination of auditory sound patterns form an intercorrelation cluster that is assumed to represent crystallized intelligence (gc, Stankov & Horn, 1980). The relationship between listening verbal comprehension and maintaining and judging rhythm (which is expected to have a moderate relationship to gc) seems to support this hypothesis. However, temporal tracking was identified as an indicator of fluid intelligence in other studies (see e.g., Stankov, 1983; Carroll, 1993). Memory for sound patterns and discrimination of auditory sound patterns seem to represent fluid intelligence (gf). Speed under distraction as well as maintaining and judging rhythm could indicate a broad auditory function similar to a broad visual function that has already been identified.

The primary level factors making up Ga require holistic comprehension of sounds and patterns among sounds in many different ways. They have to be differentiated from auditory acuity tests (e.g. pitch and loudness discrimination). Within auditory acuity tests, subjects have to deal with mutilated and incomplete sounds. This kind of ability dimension is characterized by variables pointing to very elementary processes of simple discrimination and seeming to represent organization among sensory detector functions of hearing (low in hierarchy). In additional analyses of Horn and Stankov (1982), listening verbal comprehension is not part of Ga. A major proportion of variance in this factor seems to be involved in the verbal intellectual comprehension represented by gc and in sound discrimination. It does not seem surprising that several auditory tasks load on gf and are expected to be related to working memory. Auditory ability tasks require a capacity for maintaining awareness, and good reasoning requires maintaining the elements of a reasoning problem within the span of immediate apprehension. In 1994, Stankov classifies the auditory primary factors into three layers. On the first layer, sensory detection tasks (e.g., pitch discrimination) can be classified. The second layer consists of tasks expected to tap perceptual processes (e.g., SPUD). The third layer contains tasks such as tonal reordering and cloze, which affect higher order intellective processes (see Stankov, 1994).

Earlier researchers expected verbal tasks to be better performed by the left hemisphere and tonal tasks by the right hemisphere. Stankov (1980) investigated whether one ear (and the opposite hemisphere) is superior in performing a certain auditory task. He worked with four primaries of the auditory ability, namely temporal tracking, SPUD, maintaining and judging rhythm and tonal memory. He assumed Ga and Gv to be broad perceptual factor and located Gv processing mainly to the right hemisphere based on former research. His findings reveal that tonal memory was better performed by the right hemisphere and corresponding left ear. Temporal tracking and verbal comprehension, however, were better performed by the right ear and corresponding left hemisphere. SPUD and "maintaining and judging rhythm," as well as other auditory factors did not show any ear and hemisphere preference. Therefore, former assumptions could be confirmed only partially. Stankov (1980) also claims that Gv is different from Ga. He assumes that lateralization is not typical for Ga. Rather, competition taking place on a perceptual level seems to be important. Confirming findings are shown with regard to differences between AIT (auditory inspection time) and VIT (visual inspection time) tasks (see below).

Some of the tests show correlations with musical experience, but it is not necessary to be musically trained to be able to complete the auditory tasks. However, it seems plausible that the degree of musical experience of the subjects alters the results as well as the factor structure. Whereas musically inexperienced subjects are expected to listen to musical stimuli melodically and rhythmically, musically experienced people are assumed to include harmonies in their judgments as well (Shuter, 1968). In pitch memory tasks, musicians showed greater right posterior temporal and supramarginal activation (namely short-term auditory storing), whereas non-musicians had greater activation on the left secondary auditory cortex (namely early perceptual brain regions) (Gaab & Schlaug, 2003). Performance between the two groups was quite similar. Conclusively, cognitive and perceptual processing seem to differ between non-musicians and musicians.

The findings of Stankov and Horn (1980) could be consolidated in several studies (Horn & Stankov, 1982; Dun, 2000). Their approach, conceptualization, and task ideas were taken up and integrated into the WJ III (see McGrew & Evans, 2004; Schrank, 2006; McGrew, 1994). The auditory processing factor (Ga) is measured with two marker variables, namely "sound blending" (i.e., ability to integrate and speak whole words that are presented auditorily in parts; phonetic coding) and "incomplete words" (i.e., ability to name a complete word after hearing a recording of the word with at least one missing phoneme; phonetic coding). Both tests were taken from the Stankov and Horn (1980) battery. The subtests "auditory attention" (i.e., speech-sound discrimination, resistance to auditory stimulus distortion), "sound patterns-voice" (i.e., sound discrimination), and "sound patterns-music" (i.e., sound discrimination, music discrimination and judgment) are mentioned to be Ga indicators, as well (Schrank, 2006). However, in most of the analysis, only the phonetic coding factors (sound blending and incomplete words) were included (see also McGrew, 1994). With fewer than three indicators, identification problems emerge since the factor will probably be underidentified (e.g. Kenny, 1979; Bühner, 2006; for an overview see Loehlin, 2004). The WJ III uses auditory material in the other hypothesized factors, as well (i.e., gc, gf, STM, LTM), without being associated with Ga. In addition, some of the tests are indicators of several factors. Thus, the tasks applied in the WJ III suggest a facet design, including a modality facet (auditory, visual) and an operation facet (i.e., gf, gc, STM, LTM). This, however, is not used for the WJ III test. Rather, the proposed factors are regarded as being at the same level. Ga was even identified as a subcomponent of Gc.

Although I appreciate the integration of auditory abilities within the WJ III, the test structure and its empirical evidence does not seem convincing. In addition, the two Ga marker tests stem from the Stankov and Horn approach (1980). In contrast to Watson et al. (1982, Surprenant & Watson, 2001), who focused mainly on perception abilities, Stankov and Horn also included auditory tasks intended to measure memory and reasoning. Thus, until now, Stankov and Horn were the only researchers who tried to measure auditory abilities extensively. Therefore, the auditory part of this book will be based on the original work of Stankov and Horn (1980). The systematic nature and methodological foundation of the Stankov and Horn approach are further reasons for this choice. Nevertheless, it is valuable to draw attention to the much better explored and more progressive domain of musical psychology compared to the psychometric intelligence domain. It is important to take the results within musical psychology into account for further development of an appropriate instrument for the assessment of auditory intellectual abilities as well as for a validation tool of auditory SI.

2.5.4 An Insight into Models and Tests of Music Psychology

Theories and Models of Musical Abilities

In the research tradition of musical abilities, hierarchical and non-hierarchical theories have to be distinguished. Seashore et al. (1960) as well as Mainwaring and Bentley (1955, cited in Shuter, 1968) supposed musical abilities to depend on specific basic capacities of time, intensity discrimination, and memory of pitch. Drake (1939) and Wing (1948) took a different view and proclaimed a general musical ability factor. Others act on the assumption that there are group factors. Holmstrom (1969) reanalyzed some older datasets using factor analysis (Varimax rotation) and found three factors. The first factor, "Alpha," was interpreted as a primary perception factor and expected to have a physiological basis that is only slightly influenced by musical experience. Tasks of tonal memory had their highest loadings on the second factor "Beta." The third factor, "Gamma," with loadings of the tasks of rhythm, pitch and memory, was interpreted as a broad music factor. "Gamma" was highly correlated with intelligence.

Franklin (1956) argued that musical talent includes two parts: "mechanical-acoustic" talent (i.e., ability to discriminate with regard to pitch, timbre, time and intensity; see pitch differences in the Seashore test) and "judicious-musical" talent (ability to discriminate at the service of music, see also Wing test). Apparently, the mechanical-acoustic talent is more basic compared to the judicious-musical talent. In my view, the former can also be described as basic auditory ability whereas the latter is undoubtedly musical. Whereas the more basic auditory tests operate with single units, the musical tests prove their need for musicality working with musical sequences and musical context. An enhancement of musical talent is made by tonal-musical talent (experiences music as a whole), which Franklin (1956) locates on a higher level. Creative musical talent (i.e., musical talent as a tool subordinated to imagination and thinking) is at the top of the hierarchy, being even more complex musically and less basic auditorily. In each case, the more basic level is a prerequisite for the higher level. Davison and Torff (1994) support the view that intelligent activity in music is context dependent. They classify musically intelligent activity within three levels: (1) perception (i.e., discrimination while listening to music), (2) production (i.e., musical thought expressed in composition and performance), and (3) reflection (i.e., critical thinking behind re-envisioning, reconceptualizing, and re-working, leading to coherent musical composition or interpretative performance).

Musical Ability Tests

Tests of musical ability were mainly developed to select students of music. The most notable tests have been the Seashore Test of Musical Talent (Seashore, 1919; Seashore, Lewis, & Saetveit, 1960) the Standardized Test of Musical Intelligence (Wing, 1939), the Gordon Test (Gordon, 1965, 1989), the Bentley Test (Bentley, 1966), and the Drake Musical Aptitude Test (Drake, 1933a, b). All these tests and, correspondingly, several factor analytic studies on these tests, were developed for use in music sciences (Horn & Stankov, 1982) rather than for measurement of intelligence operations with auditory content. However, orientating on Franklins taxonomy, some of the subtests contain auditory tasks rather than musical ones. A selection of the well-known musical ability tests is presented in the following.

a) Seashore Measues of Musical Talent(s)

Seashore (1919) published a first standardized version of a musical screening instrument. Seashore focused on the acoustical aspects of musical aptitude (atomistic, Gordon, 1998); only one of his suggested subtests (i.e., tonal memory), requires more than a comparison between two tones. Subtests of the Seashore Test classified in two series (A and B), differing in degree of difficulty, examine the discrimination abilities concerning frequencies, intensity, duration, rhythm, timbre, and musical memory. For the total test, a reliability coefficient of $r_{tt}=$ .89 is reported (see Franklin, 1956). The internal consistency of the subtests depends on the age of the participants and is sometimes very low (Franklin, 1956). In some of the subtests, clear ceiling effects emerged among participants with musical experience. In nearly all subtests, participants with musical experience (N=131, Kormann, 1985) score higher than the normative sample (N=1550, Butsch & Fischer, 1966). Karlin's (1942) results seem to support Seashore's assumption of a hierarchy of talents that are independent from one another. In a factor analysis that included different auditory measures, eight separable factors of musical ability could be extracted: discrimination ability concerning (1) *frequencies*, (2) *intensity*, (3) duration, (4) rhythm, (5) timbre, (6) musical memory, (7) *auditory analysis*, *and* (8) *synthesis*. According to French (1951, cited in Stankov, 1971), four factors are well established: pitch quality (see 1), loudness (see 2), auditory integral (see 8), and auditory resistance (see 3). Shuter-Dyson (1982) reports correlations between the test and expert ratings ranging between r=.34 and r=.47. The quality of the stimulus material of the Seashore Test is rather bad and only available on phonograph. Instructions are spare and studies of the test were only administered in the context of musical education. The Seashore subtests were criticized as being too basic for a musical test, as they require only discrimination abilities (Rothe, 1991, cited in Kormann, 2005).

b)   Standardized Test of Musical Intelligence (Wing, 1948)

Wing's purpose was to cover the scope of musical abilities with a short series of tests (Shuter-Dyson, 1982). In 1939, he published an instrument with seven subtests that were available on tape until 1961. In contrast to Seashore, he conceptualized musical stimuli as containing a *source* and a *content* of sound. Whereas Seashore used an electronic instrument for his stimulus material, Wing chose the piano. With respect to the content, Wing used musically related pitches, whereas Seashore's pitches were unrelated. For about 80 minutes, subjects have to work on the following subtests: chord analysis, changes of pitch, memory for melodies, and tests of rhythm, harmony, dynamics and phrasing (judging the more appropriate grouping of notes by pauses, legato, staccato, etc.). Chord analysis and pitch change can be regarded as atomistic; the remaining subtests are rather musical. In Wing's opinion, musical memory consisted of the interplay between tonal and rhythmic elements. He regarded rhythm as natural and subordinate to melody (melody requires rhythm). Split-half reliability for four of the subtests (rhythm, harmony, dynamics and phrasing) was only between .28 and .50. The total score of the test correlates with teacher ratings in the range between .64 and .90. According to Shuter-Dyson (1981), the subtests chord analysis, changing pitch and memory are the most useful measures (see also Kormann, 2005).

c)   Drake Musical Aptitude Tests (Drake, 1933a, 1939b, 1939; see also Siegel, 1958)

Drake's conception of musical talent is similar to that of Wing in expecting a general musical ability factor. In a first stage of development, the Drake tests consisted of four subtests, namely melodic memory (i.e., two-bar melodies have to be compared to four alternative melodies), retention (i.e., memory for elemental factors, test of absolute pitch or memory for isolated tones), intuition (i.e., presentation of ideas/feelings by means of music), and interval discrimination. Thus, both, auditory acuity and musical expressiveness are included. When the test was published in 1954, only melodic memory (then known as musical memory) was carried over. The additional test was called rhythm, which could be applied in two forms, A and B. In form A, a pre-determined tempo had to be maintained by the subjects for varying periods of time. Form B required the maintenance of a tempo against a second distracting rhythm. Reliability for the two tests is mainly reported around .85 to .95 (Md=.84). There seems to be no training improvement (Gordon, 1961). The subtests show only low correlations, which disproves Drake's assumption of a general factor. Drake's rhythm test and Seashore's rhythm test correlate only between r= .02 and r= .11. Musical memory and rhythm demonstrate a low correlation with age and intelligence (r= -.07 to.10). They show moderate correlations (r~.35) with musical experience and a wide range of correlations (.31 - .91) with teachers' ratings of musical talent (Shuter-Dyson, 1982).

d)   Bentley Test (1966; German version of the test Jacoby, 1986)

Bentley (1966) published the "Measures of Musical Abilities." The measures intend to measure some aspects of musical giftedness, namely pitch discrimination (k=20 tasks; increasing level of difficulty, differences in double oscillations per second between 26 to 3), tonal memory (k=10; Which tone of a five-tone melody was changed in the second presentation of that melody?), chord analysis (k=20; Does the chord consist of three, four or five tones?) and memory for rhythm (k=10; Which of five rhythm times was changed in the second presentation of that rhythm?). The test was developed for children between 7 and 14 years old and is based on norms of 2000 school children. The subtests show low intercorrelations. Retest reliability after four months was r=.84 and .83 after one year (McLeish, 1971, cited by Shuter-Dyson, 1982), and validity (criterion: examination marks) r=.94 in a sample with 70 boys of 11 years.

e)   Gordon Tests (1965, 1989)

Gordon (1965, 1989) regards music aptitude as the potential to achieve in music. In order to measure this aptitude, he developed tests of musical giftedness in a developmental (e.g. Primary Measures of Musical Audiation, PMMA) and an established (Musical Aptitude Profile, MAP) "stadium." The MAP (1965) for testing children aged 9-17 years, examines tonal imagination (harmony and melody), rhythmic imagination (tempo and metrum), and musical judgment (phrasing, balance, style). The PMMA (1979) for 5-8 year-old children measure tonal imagination and rhythm abilities. Gordon could show that students who have a high level of pitch discrimination and students who perform well in time discrimination do not necessarily perform well on the MAP. But students performing well on the MAP have high levels of pitch and time discrimination (Gordon, 1998). Thus, basic discrimination processes seem to be a necessary but not sufficient condition for musical performance. This is another indication that we should separate musical and auditory abilities. Gordon also regards rhythm aptitude as a profoundation of musical aptitude. Rhythm aptitude is a necessary condition to show high overall musical achievement. Deriving from theoretical considerations and empirical findings, Gordon subsumes tonal, rhythm and aesthetic-interpretive components under stabilized musical aptitude. The first two components are rather basic, whereas the third requires both tonal audiation and rhythm ability. The subtests' reliability values range from .66 to .85; the total test score has a reliability score between .90 and .96 (Shuter-Dyson, 1982). Predictive validity of the MAP for judges' ratings of the rhythmic, melodic and expressive aspects of previously prepared etudes with and without teachers' guidance and of sight-reading of students as well as scores on a music literacy test is .75. Shuter-Dyson reports a median validity of .79 for the total scores predicting teacher ratings.

f)   Test of Buttsworth, Fogarty, and Rorke (1993)

Buttsworth et al. (1993) present a test of musical ability intended to be used for the development of musical ability through formal training programs. Specifically, it deals with one vital aspect of aural abilities, intonation (playing in tune). Buttsworth et al. highlight that intonation is one of the most frustrating problems in, but also one of the most important aspects of, successful musical performance. They developed 14 tests containing 30 test items each. Four of the tests were expected to assess unlearned aural skills, mostly pitch discrimination. The remaining ten tests were assumed to depend on prior experience, mostly dealing with intonation skills. The test battery should capture variance associated with two broad factors: pitch discrimination and intonation. However, some of the tests either had reliability problems or were of an inadequate difficulty level, so that they had to be excluded. Only three of the tests were able to explain 36% of the variance produced by aural training scores. Two of the tests dealt with identification of out-of-tune tones in dyads and triads; the third required subjects to decide whether the melodic or harmonic form of the minor scale was used in a tonal sequence. The authors conclude that intonation ability represents a basic ability for later learning and a variety of aural skills (Buttsworth et al., 1993).

What Can We Conclude Regarding Theories, Models and Tests in Musical Psychology?

First of all the tests differ with regard to their scope. The Wing test seems to be the broadest measure, including not only discrimination and memory abilities but also more complex, music-specific tests such as harmony. Bentleys' tests appear to be similar but cover a narrower spectrum of discrimination, memory and analysis tests. The other tests, although including many subtests (e.g. Seashore and Buttsworth et al.) are rather specific. Gordon's test concentrates on the more complex musical abilities and includes imagination and judgment measures, Buttsworth et al. focus on intonation ability as a very specific aspect of musical ability, and Seashore includes mainly discrimination tests. Apart from the scope of the tests, it is surprising that many subtests do not seem to be much different from tests described in Stankov and Horn (1980) as well as in Watson et al. (1982). The Seashore test is most difficult to separate from auditory ability measures (see chapter 2.5.3). This assumption is supported by analysis revealing ceiling effects for musicians and also providing confirmation for the separation into mechanical-acoustical tests and judicious-musical tasks. With regard to Bentley's test, only his chord measure seems to be music specific and can easily be discriminated from basic auditory abilities.

These considerations complicate the discrimination between auditory and musical abilities. There are difficulties in defining the differences and developing appropriate tests. Moreover, the question emerges whether differences between the two constructs indeed exist. With respect to the factorial structure resulting of analysis of the tests in musical psychology, Stankov (1971) noticed that specific factors (such as pitch, loudness, timbre and rhythm) seem to appear if a test requires pure discrimination on a psychophysical basis. A general factor of broad group factors seems to emerge when the tasks involve complex processes to a higher degree. Factor analytic studies including musical ability tests also confirm the separation between mechanical-acoustical tests and judicious-musical tests. Franklin (1956) carried out two factor analytic studies with 79 (1st study) and 157 (2nd study) elementary teachers applying the methods of successive approximation (1st study) and simple structure rotation technique (2nd study). In the second study, the Seashore and Wing pitch tests representing basic auditory and advanced musical abilities loaded on separate factors. Besides this finding within the pitch discrimination ability, he could identify a tone memory factor, a melody and harmonic factor, a rhythm and intelligence factor, and a factor including tests which are judged as being particularly judicious-musical (Wing tests). Franklin (1956) regards the ability of pitch discrimination as a precondition for other musical tasks (e.g. tonal memory). This may account for the relationship emerging between tasks that measure different aspects. According to Bruhn (1993), classical music tests (e.g., Gordon, Seashore or Bentley) are developed to measure musical talent. However, with tasks dealing with simple differences between tones and tonal sequences, the tasks concern rather musical memory (comment added: auditory memory) and thus cover only one aspect of musical talent.

2.5.5   The Relationship of Auditory and Musical Abilities to Academic Intelligence

This section complements the findings with respect to auditory and musical ability but focuses mainly on the relationship of these constructs to AcI. Results concerning auditory abilities are reported first, then combined with those concerning musical abilities.

Auditory Abilities and Academic Intelligence

Relationships between auditory abilities and AcI mainly refer to the tasks of Stankov and Horn (1980) and to the TBAC (Watson et al., 1982; Surprenant & Watson, 2001). Horn and Stankov (1982) report correlations of Ga with a general visual factor (.44), hearing (auditory) acuity (.28), fluid intelligence (gf; r=.39) and crystallized intelligence (gc; r=.54). Ga seems to be more closely related to gc than to gf (Horn & Stankov, 1982). However, according to Stankov (1986), Ga due to loss in auditory acuity decreases with advancing age and therefore differs from gc, which remains rather stable until old age (Stankov, 1986). Dun (2000) carried out a study with 92 first year psychology students applying the auditory tasks described in Stankov and Horn (1980). She included a total of eighteen tasks in her test battery. Four of the tasks can be recognized as markers of gf and gc; four were chosen from the Referenced Tests of Cognitive Factors (Ekstrom, French, & Harman, 1976) in order to measure visual ability; and the remaining nine tasks were established markers of broad auditory ability. Dun reports evidence of a broad auditory factor that correlated with gf (.55), with gc (.36), and with visual abilities (.43). She did not find a relationship between speed and Ga. The particularly high correlations with gf support the results obtained in Horn and Stankov (1982) and are expected to be due to the requirements on working memory that are demanded by the auditory tasks. However, the moderate correlations between broad visual and broad auditory ability, in her view, may also stem from similar construction principles: auditory task development was orientated on the development of visual tasks and on established musical tests.

Deary, Bell, Bell, Campbell, and Fazal (2004) report correlations between .28 and .40 of the TBAC loudness discrimination test and psychometric intelligence tests (Mill Hill Vocabulary Test, Raven, Raven, & Court, 1982; Cattell Culture Fair Intelligence Test, Cattell & Cattell, 1973; Digit Symbol Test, Wechsler, 1981). In another experiment implemented by the same authors, the Seashore test was used as an auditory sensory discrimination measure. Again, the correlation between the sensory auditory factor and a general intelligence factor was about .68 and highly significant. Deary et al. (2004) conclude that something in sensory discrimination tests appears to be substantially shared with psychometric intelligence tests. Deary (2000) summarizes the correlations found between auditory sensory pitch discrimination and psychometric intelligence. With the exception of one study (Deary, Head, & Egan, 1989) they ranged from .14 to .57 (Watson, 1991). Subjects who scored higher on psychometric intelligence required shorter stimulus duration to make accurate pitch discriminations (Deary, 2000). Conclusively, Spearman (1904) seemed to be right in his assumption that general sensory discrimination and general intelligence have a common, more fundamental source (Spearman, 1904).

Musical Abilities and Academic Intelligence

Since standardized tests of musical abilities exist, a large number of studies about the relationship between musical abilities and AcI have been carried out. Inspecting the results, Stankov (1971) draws the conclusion that the correlations between musical abilities and intelligence are mostly positive and around .30. However, he remarks that correlations may depend on the level of tasks and that correlations between auditory abilities and AcI may be due to common speed variance. In existing tests of musical abilities (see section 2.5.4), tasks are mostly on a low-level of sensory discrimination. When related to low level intelligence test tasks (e.g. processing speed tests), correlations increase. Comparable with the differentiation problems between auditory and musical abilities, major tests of musical ability do not depart much from sensory psychology tests (Franklin, 1956). McLeish (1950) found out that speediness in higher levels of cognition has an influence on the Seashore memory and discrimination tests. Music is extremely dependent on time: irregularities in tempo destroy the character of music. Therefore, speed seems to be more important for musical abilities than other components of intellectual abilities. However, not only the task level and time dependence seem to have an impact on the relationship between musical abilities and AcI. Lynn, Wilson, and Gault (1989) discovered that performance in tasks of Wing's Standardised Test of Musical Intelligence correlated with the results in Raven's Standard Progressive Matrices (chords analysis r=0.27; pitch change r=0.40; pitch memory r=0.37; N=97). For his analysis, he used the accuracy rather than the speed as a performance measure. Subjects did not have a time limit to complete the tasks.

Wing (1948) found that lower values in tests of intelligence were associated with lower values in musical tests. However, higher IQ is not sufficiently accompanied by high musical ability. Intelligence therefore seems to be a necessary but insufficient condition for musical ability; given a minimum intelligence level, IQ does not have an additional positive impact/influence on the degree of musical ability. According to Kormann, above-average musical giftedness requires a least a slightly above-average academic intelligence IQ. Wing (1948) assumes musical intuition (fast comprehension of music or musical tasks) is one form of intelligence even if it is not measured in standard tests of intelligence dealing with reasoning. Edmund's (1960, cited by Stankov, 1971) findings confirm these results. The findings of these underlying assumptions provide evidence that the important auditory domain of intelligence is not measured through well-established intelligence tests.

Several authors (Fleishman et al., 1958; Franklin, 1956; French, 1951; Hanley, 1956; Harris, 1969; Karlin, 1942; Kelley, 1964; Shuter, 1968; Solomon et al., 1960; Stankov, 1971; White, 1954; Woodrow, 1939) carried out research studies about auditory abilities within their nomological network of other intellectual abilities (vocabulary, spatial, speed, speech and perception, visual abilities). Stankov (1971) concluded from those findings that apparently, intuitive notions about the similarities between auditory and visual tests do not correspond to similarities in the functions involved. He further assumed that abilities high in hierarchy (e.g. verbal comprehension) can be measured equally well through either of the modalities, visual or auditory. On a lower level, however, variables of the two modalities will have less in common. This corresponds to the assumptions the radex model proposes (see chapter 2.1.4). As soon as complexity rises, abilities move to the center of the radex, they correlate higher, and they consequently share more common variance. Peripheral, and more specific, abilities move out of the center and therefore should share less common variance. A study by Kormann (1971) showed that 37 of 48 correlation coefficients between musical tasks and measures of AcI were significant; rhythm memory and AcI correlated with r=.54. AcI reasoning seems to be related especially to musical abilities that require comparison and counting. However, musical productivity (creativity) did not correlate with tests of AcI at all (Kormann, 1971).

With respect to the relationship between musicality and intelligence, it may be that an underlying AuI serves as a precondition for musicality (musical ability/skills) and additional abilities requiring hearing. Maybe the relationship between traditional intelligence tests and musical ability tests is not as high as findings let us assume, because traditional intelligence tests lack of an AuI dimension.

On Auditory Inspection Time and Intelligence

Representatives of the mental speech tradition focused on simple auditory ability measures of mental speed, so-called auditory inspection time (AIT) tasks. Mental speed researchers share the view that "general intelligence" is mainly determined by the speed of information processing in the brain (for references, see e.g., Deary, 2000; Eysenck, 1987; Jensen, 1982b; Neubauer, 1995; Vernon, 1983). Inspection time refers to the length of exposure time needed to correctly discriminate between two stimuli. Most of the AIT measures require sensory discrimination concerning loudness, pitch, time, or localization. In auditory pitch discrimination (AIT-P), a low- and a high-frequency tone presented at various durations have to be differentiated. The task is relatively similar to common pitch discrimination but explains unique variance (Olsson, Björkman, Haag, & Juslin, 1998). AIT tasks were found to be correlated with general intelligence (Deary, 1994, 1995, 2000; Deary & Stough, 1996; Irwin, 1984; Raz, Willermann, & Yama, 1987; Spearman, 1904). The strength of the correlations depends on how AIT is measured: Raz et al. (1987) found correlations higher than the usually -.30 relationships (see Hunt, 1980) ranging between -.42 and -.54 between pitch discrimination and performance on Cattell's Culture Fair Intelligence Test (Cattell & Cattell, 1973). They argue that high intelligence is associated with a greater resolution of sensory information. Raz et al. (1987) and Deary (1994) agree with the perspective of Spearman (1904), who claimed that auditory abilities (in particular the detection of thresholds for sound frequencies) constitute the basic processes of intelligence. Within the AIT types, empirical findings support stronger and more consistent relationships of AcI with loudness discrimination compared to pitch discrimination. On the contrary, AIT-P tasks correlate more highly with general musical ability (i.e., more complex musical tasks regarding the results mentioned above). Problems with pitch discrimination arise with participants having absolute pitch ability. Helmbold and Rammsayer (2006, see also Rammsayer & Brandler, 2002) examined the relationship of psychophysical temporal tasks and AcI. They applied auditory performance measures of interval timing, rhythm perception, and bimodal temporal-order judgment, for example, in rhythm perception subjects had to indicate whether the presented rhythm was perceived as "regular" (beat-to-beat interval appeared to be of the same duration) or "irregular" (deviant beat-to-beat interval). They found the auditory timing tasks to be positively related to psychometric intelligence (figural reasoning: r=.47, Wiener Matrizen-Test, WMT; Formann & Piswanger, 1979; numerical speed test [Zahlen-Verbindungs-Test, ZVT; Oswald & Roth, 1987]: r=.36). An additional study (Rammsayer & Brandler, 2002) revealed that high IQ individuals are better in duration discrimination of auditory intervals, in temporal order judgments and temporal resolving power for central sensory information. A study of Deary et al. (1989) revealed a higher AIT-IQ correlation in verbal than in nonverbal IQ tests. That points into the direction of a common underlying mechanism between verbal and auditory processing. According to Deary et al. (1989), this result mirrors verbal ability operating as a cumulative average of past levels of processing efficiency and explaining less idiosyncratic variance than a more fluid task. Verbal ability scores allow more resources to be freed for consolidation of verbal information when information intake is faster and discrimination more accurate.

In summary, the mental speed approach has to be considered rather critically since empirical results do not confirm the view of a basic speed factor that determines intellectual performance and reduce the complex interplay of intelligence subconstructs unrealistically. However, findings obtained with AIT tasks may be important with respect to the relationship of different types of AIT tasks to AcI and musical abilities as well as with regard to the relationship between auditory and verbal latent variables.

2.5.6 Integrative Considerations on Auditory Ablities and their Relationship to Academic Intelligence

The construct "auditory abilities" seems to include everything that makes use of acoustic cues (see also Carroll, 1993; Stankov, 1994). These cues might be spoken language, as well as pure tones or complex music compositions. However, the abilities (or skills) can be differentiated according to the knowledge and skills they presuppose. A musician should not have any problems in identifying a presented chord. For a layperson who never played an instrument or sung in a choir it may be an unsolvable task. Correspondent to AcI, auditory tasks independent from prior knowledge should be adequate indicators of auditory intellectual abilities (auditory intelligence). That does not imply that people who are trained in music should not have advantages in the solution of not only complex musical but also basic auditory tasks.

Basic abilities can be further differentiated according to the stimulus material they rely on. Stimuli might be pure tones, familiar environmental sounds, and basic language (speech). Dealing with basic tones should be more closely related to musical abilities, whereas language-based (speech) tasks should have a closer relationship to tasks dealing with written verbal material. In terms of facet theory, besides the content dimension, an operation facet can be built. Within the cognitive operation, comparable to AcI facet models, discrimination, memory, reasoning and creativity abilities may be distinguished. Following these considerations, a preliminary model of auditory abilities can be developed (see Figure 2-10).

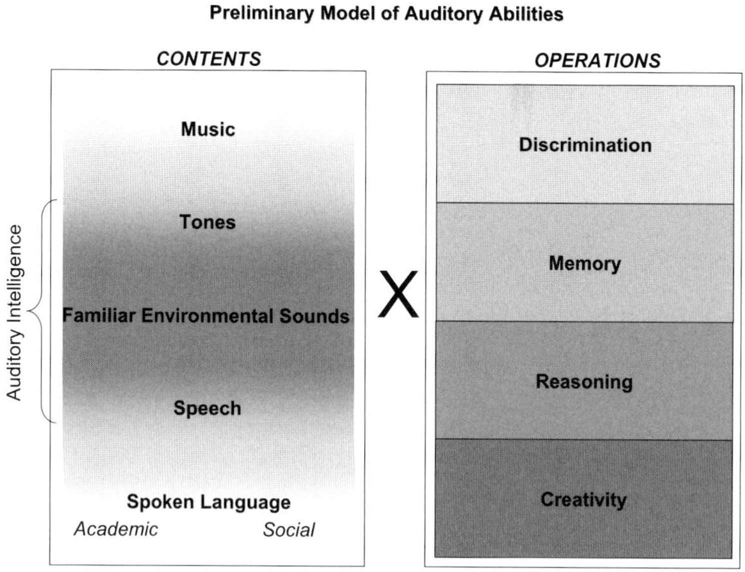

Preliminary Model of Auditory Abilities

Figure 2-10: Preliminary Model of Auditory Abilities

According to this preliminary and definitional model, auditory abilities include music, pure tones, sounds, speech and spoken language as content domains (stimulus material). Spoken language might occur within academic as well as social abilities. These content domains can be combined with operational domains, namely discrimination (corresponding to academic perception), memory, reasoning and creativity. The auditory intelligence domains tones, noises, and speech remain as auditory content expected to be rather independent from (musical) experience and different from already well-established verbal AcI. Consequently, in this book, auditory intelligence is defined as the ability to discriminate, remember, reason and work creatively (on) auditory stimuli, which can be tones, noises and speech. Auditory intelligence is separated from musical abilities, but nevertheless partly overlaps because musical material mainly consists of single tones. Correspondingly, speech tasks are distinguished from auditory language tasks, but are expected to overlap because language contains several speech units. However, this model should only serve as a preliminary basis of orientation. Transitions between auditory intelligence and musical abilities as well as verbal academic ability are smooth. Therefore, the operationalization (see chapter 4.2) of auditory intelligence should be rather broad, including partly musical abilities and spoken language abilities. Auditory intellectual abilities seem to be positively correlated to but separable from classical AcI. Taking up Stankov's (1971) and Horn's (1967) suggestions, auditory tasks should be equivalent to tasks of AcI in level in order to minimize undesired variance. In my opinion it is not yet clear whether auditory tasks not only differ in content but also require completely new operations. If so, they need completely new task ideas to measure them properly. However, in this book, past results have to be taken up to continue research systematically.

2.6 Social Intelligence Meets Auditory Intelligence

2.6.1 On the Relevance of Social Auditory Abilities

In our daily life, we can often hear how a person feels by listening to the tone of voice (e.g. on the phone: "You sound good today."). This chapter focuses on social and emotional stimuli expressed and received through voices and combines two not yet well-established constructs, social and auditory intelligence. Effective interpersonal relationships and social performance require individuals to accurately decode nonverbal expressions of emotions in other people and remember what they said and how they expressed it. It is almost impossible to discuss emotions without considering the social context in which they occur (White, 2000). Social relations produce emotions in different ways (Kemper, 2000) (e.g. reading a letter from a loved one, making compliments on a neighbor's new dress) and also are described as "social emotions" (Brandstätter, 1990). In an intercultural study, Scherer, Wallbott, Matsumoto, and Kuhdo (1988) found that in Japan, Europe, and the USA more than 50% of the emotional episodes were elicited by others (especially true for joy, anger and sadness). A representative inquiry with American students revealed that guilt, shame, and embarrassment in more than 80% of cases were elicited by others (Tangney, Miller, Flicker, & Barlow, 1996). The quality of a relationship is determined through the affective intensity of the interaction. According to Banse (2000), social emotions have the function of adapting the behavior of people to the necessities of living together. As within psychometric intelligence research, empirical investigations within this field are rare, I will mainly follow results obtained in emotion research with a special focus on emotions expressed through speech. Speech can be described *auditorily* (i.e., aspects of sound as they are perceived by people such as pitch and loudness), *acoustically* (i.e., properties of sound independent of perception such as fundamental frequency and intensity) and *articulately* (i.e., production of speech such as subglottal pressure, vocal effort). In my descriptions, I focus on auditory and acoustic aspects of speech. Vocalization and voice quality together are labeled "paralanguage" (Trager, 1958, p. 4, cited by Kramer, 1963). Prosodic features of speech are any nonverbal features including loudness, pitch and rate (Frick, 1985).

We associate social processes in the auditory domain with communication using language. For example, the ways of speaking (i.e., use of dialect, pauses, intonation, intensity) of two interaction partners increasingly resemble each other when they feel sympathy for each other but diverge when feeling antipathy for one another (Giles, Mulac, Bradac, & Johnson, 1987). Dropping or rising the voice helps the interaction partner to gather the meaning of what is said. Likewise, a speeded manner of speaking emphasizes the urgency of a situation (see Shintel, Nusbaum, & Okrent, 2006). Summarizing past studies, a person's changing emotional state and stable personal characteristics, as well as a speaker's age, height and weight can be judged with better than chance accuracy from nonverbal properties of the voice (see Kramer, 1963; Krauss, Freyberg, & Morsella, 2002; Lass & Davis, 1976). Males rated the social attractiveness of a woman more highly when her speech rate was higher than their own. Apparently, there are perceptual cues in the voice (e.g., pitch, loudness, breathiness, rate, intonation, resonance, fundamental frequency) that reflect the speaker's characteristics. All in all, the perceived social attractiveness and competence of a speaker were evaluated as higher when speech parameters were similar to the evaluator's own (Feldstein, Dohm, & Crown, 2001; Kallinen & Ravaja, 2004; Nass & Lee, 2001). Lower voice levels in adolescents were associated with lower self-worth in a study implemented by Harter, Waters, Whitesell, and Kastelic (1998). Speakers can identify smiling from the voice alone. Listeners seem to have precise and consistent criteria for what contrasts happy and sad tones of voice (Tartter, 1980). The voice helps to reveal whether someone is lying or telling the truth, whether a sentence is meant like it was said or is rather ironically spoken (e.g. Ekman, O'Sullivan, Friesen, & Scherer, 1991). When emotionally aroused, people seem either to be silent or to talk a lot, which is evident in 27 cultures on five continents (Wallbott & Scherer, 1988). Sad sentences are longer than neutral, and angry sentences are significantly shorter (Reilly, McIntire, & Seago, 1992). One indicator for deceit is a rising voice (e.g. Ekman, Friesen & Scherer, 1976). Thus, it becomes evident that the voice reveals a great deal of information about a person, their feelings, thoughts, actions and relationships, and that it is important to a person's auditory SI.

2.6.2 Visual vs. Auditory Channel – Difference in Importance?

In spite of its obvious importance, the voice has received far less interest than the face (Baum & Nowicki, 1998; Scherer, 1986). There may be several reasons (e.g., lack of adequate methodology, difficulties in defining relevant parameters, in graphic representation, and in the distinction between the linguistic and paralinguistic domain). The examination of the fleeting auditory perceivable voice signal is methodologically much more costly than the observation of facial expressions (Scherer & Wallbott, 1990). Besides the methodological reasons, for a long time visual abilities were regarded as more relevant. Why?

Mehrabian (1972) and others claim that observers rely more on visual than on vocal behavior in making judgments. Mehrabian (1972) used regression analysis and found out that of a message's impact, only 7% can be attributed to verbal content. The vocal channel accounts for 38% and the visual channel for 55% of the variance. Nonverbal channels (*how* something is expressed) consequently seem to have a much higher impact than the actual verbal expression (*what* is actually expressed) (see also Video-Primacy hypothesis, Krauss, 1981, cited in Wallbott, 1995). Findings of DePaulo, Rosenthal, Eisenstat, Rogers, and Finkelstein (1978) show evidence that, when there is inconsistency between auditory and visual nonverbal information, subjects were more influenced by visual cues than by auditory cues except for very discrepant messages favoring auditory cues. However, the actual importance of a channel depends on the social context (Ekman, Friesen, O'Sullivan, & Scherer, 1980; O'Sullivan, Ekman, Friesen & Scherer, 1985), the degree of consistency across channels, and on the intimacy of the communication (see Hess, Kappas, & Scherer, 1988). For example, O'Sullivan et al. (1985) found that voice is more highly correlated with honest speech, whereas content is more correlated with deceptive speech. In social exchanges among nonintimates, the verbal response directs the course of the interaction, whereas in more intense relationships, verbal communications about internal events are ignored. In judging other people, both verbal and nonverbal cues are important. Complementary to the context dependence of a channel's relevance, there are even findings indicating a higher importance for verbal rather than visual information (Domangue, 1978). Maier and Thurber (1966) found that accuracy was highest when an interview was read (77% accuracy) and listened to (77%) compared to an accuracy of only 58% when participating in the interview. The authors conclude that visual information distracts attention from the important information, consequently reducing accuracy. Children three and four years old have a strong preference for prosody over facial expression when revealing emotions in their story telling (Reilly & Seibert, 2003).

Voice recognition may be particularly important in the clinical context. People with an acquired inability to recognize faces (prosopagnosia) and all other visually impaired people have to rely strongly on voices for identification (Bodamer, 1947, cited by Schweinberger & Sommer, 1997). Furthermore, for several proficiencies depending on the auditory channel (e.g. telephone counsellors), social and emotional auditory abilities are of major importance. Recognizing the emotional state and drawing conclusions about the dialog partner's personality are important conditions for telephone counsellors and salesmen in order to deal most effectively with their customers. Forty female telephone counsellors performed significantly better concerning portrayed emotions in vocal stimuli when compared to 40 female face-to-face counsellors (t=2.55; p=0.013). They were not better in recognizing emotions from visual cues (Wallbott, 2003). Besides emotion recognition, there are also hints that problem solving can be more effective in telephone communication compared to direct interaction. Limited to vocal communication, there is less distracting information that keeps people from focusing on relevant problems (Wallbott, 1995).

Generally, positive emotions and attitudes (e.g. joy and positivity) are better recognized visually, whereas negative emotions (especially anger, but also sadness, indifference and dominance) are better recognized in the vocal channel (e.g. Wallbott & Scherer, 1986; Rosenthal, Hall, DiMatteo, Rogers, & Archer, 1979). That is probably due to adaptive advantages such as the ability to warn (fear) or threaten (anger) over large distances using auditory rather than visual methods (see e.g. Johnstone & Scherer, 2000; Tooby & Cosmides, 1992). The verbal channel was identified as being the most controllable, followed by the face and the body and finally the voice as the channel with the least possibility of control. The less controllable a channel is, the more accurate it should be in revealing the true message (see Ambady & Rosenthal, 1992). In summary, focusing on only visual stimuli when dealing with social intellectual abilities cannot be justified, considering the extensive proof of the significance of the auditory channel.

2.6.3 Emotion Theories – Basic Concepts

Dealing with emotions, for example expressed through the voice, it is crucial to define how many emotions exist and how they can be classified. There are two major hypotheses in emotion research. Some theorists reduce emotion theories to "basic emotions," namely anger, sadness, fear, disgust, surprise and joy, that are expected to be psychologically and biologically fundamental (not further reducible, relying on psychic mechanisms that emerged from natural selection, see Reisenzein, 2000). In the reductionist's opinion, all other emotions are based on these fundamental emotions; consequently, only the basic emotions need to be described and analyzed (Izard, 1977; McDougall, 1908, 1960; Plutchik, 1994; Tomkins, 1962). Other theorists argue that in addition to basic emotions there are secondary emotions consisting of basic emotions and additional elements (e.g. cognitions and behavior tendencies). Repentence, for example, is regarded as sadness caused through the evaluation of a past action as morally wrong (Johnson-Laird & Oatley, 1989). Data confirm the second approach rather than the assumption of discrete basic emotion theorists (Meyer, Schützwohl, & Reisenzein, 1997). There is growing consensus among emotion psychologists that emotion needs to be viewed as a multicomponent entity (e.g. Frijda, 1986; Lazarus, 1991; Johnstone & Scherer, 2000).

According to Plutchik (1994), emotions vary in intensity (e.g. fear vs. panic), in similarity (e.g. shame and guilt are more similar than love and disgust) and in polarity (joy vs. sadness). Emotions have to be distinguished from the affective states, moods, attitudes, and personality traits of the speaker. At present, there is no consensus about the number and degree of differentiation between emotions (Schmidt-Atzert, 2000). Shaver, Schwartz, Kirson, and O'Connor (1987) used the prototype approach to specify scripts of five basic emotions, namely love, joy, anger, sadness, fear and surprise. They found these emotions to overlap substantially with emotion examples mentioned spontaneously by laypersons and with the emotions children first learn to name (Bretherton & Beeghly, 1982). The emotions listed by more than 40% of 200 subjects were happiness, anger, sadness, love, fear, hate, and joy. Ekman (1984) differentiated between fear, anger, surprise, disgust, sadness, and happiness, also known as the six basic emotions. Epstein (1984) does without surprise and disgust and suggests love and affection instead. In a study carried out by Bretherton and Beeghly (1982), 28-month-old children were able to distinguish between love, like, mad, scared, happy and sad (see also Harris, 2000). Schmidt-Atzert (2000), using the differential emotions scale (see Izard, 1977), could establish nine (i.e., fear, anxiety, restlessness, sadness, shame, joy, affiliation, sexual agitation, surprise) of ten emotions empirically. There were some problems, however, with the disgust items. Russell (1980) classifies emotions within a circumplex model that consists of the dimensions agitation-quietness and pleasure-displeasure. Reisenzein and Hofmann (1993) selected 23 emotions (e.g., interest, joy, surprise, distress, anger, fear, shame, disgust, contempt, and guilt among others) orientating on cognitive models (e.g. Izard, 1977; Weiner, 1986) and empirical criteria (e.g., emotional states that are typical examples of emotions in the layperson's view). According to Reisenzein and Hofmann (1993), a good model should approximate the subjects' natural ability to distinguish emotions based on appraisal of relevant situational information. It is obvious, that the suggested models are quite similar in including basic emotions (see e.g. Ekman, 1984) and complement these through a number of additional ones. Newer emotion theories describe emotions as processes including different reaction components or modalities (Scherer, 1990). Scherer (1996, 2003) suggests a component-process-model based on the Brunswik lens model. It contains five emotion components (i.e., cognitive, neurophysiological, motivational, expressive, emotional), which are based on five subsystems (i.e., information processing system, supply/provision system, guiding system, action- and monitor system) and have specific functions (i.e., stimulus appraisal, system regulation, performance preparation, communication of reaction and intention, reflexion and control). Emotion is regarded as a series of interrelated adaptive changes in several organismic subsystems following antecedent events evaluated to be of major importance to an organism's goals. Emotion process is seen as a sequence of highly variable, quickly changing emotional states (Scherer, 1986). Banse and Scherer (1996) used empirically generated scenarios including 14 emotions. Ten out of the 14 contained pairs of the same emotion family, with five differentiations altogether. Their model makes concrete predictions that refer to changes in the most important acoustic parameters for the 14 emotions (see section 2.6.4). A detailed overview about a plethora of different emotion theories and their assumptions is provided by Scherer (2000). In my considerations and test development, I rely on the model of Scherer, since his research seems to be thorough and sound, and since principles of Brunswik symmetry are considered. Moreover, Scherer and colleagues were the only ones who provided an emotion in voice recognition test with German intonation (pronunciation).

The lack of consensus makes it difficult to compare existing studies. Scherer (1986), for example, proposed a distinction between quiet happiness and elated joy, between cold and hot anger, dejected sadness and desperate grief, and so on. When, in a study, the emotion of joy is reported, it remains unclear whether it refers to quiet happiness or elated joy. Additional problems encountered when comparing or summarizing studies concern their degree of reality (reality vs. portrayed), their measurement and statistical procedures. Often, interindividual differences concerning the meanings of emotion labels lead to differences in judgment. Reisenzein and Hofmann (1993) used comparative model testing in order to control for these possible confounding factors. They found out that subjects can discriminate between emotions rather well. Laypersons were not significantly worse in emotion discrimination compared to trained observers. Ambiguous and complex situations, however, are harder to discriminate, as it is especially difficult to decide which of the simultaneously occurring emotions dominates.

2.6.4 The Objective Measurement of Social Cues/Emotions in Voices

In the past, researchers have tried to identify objective components for emotion recognition in voices. Johnstone and Scherer (2000) differentiate between four groups of measuring the encoding of voice. (1) Time-related measures expect rate and duration of vocal sounds and pauses to vary for different emotions (e.g. extraverted American speakers produce fewer hesitation pauses than introverted speakers). (2) Intensity-related measures reflect the amount of energy in a speech signal, the effort required to produce speech and the perceived loudness (e.g. lower intensity is related to submission). (3) Measures related to fundamental frequency (F_0) examine the number of cycles per second in a periodic sound that strongly determines pitch of voice (e.g. higher fundamental frequency seems to be associated with a competent and dominant personality in male Americans and with discipline and dependability in male German and female American speakers, Scherer, 1979). (4) The combined time-frequency-energy measures use formants to identify emotional states. Forming the individual sounds (phonemes) of a language, each phoneme can be characterized by the amplified frequencies corresponding to that phoneme (formants). The amount of resonance (formant amplitude) and the range in the given formant (formant bandwidth) may change considerably with different emotional states. As a suprasegmental feature of speech, prosody includes intonation, loudness, pitch, and rate of speech (tempo) (e.g. Michell, Elliot, Barry, Cruttenden, & Woodruff, 2003). It co-occurs with the lexically conveyed message and therefore reveals whether a sentence corresponds to its content or whether it is meant ironically (Reilly & Seibert, 2003). Banse and Scherer (1996, 2003) relied on such objective parameters and used empirically generated scenarios to test the predictions of changes in the most important acoustic parameters for the 14 emotions. High-stress conditions or mental workload were associated with higher F_0, higher intensity values and faster speech rate than low-stress conditions. Sadness and boredom have been found to show low F_0, F_0 variability, intensity and speaking rate. Compared to a neutral condition, the "fundamental frequency, F_0" rose when the emotions joy, anger and fear were expressed. The *intensity* of the voice was reduced when sadness was expressed compared to the other emotions. The portion of high frequency energy (> 635 Hz) was higher when anger was expressed compared to other emotions. Banse and Scherer (1996) could distinguish between different emotions with comparable arousal levels such as rage, panic, and elation, via their acoustic profiles. Confusion patterns could show that confusion within the same emotion family is more probable than between emotions from different emotion families. For example, disgust is confused with nearly all other negative emotions (Banse & Scherer, 1996). The end of a prosodic contour has a special significance in the discrimination of emotions. Rising pitch at the end of a phrase may either indicate a question or express uncertainty, politeness, or submission (Frick, 1985). Falling contours are in turn associated with pleasantness (Scherer, 1974).

Considering the review of findings, vocal parameters seem to be promising indicators of physiological arousal (e.g. Scherer, 1979, 1986; Frick, 1985). On average, acted emotions in voices could be classified with an accuracy of 60% (chance level: 12%) by the hypotheses the model makes. This value is based upon 30 studies that were implemented in the early 80s (Scherer, 1989) and was supported by later studies (e.g., 65%, van Bezooijen, 1984; 56%, Scherer, Banse, Wallbott, & Goldbeck, 1991). The best recognition rates could be obtained for sadness (72%) and anger (68%), followed by joy (59%) and fear (52%). However, people who are good at emotion recognition also show rates of about 56% correct assignments. Thus, they are even better than objective emotion diagnostic tools. It can be assumed that judges intuitively choose more complex judgment and information integration strategies than is possible in objective emotion assessment. Even when controlled for emotion differentiation (see above, global joy vs. differentiation between elation and happiness) recognition rates do not rise higher than 55-56%. The recognition rates are about 15% lower compared to recognition rates that were found for the recognition of facial expressions (Scherer, 1999). Besides the degree of emotion differentiation, one major problem in studies was their focus on emotion discrimination rather than on actual emotion recognition. Being able to discriminate between alternative emotions does not automatically mean that the person is also able to identify a single emotion. Other errors occur with emotions similar in valence (e.g. pride and interest). Although standardized spectral parameters can be regarded as very important in the measurement of qualitative differences between emotions, there is no common agreement about the appropriate parameters that should be measured, nor about the appropriate length of a prosodic contour.

Moderating Variables

Studies on objective emotion measurement suggest several variables and parameters that influence the auditory recognition rate.

a)   Familiarity and length of stimulus presentation (duration)

Recognizing unfamiliar voices from a previous presentation may engage perceptual or cognitive mechanisms quite different from those involved in the recognition of familiar voices (Schweinberger & Sommer, 1997). Performance for famous voices improves with increasing stimulus duration. The most rapid improvements were observed during the first seconds of stimulus presentation (Schweinberger & Sommer, 1997). Ambady and Rosenthal (1992, 1993) showed that samples of nonverbal behavior with a duration of only half a minute allow observers to form an impression of a person's affective state and interpersonal attitudes correlating highly with objective criteria or long-term observation judgments. Moreover, the longer people know each other, the better they get at communicating emotions prosodically (Hornstein, 1967). However, there are also studies that did not find an influence of acquaintance on the recognition of emotions (Scherer, London, & Wolf, 1973).

b)   Context

Emotion psychology suffers from the serious difficulty of studying emotions in a (real-life) social context (Scherer & Wallbott, 1994; Wallbott & Scherer, 1989). In most of the studies on vocal emotion recognition, subjects are presented with isolated stimuli of nonverbal expressive behavior, rather than dynamic and static context stimuli such as the situation, related persons' behavior and changes in the course of time (Wallbott, 1986). However, in daily interaction situations, we experience nonverbal behavior within the social context. The knowledge of the context in which the communication occurs determines the translation of the received message (Kappas, Hess, & Scherer, 1991).

c)   Culture

Auditory emotion expressions by people of a certain culture are recognized above chance level by people of different cultures. Scherer et al. (2001) documented an accuracy value of about 66% across all emotions and countries using German actors and evaluators from nine countries in Europe, Asia and the USA. Their findings were interpreted as a proof for the existence of universal, culture-independent rules for vocal characteristics concerning specific emotions. Nevertheless, language-specific paralinguistic patterns of the vocal emotion expression do exist. The more different languages are, the lower the emotion recognition accuracy was. In German voice samples, the recognition rate among Germans was 74% whereas only 52% of the emotions were identified correctly by Indonesians. Joy was much harder to recognize (42%) than the other emotions (around 70%). In summary, the results indicate that there are universal inference rules from vocal characteristics of specific emotions across cultures. However, it is possible that understanding the verbal content is a crucial precondition for the correct interpretation of prosodic features.

d)   Speech material generation technique

In the past, there have been different approaches in the generation of speech material: natural vocal expression, induced emotional expression, simulated emotional expression and masking techniques (Scherer, 2003; Campbell, 2000). Table 2-9 gives a short description of each of the four methods and provides a summary of their advantages and disadvantages.

Several techniques were applied to mask speech. In *voice content masking* the speaker recites standard meaningless material (e.g. alphabet or numbers) or some standard meaningful but affectively ambiguous or neutral material (a word, phrase, or one to two sentences) with different moods or tones of voice. *Filtering* (Rogers, Scherer, & Rosenthal, 1971) removes selected bands of frequencies. Low-pass filtering, for example, removes the higher frequencies of speech upon which word recognition depends. Intonation, rhythm, tempo, and loudness of the voice remain the same, while speech intelligibility is lost. Compared to ordinary speech, the voice sounds calm and steady, muffled and slightly distorted. However, the upper and lower overtones of speech contribute to the personal tone or timbre of a person's voice (Ochai & Fukamura, 1957, cited by Kramer, 1963). Applying *randomized splicing* (Scherer, 1971), spoken language is cut in pieces so that words are scrambled. The voice sounds natural, but more pleasant, more peaceful and nicer than ordinary speech. The content cannot be understood. Additional possibilities are *playing backwards, pitch inversion* and *tone silence coding*. Scherer, Ladd, and Silverman (1984) found that politeness was still recognizable in the most severely masked speech samples. Natural emotions were used in the clinical context with depressed people and during psychotherapy (see e.g. Hargreaves, Starkweather, & Blacker, 1965; Roessler & Lester, 1976), and rarely with unimpaired people (Huttar, 1968). On the one hand, speech samples obtained in naturally occurring emotions may not have been sufficiently emotional to yield discrete vocal cues pronounced sufficiently to show up in acoustic analysis. On the other hand, simulated emotions with instructed encoders may not be natural enough, especially when actors are asked to produce the stimulus material. Emotions may only be identified because posers overemphasize powerful cues, particularly arousal, but miss more subtle cues, that differentiate discrete emotions in natural settings (Scherer, 1986). Kappas et al. (1991) criticize the focus on portrayed emotions in past studies. Thus, it remains relatively unclear how far results obtained with acted utterances can be transferred to natural

110

occurrence (Kappas et al., 1991). Until now, systematic studies on the relationship between acted and natural emotions are scarce (see Halberstadt, 1986).

Table 2-9: Description of Speech Material Generation Techniques

Technique	Short description	Advantages	Disadvantages
Natural vocal expression	Material is recorded during naturally occurring emotional states (e.g. in dangerous flight situations or affectively loaded therapies)	- high ecological validity - especially useful in clinical context	- brief voice samples, small number of speakers and bad quality - emotions are not always obvious - appraisal of an event is individually different - several emotions may be reflected simultaneously - lack of control in speech material (see Williams & Stevens, 1972)
Induced emotions	Emotions are induced (e.g. via stress induction, presentation of emotion-eliciting slides or films)	- comparable voice samples for all participants	- often only weak affect - appraisal of an event is individually different
Simulated vocal expressions	Voice samples produced by actors	- yields intense, clear, prototypical, and unambiguous expressions	- danger of over-emphasis - lack of more subtle (natural) cues
Masked speech (Techniques are described in further detail in the text.)	Removes speech intelligibility	- allows the use of natural speech rather than artificially posed emotions	- unclear how far it is comparable to reality - unclear whether additional processes (general discrimination and hearing ability, etc.) play a role as well.

e)   Group differences

Several studies have shown that persons differ with respect to their ability to decode emotions from facial expressions and other nonverbal channels (Hall, 1978, 1984; Rosenthal et al., 1979; Russell & Fernández-Dols, 1997; Wallbott, 1998). Among laypersons the hypothesis often emerges that people who have lost their sense of hearing or their vision are forced to compensate for that loss by increased investations in other channels (deficit hypothesis). However, several studies revealed no differences between blind people and normal hearing subjects in identifying emotions and familiar environmental sounds. Sometimes, visually impaired people even performed worse (see Blau, 1964 cited by Wallbott, 2003; Minter, Hobson, & Pring, 1991; Rosenthal et al., 1979; Wallbott, 2003). Research about gender differences with regard to vocal expressiveness and emotion recognition reveals inconsistent results. There are findings, showing that men may convey emotions more clearly through specific vocal characteristics (e.g. harshness, laxness, intensity) than women. Other studies, however, did not show any differences (Brody & Hall, 2000). Females reporting to experience positive emotions intensely and receiving rewarding feedback, produced speech that showed higher vocal-emotion-related parameter values (e.g., F_0) than comparison subjects. In male subjects, expression of emotion was more clearly related to negative emotional intensity (e.g., failure) (Bachorowski & Owren, 1995).

2.6.5 Measurement Approaches in Emotion Research

In EI and SI research, instruments developed and results obtained in the emotion research tradition were almost completely neglected in studies. However, a plethora of tests within this field, often labeled as interpersonal sensitivity, do exist (e.g., Communication of Affect Receiving Ability Test, CARAT, Buck, 1976; Japanese and Caucasian Brief Affect Recognition Test, JACBART, Matsumoto, LeRoux, Wilson-Cohn, Raroque, Kooken, & Ekman, 2000; Facial Action Coding System, FACS, Ekman, Friesen, & Hager, 2002; Standardized database of facial expressions, Ekman, 1973; Emotional Stroop-Test; McKenna & Sharma, 1995, 2004). Interpersonal sensitivity used as a construct in emotion research is defined as the correct identification and comprehension of social stimuli (perception, inference, decoding, deception) (see Bernieri, 2001) and thus apparently overlaps with the SI subconstructs we are interested in. Table 2-10 summarizes the most famous tests relying on auditory material that were developed within the tradition of emotion research.

Table 2-10: Auditory Tests in Emotion Research

Test name	Definition/ Model	Dimensions/ Material	Scales	Results/Studies
Profile of Nonverbal Sensitivity (PONS; Rosenthal, Hall, DiMatteo, Rogers, & Archer, 1979)	Nonverbal sensitivity Content of scenes can be classified according to positivity (positive vs. negative) and dominance (dominant vs. submissive)	Dimensions: understanding (perception) Material: auditory, video, pictorial	Short audio and video extracts have to be judged according to the emotion, cognition and content that is displayed in the section. Auditory: 20 items, each randomized spliced and content filtered	Psychometry: - Alpha: full PONS: .86 (220 Items); audio: .17-.30 (Hall, 2001) - Retest-reliability: Md= 69 (6 studies) Convergent validity: - measures of person perception (programmed cases task, nonverbal decoding tasks): r= .28 - no correlations with dispositional empathy measures Discriminant validity: - cognitive complexity: r (Md)=.28 (two studies) - no correlations with AcI (IQ, SAT, Vocabulary, school achievement) Md r= .14 (15 samples) - personality variables (adjustment, extraversion, encouraging etc.): r=.22 (24 studies) Criterion validity: Greater professional advancement was associated with lower PONS scores, for clinicians (-.62) and teachers (-.66). Additional remarks: - Women perform better than men (in 80% of the samples). - Voices of women are easier to judge. - Training improves performance.
Diagnostic Analysis of Nonverbal Accuracy (DANVA, Nowicki & Duke, 2001, 2007) and DANVA2 DANVA-AP (auditory and pictorial)	Measurement of emotional sensitivity based on affect in voice and face	Dimensions: perception, understanding Material: auditory and pictorial	Systematically samples two levels of intensity (high and low) of four emotions (happy, sad, angry and fearful)	Psychometry: - Alpha between .64 and .83 - Retest: two months r = .84, (n = 45); (Nowicki & Carton, 1993); six weeks: .83 (N=68) - Mean accuracy increased with age between 4 and 19 years. In eldery people it increases gradually following a cubic function (Baum & Nowicki, 1998) Convergent validity: - only minor correlations between the subtests - relation to similar tests: r= .48 und .58 - no correlations with social perception auditory Discriminant validity: - no correlations with AcI, but correlations with academic achievement (Nowicki & Duke, 1989) - no correlations with general auditory processing (tone discrimination, Baum & Nowicki, 1998; r=.03) - Correlations with social competence criteria, such as conflict involvement .25 - .52 (more errors in DANVA, more conflict involvement, less effective strategies)

Table 2-10: Auditory Tests in Emotion Research, continued

Test name	Definition/ Model	Dimensions/ Material	Scales (mentioned in test)	Results/Studies
Index of Vocal Emotion Recognition Test (Vocal-I; Scherer, Banse, & Wallbott, 2001; Scherer, in press); Item material of the GVEESS.	Subjects have to identify emotions in meaningless sentences that are spoken by male and female German radio actors.	Dimensions: perception Material: auditory Two senseless sentences were spoken. Use of the scenario approach to get sentences as naturally acted as possible.	joy, sadness, fear, anger, neutral	Validity: - no correlation with EI ability measures (MSCEIT, emotion perception) - same confusion matrices and recognition patterns in nine different countries (Germany, Switzerland, France, Great Britain, USA, Italy, Spain, Indonesia, the Netherlands) - Anger was recognized most easily (recog. rate: 76%), followed by neutral, sadness, fear, and joy (42%). Joy was most often confused with neutrality. - Women performed significantly better (Scherer, in press). - Overlap with facial recognition (Facial-I): $r = .24$ ($N = 1,264$; $p < .001$) (Scherer, in press). - Correlation: Gf - vocal, $r = .18$ ($N = 1,311$; $p < .001$), recognition Criterion validity: 3% advantage (t significant at $p < .01$) for employees in non-management positions for the recognition of vocal anger expression
Multimodal Emotion Recognition Test (MERT; Bänziger, 2005; Bänziger, Grandjean, & Scherer, 2005)	Evaluation of the perception of dynamic face and voice expression	Dimensions perception Material: video, audio, audio-video picture	10 acted emotions, each represented in four modalities facet design with 120 items (3 clips x 10 emotions x 4 modalities)	Psychometry: - Retest of the MERT after 6 weeks - confusions among emotions emerged mainly with emotions of the same family (subjects: N=73 (63 female) had to choose one of 10 emotions) Validity: - no significant correlations of the MERT with the NEO-FFI and the STAI - MERT correlates with BIS / BAS between .26 (audio; audio-video) and .31 (video). - correlation between PONS and JACBART with MERT (N= 70): r=.50

Conclusions With Regard to the Instruments

The available instruments can be criticized in different ways. The PONS uses only one person for stimulus generation, the content-filtered and random-spliced masking techniques lack ecological validity, and it does not include the measurement of specific emotions. The rating of affects is combined with a forced choice. This implies that if one recognizes the affect displayed correctly it is possible to make a mistake in choosing the wrong MC option. The PONS does not show evidence of sufficient reliability. Neither the PONS nor the DANVA include the social context (see Nowicki & Duke, 2001).

As evidenced by the information provided in Table 2-10, the instruments dealing with recognition of emotions and socially relevant stimuli in voices clearly concentrate on the perception domain including some aspects of social understanding. With the exception of the findings reported in Bänziger et al. (2005, r=.50), the intercorrelations between the instruments are rather low, ranging between -.09 and .20 (see Ambady, LaPlante, & Johnson, 2001; Hall, 2001; Scherer, 2003) indicating a lack of convergent validity. This lack may be due to variable theory and method application (i.e., concerning construct definition), the duration and method of stimulus presentation, (i.e., spontaneous vs. acted emotions), the channel (face, eyes, gesture, voice), the definition of the criterion, and the consideration of guessing probability. An additional reason may be the amount of (different) subconstructs that are subsumed under interpersonal sensitivity, such as attentional accuracy, ecological sensitivity, sensitivity to deceit and to the identification of emotions, interpretation of cues (see e.g. IPT-15 vs. PONS), and empathic inference (=everyday mind-reading, Ickes, 2001) (see Hall, 2001). Not only are the intercorrelations among the instruments of this research tradition low, but the relationship to AcI and personality are low as well. It would thus be quite interesting to examine what these kinds of instruments actually measure.

How are Social and Emotional Intelligence Related to Research from Emotion Theory?

There are almost no empirical studies that relate measures commonly used in emotion research to measures of SI and EI. Nor did I find theoretical conceptions about how they may be related in the literature. However, there are some rare exceptions published recently. In the view of Scherer (in press), highly emotionally competent individuals are characterized by optimal functioning of the emotion mechanism with respect to both emotion perception and emotion production. According to Scherer, "emotion production refers to the total pattern of bodily and behavioral changes that characterizes the adaptive function of emotion, allowing the organism to cope with events of major relevance for well-being" (p. 175). The visible bodily and behavioral changes provide important information about the individual's reaction and potential behavioral intention to social interaction partners. A precondition of this emotion signaling in social intercourse is the accurate perception and interpretation of other peoples' emotional states. Scherer (in press) postulates three components that are expected to have an effect on these two functions: appraisal (i.e., evaluating events in an accurate fashion with respect to the personal implications of the events and one's ability to cope with the consequences), regulation competence (i.e., the capacity to react in an appropriate fashion with respect to promising action tendencies and situational contingencies), and communication competence (i.e., the ability to produce emotion signals in accordance with strategic aims and cultural norms and to correctly infer the emotions of others on the basis of outward expression and to empathize with others under appropriate circumstances). It is apparent that these components overlap with both emotional and social intelligence. The perceptual function is what we assume to be a part of an underlying intelligence (cognitive). The production function can be seen as the potential (intelligence) that is transformed into action (e.g. social behavior). Scherer's appraisal component should also play a major role in social and emotional understanding (cognitive) whereas regulation and communication are expected to be more important in the actual behavior. According to this perspective, I would expect a relationship between auditory emotion perception tasks (e.g. items of the VOCAL-I, see Table 2-10) and our SI perception domain as well as between appraisal tasks (e.g. PONS test, see Table 2-10) and our social understanding dimension. Recent empirical results (Roberts, Schulze, O'Brien, MacCann, Reid, & Maul, 2006), however, indicate that instruments of the psychometric tradition (the MSCEIT) and measures that were developed in the emotion research tradition (VOCAL-I) load on different latent variables.

2.7 Objectives for Test Development

2.7.1 General Ideas

Two questions are subsumed under construct validity: (1) To what extent does the test measure a trait that exists? (validity of the test) (2) How well does the proposed interpretation correspond to what is measured by the test? (validity of the construct). The evidence of the two kinds is usually not separable (see Loevinger, 1957; Cronbach & Meehl, 1955). Therefore, conceptualizations and models of both SI and AuI were formulated recommending how to measure these constructs. The results obtained with these measures may suggest revisions of the models, which in turn, may provoke thought about whether we measured what was intended. Test and theory development underlie the following specifications:

- The SI and AuI test should tap a wide range of the abilities that we regard as manifestations of those constructs. They should be content valid.
- The constructs are regarded as latent, with indicators that we will attempt to identify and measure. The specific abilities were chosen to represent the construct according to the discussion of the constructs (see chapters 2.3 – 2.6) as exhaustively as possible, but often

we had to sample and postpone the development of tasks representing the universe to a later time.

- Available and recommendable tasks that fit into the model were taken from existing tests. The remaining gaps were filled with new developments orientated on the selected instruments, the corresponding literature, and tasks that we thought would be appropriate to measure the construct.

- At this point, the immediate use of these tests is likely to be for research; applications (e.g., in school testing, personnel selection and training) should follow at a progressive stage of test development.

- Both tests will be developed and structured so as to be useful primarily for adults aged 20 to 40 years.

- All abilities tested will be assessed by multiple items that will be subjected to analyses of their psychometric properties by conventional methods of the Classical Test Theory (CTT). Specifically, we will be attempting to develop measures that have a high degree of internal consistency.

2.7.2 Development of a Social Intelligence Test

Since existing instruments of social intelligence did not meet our requirements of being realistic, including representative material, relying on clear definitions and a theoretical model, and being methodologically thorough, we decided to develop a new SI test. The construction of a new measure was already suggested by Wong et al. (1995), who proposed developing more appropriate measures in order to examine SI. With the exception of some tasks that could be adapted relying on previous work (Weis, 2002), the test had to be completely newly developed. With this test, we aimed at overcoming past problems and in turn allowing the profound investigation of the still unsatisfactory and unanswered questions (e.g., concerning subconstructs and validity against AcI). The following objectives should be a guideline for the development of a new SI test and the implementation of a corresponding study.

1) *The test should concentrate on cognitive aspects of SI. It clearly excludes social behavior from its scope.*

Whereas tests of AcI measure cognitive preconditions of academically intelligent behavior, according to many authors SI tests should measure socially intelligent behavior. Consequently, the goal of SI tests is much higher than for tests of AcI. However, it makes sense, correspondingly to AcI, to develop tests of the purportedly measurable cognitive preconditions for a person's socially intelligent behavior first, and in a second step, validate these instruments within social situations with persons who are willing to show socially intelligent behavior. Therefore, we focus only on the cognitive requirements necessary to show socially intelligent behavior.

2)   *The test should be a performance measure.*

Focusing on multiple cognitive aspects of social intelligence, we can choose between self- and other-report measures and performance measures, since behavior measures are out of the question as explained above. Knowledge tests cannot be applied, since the cognitive operation should be measured rather than the crystallized knowledge (see framework of Süß, 1996, 2001; third criterion). Ability measures represent the individual's performance level on a task, whereas self-report measures are filtered through a person's self-concept and impression management motives. Because of former results concerning self-report and other-report measures (high correlations with personality, no emerging social intelligence factor) and the problems that appeared when relating them to AcI, we intend to assess SI with a performance test (see framework of Süß, 1996, 2001; second criterion). Corresponding to Carroll (1993), an intelligence test should assess actual ability to perform well at mental tasks rather than one's self-reported beliefs about these abilities (Carroll, 1993; Neisser et al., 1996). We are interested in maximum performance, correspondent to AcI tests.

3)   *Underlying theoretical model*

For a successful study of SI and further insights into the construct, one has to start with definitions of the construct and develop a model that may serve as a basis for test development and empirical studies. Therefore, this book is based on the model of Süß et al. (2005, see also Weis & Süß, 2007), including the corresponding definitions and subconstructs of social understanding, social memory and social perception. As may be expected, scoring divergent productions proved considerably harder than scoring cognitions, as in the former case a best answer hardly exists, and the subjects' responses must be evaluated by independent judges for quality and quantity (similar to AcI creativity tests). Thus, in our studies, social flexibility is excluded because of economical reasons and minimal empirical results. Social knowledge is also excluded because of its special role in that it explicitly depends on prior knowledge and therefore is not a "pure" cognitive operation.

4)   *Application of a MTMM design including written, auditory, pictorial, and video-based material*

By means of the application of a multimethodal design relying on written and spoken language as well as on pictures and videos the theoretical model of Süß et al. (2005, see also Weis & Süß, 2007) is extended to a hierarchical facet model. The advantages of facet models have been specified in chapter 2.1.4. Archer and Akert (1980) could show empirically that every channel contains meaningful information and that there is an information redundancy (the same information is imparted by different channels and cues). They assume that even small pieces of information imparted through different channels are interpretable and sufficient to come to the correct conclusion of the situation and of peoples' behavior. In the view of Ambady and Rosenthal (1992) information of too many channels at the same time may be rather distracting. On the contrary, Ekman, O'Sullivan, Friesen, and Scherer (1991) report the highest accuracy for the detection of deceit when all channels are involved. Obviously, there is no common opinion and empirical results are contradictory. Therefore, in our SI test, different channels should be involved separately but referring to the same situations. Future studies may combine the channels systematically. One could argue that written material from former studies of SI (e.g. Chapin, 1967; Gough, 1968; Orlik, 1978; Riggio et al., 1991; Shanley et al., 1971; Wong et al., 1995) is not worth further investigation. However, although many problems arose with written material in the past, there are practical as well as theoretical reasons to include it (see also Wong et al., 1995). One of our main methods of communication is via email. That makes it especially important to understand and react adequately to social cues and to avoid misconceptions. Semantic content was important to the identification of sadness (Apple & Hecht, 1981), and the verbal channel was most accurate to communicate the distinction expressive-inexpressive (Ekman et al., 1980). With regard to theoretical reasons, the question of whether SI measured with written material is separable from AcI could not be assessed exhaustively because of theoretical (lack of theoretical model) and methodological (lack of a test including realistic material, inclusion of social context) shortcomings. Empirical studies provided evidence, that verbal information is particularly important in longer exposures to social cues leading to a greater accuracy (Ambady & Rosenthal, 1992). Research based on newly developed realistic written SI tasks that include the social context and are developed thoroughly should be worthwhile to further address the question of the relationship between social verbal intelligence and AcI. Another reason for the use of written language concerns the operational domains. Is there a relationship to AcI in all operational domains (understanding, memory and perception) of SI, including written material?

5)   *Inclusion of the social context*

Statements about the SI of a person require consideration of historic and cultural elements, and even different conditions of life, as well as a notice of personal aims someone brings into the context of a situation. Intelligence is not intrinsic to a person but must be contextually defined (Ford, 1982) and is to a large part determined by social or personal values rather than by objective, scientific criteria. Consequently, a person's behavior can never be judged as socially intelligent or unintelligent. Statements can only be made regarding the specific situation. This makes it once again important to search for underlying characteristics of SI, because all other behaviors are context dependent and thus cannot be empirically investigated in a way that is generalizable and valid across situations, aims and people. For the measurement of underlying characteristics, possible social situations have to be covered as completely as possible. A person who is able to understand someone's feelings, thoughts, and relationships to other people correctly in different social situations and with different kinds of people is, in our view, expected to be socially intelligent. Therefore, stimulus material for our test should be chosen according to its representativeness of possible social situations. A kind of a taxonomy on social situations should be provided (or alternatively, if not available, newly developed) that can be covered as completely as possible by the stimulus material.

6)   *Realistic (non-acted) material*

For most of the existing tests, actors generated the stimulus material. With actors, typical conflict and cooperation situations can be displayed (see e.g. VISION, Runde & Etzel, 2005, chapter 2.2.3) clearly and unambiguously. However, it has to be queried whether acted social situations correspond to reality. In daily life, we often encounter social situations that are not as extreme and exaggerated as shown in acted situations. On the contrary, daily social situations and emotions are often much more subtle. Besides bypassing the problem of overemphasis that arises with actors, another advantage of the use of realistic stimulus material is the lack of transfer problems between the test and the social behavior that is shown in real life (important for criterion validation, training etc.). In our study, we decided to use realistic situations instead of actors. The collection of realistic material is much more costly and requires much more effort. How that was done is described in chapter 4.1.

7)   *Objective scoring*

In chapter 2.2.3, I mentioned that the scoring of SI tasks should be as objective as possible. This seems to be easier with regard to social perception and social memory tasks than for social understanding tasks. Perception tasks should include reactions to objectively present stimuli in the material. Social information that is tested in social memory tasks should be obvious in the stimulus material, which has to be remembered. For social understanding there are no equivalent systems to determine the correct answers on the tests. The items of such tasks are much more complex, requiring alternative scoring procedures, namely (1) target scoring, (2) consensus scoring, and (3) expert scoring (see chapter 2.2.3).

For our social understanding test we decided to focus on target scoring to avoid the negative implications of consensus scoring (see chapter 2.2.3) and expert scoring (dependence on a usually small group of experts' opinions and is an opinion rather than being objective). The approach mentioned by Legree et al. (2005), who take the perspective that consensus scoring may be an adequate procedure for some domains (i.e., with neither experts nor object knowledge; for controversial subjects) is not recommendable for several reasons. First, including only novices in the sample may result in strong intra- and interindividual disagreement among subjects and with an experts' view. Second, the procedure may not apply when the target has extra information that is not available to the outside observer (see chapter 2.2.3), which is true for the approach we used, which will be presented in chapter 4.1.3. According to Kang et al. (2005), "consensual definitions of SI have not been forthcoming in the literature" (p. 112). However, since consensus-based scoring does not imply much effort it may be an easily gained additional source of information we can use with respect to the correspondence between target and consensus scoring (see chapter 2.2.3).

8)   *Representative sample*

a) Age range between 25 and 40 years

It is interesting that most of the studies in the domain of SI have been conducted with young people. Out of 44 studies published before 1983, forty studies used students (primary school students, high school students, undergraduate students, graduate students) as subjects (Landy, 2006). Only five studies, four of them using the Guilford and O'Sullivan tests (1965), were conducted with high school students and revealed an independent SI factor compared to AcI. All of the graduate and undergraduate students were psychology majors. Landy (2006) criticizes correctly that this selection of participants is not representative. Even after 1983, most studies have been implemented using (psychology) students (see references chapter 2.2), often for economical reasons (availability of psychology students, lower costs). At least one of our studies should involve adults, who have to prove their SI in a variety of privat (e.g., family) and public/working situations.

b) Different levels of education and proficiency

Focusing on psychology majors, proficiency and level of education did not vary considerably in past studies. However, results of some investigations show that there are differences concerning education and proficiency. For example, profiles of sophisticated samples showed good performance on video and poorer performance on audio while profiles of the unsophisticated showed the reverse pattern. Rosenthal et al. (1979) assume that reading the tone of voice is a rather unsocialized skill compared to reading visual cues (in western standards). However, regarding the results from an evolutionary standpoint they seem to be counterintuitive: Nonverbal language starting from this viewpoint should emerge as being more basic. Our aim is to examine social intelligence at least in one study with a group of adults covering different proficiencies.

2.7.3   Composition and Construction of an Auditory Intelligence Test (AuIT)

I assume auditory intellectual abilities to be classified according to the cognitive operation they require (discrimination, memory, reasoning and creativity) and according to the material that was used (e.g., tones, familiar environmental sounds and speech) (see chapter 2.5). The Stankov and Horn (1980) test battery is still the broadest that exists and covers several of the operational and content domains mentioned. Therefore, my purpose is to take the Stankov and Horn tasks as a basis and develop additional tasks for cells that are not covered by their subtests. Several objectives arise starting from this point that will be explained briefly below, since most objectives that are also valid for the AuIT have already been described in the context of SI.

1)   *Performance-based measurement*

Auditory intelligence should be measured based on performance instead of using self- and other-report measures or knowledge tests (see Süß, 1996, 2001; second criterion).

2)   *Operational domains*

Tasks should tap the three operational domains discrimination, memory and reasoning. Similar to SI, an additional auditory creativity dimension is expected, which would be measured, for example, with composition tasks. However, the creativity domain exceeds my and our limits because of economical reasons including scoring difficulties, test time, and effort. Therefore, the creativity domain is reserved for future research.

3)   *Content domains*

At least two content domains, speech and tones, should be included forming according to Figure 2-10 the poles of what I defined as "auditory intelligence." It would make sense to examine the familiar environmental sounds in addition if enough resources are available.

4)   *Level of tasks*

As suggested by Stankov (1971) and Horn (1967), the level of auditory tasks should be equivalent to tasks of AcI in order to minimize undesired variance. That means developing tasks with a mean difficulty of .50 covering different degrees of difficulty.

5)   *Musical experience*

The tasks should be soluble without musical knowledge (see Süß, 1996; 2001; third criterion). However, we cannot make sure that people with musical experience do not have advantages in solving tonal tasks.

3 Research Questions

I already indicated that task development and selection of both constructs, SI and AuI, is intended to take place on a level comparable to AcI. With respect to the questions that should be answered with the test of SI and AuI, the constructs should be compared at the same level, such as expected primary factors with primary factors and secondary factors with secondary factors (e.g. AcI memory with SI memory and AuI memory). Thus, factors should be Brunswik symmetrical (see Wittmann, 1988).

3.1 Social Intelligence

3.1.1 Inner Structure of Social Intelligence

We expect a coherent SI structure with a general positive manifold including all SI dimensions (hypothesized SI model, Süß et. al; Weis & Süß, 2005). Since we know that SI is a multidimensional construct, we expect the dimensions of social perception, social memory and social understanding to be moderately correlated. Besides this main question it should be tested whether the nonverbal material domains (pictorial and video-based) and the language-based materials (written and auditory) build two combined entities or whether, alternatively, written and auditory split into two factors.

3.1.2 Relationship between Social and Academic Intelligence

Wechsler (1958, p. 75) queried whether "social intelligence is just general intelligence applied to social situations." In our view, however, SI should form a separate ability domain. Since our test includes the social context, we can test Wechsler's assertions. According to Carroll (1993), SI measures should correlate at least moderately with AcI to be regarded as an aspect of intelligence. However, in Lee et al.'s study (2000, see above), SI and AcI were not at all correlated. According to Carroll (1993) and Lee et al. (2000), these findings question whether or not SI can be regarded to be an intelligence. As already mentioned (see chapter 1.2 and 1.3), criteria have to be specified in a way that clearly defines the manner in which a construct will (and if so, how strongly) or will not be related to AcI. However, there is no clear criterion that stresses the strength of correlations between constructs necessary for defining it as intelligence. Intelligence according to the definition as being underlying and stable, relatively general and to a comparatively higher degree genetically predetermined does not prescribe guidelines for the strength of correlations with AcI. In my opinion, to be treated as an intelligence, correlations with AcI are not needed if the criteria described in Süß (1996) are fulfilled. To find an ability construct meeting the criteria and being not at all correlated with AcI, in my view seems even to be preferable, as a greater portion of variance can be explained. High correlations with AcI, on the contrary, seem to prove that nothing novel is measured. In order to be handled as an ability construct different from AcI and others, I suggest moderate correlations at the most. Of course, the correlation-related proportion of variance explained by other variables should also be taken into account and serve as even better proof.

With regard to our study, we expect SI to form a completely different construct, and consequently to be clearly separable from AcI. However, we also expect low to moderate correlations, because we expect cognitive operations of AcI and SI (e.g. memory) to share some parts of variance. In more detail, we assume social understanding as the core facet of social intelligence to show, compared to other social intelligence domains (i.e., social memory, social perception), the lowest correlations with AcI, since it is expected to be most different from academic intelligence dimensions. Concerning the content domains, I expect the highest correlations between social written abilities and verbal AcI. Since I expect SI perception and SI memory as well as SI written to share more common variance compared to SI understanding and the other SI content domains, I wonder whether SI perception and memory applying written material can be separated from AcI. Nonverbal as well as social auditory abilities should demonstrate lower correlation with the BIS contents. However, all social content domains should be weakly correlated with verbal AcI, because in SI tasks, written task instructions, answer sheets etc. are used. We assume minor correlations between academic figural-spatial and SI pictorial, and even lower correlations with video-based material.

3.2 Auditory Intelligence

3.2.1 Inner Structure of Auditory Intelligence

I expect that auditory intelligence can be described applying two facets analogous to the BIS model: A content facet including speech and non-speech material and an operation facet that splits up into auditory discrimination, memory and reasoning. All domains are expected to be correlated but nevertheless separable. Comparable to SI, the content and the operation model should be tested separately because of restrictions concerning degrees of freedom.

3.2.2 Relationship between Auditory Intelligence and Academic Intelligence

The auditory ability dimensions are expected to be separable from AcI (represented by the BIS model). There are several possibilities for how auditory abilities could be related to the BIS model:

1) They form an additional content domain in addition to verbal, numerical and figural-spatial.

2) They form a completely new operation.

3) They form a new facet (together with the precedent visual abilities).

4) They cannot be classified within the facet structure

Of course, not all of the possibilities can be tested in the present study. For now, I expect auditory abilities to make up an additional content domain within the BIS model including speech and tonal material. Speech-related auditory abilities are assumed to show higher correlations with verbal AcI and with the corresponding operations they are expected to measure. Tonal auditory ability is expected to correlate with figural and numerical AcI contents, since tonal material is assumed to require internal representation (cognitive strategy), which might be imaginative (visual, figural-spatial) or numerical (counting tones) and is applied to the scale and distances between tones. With regard to operation domains, firstly, I expect auditory discrimination to be related to AcI speed, auditory memory to be related to AcI memory, and auditory reasoning to be related to AcI reasoning. However, I assume the correlations between the two suggested intelligence constructs to be low to moderate as they do not share the same content material. It is also possible that auditory intelligence tasks form a completely new operation on top of the auditory content or make up a new facet together with visual abilities. If auditory abilities form a new operation, the auditory operation domains (discrimination, memory and reasoning) are expected not to be correlated with the AcI operations processing speed, memory and reasoning (or to demonstrate only minor correlations). It is also possible, that the facet structure is not appropriate to classify auditory intelligence into the BIS framework.

3.3 Social Auditory and General Auditory Abilities

I expect social auditory abilities to be separable from but positively intercorrelated with general auditory abilities. The relationship between social auditory abilities and general auditory abilities reflects the relationships of the superordinate model that includes all academic and social intelligence factors. The strongest overlap is expected between the two auditory memory factors (general auditory memory and social auditory memory) since they are most similar with respect to the cognitive operation. With regard to contents, both auditory speech and auditory tonal tasks are assumed to correlate with social auditory tasks. However, because of the use of language in both general auditory speech tasks and social auditory tasks, factors including speech should correlate more strongly than the tonal factor with the social auditory abilities.

4   Test Development

This chapter describes the development of the Magdeburg Test of Social Intelligence (in the following abbreviated with "MTSI" (Süß, Seidel, & Weis, 2008, see also Süß, Seidel, & Weis, 2007)) and of the Auditory Intelligence Test (in the following abbreviated with "AuIT", see also Seidel & Süß, 2007). The main focus is on the development of social written and social auditory tasks.

4.1   Development of the Magdeburg Test of Social Intelligence (MTSI)

For the development of the MTSI (Süß et al., 2008), an extensive research plan was worked out. In this book, the test ideas for the written and auditory social intelligence tasks will be described in more detail. For more information on the pictorial and video-based tasks see Weis (2008). In the following chapter, the main steps of test development and the modifications that were made for the first main study are described with respect to the social understanding tasks as well as for the auditory and written memory and perception tasks.

4.1.1   Test Design

In order to meet the objectives described in chapter 2.7, a test design was developed that included the three operational domains of (1) social understanding, (2) memory, and (3) perception and that relied on written and spoken language and pictorial and video-based material. In the following, the term "different types of material" is used in order to refer to the separation of auditory, video-based, written, and pictorial content domains. Each cell resulting from cross-classification of operations and contents should be represented through two tasks. In the first study, however, we restricted our development on at least one task for each cell. In a next step, the cells should be completed by additional tasks using the results of the first validation study. In this chapter the test development is illustrated by some examples; the complete test will be presented in the context of the second study (see chapter 1). Table 4-1 represents the test design with the abbreviations that will be used in the text that follows.

Table 4-1: Overview of the Social Intelligence Test Design and the Corresponding Abbreviations

	Content domain			
Operational domain	*written language (w)*	*spoken language (a)*	*pictorial (p)*	*video-based (f)*
Social understanding (SU)		Scenario approach		
Social memory (SM)	SMw1+2	SMa1 SMa2	SMp1 SMp2	SMf1+2
Social perception (SP)	SPw1 SPw1	SPa1 SPa2	SPp1 SPp2	SPf1 SPf2

Note: SMw=Social memory written; SPw=Social perception written; SMa=Social memory auditory; SPa= Social perception auditory; SMp=Social memory pictorial; SPp=Social perception pictorial; SMf= Social memory video-based; SPf=Social perception video-based

We chose a scenario approach for the design of the social understanding (SU) tasks. The reasons for selecting this approach were the following: Social understanding deals with the interpretation and judgment of other peoples' feelings, thoughts, and relationships (see chapter 2.2.2). On the one hand, it is important to judge a person's behavior, and accompanying thoughts and feelings, correctly in an arena of knowledge at a relatively early point. On the other hand, it is also important to refine one's interpretation of the person's feelings, thoughts, and actions when more background information is available. A person may behave differently in private and public settings. The behavior may also depend on the people the person deals with (e.g., husband/wife, children, relatives, friends, acquaintances, colleagues and superiors) as well as on the number of people interacting in a certain situation (e.g., dyads, small groups and larger groups). It is difficult to cover all these aspects with a variety of people in one or two tasks separating the different types of material. Therefore, we chose a scenario approach that presents one person in further detail in different settings involving all kinds of material we selected. We decided to investigate the different channels separately (e.g., presenting video without sound, pictures without text, etc.) in order to get as much information as possible about each type of material and about the effects of a certain sensory channel (see chapter 2.7.2 for further reasons).

4.1.2 Taxonomy of Social Situations

In order to represent the context adequately and systematically (see chapter 2.7.2; Dewey, 1909, cited by Landy, 2006) by selecting appropriate and representative material, we searched for a taxonomy of possible social situations. Such taxonomies are rare; for an example see Bronfenbrenner et al. (1958) who distinguished object and referent dimensions and included variations of the content and the time. Despite of extensive literature review, we found only one classification we could rely on. Runde and Etzel tried to cover as many social situations as possible with their taxonomy that also serves as a basis for their instrument VISION (Runde & Etzel, 2005). They differentiate between three dimensions: (1) The content dimension is described by parameter values (or: specifications, characteristics) job, family, friends and public life. (2) The structure dimension differentiates between a group and a dyad and (3) the quality dimension involves two conditions, competitive and cooperative behavior. Our own taxonomy is based on the Runde and Etzel (2005) system but is enlarged and modified on the basis of literature studies in the domain of social cognition (e.g., Abrams, & Hogg, 1999; Aronson et al., 2004; Forgas, 2000). Figure 4-1 presents our classification system for possible social situations.

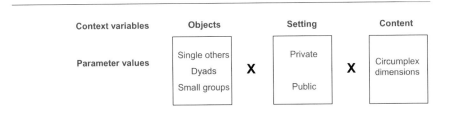

Figure 4-1: Taxonomy of Possible Social Situations (Süß et al., 2007)

The "objects" dimension describes the number of interacting persons. We include single others as a characteristic of this dimension, accounting for monologues, emails, pictures with emotional expressions emerging in situations in which single persons are not seen or heard by other people. However, in contrast to tests of emotional intelligence, the expressions, behavior etc. of single others are always elicited by human beings rather than being free from social interaction (see e.g., emotions in the MSCEIT elicited through landscapes). Small groups are, according to the literature in social psychology, groups including between two and nine persons (Witte, 2005). According to Witte (2005), larger groups (e.g. sport clubs or school classes) can also be considered as small groups dependent on the duration of acquaintance and the time spent together. The more intense the contact is, the larger the number of people that can be encompassed by the idea of a "small group." Small groups are chosen as object dimension since they have their special laws of behavior different from the individual and a larger social context and because the interaction in such groups is expected to influence decision-making (see Bronfenbrenner et al., 1958). In our taxonomy, however, we do not classify dyads as small groups, but regard them as a separate entity. We differentiate between private and public "settings" as social systems and include family and relatives, friends and private acquaintances within the private category. The public domain subsumes job situations, as well as daily public life (e.g. shopping, going by train or bus, interactions in administration offices or departments). The "content" of a situation is classified according to the interpersonal circumplex, which is made up of two main dimensions, status (assured-dominance vs. passive-submissiveness) and love (warm-agreeableness, see

Wiggins, 1979). Status is also described as control (Kiesler, 1983), power (Wiggins, 1979) and agency (Wiggins, 1991); love is known in terms of affiliation (Kiesler, 1983) and communion (Wiggins, 1991). The dimensions are characterized as follows. (1) Power: dominance is expressed through steady and raised voice, speech interruptions, presentation of information, expression of opinion, leading and delegating behavior, and getting quickly to the relevant point of an interaction. Submissive behavior is shown through the application of soft language and patient behavior that lets others precede (speak and act). It tends to conform with the opinion and meaning of others, does not directly express the wishes of the actor, and avoids responsibility. (2) Love: an agreeable behavior is characterized by attentive listening, smiling, a positive attitude, talking to other people, making compromises, showing correspondence (of opinions; agreement) and expressing affiliation and sympathy. Quarreling is expressed through demanding and sarcastic behavior, not answering to questions, witholding information or providing wrong or inaccurate information. The interpersonal circumplex is supported by 40 years of psychological research and has been successfully applied in a variety of studies with widely different settings (e.g. Carson, 1969; Foa, 1961; Kelley, Holmes, Kerr, Reiss, Rusbult, & Van Lange, 2002; Kiesler, 1983; Leary, 1957; Wiggins, 1996; Wiggins & Trobst, 1997). The circumplex goes back to the Interpersonal Adjective Scales (Wiggins, 1979), classifying and categorizing words describing the way, people interact. The axes can serve either for the description of an individual/group or for the classification of a situation (see Wiggins, 1991). An example description for a status situation in public life can be "strivings for mastery and power that would enhance and protect the differentiation of the individual, accompanied mostly by dominant, seldom by submissive, behavior. An example of a description for love in private settings might be "strivings for intimacy, union and solidarity with a social or spiritual entity, and communality would be partly reflected in frequent agreeable behaviors and infrequent quarrelsome behaviors". A certain interpersonal behavior can be classified in the two-dimensional space through marking the co-ordinates. Often, the interpersonal circumplex dimensions were examined through self-report measures (e.g. Inventory of Interpersonal Problems-Circumplex; IIP-C, Alden, Wiggins & Pincus, 1990), which was also used in this book. The circumplex dimensions are expected to cover parts of the broader structure of the Big Five in further detail, namely agreeableness and extraversion. The dimensions extraversion and agreeableness depend directly on the presence of other persons: Both dimensions seem to determine the extent of social stimulation and the preferred way of social interaction. The circumplex dimensions interact with the setting. Moskowitz (1994) found that in public situations, the status of the interaction partner was of prime importance, whereas in private situations, the degree of intimacy (closeness) was decisive. Social norms play a greater role in public situations than in private situations. In the private domain the person has a larger margin of freedom to behave according to personal tendencies. The source of information, applying our taxonomy, always stems from a person-situation interaction. According to Wiggins (1979), interpersonal events may be defined as dyadic interactions that have relatively clear-cut social (status) and emotional (love) consequences for the self and other people.

With respect to our task material, we do not expect, that in each task all possible combinations of object, setting, content and question mentioned in the taxonomy (see Figure 4-1) are covered. However, systematic variation can also be managed by covering the cells across tasks (instead of presenting each combination within one task).

4.1.3 Social Understanding Tasks (SU)

Each scenario deals with one target person shown in both private and public life interacting with different people. Various situations and background information about the person provide context information. Judging a person across different situations should lead to a higher degree of reality (more extensive impression of the person) and consequently to better conditions for high verisimilitude. For the material collection, two persons accompanied the target person for two or more days and collected video, audio, pictorial, and written material of that person in different private and public situations with different people. One person concentrated on filming, the other on generating questions related to interesting parts of the situation. In order to collect as much information as possible in limited time, target persons were asked to make a schedule of situations that might reasonably be expected to be encountered during the period reserved for recordings. Before recordings were made, all persons present were asked to sign a letter of agreement for later use of the material. In order to minimize effects of recordings on natural behavior, we did not use the first 10 or 15 minutes for item generation and questions. However, all our target persons told us, that after a short time and a few recording sessions, they tended to forget the camera and behaved naturally. As soon as possible after finishing the recordings of one situation, the target person was asked about her feelings, thoughts, and relationships to other persons present in selected parts of video, audio, pictures, or written notes. Some questions that emerged later on during test development were answered in a second meeting and/or via email/phone. We generated standard questions for each modality involved for a particular person and situation. The questions served as an orientation but were adapted according to the specific situation and people. Beyond standard material, there was always a possibility of completely different questions arising in the special situation. The content of the questions concerned cognition, affect, and behavior. The questions differed slightly according to the kind of material (written and spoken language, pictures, videos). Consequently, a 3 (question contents) x 4 (material) matrix with 12 cells was applicable. In addition, we developed evaluation questions dealing with metacognitive issues. In Table 4-2 an excerpt concerning language-based items from our question catalogue is presented. For comparable questions concerning video-based and pictorial material, see Weis (2008).

Table 4-2: Questions for Target Persons (Verbal and Auditory Material)

Cognition	Affect	Relationship to other people	Evaluation/Metacognition
What do you want to attain with the text you wrote/with what you said? (purpose)	Which feelings did the expression of person x elicit?	How important is the topic/correspondent person for you? Why?	How did you think, during writing, how the text/what you said would appear to the person who reads/hears it? (metacognition)
How do you explain your remark (comment/ expression) in the situation? (explanation)	How do you feel with regard to the person you correspond/talk with?	How much sympathy do you feel for the correspondent person? Why?	How probable do you think it is that you attained your aim (with what you said or wrote)? (metacognition)
How would you describe your attitude concerning this person/this topic? (attitude)	How comfortable do you feel with regard to your own expressions/the situation/the expressions of the other(s)? Why?	How typical is this way of writing (e.g., email, letter)/way of conversation/talking for you?	Did you think any thoughts different from what you wrote/said? What? (Difference between expressed behavior and thoughts/feelings)
	Describe the mood you were in when writing the text (email/ letter)/ talking to the other person ...?	How familiar are you with the topic of writing (e.g., complaint, loveletter)/of the conversation?	At any point in the conversation do you now wish you had said something different? What? Why?
		Would you have expressed anything different in another situation (other person of correspondence, different topic)? What?	Do you believe that you were able to say what you wanted to say? Why (not)?

Once the questions were generated, the target person had the opportunity to view the scenes and pictures again and to hear the audiofiles in order to be reminded of the exact situation. The target person and the accompanying persons were permitted to exclude material and information they did not want to be exposed but none of them seized that opportunity. Target persons were asked to name the cues in the material indicating their feelings and thoughts in the situation and their relationship to others. In addition, a short self-presentation including some basic information about the person's age, proficiency, family status and favorite hobbies was recorded. That information was intended to provide some background information for the test and help the subjects get an impression of the voice and the physical appearance of the target person. At the end of the recordings, the target persons were asked to complete some additional questionnaires: the NEO-Five Factor Inventory (NEO-FFI, Borkenau & Ostendorf, 1993), the Inventory of Interpersonal Problems-Circumplex (IIP-C, Horowitz, Strauß, & Kordy, 2000), the Prototypical Acts on SI (Amelang et al., 1989), a social desirability questionnaire of the Freiburg Personality Inventory-Revised (FPI-R; Fahrenberg, Hampel, & Selg, 2001) and a biographical questionnaire. The answers of the target persons to our questions after each scene, as well as the answers they gave in the questionnaires, served for generating items later on. Answers to the questions concerning the scenes should be given on a visual scale in order to be able to transfom them to different kinds of scales (e.g., 6-point or 7-point scale). We took care to use high quality equipment in order to maximize the quality of the stimulus materials. Video recordings were made with a videorecorder (Panasonic NV-GS50) and pictures were taken with a Minolta Dimage A1. Audiofiles were finish-worked with the program CoolEdit 2.0 and saved as wav-files (quantization 16Bit, sampling rate 44KHz, mono).

Selection of Appropriate Target Persons

Our main criterion for selection of the appropriate persons was that they be typical in gender, age, proficiency and education of the sorts of persons our student subjects might encounter as they go around their daily lives. We did not want unusual, exotic persons for our targets, especially at this beginning point in our efforts. The descriptions show in Table 4-3 represent, of course, only our first scenarios, eventually they should be complemented by an expanding array of target persons if our general approach proves to be successful. We chose as targets persons that are well known to at least one of our team and on whose information we could rely. Of course, that does not guarantee that the person's self-assessment and those of others' do not diverge. To assess the likely veridicality of the target persons' answers, we also asked them to complete a social desirability scale. In addition, we collected extra information on the scenes. Table 4-3 presents an overview of characteristics of the first four persons we recorded in their daily private and public lives. None of the recordings was done in Magdeburg since we wanted to minimize the possibility that one of the target persons is known to the test takers.

Table 4-3: Overview of Scenario Target Persons (First Study)

Name of person	Gender	Age	Proficiency
Christian	male	23	student of law
Rita	female	24	medical-technician
Kathrin	female	26	student of psychology
Martin	male	33	independent dancing teacher

Selection of Material

The material obtained from target persons was edited to enhance quality (e.g., noise reduction in audio files) and to ensure anonymity (e.g., removing of names and places) and was then separated into segments constituting what we judged to be adequate and coherent stimuli. The questions we had formulated were assigned to the correspondent material. In a team of at least six psychologists and psychological assistants we evaluated and discussed each scene and the corresponding questions. A scene was selected for use only when there was a consensus on its appropriateness and that relevant cues to the answer of the target person could be identified in the task material. The selected scenes were revised again and then combined into an approximately 20 minute sequence. Finally, all materials were integrated into a software package that was adapted especially for the use in our study (WMC program, see also chapter 6.1). With the exception of the self-presentations of the target persons in the beginning of each scenario that combined videos, and sound, all materials (written, auditory, video and pictorial) were presented separately. The answer sheet was prepared with an initial short scene description followed by different kinds of questions (open, 6-point rating scale, multiple choice). At the end of the session, the subjects were asked to judge the presented target person according to the Big 5 and the Interpersonal Circumplex. Once the scenarios are established, the content of the social understanding scenario scenes could serve as a subtest of long-term memory.

Example of the Task

Box 4-1: Example of a Social Understanding Task (SU)

First, a short introduction (written, video, and sound) of the target person "Rita" serves the familiarization with the appearance and voice of Rita.

In a short conversation with a colleague and friend of hers she talks about her experiences with her former job.

After listening to the conversation, subjects have to answer questions that concern Rita's feelings and degree of sympathy for her former boss, and her opinion about the job in general. The questions have to be rated on a 6-point rating scale.

Scoring of Answers

Persons being tested later were asked to respond to questions and fill out questionnaires as they thought the relevant target person might have done. Scores on the tasks were then generated by comparing the answers of our subjects to those of our target persons. The deviation between the target person's answer and the subject's answer produces the itemscore. The smaller the deviation the better the score. Since we got the answers of our target persons to our questions about emotions, cognitions, and relationships to other people we had a rather objective criterion by means of which to evaluate the answers of our test takers instead of taking the "common sense" as the best answer. As already mentioned, to ensure the best conditions for the veridicality of the target person's answers, we chose persons who were familiar to us. These persons completed a social desirability scale, we have started to collect peer-ratings on them, and we will get some expert ratings in the future.

4.1.4 Social Memory Tasks (SM)

Social memory is the ability to store and recall social information. In order to discriminate social memory clearly from social perception and from social knowledge (see also chapter 2.2.2) items (questions) and task material have to be explicit and unambiguous without requiring any kind of interpretation or judgment that is part of social understanding. Perception without interference has to be taken for granted. In the social memory tasks, the material contains exactly the information (word, sentence, picture, movement, etc.) that is asked for later on. The social context is taken into account, and items cover the cells of our taxonomy as well as possible. Table 4-4 presents the conceptual scheme for written and auditory social memory tasks.

Table 4-4: Test Ideas of Written and Auditory Social Memory Tasks

	Written	Auditory
Material	*Task 1*: one-sided correspondence including emails, letters, involving socially relevant content	*Task 1*: one-sided expressions, monologues
	Task 2: two-sided correspondence including emails, letters, involving socially relevant content	*Task 2*: telephone dialogues, conversations with two and more people
Question type	open	open
Scoring	percent of right answers based on a key of analysis for evaluation	percent of right answers based on a key of analysis for evaluation

For both modalities, task 1 and task 2 can be differentiated with respect to the manner of communication. Whereas the first task deals with only one person, in the second task two or more people communicate. In the following a more detailed rational of each of the memory tasks is presented.

Social Memory-Auditory: Test Description

Subjects listen to sound sequences including a different number of people. Subjects are encouraged to listen carefully and try to remember as much socially relevant information as possible. After listening, subjects have a certain amount of time to answer questions to each presented sound file (conversation). Questions are answered in open format. We tried to cover our taxonomy with questions that involve all modalities (cognition, affect and relationship to other people). See Box 4-2 for an example. Table 4-5 presents an overview of the sound files included in the task.

Box 4-2: Example of an Auditory Social Memory Task (SMa)

> *Example*:
>
> The first conversation deals with a conflict between a boy who carries out his alternative service and his colleagues who evaluate his working behavior. In the colleagues' opinion he does not work autonomously enough and extends his breaks beyond time allowed. The narrator talks about a meeting, in which he, his superior, and his colleagues are present. The narrator rejects the accusations.
>
> Possible questions that are asked: Who complains about the narrator?
> How did the superior behave during the discussion?

Table 4-5: Test Construction Rational of the Task Auditory Social Memory (SMa)

Task	Gender	Private	Public
1) monologues: one person	male	*Conversation 2* (1:48 / 5 / 6) about holiday with girlfriend	*Conversation 1* (1:36 / 5 / 8) about conflict with colleagues and superior
	female	*Conversation 3* (1:48 / 5 / 7) about a friend who has personal and financial problems	*Conversation 7* (1:50 / 5 / 7) report about feedback for a trainee's performance
		Conversation 10 (1:57 / 5 / 5) telephone conversation about parents	
2) conversations: dyads and small groups	homogeneous	*Conversation 4* (1:54 / 5 / 7) small group discussion about a TV program	*Conversation 5* (1:50 / 5 / 8) future profession: industry vs. university
		Conversation 9 (2:11 / 5 / 8) about a female sales assistant a man met in a shop	*Conversation 8* (2:12 / 5 / 5) girl looks for a gift for her mother
			Conversation 11 (2:14 / 5 / 5) changes in life
	heterogeneous	*Conversation 12* (1:42 / 6 / 7) about a wedding	*Conversation 6* (1:46 / 5 / 5) about a gift a member of the work group received

Note: In parentheses: (duration / number of questions/number of possible points); A summarizing note on the content of each sound file is provided within the cells. homogeneous: either women or men; heterogeneous: women and men mixed.

Social Memory-Written: Test Description

In the social written memory task, four text modules are presented. Each text has to be read carefully in a limited amount of time. Subjects are instructed to concentrate to remember the socially relevant details as accurately as possible. After each text, subjects have a limited amount of time to write down their answers to several open-ended questions. An example is presented in Box 4-3. Table 4-6 shows the test construction rationale.

Box 4-3: Example of a Written Social Memory Task (SMw)

> [...] Surprisingly, vacation was also good for me. I never thought that I would like skiing. I participated in a beginner's course with an actually kind skiing instructor. He explained skiing well. Unfortunately, he always felt the need to touch women. That is something, I can absolutely not tolerate. One of my colleagues also participated, but she gave up on the third day. The major reason was probably her weight. I felt so sorry for her because I talked her into coming with us. Tomorrow, I am going to see her again at work, I hope she will not be mad at me. [...]
>
> Possible questions are:
>
> Which positive information does the narrator write about the skiing teacher?
> Why did the narrator feel sorry that one of her colleagues gave up?
> What does the narrator hope when she meets her colleague again?

Table 4-6: Test Construction Rational of the Task Written Social Memory (SMw)

	Private	**Public**
One-sided correspondence	*Text 1*: skiing holidays (231 words)	*Text 2*: objection against a school reference (342 words)
More-sided correspondence	*Text 4*: letter correspondence between friends (355 words)	*Text 3*: consultation offer/order (333 words)

4.1.5 Social Perception Tasks (SP)

Social perception is the ability to perceive social information about persons and context as fast and accurately as possible (similar to perceptual speed in academic intelligence) (see chapter 2.2.2). In order to separate social perception clearly from social memory, all relevant information must be available, obvious, unambiguous, and objective. Possible cues to react to are, for example, a laughter in a conversation, a change of speakers, an emotional word etc. This quick responsiveness is particulary important with regard to the distinction of social perception from social understanding. In the same way as for social understanding tasks, the social context should be taken into account, and items should cover the cells of our taxonomy as well as possible. Within all social perception tasks, targets are presented in advance of the item material. People have to react as soon as previously presented targets emerge.

Test Idea Auditory and Written Social Perception Tasks

Table 4-7: Description of the Preliminary Auditory and Written Social Perception Tasks

	Written	**Auditory**
Material	*Task 1*: On the right hand side of the screen a short text with social content emerges (extracts of emails, letters, diaries,etc.). On the left hand side, a question that has to be answered on the basis of the text on the right hand side is presented (e.g. Is the future of Liz topic of the text passage? – answer with "yes" vs. "no") *Task 2*: Sentences, phrases, chats, etc. are presented. Reactions have to be made according to the content (social content vs. non-social content; positive vs. negative emotion)	*Task 1*: Reaction to target cues in conversations; possible target cues: names of people, interruptions, laughter, talking at the same time, etc. *Task 2*: Presentation of voices. Reaction to changes of pitch, tempo, emotions
Scoring	Reaction time and accuracy	Reaction time and accuracy

For the written social perception tasks, it is important to show the target questions before presenting the item content. Target questions are available until the item is answered in order to avoid memory effects. Moreover, reading speed has to be controlled. Perception tasks are quite short in duration. Once started, it is difficult to explain the task again to someone who did not understand it properly. Therefore, the task has to be practiced to ensure proper understanding before starting the test.

Auditory Social Perception Tasks

In the social auditory perception task, subjects have to perceive specified facts and react to the stimulus as fast and accurately as possible as soon as it has been perceived. Facts can be names of persons, the voice of a child, rejection or agreement, laughter, etc. The number of people talking within the sound files differs.

The conversations and corresponding stimuli that have to be perceived differ in complexity. In six of the conversations only one stimulus has to be monitored; the same number of conversations requires reaction to two stimuli. In one additional conversation, three stimuli have to be monitored. Four examples serve for practicing the task. In three of them one stimulus has to be monitored (agreement, laughter, change of speaker), in the fourth, subjects have to practice the reaction to two stimuli (laughter, voice of a woman). In the following an overview of the conversations (see Table 4-8) and the corresponding stimuli (see Table 4-9) is presented.

Table 4-8: Rational for Auditory Social Perception (SPa)

	Sex	One cue	Two cues	Three cues
Homo-geneous	male	1) Telefone conversation: Niklas/Steven; dyad (8) 2) Politics conversation; small group (6)	3) Conversation at a summer evening party; small group (7) 4) Conversation with a colleague about a new bike; dyad (12)	---
	fe-male	5) Conversation about a wedding dress; small group (7) 6) Telephone conversation about a job/application; dyad (10)	7) Tea time conversation; small group (8) 8) Conversation while regarding photographs; small group (11)	13) Conversation during breakfast; small group (10)
Heterogeneous		9) Explanation of a game on holidays; small group (9) 10) Reaction of a father to his baby daughter; dyad (9)	11) Conversation at a party about a flat and furniture; dyad (8) 12) Conversation at a birthday party about hairdressers; small group (10)	---

Note: The situations recordings took place involved dyads and small groups. In parentheses, the number of cues in a conversation is shown.

Table 4-9: Overview of the Different Types of Cues in Auditory Social Perception (SPa)

Type of cue	Number of items	Conversations
laughter	15	3, 7, 8,
names	18	3, 8, 9, 13
agreement	18	1, 11, 13
interruptions	10	2, 13
reaction to voices	23	7, 10, 12
rejection	6	4
admiration	7	5
filling words (like ehm)	10	6
SUM	107	

Note: Modified according to Papenbrock (2005)

Written Social Perception Tasks

We also worked to develop stimuli to elicit target-oriented reactions for the social written perception task. I decided not to present single social/emotional words to be judged but instead elected to select sentences so that items could include at least some social content.

Using sentences, however, implies that reading comprehension and reading speed are expected to influence the performance on the social perception tasks. I tried to minimize both influences and also included measures of reading speed as a reference (e.g., a possible covariate). The task will be described in Box 4-4.

Box 4-4: Example of a Written Social Perception Task (SPw)

Example 1 (statements, complexity part 1, private setting):
On the left hand side a statement appears:
Running in twos does not seem to be as effortful as alone.

On the right hand side a short statement appears:
On Wednesday, I was running with a friend. It is really fun to run in twos and is not as much effort as running alone. After running I felt quite fit.

Answer: "right"

The second part of the task is similar but uses questions instead of statements. One (level 1) or two (level 2) questions arise, that have to be answered with "yes" or "no". In the case of two questions, the overall answer is only "yes", if both questions can be answered with "yes." If one of the two questions has to be answered with "no", the overall answer is "no". Answering occurs by key pressing.

Example 2 (questions, complexity part 2, public setting):
On the left hand side two questions appear:
- Did the author agree to be the only representative at the conference?
- Is *Mr. Moss* mentioned in the text?

On the right hand side a short statement appears:
I don't venture to hope that Mr. Moos has time the 28.11. I already agree to attend the conference alone.
Answer: "wrong"

At first, a target statement arises on the left hand side of the computer screen. The question deals with social/emotional issues. Then, extracts of emails and letters are presented on the right hand side of the computer screen. The task is to scan the short text extracts and judge the statement according to its correctness (wrong or right). The judgment can be made without interpretation only on the basis of the short text. Memory effects should be excluded because the question and the extract are visible until the item is completed. Subjects are instructed to press a key for each answer (wrong or right) as fast and accurately as possible. The second level of increased complexity contains two statements that have to be judged. Only if both statements are right should the overall answer be "right." If one of the statements is wrong, the overall answer is "wrong." Table 4-10 shows the different parts of the written SP tasks.

Table 4-10: Overview of the Written Social Perception Task (SPw)

Task 1: Statements		Setting	
		private	public
Complexity level	one statement	9 items	8 items
	two statements	7 items	7 items
Task 2: Questions		Setting	
		private	public
Complexity level	one question	8 items	8 items
	two questions	7 items	7 items

4.2 Development of the Auditory Intelligence Test (AuIT)

The idea for the development of the test of general auditory abilities arose in the discussion about validation of the social auditory intelligence tasks (see also Seidel & Süß, 2007).

4.2.1 Selection of Tasks

First, tasks from the Stankov and Horn battery (1980) were selected that fit in well in our taxonomy and represented the factors identified by Stankov and Horn (1980, see chapter 2.5). Representativeness of the tasks for a factor was evaluated in terms of their loadings and communalities. Moreover, the loading on a common, more general auditory factor was considered. Among the suitable tasks, we again selected according to the reliability value (Cronbach's Alpha and Retest, see Carroll, 1993; Stankov & Horn, 1980; Horn & Stankov, 1982), length, and heterogeneity (to cover as many aspects as possible of our definition of auditory ability; see recommendation by Loevinger, 1957). Moreover, the correspondence to tasks of academic intelligence was attempted. For the auditory tasks, parts of the scale and written notes were available and provided by Lazar Stankov. Auditory recordings did not exist any more. As not all original items were still available, we tried to complete the tasks and introduced some modifications that seemed to be reasonable to us. Alexander Trinko[1], musician at the University of Magdeburg, helped us to complete the score including the development of new items and the implementation of modifications.

---

[1] I gratefully acknowledge the help of Alexander Trinko, Institute of Music Psychology, University of Magdeburg, in the implementation of auditory tonal tasks.

4.2.2 Completion of Tasks

Within auditory intelligence (see chapter 2.5), the focus was on tonal (nonverbal) tasks, because language-based tasks seem difficult do differentiate very sharply from verbal AcI tasks as well as SI tasks. The aim was to cover each nonverbal cell with at least two tasks and each cell requiring language with at least one task. Not all cells could be covered as we required by relying solely on the tasks of Stankov and Horn. Thus, we decided to supplement the memory cell of the classification system through a newly developed task, "audiobook". The task "recognition of familiar environmental sounds" was also added to get an idea of the corresponding content domain (see chapter 2.5.6). We focused on tonal and speech content as being the boundaries to explore the ins and outs of auditory intelligence especially with regard to verbal AcI. In addition, we chose an auditory inspection time task (pitch and loudness discrimination, AIT-P/AIT-L, Deary et al., 1989; Olsson et al., 1998) to complement the battery, because extensive research has been done with auditory sensory discrimination. Speech perception includes an additional task, "detection of repeated voices", that corresponds to the task "detection of repeated tones" in the nonverbal perception domain. Since it includes voices, it is expected to mark the transition to social auditory abilities. The reasoning nonverbal cell also includes a third task, chord decomposition. This task, though including auditory nonverbal material, is assumed to represent the transition to musical abilities. According to Stankov (1994), within psychological research, auditory abilities can be measured on three levels, namely sensory, perceptual, and higher-order processes. We split between memory and reasoning as higher order processes and subsumed the sensory perceptual abilities under the concept of "discriminative abilities". The following matrix (see Table 4-11) represents all auditory tasks, that are described thereafter. In order to simplify matters, the task recognition of familiar environmental sounds was subsumed under the nonverbal category, since it does not involve speech material. Actually, it makes up an own category (see chapter 2.5.6).

Table 4-11: Classification Matrix of Auditory Intelligence Tasks

	Perception	Memory	Reasoning
Tonal/ Nonverbal	• Detection of re- peated tones • AIT-P/AIT-L (discrimination of pitch, Olsson)	• *Recognition of fa- miliar environ- mental sounds* • Rhythm reproduc- tion • Tonal figures	• Tonal series • Tonal analogies • Chord decomposition
Speech	• Masked words • Detection of re- peated voices	• *Audiobook*	• Disarranged sen- tences

Note. The newly developed tasks are highlighted in italics.

In order to get an impression of the tasks, a short description of each task appears below. Directly after the name of the task, in parentheses, are the operation and content domains according to the classification system, as well as the corresponding factor according to Stankov and Horn (1980, see chapter 2.5.2 and 2.5.3).

a)   Detection of repeated tones (discrimination, nonverbal; factor: temporal tracking)

An eight-tone melody with four different tones is played. Except for one, all tones are presented at least twice. Subjects have to indicate which of the eight tones is presented only once (Stankov & Horn, 1980). The task includes 17 items. Some items were newly developed as not enough items were already available. The task was classified within the discriminative abilities because of its task requirements (detection of a stimulus within a sequence of tones), although empirical analyses (see chapter 2.5.3) revealed relationships with gf/gc and working memory.

b)   AIT-L /AIT-P (discrimination, nonverbal; factor: discrimination among sound patterns)

There are different possibilities for measuring auditory inspection time. Mainly, auditory discrimination of pitch (AIT-P) or loudness (AIT-L) have been used. In an AIT-L task, a tone indicates the beginning of the item (832 Hz, 500 ms), followed by a short break (1000 ms). Two tones of different intensity (loudness) (60 dB and 57 dB) are presented immediately, one after the other, and then masked through rustle. Participants have to decide whether the louder or the softer tone was presented first. Pairs of tones are presented within 11 blocks, including 120 items altogether, with decreasing duration of presentation (200 ms, 150 ms, 125 ms, 100 ms, 85 ms, 70 ms, 55 ms, 40 ms, 30 ms, 20 ms, 15 ms). The succession of tones (high intensity → low intensity or low intensity → high intensity) occurs by chance. The pitch of the tones remains constant at 832 Hz (Deary et al., 1989; Olsson et al., 1998). In a similar way, in an AIT-P task, a tone indicates the beginning of the item (832 Hz, 500 ms) followed by a short break (1000 ms). Two tones of different pitch (880 Hz and 784 Hz) are presented immediately, one after the other. Participants have to decide whether the tone higher or lower in pitch is presented first. Pairs of tones are presented within 11 blocks, including 120 items altogether, with decreasing duration of presentation. The succession of tones (high pitch → low pitch or low pitch → high pitch) occurs by chance. The intensity of the tones remains constant at 60 dB (Deary et al., 1989; Olsson et al., 1998).

c)   Recognition of familiar environmental sounds (memory; familiar environmental sounds (nonverbal); new)
Subjects are instructed to remember as well and as accurately as possible, twenty target sounds presented in succession and interrupted only by a short silence. Thereafter, 45 sounds (after pilot studies of 55) sounds are presented. Each sound has to be judged as to whether it belongs to the previously presented set of sounds or not.

d)   Rhythm reproduction (memory, nonverbal; factor: maintaining and judging rhythm)
Twenty rhythms, varying in length and complexity, are presented. Participants have to reproduce each rhythm using the keys of the computer (Drake, 1954, see Shuter-Dyson, 1982; Stankov & Horn, 1980). In contrast to Drake's (1954) and Stankov's and Horn's (1980) task, which required subjects to reproduce the rhythm as long as the original stimulus was beaten out, in our task the rhythm has to be beaten only once.

e)   Tonal figures (memory, nonverbal; factor: immediate auditory memory)
Participants hear a sequence of four tones in descending or ascending order. Thereafter, four alternative sequences, each including four tones, are presented. The one that includes the same notes as the target sequence is to be chosen (Stankov & Horn, 1980). The task includes 17 items.

f)   Tonal series (reasoning, nonverbal; factor: auditory cognition of relationships)
Four tones are played one after another in a particular order (ascending, descending or other). Four answer alternatives follow, each including one tone. The tone that completes the series logically (not musically) has to be selected (Stankov & Horn, 1980). In contrast to the original task, our 21 item task includes four instead of three options.

g)   Tonal analogies (reasoning, nonverbal; factor: auditory cognition of relationships)
The pitch difference of two tones played in succession has to be remembered. Four alternatives are then presented, including two tones with the critical pitch difference. The alternative containing the two tones equivalent to that of the first two tones has to be selected

(Stankov & Horn, 1980). The modified version involves four answer alternatives instead of three. The task consists of 17 items, some of which were newly developed.

h)   Chord decomposition (reasoning, nonverbal; factor: auditory cognition of relationships)

A three-tone-chord is followed by four answer alternatives including three tones each. Participants have to choose the alternative that contains the three notes presented in the three-tone-chord (Stankov & Horn, 1980). To supplement the original task, some new items were developed. The whole task contains 14 items.

i)   Masked words (discrimination, verbal; factor: speech under distraction, SPUD)

Isolated words differing in frequency (frequent two syllable words – infrequent two syllable words – one syllable words) and spoken with different intensity, have to be recognized against a background noise also varying in intensity (quiet – middle – loud). The words that were identified against the noise must be written down (Stankov & Horn, 1980). The kind of background noise at a party (instead of a cafeteria noise as in the original task) goes along with a variation in word frequency. The task includes 35 items. A similar task is also used in Gygi, Kidd, and Watson (2004). Unlike our task, in their study, they used high and lowpass filtering techniques and short sentences (431 to 3945 ms) instead of single words.

j)   Detection of repeated voices (discrimination, verbal; factor: temporal tracking)

A separate word (like "april" or "chair") is spoken eight times in succession by four speakers. One of the four voices is only presented once. That voice has to be identified (Stankov & Horn, 1980). The task contains 25 items. This task was classified within the discrimination domain for the same reasons as described for the task "detection of repeated tones" (see above).

k)   Audiobook (memory, verbal; new)

A 312 word text, excluding social content, is read. Participants are allowed to hear it twice and thereafter have to answer 14 questions concerning the content of the text (in the first study an open-ended answer format was used).

l)   Disarranged sentences (reasoning, verbal; factor: auditory verbal comprehension)

A sentence with disarranged words is presented. Participants have to write down the sentence with the correct order of the words (Stankov & Horn, 1980). We translated most of the original sentences into German language but also generated some new items. The task contains 19 items.

In collaboration with the musician Alexander Trinko, we arranged for the completion and order of the tonal auditory task items to be presented according to the following principles: Items were classified into three levels of difficulty (easy – middle – difficult). Within these levels, several parameters were manipulated. Easy items involve a clear harmonical structure (e.g. C-Dur), work with a clear leading tone, and distractors can be identified by focusing on the last tone. Time is easy with regard to rhythm (2/4); it contains only trioles. Fast syncopes are introduced only in the last items of that difficulty level. Items in the mid-range of difficulty also include foreign tones that do not belong to the harmony. The order is changed: tonal sequences are no longer melodies but are still tonal, sometimes phrygian. Moreover, dissonances are introduced and leading tones are not dissolved. With respect to rhythm, time gets more complex by using an additional beat (3/4). Additional breaks, neighborhoods with trioles as well as the use of eighth and sixteenth notes makes the sequences more difficult. In the items with the highest degree of difficulty, there is neither a harmony nor a melody. The items make use of abstract tones, great jumps as well as similarities between target and distractors, non-chords and inversions. Also to test rhythm more fully, syncopes, breaks between basic beats, and quintoles are employed.

Difficulty levels were fixed based on findings in the literature. Tonal sequences (songs etc.) are remembered better when they have a clear orienting structure with a predominant tonic chord. If tonal structure is lacking or obscured by rhythm the recognition and recall, performance is considerably worse (Boltz, 1991). We also took into account that primacy and recency effects are larger for auditory than for visual stimuli (Bruhn, 1993), the first and last tones thus are more prominent.

4.2.3 Integration of Items into the Presentation Program

Tonal tasks were realized with the program Cakewalk Pro Audio 7.00. For all tonal tasks except the rhythm task, we used a piano tone as most people may be expected to be familiar with piano tones, and compared to other instruments (e.g. the flute), the tone does not fade out. The rhythm task was realized with the "wood drums" sound chosen from the Cakewalk program. For the language-based tasks (recognition of repeated voices, masked words) students read selected words and were recorded on a dictating machine (Sony ICDSX20). The text of the task audiobook was read by several students, and we selected the one with the clearest language. Voices were recorded by the already mentioned dictating machine. Datafiles were cut and arranged with Cooledit 2.0 and saved in wav-format (16Bit, Sampling rate 44KHz, mono). The general auditory tasks and the social auditory tasks were integrated in the WMC program, a special software (see next chapter 6.1).

5 Methodological Approach

5.1 Preparatory Data Analysis

The detection of outliers was done with graphical analysis, box plots, frequency distributions, and scatter plots applying Systat and SPSS. After systematic exclusion of reasons such as data entry errors, improper functioning of instruments, administration and instruction I used the following strategy that is orientated on Roth and Switzer (2002). Outliers and influential cases were eliminated as soon as they deviated considerably from the rest of the distribution leading to distortions resulting in altering of the covariance matrix and/or if there were cogent theoretical reasons. As soon as distributions were shaped it is reported in the corresponding presentation of results. In baseline data (such as readspeed, see below) there were outliers with people reacting extremely slowly. Such cases were not excluded since baseline reaction times were intended for the use of correction in the social intelligence tasks and should provide a realistic measure of the individual reaction times on certain tasks. It occurred that some single values are missing unsystematically, mainly because of omissions, slips, careless mistakes, and sometimes because of a lack of task comprehension. Since we had only minor experience with the tasks, in this occurrence, I neither excluded the whole case nor performed mean substitution. In analysis of single tasks, all available cases were included (pairwise deletion). However, the listwise deletion procedure was applied in intercorrelation and multivariate analysis. Imputation was used for social perception tasks. Since these tasks are based on reaction time values, omissions are likely and require substitution in order to obtain a positive definite covariance matrix. Mean substitution is expected to produce comparatively accurate estimations and biases estimated variances and covariances towards zero. See Schumacker and Lomax (1996) for a short overview of possibilities of dealing with missing data.

5.2 Scale Construction

5.2.1 General Scale Construction

The score of a task was built by summarizing the correspondent items. Item selection included three steps: First, items that did not reach chance level were excluded. Second, the remaining items were selected according to their item-total correlation (abbreviated with r_{it}). The lowest value for r_{it} was .10. However, if possible, only items with $r_{it} >= .20$ were included in a scale. Items with lower values were also involved, if they were theoretically particularly representative for the scale. Third, a distractor analysis was performed to locate possible difficulties and concentrate on the items that proved reliability after distractor analysis. In addition, items were selected in order to represent a wide range of difficulties. Internal consistency (Cronbach's Alpha) was primarily taken as an indicator of reliability and is considered as an appropriate way in developing new tests (see Bühner, 2006). A high degree of internal consistency was a criterion of usefulness of the subtests. Since high internal consistency is normally associated with high homogeneity and may lead to unrepresentative item selection, items that were sought to reflect different important aspects of the construct were maintained. Free responses were scored by at least two independent raters.

5.2.2 Scenario Scales

A different procedure was applied with respect to the *target scores* of the scenario tasks. In these scores, the deviation of the participant's answer from the exact answer of the target person is evaluated. Zero is the best possible score; The larger the deviance, the worse the participant's performance is scored. The tasks involve items that can deviate only in one direction since the target person chose an extreme category (one or six in the 1st study and one or seven in the 2nd study). This deviance can cause a higher difference score than target person's answers located in the middle of the scale (e.g. "3" which can deviate only with 3 or 4 points, respectively). Therefore, in both studies, the differences were weighted according to the maximal possible deviation in one item to avoid an unequal weighting as in some of the items, for example, a deviation of 5 is possible whereas in other items the deviation is only 3. In addition, we paid attention to select items representative with regard to the distribution of deviation points, so that items with an extreme answer and items representing middle categories are well-balanced. Despite our theoretical preference for target scores, (see chapter 2.7) different scoring procedures were used in the first study to get an impression of their effect on the intercorrelations and the reliability. These are the alternative scoring procedures we examined:

1) *Right-wrong scores*: Only the exact answer was scored with one point. Remaining values were scored with zero.

2) *Deviation points*: The exact answer was scored with two points, a one-point difference from the exact answer was scored with one point. All other values were scored with zero.

3) *Proportion-based consensus scoring*: The answer most of the subjects chose gets the highest score. Each alternative gets the value of percent of participants who chose the correspondent option (for issues of scoring see also chapter 2.7).

Answers to open-ended questions were compared to the targets answers and judged by two independent raters. After the application of the selected scoring procedure, the items were summarized to a total written, auditory, pictorial and video-based social understanding scale across all scenarios.

5.2.3 Perception Scales

With respect to social perception scores, reaction time (RT) scores as well as accuracy scores were computed. Since RT scores are in line with the definition of the social perception dimension (see chapter 2.2), I will focus on RT scores. However, accuracy is considered by using only the correct reactions for scale construction. Results concerning accuracy scores will be mentioned in addition as far as it makes sense in the context of this book. The following procedure was taken before building the social perception RT scores (see Box 5-1). The described steps were not obligatory but applied as soon as they were needed, particularly, when scores were not normally distributed.

Box 5-1: Procedure of Trimming Reaction Time Variables and Smoothing of Distributions

1) False trials were set to missing.

2) Remaining trials with a RT value less than 150 ms were set to missing.

3) Exclusion of subjects and variables with too many missings (more than 40%)

4) RTs deviating strongly from the group mean (outliers) were set to a heuristic value.

5) Computation of the individual mean and SD and trimming by setting values that exceed "mean + 3 SD" to exactly "mean + 3 SD."

6) Calculation of group specific mean and SD, analogous trimming of the distribution ana- logue to 5).

5.3 Strategy of Data Analysis

In the context of the present work, the preconditions such as normality, linearity, variance homogeneity, etc. that have to be fulfilled in order to apply a certain statistical procedure were generally tested. Results of these tests are only reported in cases of significant deviations from these conditions. In general, SPSS was used to perform standard data analysis such as descriptive statistics, reliability analysis, graphs, and for exploratory factor analysis (EFA). EQS 6.1 was applied in confirmatory factor analysis (CFA).

In general, several steps were conducted after preparatory data analysis and scale building in order to answer the research questions (see chapter 3).
First, each construct was examined in order to clarify the inner structure. Second, it was related to the reference constructs, primarily academic intelligence. The examination was carried out with correlational and exploratory factor analysis in order to get a general idea of the structure, and with confirmatory factor analysis in order to test whether the hypothesis is

true or not. Since there was mostly confirmation of EFA results with CFA I will focus on the CFA findings in the presentation of results. For more detailed findings obtained with EFA see Seidel (2007). Third, variance explained by the academic intelligence test (and working memory tasks in case of auditory intelligence tasks) was controlled in order to examine how the construct is affected by the variance of reference constructs. In a last step the auditiry social intelligence tasks were related to the general nonsocial auditory tasks. During the analyses I always aimed at examining the corresponding model with different samples, tasks, and scoring procedures to see whether it is stable. To favor readability, I will mainly focus on the results of our second study and only summarize the first study findings. However, in general, with some exceptions second study results confirmed the first study results.

In data analysis, both types of factor analysis EFA and CFA will be used as they have both advantages. EFA "lets the data speak for themselves" (Carroll, 1995, p. 436) and thus provides important information about the relationship between variables that may serve for a comprehensive view of the data and a basis for modifications in the case that the theoretical model does not fit as it was expected. CFA's are less subject to problems in factor interpretation; they provide objective statistical tests of latent traits being superior to zero-order correlation examination among manifest variables; they partition variance into parts that are due to trait, method and error factors, thus the expected values of the correlations among latent variables are not affected by unreliabilities in manifest variables; they allow comparisons between nested models, that can lead to clear estimates of the degree of convergent validity, discriminant validity, and method variance in MTMM design (see Widaman, 1985). Since I do not want to be accused for subjectivityand arbitrariness like it is often criticized in using CFA (e.g. Holz-Ebeling, 1995) I will use a strategy with respect to both EFA and CFA that is going to be described straightaway and will only be mentioned again in the presentation of findings if it diverges from the following procedure.

In dimension reduction performed with EFA, principal axis method is chosen for *factor extraction*. According to Beauducel (2001a, see also Widaman, 1993) this method compared to principal components analysis is more robust concerning changes in the composition of variables (e.g., smaller sample sizes and communalities). I decided to apply direct oblimin (delta=0) as one of the most common and empirically proven rotation techniques (Beauducel, 2001a). A major advantage of oblique rotation methods is that they provide more information than orthogonal solutions (Beauducel, 2001a; Fabrigar, Wegener, MacCallum, & Strahan, 1999). Considering the constructs that will be examined theoretically, it is rather unlikely that variables are completely independent (e.g. within the domain of general auditory abilities). Parallel analysis will be performed as the major factor extraction criterion, since it probably leads to more reliable results than comparable extraction criteria (Scree-test, Kaiser Guttman rule) (for more information see Beauducel, 2001a; Enzmann, 1997; Zwick & Velicer, 1986).

Despite its advantages, the parallel analysis technique is conservative (Beauducel, 2001b); the number of factors is rather underestimated than overestimated. The probability of underestimation is especially evident when rotations to oblique-angled simple structure are performed and when empirical data show a strong first eigenvalue (Beauducel, 2001b). Parallel analysis (PA, Lautenschlager, 1989) was applied as factor extraction criterion and performed with the program RanEigen (Enzmann, 1997). In the case of high probability of underestimation or as soon as it is theoretically sensible, I will also report factor solutions according to the Kaiser-Guttman rule.

CFA analyses, in this book, are based on covariance matrices since they are generally preferred compared to correlation matrices (see Cudeck, 1989). Maximum-likelihood (ML) will be applied as an estimation algorithm since they are more stable and precise (Olsson, Foss, Troye, & Howell, 2000). In order to obtain relaiable results, a sample of 200 subjects is necessary; however, if error variance is low, samples with 50 to 100 subjects may be sufficient if indicators are normally distributed (Urban & Mayerl, 2003). Balancing resources and statistical requirements we strive for a sample size of close to 200 in at least one investigation. Sample sizes should always be larger than N=100. Multivariate normal distribution as a precondition for the application will be tested using Mardia's Kappa (normalized multivariate kurtosis coefficient, 1970). Results will only be reported if conditions are violated. In addition, the original Chi^2 statistic will be computed and complemented through a selection of fit indexes orientated on recommendations by Beauducel and Wittmann (2005). The authors suggest a model evaluation strategy that focuses on RMSEA, SRMR, and the Chi^2/df values for psychometric research on areas of psychology where main loadings are typically low. SRMR and RMSEA were most robust against small distortions in data simple structure (Beauducel & Wittmann, 2005). Following these recommendations, I chose to report the Chi^2/df value, the SRMR, the RMSEA, and for reasons of popularity and common use in many studies the CFI as well. If no concrete hypotheses are specified, all paths will be allowed in a structural equation model. If both EFA and CFA are performed, factor correlations will be reported on a latent level.

6 First Study

6.1 Pilot Studies

Before carrying out the first research study, the auditory tasks of both test batteries (see chapter 4.1 and 4.2) along with a preliminary version of the scenario task were pre-tested in two pilot studies, since we had no prior experience with auditory material. For item and test presentation we used the WMC (Version 0.15) program taken from a former research project at Mannheim University, Germany and adapted to the needs of the SI project (i.e., adaptation of a DOS Version into Windows)[2]. The WMC software allows saving data from all tasks that are based on reaction times (AIT, rhythm, and social perception). The preliminary scenario task was presented with PowerPoint. The main focus of the pilot studies was to guarantee the technical implementation, to gain experience with auditory material, and to test practicability and feasability of the tasks in order to optimize the first test version. In addition every computer was tested with a diagnostic program (WMCDiag) whether it is reliable enough to measure reaction times (RT).

In the first pilot study in August 2004, 29 students participated. Participants were tested for about four hours. Students' mean age was 24.76 (SD: 3.27); 69% (N=20) were female. In addition to the Aul and SI tasks, a feedback questionnaire was administered, which served for collecting students' feedback and suggestions for improvement. Each task was evaluated according to questions such as "What was good? What could be improved?", etc.. The instrument also contained questions about the comprehensibility of the scale. At the end, an overall rating/evaluation was requested. Items that reduced the internal consistency of the scales substantially, items that were too easy or too difficult (restriction of variance) and items of minor theoretical importance were excluded or modified. Additional items were developed according to the theoretical knowledge gained from first analysis. Some of the tasks including modified and newly developed items according to the findings of the first pilot study were again tested in a second pre-study in October 2004. Altogether, 17 participants with a mean age of 23.67 (SD= 2.97 years) were tested, of whom 82.4% (N=14) were female. In the following paragraphs the pilot study results are summarized. Of course, sample size is not large enough to draw generalizable conclusions but we judged the sample sufficient for testing practicability and using it for test improvement. The final selection of test items was done according to the results (item analysis) of both pilot studies and the feedback questionnaire.

Social Intelligence Tasks

With respect to the social intelligence tasks, both pilot studies indicated, that the test ideas worked out well. Beyond item reliability, item difficulty, and comprehensibility of the instructions, in general, the following changes were made:

1) Items with bad quality (person not visible or understandable) were excluded.

2) Mono files were converted into stereo files for better understanding, which was only possible with a newer version of the WMC program.

3) Items were adapted in intensity.

With regard to auditory social perception, since the task was too difficult, tasks with items containing three reaction possibilities were excluded in favor of only simple or choice reaction time. Voices were introduced before presenting the items (conversations), in case that voice identification was difficult. In auditory social memory tasks, time to answer the questions had to be lengthened in order to avoid speed effects. In addition, the conversations were reduced in length to 100 – 135 seconds. In the pilot studies, the scenario tasks were carried out as a group test so that faster students sometimes had to wait for a long time for students who worked more slowly. In order to be able to self-administer the scenario task we changed the instructions.

Auditory IntelligenceTasks

Every tonal task was practiced with two examples. The second presentation was accompanied by the score shown on the screen, and the correct option was marked with a circle line. Every nonverbal task (except for the rhythm task) was presented twice. The answers of the participants were marked on an answer sheet. Test takers were allowed to revise their choice after the second presentation. Participants were instructed not to guess but instead to make some remarks about the tasks that they could not answer or with which they had problems. The rhythm task was practiced with three examples, each presented twice. The time to complete the tasks was not limited. Each item could be started by self-administration. The answers (reactions) to the rhythm task were recorded by the computer program. The rhythm produced by the participant was compared to the rhythm presented with a tolerance of 200 ms (lower bound 70%, higher bound 130%) and absolute degrees of freedom in interval deviation of 50 ms. Absolute values have priority above relative values meaning that when absolute values are violated, the item is regarded as wrong even when relative values are within the permissable range. The reason for this procedure is that with very short intervals, relative deviations can lie within the domain of motoric skillfulness. Motoric ability is, however, not what we want to measure. The main results and revisions are

---

[2] I appreciate the work of Thomas Becker in adapting the software to our needs as far as it was possible.

summarized in the next few paragraphs, starting with the nonverbal tasks, and continuing with the rest of the general auditory intelligence tasks.

Findings of the first pilot study showed that most of the nonverbal tasks were too difficult and not sufficiently reliable. Reliability ranged from .06 (tonal series) to .77 (rhythm reproduction). We selected the items that worked out well, classified them into three difficulty levels (easy – middle – difficult), and searched for reasons for failures for items that did not function well. New items were developed according to the number of items missing in each difficulty level. Item characteristics (internal consistency, item difficulty and item-total correlation) could be improved considerably after the first pilot study. The distributions of the modified tasks were all acceptable. With the exception of chord decomposition (Alpha=.55), internal consistency improved (detection of repeated tones from .36 to .80; tonal figures from .39 to .53, rhythm reproduction from .77 to .90). However, some of the tasks still did not meet our demands with respect to reliability (tonal analogies, tonal figures and chord decomposition). Apparently, after the second pilot study, there were still items with negative item-total correlations that had to be eliminated or modified. Possible reasons for the inadequate item characteristics may well have been our lack of knowledge in the development of auditory tasks. We had to construct many items on our own, albeit with a musician's help, based on our own construction rationale for classifications and order of difficulty. For the task "tonal series", at first, we did not have any notes at all. Therefore, we developed this task together with Alexander Trinko, who tried to develop sequences of tones that should be completed musically. However, that did not work out with students having no musical expert knowledge. Fortunately, we then got the tonal score from Lazar Stankov and replaced the whole task in the second pilot study. Reliability increased from .06 to .63. In the revised tonal series task of Stankov and Horn (1980), tonal series have to be completed logically, rather than in the first version, musically. Changes that were made beyond modifications and item selections according to results of the feedback questionnaire concern the mode of presentation (speed of presentation; breaks between tones), instructions, and the feedback (summary feedback at the end of the task instead of reporting back after each item).

The speech tasks audiobook, detection of repeated voices and recognition of familiar environmental sounds were only tested once since time was limited in the second pilot study, and we had less experience with tonal tasks. Mean item difficulty was sufficient for masked words (.48; range: .03 - .97), detection of repeated voices (.43; range: .07 - .97) and AIT-L (.50; range: .28 - .83), and for recognition of familiar environmental sounds (.76; range: .35 - .97) as the random probability is .50 and the mean difficulty should be higher. Both audiobooks were rather easy (mean item difficulty of .77 and .74, respectively). Internal consistency was not sufficient for any of the tasks (range: .40: audiobook 1 to .67: masked words) but was a good point to start to improve the test, with the exception of recognition of familiar environmental sounds (.05). We excluded or modified ambiguous items and items with negative item-total correlations. Further modifications resulted from the feedback questionnaire (see chapter 6.1). The task masked words was criticized because the words could not be identified against the background noise; some of them were not spoken clearly enough. Therefore, the loudness of the background noise and the speaker's voice were adapted in order to attain better recognition rates. The degrees of difficulty were made more obvious resulting in a 3 x 3 matrix with factors: loudness of background noise, loudness of speaker, and frequency of words. The topic of the task audiobook 1, dealing with pollen allergy, was not appropriate. The text was not only too easy but also influenced by the different degree of knowledge subjects had about the topic. The test score should therefore reflect knowledge of the topic in addition to memory of the auditorily presented text. For the second audiobook, which was a report about a journey to Macao, the difficult foreign names and words were replaced and the text was shortened. For both audiobooks, time to answer the questions was too short so that the score reflected not only memory but also speed (of thinking and writing as we used open-ended questions). The sound sequences of the familiar environmental sounds test were adapted in length. In addition, grouping of distractors and targets should make the task more difficult, for example, one of four ringtones served as a target, the others as distractors (other examples: mist/rain/heavy rain/thunderstorm; car sounds like driveaway/ brake sharply/slow down). The AIT-loudness (AIT-L) was replaced through AIT-pitch (AIT-P) since the subjects had severe problems in solving the tasks and AIT-L tasks, after a first enthusiasm, were not well received in research (see chapter 2.5.5). In order to have a representative selection of tasks for the verbal reasoning domain (for a description see above) an additional auditory speech task, disarranged sentences (see chapter 6.2.3) served for test supplementation. With respect to the task detection of repeated voices, some new recordings (clearer voices) served to replace items that did not work well.

Findings of the feedback questionnaire also gave us some information about the strategies that were used to find the right task solution. With respect to nonverbal auditory tasks, several students indicated that they tried to remember the tone with the lowest and the highest pitch or clear-cut tones. Others classified tones in groups (low-middle–high of pitch). Some students imagined the tones visually on a scale (see also results reported in Danthiir, Roberts, Pallier, & Stankov, 2001) or counted the tones numerically. That indicates that we can expect some correlation with numerical and figural abilities. Moreover, some of the students told us that they mentally sang the tones in order to find the right alternative. For the auditory speech tasks, subjects used strategies like focusing on the spoken words while trying to ignore the background noise (masked words), rote memorizing of words through repetition, collecting facts, imagining stimuli visually, combining concepts with knowledge (audiobook), representing the sounds visually, combining sounds with a story, and memorizing the name of the sounds (familiar environmental sounds).

6.2 Description of the First Study

6.2.1 General Aims

The first study had two major aims: First, the evaluation of the SIM (Süß et al., 2008) and the AuIT with respect to basic statistics, reliability, and structure. The evaluation of the tests aims at providing information for task supplementation of the SI test as well since in the first study cells are mainly covered by only one instead of two tasks per cell (see chapter 4.1.1). Second, analysis should be performed to answer the questions that are mentioned in chapter 3, concerning the internal structure of SI and AuI, their relationship to AcI, and the relationship between social auditory and general auditory tasks. The study should be carried out with students as an important part of the target group (adults older than 22) for whom the tests will be developed.

6.2.2 Participants

Participants were 127 students of different faculties (psychology, economical sciences, and process engineering) all having a higher education degree ("Allgemeine Hochschulreife (Abitur)", corresponds to A–level). Their mean age was 21 years (SD=3.06, Md=20) in the range between 19 and 35 years; 53.5% were female. Table 6-1 presents the number of students of the different faculties across gender. On a two-point rating scale, 36.2% of the participants indicated having musical experience.

Table 6-1: Cross-classification of Students According to Faculty and Gender

Gender (%)	Faculty (%)		Sum
	Psychology	*Economics and process engineering*	
Male	3.15 (4)	43.31 (55)	46.5 (59)
Female	24.41 (31)	29.13 (37)	53.5 (68)
Sum	27.56 (35)	72.44 (92)	100 (127)

Note: All numbers are reported in percent; the corresponding number of students is shown in parentheses.

6.2.3 Materials

The participants worked on the SIM (Süß et al., 2008) and on the AuIT. The Berlin Intelligence Structure Test (BIS, Jäger, Süß, & Beauducel, 1997) served as a measure of AcI and was used as a reference instrument for both SI tasks and AuI tasks. For economical reasons we excluded the creativity dimension. Three baseline measures were applied to control for the influence of speed of moving the mouse, reading speed, and simple reaction time with regard to the social perception speed tasks. Information about biographical data, computer experience, and hearing abilities was collected with reference questionnaires. In addition to these complementary questionnaires, we collected data on self-report instruments such as the questionnaire of gender interests (MF subscale of the Minnesota Multiphasic Personality Inventory 2; Hathaway, McKinley, & Engel, 2000), the Prototypical Acts on Social Intelligence (Amelang, Schwarz, & Wegemund, 1989; see chapter 2.2.3), and the NEO-Five Factor Inventory (NEO-FFI) according to Costa und McCrae (see Borkenau & Ostendorf, 1993). As self-report instruments are not subject to this book, I will not deal with this question in further detail here. Results regarding these questionnaires and their relationship to the performance measures will be published in a separate paper. The following table provides an overview of the tests we applied. Each of the tests is shortly described in the following, with a focus on language-based (auditory and written) tasks.

Table 6-2: Overview of the Materials Used in the First Study

Test name	(Sub-) construct	Method			
		written	*auditory*	*pictorial*	*video-based*
SIM	SI understanding	Scenarios			
	SI memory	SMw1	SMa1	SMp1	SMf1
	SI perception	SPw1	SPa1	SPp1	SPf1
BIS (see manual for task descriptions)		*verbal*		*numerical*	*figural-symb.*
	Reasoning (processing capacity)	Word analogies (WA) Facts and opinions (TM) Word knowledge (WS) Senseless inferences (SL) Syllogisms (SV)		Number sequences (ZN) Letter sequences (BR) Estimation (SC) Reading tables (TL) Computational reasoning (RD)	Figural analogies (AN) Bongard (BG) Surface development (AW) Figure assembly (FA)
	Memory	Memorizing words (WM) Phantasy language (PS)		Two-digit numbers (ZZ) Paired associates (ZP)	City map (OG) Figure memorizing (FM) Memorizing routes (WE)
	Processing speed	Part-whole (TG) Classification of words (KW)		X-larger (XG) Seven divisible (SI) Arithmetic operations(RZ)	Marking letters (BD) Old English (OE)

Table 6-2 Overview of the Materials Used in the First Study (S1), continued

Test name	(Sub-) construct	Method		
		Aul speech	*Aul tonal*	
	Reasoning	Disarranged sentences (DS)	Tonal series (MA4) Tonal analogies (MA2) Chord decomposition (MA5)	
AulT	Memory	Audiobook (AU)	Rhythm (RH) Recognition of environmental sounds (FES)	
	Discrimination	Masked words (MW) Detection of re-peated voices (RV)	Repeated tones (MA1) Tonal figures (MA3)	

Baseline measures		
	Mouse speed	(Oberauer, Süß, Wilhelm, & Wittmann, 2003; Sander, 2005)
	Simple reaction time	(Oberauer et al., 2003; Sander, 2005)
	Readspeed	(Rüsseler & Münte, 2001)

Basic (reference)questionnaires / self report measures		
	Bio-data	
	Hearing Screening Inventory	(Coren & Hakstian, 1992)
	Computer experience	(Süß, 1996; Wittmann & Süß, 1999; Feigenspan, 2005)
	Gender interests	(see Papenbrock, 2005).
	Prototypical Acts on SI	(Amelang, Schwarz & Wegemund, 1989); chapter 2.2.3
	NEO-Five Factor Inventory	(Borkenau & Ostendorf, 1993)

Scenario Tasks

We administered four scenarios: Two female (Rita, 23 years, medical-technician; Kathrin, 25 years, psychology student) and two male persons (Christian, 23 years, student of law; Martin, 33 years, dancing teacher) were included as central target persons. The scenario started with some background information of the procedure and about the target person, followed by a short self-presentation of the target person that aimed at getting familiar with the target person's voice and appearance. Subjects have to judge the target person's cognitions, emotions, and the relationships to other people with the help of written correspondence, audio-conversations, pictures and video-scenes. At the end of each scenario, subjects are instructed to make a global rating about the target person's personality on the Big Five (NEO-FFI) and his or her general relationship to other people on the Circumplex dimensions (see Horowitz et al., 2000). The task material varies systematically according to the amount of persons in the situations (single others, dyads and small groups), the setting (private vs. public) and the situation content (e.g., comfortable vs. uncomfortable situation). The items have to be answered on a 6-point rating scale (e.g., How important is the situation for target person xy? 1 = not important at all; 6 = very important), on open-ended questions, and on multiple choice questions. With respect to rating-scaled items, answers were scored with regard to the deviation from the target person's answer (the minor the deviance the better the performance). In addition, in consensus scores answers were evaluated according to the most typical answer of the group. The more the individual answer corresponded to the groups judgment of alternatives, the better the test score. Table 6-3 presents an overview of the items that were developed for each modality. The different amount of items of each type and modality is due to the recordings of the scenes. Our aim was to find out whether the scenario approach works in general, which type of items works best etc. The procedure at this stage was rather exploratory.

Table 6-3: Overview of the Item Number per Modality in Social Understanding Tasks

	Modality				
	written	auditory	pictorial	video-based	Sum
Rating	51	56	15	70	
emotion	31	38	8	24	192
cognition	2	2	2	---	
behavior (rela.)	18	16	5	46	
Multiple choice	9	1	9	11	
emotion	---	---	---	---	
cognition	---	---	---	---	30
behavior (rela.)	9	1	9	11	
Open	4	11	3	5	
emotion	---	2	---	2	
cognition	2	8	2	2	23
behavior (rela.)	2	1	1	1	
Sum	64	68	27	86	245

Note: The numbers represent the number of items. The relative higher number of emotion and relationship items is due to the combined questions concerning different emotions (e.g., in one question, sadness, anger, joy, and disgust are tested) and behaviors (e.g. in one question dominance, activity, distance, and cooperation are tested) whereas cognition questions contain only one item (aspect), rela.=relationship.

Social Memory Tasks

The social memory items for the language-based tasks were all presented as open-ended questions because empirical findings showed that they differentiate better among subjects than other types of questions such as multiple choice and rating scales (see Funke & Schuler, 1998), that they produce a more consistent answer pattern, and result in a clearer structure (see Birenbaum & Tatsuoka, 1987). In addition, open-ended questions are particularly useful for the collection of possible answers to our questions in order to improve the items. The answers to open-ended questions can serve as a basis for the development of a MC test for a subsequent and more economical test version we aim at.

a) Memory for socially relevant information in text (SMw1)

Subjects have a pre-defined time to read a text section and to remember as many of the socially relevant details as possible. Thereafter, they have to answer open-ended questions aiming at the recall of the socially relevant details of the text. The tasks involves four texts differing in content (two are private, two work-related) and length (231 to 355 words).

b)   Memory for socially relevant information in conversations (SMa1)

Twelve conversations were displayed; their duration was in the range between 100 and 135 seconds. After listening to each conversation, subjects had to answer five or six questions within 90 seconds.

c)   Memory for couples (SMp1)

Part 1: This test contains pictures of couples that are presented in two blocks each of which involves photographs of eight couples. The task is to remember the couples as accurately as possible. Thereafter, one partner of a couple is presented followed by four pictures with different partners. Subjects have to indicate the correct partner of the person presented previously.

Part 2: Two picture sequences are presented, one contains three, the other nine pictures taken in different social settings (teacher's room, family get-together). After the presentation of the pictures, test takers have to answer questions about socially relevant details.

d)   Memory for interactions in videos (SMf1)

Four video scenes are presented on the screen showing a different number of people interacting in various situations. Test takers are instructed to remember as many socially relevant details as possible. Following the scenes, questions concerning socially relevant details of the material have to be answered within 1:15 minutes. Multiple choice and open-ended format are applied.

Social Perception Tasks

e)   Perception of socially relevant details in text (SPw1)

Sixty statements (part 1 of the task) and questions (part 2 of the task) have to be judged as right or wrong and answered with yes or no, respectively. Subjects have to respond as accurately and as quickly as possible by tapping the adequate key. Complexity is varied according to the number of questions (one or two) that have to be answered or according to the number of statements (one or two) that have to be judged. The task is practiced with eight example trials, including two examples for each part and each task level.

f)   Perception of socially relevant stimuli in conversations (SPa1)

The task contains 13 conversations including 107 perception reactions to both verbal (names, agreement, rejection, filling words, admiration) and paraverbal cues (reactions to laughter, interruptions, and voices). Before starting the test, subjects were familiarized with the type of task through working on four conversations involving 30 reactions. Task difficulty and reaction time are expected to differ according to the type of stimulus and the number of stimuli that subjects have to react on in a single conversation. Each conversation requires monitoring between one and three stimuli.

g)   Person detection in pictures (SPp1)
A person is presented pictorially and has to be remembered. Thereafter, the same person is shown in different pictures in a variety of settings. Subjects have ten seconds to click on the person's head as soon as they identified him or her appearing on the screen. The task contains seven sequences including 10 pictures each.

h)   Person detection in videos (SPf1)
A person is presented in a short video and has to be remembered. Thereafter, that person is shown in several video sequences. Test takers have to respond as quickly and accurately as possible as soon as they recognized the person that was shown in the first video. One example sequence involving ten reactions served for practicing the task. The test contains five scenes with ten reactions each.

Baseline Measures

i)   Mouse speed (Oberauer et al., 2003; Sander, 2005)
The task mouse speed intends to measure the speed and accuracy of using a computer mouse. Subjects have to press as quickly as possible with the left mouse key on a white circle point that arbitrarily emerges on the screen. The circle has to be hit as accurately as possible by clicking on its center. After ten example trials three blocks including 25 trials each follow. It takes about ten minutes to complete the task.

j)   Simple reaction time (Oberauer et al., 2003; Sander, 2005)
The space bar has to be pressed as soon as a white circle appears on the screen. Before the circle is shown, a small cross is presented in the middle of the screen. The task is practiced with five example trials, followed by 50 test trials. It takes ten minutes to complete the test.

k)   Readspeed (Rüsseler & Münte, 2001)
A text containing 198 words (120 function words, 78 content words and nouns) is presented word by word. The respective word is seen only until tapping the space bar. Participants were instructed to read the text as quickly and as accurately as possible. The reading time was recorded for each word. Following the text, three multiple choice questions involving three options each were presented to ensure that subjects did not only click through but also understood the content of the text. It takes five minutes to complete the test. For the

description of the general auditory tasks please see chapter 4.2, for the BIS description see chapter 2.1.5.

Complementary Instruments and Self-report Measures

l)   Questionnaire about personal data

Personal data was collected in a questionnaire involving information about age, sex, education, hearing ability, music experience, and grades of the last report card.

m)   Hearing Screening Inventory (Coren & Hakstian, 1992)

To ensure proper listening to the audio files, a twelve item self-report measure was applied to collect information about the individual pure-tone hearing sensitivity. The measure served as a substitute for a hearing test that is usually taken by an ear doctor. According to Coren and Hakstian (1992), the questionnaire has an internal consistency value of .82. Economical constraints and the unavailability of appropriate instruments did not allow us to apply the more accurate hearing test. With the questionnaire, those subjects who knew about having hearing problems should be identified.

n)   Questionnaire of computer experience (5 min.)

The items of this questionnaire deal with the period of time someone is familiar with a computer, the mean time spent by using the computer, the context of using computers (work, friends, courses), the knowledge and experiences in using the computer (e.g. programming, games, applications, internet, emails, etc.). It ends with a self-assessment of one's experience compared to age-related others. For references of similar versions, see Süß (1996); Wittmann and Süß (1999); and Feigenspan (2005).

6.2.4   Implementation

Equipment

The study took place in two different computer pools at the University of Magdeburg with comparable computers in each room. Each subject had an own PC equiped with earphones. For the computer-based tasks, Pentium 4 computers (1.7 GHz) with 256 MB RAM, AT/AT compatible, were used. The operating system was Windows NT. The TFT-Monitor ran on 16bit color because the WMC program requires this setting. For the auditory tasks we used earphones (Philips, SBC HP 195). The complete material, with the exception of the written language memory tasks and scenarios that were presented with PowerPoint XP, was presented with the software program WMC (version 0.15; see chapter 6.1) The answers of the auditory tonal tasks and social memory and understanding tasks were recorded with paper and pencil answering sheets. Some of the auditory tasks required additional technical settings. These are summarized in the appendix A.1. The BIS Test and the questionnaires were administered as paper and pencil tests.

Procedure

The study took about 10 hours, and was split up into two test sessions that were carried out on different days, each one lasting five hours. The first session was always done before the second. The subjects could choose between different possibilities (days and hours) of being tested for sessions one and two. The sessions were conducted by trained investigators. After having finished the second test session, each participant was rewarded with 50 Euro. Psychology students could alternatively record the hours as test participant that German psychology students have to accomplish throughout their studies.

Each session was subdivided into four blocks including three ten minute breaks in between during which times the test takers were allowed to relax and consume some drinks and snacks. In order to ensure motivation and diversion, the tasks of different modalities and different abilities/cognitive operations (AcI, SP, SM, SU, general auditory, and questionnaires) were varied. The tasks were practiced with example trials in order to ensure proper understanding. Each task was started with a different key to guarantee that subjects do not start a task accidentally or deliberately without prior instruction.

6.2.5 Data Management

One person did not participate the second day of the study and was excluded from analysis. Because of missing values (e.g. lack of task comprehension, careless mistakes), some of the psychometrics are based on less than 126 subjects. How I dealt with missing values was reported in chapter 5.1. Technical problems occurred while administering the task "Masked words". Thus, we could do the analysis with 57 cases only. Some data got lost irreproducibly on some of the computers because of technical problems that occurred in the readspeed task with the data saving procedure. In some of the first test sessions, a former version of the social written perception task was erroneously administered. In this version, the time to answer was limited to eight seconds. Many test takers were not able to complete the task within this time. The final version allowed 12 seconds answering. One hundred and five subjects were tested with the latest version (12 seconds) whereas 21 completed the former version.

6.3 Main Results of the First Study

The presentation of results will focus on the second study. However, the main results of the first study will be summarized in order to understand the modifications that were introduced before carrying out the second study. The interested reader will find the detailed results of the first study in Seidel (2007) and Süß et al. (2007).

6.3.1 Social Intelligence

Psychometric Properties

Social Understanding

In a first step, the different scoring procedures that were applied in scoring social understanding items, namely target scoring, consensus scoring, and deviation points (see chapter 2.7 and 5.2) were evaluated. Subjects' answers to open-ended questions were compared to the targets answers and judged by two independent raters. Correspondence of independent raters was more than 95%. The target scores were weighted as described in chapter 5.2.2.

Target scores proved to be the most reliable compared to all scoring methods that were applied. Theoretically, target scores are the most recommendable as well, since they orientate on an external target instead scoring according to a group depended common opinion and thus do not depend on the sample. Compared to deviation points and right-wrong scores they make use of the whole available information. The more differentiated the scale is, the better the reliability value; correspondingly, with right-wrong scores we encounter the most extensive information loss. We also learn that using only rating scales is not worse compared to the application of all kinds of scales (multiple choice and open-ended questions). With the exception of the pictorial scale, almost all selected items are rating scaled. Involving only rating scaled items in the scale affects only the pictorial score of which the reliability value increases. A detailed comparison between multiple-choice (MC) items, open-ended questions, and rating scale items, is not possible, since we did not have enough MC items and open-ended questions. You will find the comparison between the different scoring procedures in the appendix B.1.1. Resulting from these findings, the following analyses will concentrate on target rating scores and include consensus scales for some additional analysis. The pictures score ($Z=1.49$, $p<.05$ target scoring; $Z=1.97$, $p<.01$, consensus scoring) was not normally distributed.

When considering how many items of each type of material, type of scale, and content of question (emotion, cognition, and relationship/behavior) were selected from the original number of items that were developed, we find the rating format working well for all material scales, in particularly for pictures and video-based items. However, the proportion of selected auditory and written items is highest for open-ended questions. Multiple-choice format seems to be the least reliable. However, we have to consider that the largest available database is on rating format as we used it most often in our scenario questions. With respect to the item content, emotion items seem to work best, followed by cognition items. With regard to the emotion items, it is not yet clear how the composition of emotions that have to be evaluated in one task influence the judgment of the other emotions (e.g. does it make a difference whether only two negative emotions have to be judged or whether a positive emotion is involved in addition). The numbers can be found in appendix B.1.2.

The correlations *within* the consensus-scored and target-scored material scales are moderate to high except for the personality scale. The global personality rating of a person seems to be different from a scene dependent rating of the target person's cognitions, emotions and relationships/behaviors to other people. Correlations are highest between the video-based and the auditory scale and between the auditory and the written scale.

The correlations *between* consensus-scored and target-scored scales are the highest within the auditory and the written modality scales (r=.82 for both scales). The findings indicate that the scale construction based on objective cues in the task material was successful as both target persons and students judge the feelings, thoughts, actions, and relationships similarly. Again, the target personality scale seems to be neither related to the SI material/content scales nor to the consensus-based personality scores (r=-.14). This is another hint of the difference between a total personality judgment and the judgment of the target person with regard to cognitions, emotions, and relationships in different scenes. In addition, there seems to be a difference in how the target person regards his or her own personality and how a group of students judges it. Possible reasons for these differences may be that people form a picture of the target person very quickly that differs from the objective and more detailed judgment in a certain situation. The personality scale (target score) correlates with .04 (p=.64) non significantly with the IIP-C score (circumplex judgment, part of the behavior dimension), I expected to be correlated more highly with the personality estimation than with the judgement of emotions and cognitions. Unclear instructions may also be the reasons for these low correlaions: the task of the subjects was to put themselves into the target person's place and to judge the scenes and personality according to the target person's view. However, students often reported that they judged the target persons in their own perspective. Thus, instructions should be made clearer in the second study. Additional analyses aso revealed no stronger correlations between the personality estimation and items at the end of a scenario disproving the assumption that test takers have a more valid picture of the target person at the end compared to the beginning of a scenario task (see Weis, 2007). Bronfenbrenner et al. (1958) distinguish between analytic and non-analytic judgments, which may also be the reason for the differences between the personality judgment dimension and the content specific SU scales. Whereas in analytic judgments the judge is required to conceptualize and to quantify specific characteristics of the subjects, in non-analytic judgments, the judge responds in a global way. Thus, differences may result as a consequence of the different classification: the personality dimension can be classified in the non-analytic domain and the other SI scales require specific, analytic judgments.

Taking into account the findings obtained through analysis of psychometrics, the following scores and procedures will be applied for further analyses: Target scoring was chosen as being of prime importance. When useful, consensus scoring will be applied in addition. Moreover, I will focus on rating scales without the inclusion of MC items and open items, as rating-scaled items have proven to differentiate best across all contents. With the use of open answer questions, we encounter economical problems (e.g., effort of scoring the answers). The ability that should be assessed may also be intermingled with the speed of writing and verbal academic intelligence.

Social Memory

The answers to the open-ended questions were scored by two independent raters according to an assessment profile that was developed by investigating the completed questionnaires (answer sheets) of a random sample. Answers were only judged as completely correct when they were equal to the presented sound file or to the presented text and did not involve any interpretation. Partially correct answers were scored with half of a point. Two independent raters judged the answers according to the scoring suggestion. The raters agreed in 98% (auditory) or 99% (written) of the items. With respect to the remaining items a consensus agreement was attained and conclusions for test optimization with respect to unambiguity were inferred.

Table 6-4: Psychometrics of the Auditory Social Memory Task (SMa)

Task	Number of items	Skewness/ Curtosis[4]	Mean difficulty (SD)	r_{it} range	Cronbach's Alpha
SMa1 Total score	61 (62)[1]	-.94/1.49	.52 (.09) [.06; .97]	-.05 - .45	.78
Revised total score 1	[2]33 (rev1)	-1.12/1.83	.57 (.24) [.19; .92]	.16 - .48	.78
SMw1 Total score	38	-.60/.93	.46 (.10) [.11; .70]	.02 - .41	.73
Revised score	26	-.63/.53	.49 (.13) [.17; .93]	.16 - .46	.74

Note. Item numbers in parentheses indicate the corrected number after selection; [4] Skewness is presented first; the second value represents curtosis, SE (Skewness): .22; SE (Curtosis): .43

The reliability of the revised scores (see Table 6-4, in italics) can be regarded as sufficient and they were chosen for further calculations. Some of the single conversations and texts suffer from bad reliability and low item-total correlations. The unsufficient values may be attributed to item formulations, sound quality of conversations, ambiguity of instructions, and the limited time to answer the questions (1 ½ minutes) with respect to written memory tasks. The limited answer time may have caused many omissions. (The most omissions were obeserved with the last questions of each text.).

Social Perception

The values of both social written and social auditory perception tasks were trimmed according to the steps described in the chapter 5.2.3. Since the simple ability to press a key as quickly as possible or the speed of reading (social written) is expected to be mixed up with the actual social perception ability, for each task, an additional performance score was computed that is controlled for simple reaction time (SRT) or readspeed respectively. The sum of the modified standardized values was finally standardized in order to obtain a total score controlled for SRT and/or reading speed. In case of social auditory perception, the two values (with SRT and without controlling for SRT) correlate with .92. In order to obtain a readspeed corrected written social perception performance score, the variance of the readspeed accuracy and speed score were partialed out using regression analysis. The same procedure was applied for both parts (statements and questions) of the task. Reading speed was measured by the "Readspeed Test" (Rüsseler & Münte, 2001). The original written social perception score correlates with .94 with the score controlled for the readspeed variance, thus controlling for readspeed variance does not change the quality of the original score.

The social auditory perception task includes items that can be classified into groups of different stimuli (e.g., laughter or names). The task also takes complexity into consideration (paying attention to one, two, or three stimuli; see chapter 4.1.5). The different types of stimuli were combined into a general auditory perception value using z-transformation since mean reaction time differed significantly. Reactions to "rejection" took the longest whereas reactions to "filling words" and "agreement" were fastest. The total score is sufficiently reliable. With regard to the single scales, reliability would need improvement, in particular the scales "admiration" and "filling words." The most reliable scales were those including reactions to "agreement", "voices", and "rejection." The social written perception task distinguished between two levels and between questions and statements subjects had to react to. The mean reaction time of level 1 (paying attention to one statement/question) is lower than the reaction time for level 2 (paying attention to two statements/questions) which is in line with the expectations. Moreover, test takers seem to react slightly faster to statements than to questions.

The social perception tasks can also be evaluated regarding the accuracy of task performance. With regard to auditory social perception, the mean value for a combined accuracy score amounts to .70 (SD=.24; range: .06 to .98; N=118). The total score has an alpha value of .94 with r_{it} ranging between .05 and .70. The reduced score involves 82 items and shows a r_{it}-range between .20 and .63. Alpha decreases slightly to .93., the mean value increases to M=.77 (SD=.24; range: .35 - .98). The accuracy value of the written social perception task is exceptionally high (>= .80). For further information about the accuracy scores see Seidel (2007).

Table 6-5: Psychometrics for Scales of the Auditory Social Perception Task (SPa)

Task	N	Number of items	Skewness/ Curtosis [3]	RT range (min./max.)	Mean RT (SD) [1]	Cronb. Alpha
SPa1 Combined z-score	125	136 (109[2])	-.02/-.20	-2.74 - 2.37 (578.57- 965.84[2])	---	.85 (.88[2])
SPa1 Score controlled for SRT	125	136	.15/-.22	-2.55- 2.71	0.00 (1.00)	---
SPw1 Combined score	109[4]	35	-.20/.16	3998.43 - 6995.84	5488.72 (631.50)	.81
SPw1 Score controlled for Reading speed	109[4]	32	-.29/.32	3491.59 - 7182.97	5442.19 (700.57)	.83

Note: N=125; [1] after trimming; [2] after item selection; The combined score was computed by summarizing z-scores of single scales. [3] Skewness is presented first; the second value represents curtosis. Social auditory perception: SE (Skewness): .22; SE (Curtosis): .43 ; Social written perception: SE (Skewness): .23; SE (Curtosis): .46. [4] In chapter 6.2.5, I already mentioned that some of the participants worked on an older version of the written social perception task that allowed only 8 seconds to react on the questions instead of the intended 12 seconds. Since the program saved only reactions within the time limit, subjects with 50% and more missing values were excluded from analysis. That is why the number of participants is reduced to 109 persons. In addition, 22 items with more than 40% missing values were excluded from analysis.

For the following analyses, I will focus on reaction time measures, corrected by simple reaction time and readspead. Nevertheless, for some analyses the original reliability corrected scores are reported. With the exception of the pictorial social understanding score, all SI total test scores were normally distributed. A closer examination of this task shows that the deviance from normal distribution is minor. Therefore, despite of the violation of normality by one task, I will apply Pearson intercorrelations while taking attention in interpreting the results related to that task. The same occurs with the application of multivariate statistic procedures.

Internal Structure

Research Questions:

SI-1_1) Does data support a coherent SI structure by showing a general positive manifold (more specifically moderate correlations) including all SI dimensions?

SI-2_1) Do the content domains form separate factors or combined entities (such as nonverbal vs. language-based)?

Correlation analysis (see appendix B.1.3 for the full correlation table) confirmed the expectation of a positive manifold with respect to SU and SM that are obviously related and share common variance. It is not valid for the social perception tasks and their relationships to the remaining SI variables. These tasks seem to measure something different.

CFA confirmed the two factors SU and SM (e.g. model using SU target scores: Chi² (df)= 39.045 (19); p=.004; CFI=.902; RMSEA (CI 90%)=.037 (.050, .134); SRMR=.076). Since the personality scale is not correlated with the remaining SU variables it was excluded from CFA. Nor a third nonverbal perception component was included, since we have only one indicator of each nonverbal perception domain, pictorial and video-based perception. Social memory and social understanding were found to be correlated with .29 (target-scored SU) or .36 (consensus-scored SU) respectively. Loadings are satisfactory, except for the pictorial scales (SMP: .26 and SUP .33) and the video-based social memory scale (.45). The model fits the data well, also when applying different scoring methods for social understanding variables; the model using consensus scoring fitting data even better (Chi² (df)= 27.518 (19); p=.093; CFI=.952; RMSEA (CI 90%)=.061 (.000, .107); SRMR=.073).

According to my expectations (see also chapter 3 and research question SI-2_1), nonverbal abilities (pictorial and video-based), written, and auditory abilities should form separate factors. Whereas videobased and pictorial abilities are expected to mingle, auditory and written abilities are assumed to form correlated factors that exist separately from each other. Structure analysis using the tasks of one method across different cognitive operations (SP, SM, and SU) does not yield a clear and trustworthy structure. Neither two-factor models (nonverbal factor including pictorial and video-based material) nor models including three factors (auditory, nonverbal, written) nor models containing all four method factors show a sufficient fit to the data. One problem seems to be with the social understanding tasks since their contents cannot be completely distinguished. This is due to the scenario type of task as even though materials are separated, the answers to content specific questions influence each other. With regard to the memory and the perception tasks, content variance may be suppressed by operation variance similar to the problem Jäger (1982, 1984) encountered developing the BIS. Whether the content structure of the SIM (Süß et al., 2008) is covered by its operations, could be examined with hypotheses-guided aggregation of variables belonging to one method but containing heterogeneous operations. For the application of parceling technique at least six variables of each method are needed (to form at least three parcels with at least two variables). At this point of test development, we have only two variables for the measurement of each content factor when doing without the SU variables. I do not take task splitting into account because technical dependence on halving the tasks would distort the results. The common task specific variance would have an influence on the factor structure. When only including the memory and the perception tasks in a CFA, the content model does not fit the data. Using modification indexes, a one-factor model is suggested that contains the memory variables only. Therefore, here and now, we cannot make clear statements about the relationship between nonverbal, auditory, and written social abilities. We either cannot confirm the supposed within structure of language based abilities.

Social Intelligence Related to Academic Intelligence

Research Questions:

SI-3) Is SI separable from academic intelligence? – We expect at most moderate correlations.

SI-4) Does SI memory overlap more strongly with academic intelligence since their oprations (common use of memory) are more similar compared to SI-understanding and SI–perception?

SI-5) Do the SI tasks intercorrelate more highly than with the corresponding AcI domains?

In order to examine these questions, the two-factor SI model was related to AcI, represented by the BIS model (Jäger, 1982, 1984, see chapter 2.1.5). Correlational, exploratory and confirmatory factor analyses were performed. See appendix B.1.4 for the intercorrelation table.

The correlations between the SI tasks and the BIS cells (combinations between the cognitive operations reasoning, memory, and speed with the contents, namely figural-spatial, numerical, and verbal) partly explain the missing correlations that were expected between social perception with social memory and social understanding. Social perception measured with written material (SPw) correlates significantly with verbal and numerical speed of the

BIS. The variance written social perception tasks explain seems to be due to Acl speed. In addition, verbal memory and figural reasoning seem to explain parts of the written social perception variance. The correlation of SPw with verbal memory may also be due to the common verbal variance. This points to the assumption that the written social perception task is too complex or difficult so that higher-order processes such as memory and reasoning partly determine the performance in the task. For task modification this implies that the task has to be simplified, trying to make the specific social part more obvious.

Similar to written social perception, the perception of videos and pictures correlates with figural and verbal speed of the BIS. It is striking that the memory tasks correlate moderately with verbal speed indicating that the time limits for answering the questions have been too short so that the tasks measure speed beyond memory. With the exception of the SI video-based memory tasks all SI memory tasks correlate significantly with Acl verbal memory. They share common variance because they require the same cognitive operation (memory). Answering the open-ended questions requires participants to write down the facts remembered and the open-ended questions favor people who possess higher verbal skills and are able to express themselves comparatively better. This results in a higher proportion of verbal variance explained by the memory tasks. The SI auditory memory tasks also correlated with Acl speed verbal. A possible reason may be that the BIS does not involve indicators of an auditory performance domain; consequently, the auditory tasks find a "partner" in verbal tasks. Surprisingly, the core facet of SI, social understanding, does not seem to have anything in common with Acl (BIS cells). Alternatively, we can expect that the SI contents are balanced through the scenario approach as former information about the target person presented either through pictures, videos, conversations or emails influences later judgment of the scenes.

Including Acl memory, reasoning, and speed parcels as well as SU and SM scales, exploratory factor analysis suggests four factors. The first factor can be interpreted as social memory factor (22.52 % explained variance). With the exception of SI pictorial memory, all SI memory scales show their highest loading on this factor (probably due to low reliability). The social understanding tasks form the second factor (15.29 % explained variance). The third factor describes Acl-reasoning (10.16 % explained variance). The fourth factor subsumes Acl-memory tasks (8.53 % explained variance). The BIS speed tasks do not make up a separate factor. Parts load on the social memory factor (verbal speed; probably due to common verbal variance and speed limits in social memory tasks), academic reasoning (numerical speed; common finding according to Schaie, 1994 and Süß, 1999) and academic memory (figural speed).

Despite the problems of the speed factor revealed by exploratory factor analysis, the hypothesized BIS structure was proved and confirmed. The model fits the data very well (Chi²=42.25, df=32; p=.106; CFI=.971; SRMR=.05; RMSEA= .052, CI: .000, .091). However, a quite high correlation (r=.68) between the reasoning and the speed factor confirms the results of the EFA. Compared to the normative sample, in our study, BIS standard values are lower in speed tasks concerning words (KW, OE) and numbers (RZ, SI), and in reasoning tasks, particularly those applying numerical material (RD, SC, ZN). This already anticipates the high correlation between BIS–R and BIS–S. In our study, participants performed better in verbal reasoning tasks (SL, SV, TM, WS), figural reasoning tasks (AN, AW), and memory tasks (OG). This is particularly evident for the numerical memory (ZP, ZZ) and for the speed tasks (BD, TG) (for abbreviations of tasks see chapter 6.2.3).

Proven to be reliable, the BIS model was related to the SIM (Süß et al., 2008) model. In all analyses, social perception was excluded. In the complete SI-AcI model, SU (target scores) and SM are contrasted with the BIS factors memory, reasoning and speed. Allowing all factor intercorrelations, analysis reveals unnecessary non-significant correlations between BIS-R and SU (r= -.06) and BIS-M and SU (r=.12). The best fitting model (Chi²=176.838; df=128; p=.003; CFI=.918; RMSEA=.057, CI90%: .035;.077; SRMR=.073) applying target scores does without these nonsignificant paths and since it is not significantly worse (ΔChi²=1.051, Δdf=1 < Chi$_{crit.-95}$=3.84) would be preferred for reasons of parsimony. Thus, the core facet of social intelligence, SU is completely independent from AcI. Intramodel correlations remain stable for both the AcI and the SI model. The SI memory factor correlates with .40 with the AcI memory factor, with .43 with the AcI reasoning factor, and with .38 with the AcI speed factor (see question SI-4). Although the model with a separate social memory factor can be confirmed we have to query whether social memory is a specific social ability rather than being a compound trait made up by various parts of AcI. This question seems worthwhile to investigate since the SI factors, social memory and social understanding, correlate lower than the SI memory factor correlates with the mentioned AcI factors. Therefore, a regression model was computed with SI-M being the dependent variable that is predicted by BIS-S, BIS-M and BIS-R. Obviously, only parts of the social memory factor are explained by the BIS operation factors (regression weights: .22 (BIS-R); .24 (BIS-M); .13 (BIS-S)). The largest proportion remains unexplained. Thus, there is still room for specific social memory variance.

Excluding the BIS-B factor completely and involving only the purportedly related memory and understanding/reasoning factors improves the model fit. Using consensus scores instead of target scores leads to a better model fit for both models including (Chi²=159.361; df=128; p=.031; CFI=.95; RMSEA=.046, CI 90%: .015; .067; SRMR=.074) and excluding BIS-B (Chi²=91.559; df=84; p=.268; CFI=.982; RMSEA=.027, CI 90%: .000;.059; SRMR=.069). The

SI structure with the two factors, SM and SU, remains stable when BIS variance is controlled. The fit is only slightly worse compared to the model without partialing out the BIS variance. Again the consensus-scored model (Chi²=31.356; df=19; p=.037; CFI=.910; RMSEA=.074, CI 90%: .018;.118; SRMR=.087) had a better fit compared to the model that uses target scores for the SI-SU scales. Compared to the original SI model, in particular, the social understanding part of the model remains stable.

To sum up, there is some confirmation for the assumption that measures of SI and AcI are correlated low to moderately (see research question SI-3_1 and chapter 3). Social understanding does not show any relationship to AcI at all whereas social memory is moderately correlated with BIS-M and BIS-R. However, SM has some unique variance as well. With respect to social perception we can only refer to the intercorrelation matrix to derive indications for or against the confirmation of our expectations. As already mentioned, SPw is related to both BIS numerical and verbal speed ($r_{SPw-BIS-Sn}$=.20 and $r_{SPw-BIS-Sv}$=.35 respectively) as well as to verbal memory ($r_{SPw-BIS-Mv}$=.30) and figural reasoning ($r_{SPw-BIS-Rf}$=.22). SPp shows correlations with BIS-speed verbal ($r_{SPp-BIS-Sv}$=.33) whereas SPf correlates with speed figural of the BIS scores ($r_{SPf-BIS-Sf}$=.22). Interestingly, there is no correlation between auditory speed and AcI speed. Auditory variance is not covered through the BIS tests. Parts of the social perception variance thus seem to be due to AcI speed. Therefore, resarch question SI-5_1 can only be answered in favor of the SU factor which has its strongest relationship with SM. SM on the contrary has more in common with AcI than with SU. This meets the expectations made in chapter 3 (see also research question SI-4_1), according to which social understanding shows the lowest correlations with AcI compared to SI perception and SI memory.

I expected all SIM (Süß et al., 2008) content scales to be weakly intercorrelated with BIS-verbal (see chapter 3). Regression analysis was used to build factor scores of both the BIS content scales and the SI content scales. All SIM (Süß et al., 2008) content scales correlated significantly with the BIS content scale "verbal" (N=101). Correlations between SI-written and AcI-verbal was most highly ($r_{SIw-BISv}$=.62, p<.001), followed by SI-auditory ($r_{SIa-BISv}$= .50, p>.001), SI-pictorial and SI-video-based (both $r_{SIw-BISp/f}$=.31, p=.002), thus providing some proof for my expectations.

Summary of Findings

In summary, the social intelligence tests worked out well. However, some of the scales have to be improved. With regard to the social understanding tasks, rating scales proved to be the most successful. Although open-ended questions were useful, too, they imply problems reaching beyond economics: Open-ended questions favor people who are fast in writing, good at verbal comprehension, and verbal fluency. The same is true for social memory tasks. Therefore, open-ended questions should be transformed into a different format. The correlation of SM tasks with AcI speed can be reduced allowing more time for answering the questions. Social perception tasks seem to measure rather AcI speed than social perception. Additional socially complex items could help to reveal the specifically social part of the perception ability. On the contrary, the complexity of written social perception tasks needs to be reduced. Working on the social perception tasks seems to be worthwhile in the context of structure analytic results, too. Maybe, some task changes allow to answer the question of whether a social perception ability does exist more reliably. The first study confirmed the two factors, social memory and social understanding, of the multidimensional SI construct. Despite its relationship to AcI operations, analyses controlling for AcI variance and a regression analysis predicting SI-SM with the BIS operations indicate that SM has specific reliable variance that is unexplained by AcI. I now turn to the findings obtained with the auditory intelligence tasks (see also Seidel & Süß, 2007).

6.3.2 Auditory Intelligence

Psychometric Properties

Internal consistency of the auditory intelligence tasks is rather low. Three of the tasks have severe reliability problems (tonal analogies, chord decomposition, recognition of repeated voices). The remaining auditory tasks showed reliabilities (Cronbachs Alpha) between .60 (audiobook) and .88 (AIT), and are similar to the split-half reliabilities reported in Stankov and Horn (1980).

Table 6-6: Psychometrics of the Auditory Intelligence Tasks (First Study)

Task	Number of items [1]	Skewness/ Curtosis [5]	Mean difficulty (SD)	Difficulty range	Item-total- corr. range	Cronb. Alpha [3]
Detection of repeated tones (MA1), N=125	17 (15)	.10/-.62	.47 (.22)	.16 - .75	.24 - .46	.73 (.74)
Pitch discrimination (AIT-P) N=126	120 (80)	.57/-.62	.64 (.16)	.56 - .71	.47 - .77	.84 (.88)
Tonal figures (MA3), N=126	17 (11)	.03/-.66	.52 (.23)	.33 - .66	.20 - .41	.63 (.66)
Rhythm reproduction N=126	20 (19)	.35 (.21)/-.29	.41 (.19)	.02 - .84	.22 - .62	.82 (.82)
Recognition of familiar environmental sounds N=126	55 (36)	-.80 (.21)/.15	.83 (.11)	.65 - .98	.10 - .40	.63 (.70)
Tonal analogies (MA2), N=126	17 (7)	.25/-.27	.43 (.23)	.28 - .58	.12 - .26	.19 (.43)
Tonal series (MA4), N=126	21 (13)	-.31/-.83	.63 (.21)	.33 - .84	.15 - .45	.65 (.69)
Chord decomposition (MA5), N=125	15 (11)	.84/.84	.39 (.20)	.25 - .47	.14 - .34	.51 (.54)
Masked words N=57	35 (24)	.03 (.32)/ .47 (.62)	.44 (.16)	.07 - .98	.20 - .49	.75 (.79)
Detection of repeated voices N=126	25 (11)	.29/.07	.44 (.17)	.17 - .90	.14 - .30	.36 (.48)
Audiobook N=125	14 (11)	-.71/.39	.70 (.15)	.30 - .98	.21 - .42	.60 (.60)
Disarranged sentences, N=124	19 (16)	-.65/1.40	.61 (.14)	.12 - .95	.18 - .40	.66 (.67)

Note: S1= first study; [1] In parentheses: after Item selection; [2] in parentheses: after correction; [3] scale was extended to k=15 and k=20 (in parentheses), respectively; [5] Skewness is presented first; the second value represents curtosis, SE (Skewness): .22 if different, it is reported in parentheses; SE (Curtosis): .43; the tasks pitch discrimination, rhythm reproduction, recognition of familiar environmental sounds, chord decomposition, and detection of repeated voices are not normally distributed.

For further analysis reliability corrected scores of the tasks will be used. In the application of multivariate analyses, the tasks with severe reliability and distribution problems were excluded. The task masked words was excluded in the main correlation table because technical problems allowed us to analyze only the data of 57 subjects.

Internal structure

Research Questions:

AuI-1_1) Can the two expected facets (operation: discrimination, memory, reasoning) and content (nonverbal; speech) be shown?

Correlation results indicate that we did not succeed in developing tasks representing the three operational domains reasoning, memory and discrimination or that such operation factors simply do not exist (see appendix B.2.1 for the correlation table). More likely, we can expect a general auditory factor or two content factors (verbal vs. nonverbal) since tasks including speech seem to be measure different abilities compared to tonal tasks and further auditory tasks dealing with non-speech material (e.g. rhythm). However, the correlation pattern should not be overinterpreted since some relationships may be due to distribution and reliability problem.

Such as with social intelligence, in auditory intelligence the internal structure was examined applying EFA and CFA. Since the reliability of the tasks detection of repeated voices, tonal analogies, and chord decomposition is by far too low, these tasks are excluded from further analysis. The three remaining tasks that suffer from distribution problems are included in the analysis because they deviate only slightly from normal distribution. Because of its limited number of cases, analysis was done without the task masked words. Dependent on the extraction criterion used we find either a one-factor solution (parallel analysis; general auditory) or a two-factor solution (Kaiser-Guttman rule). As parallel analysis is conservative when only few variables are included, I refer to the two-factor solution here which also confirms past empirical results. Regarding the two-factor solution, there is an obvious difference between speech tasks and nonverbal (=tonal and rhythm) tasks. With the two-factor solution, 54.17% of variance can be explained. The first factor has an eigenvalue of 3.19 and explains 39.84% of the variance. The second factor with an eigenvalue of 1.15 explains 14.33% of the variance. Again, the task familiar environmental sounds cannot be classified in either the speech or the nonverbal factor corresponding to the task classification described in chapter 2.5.6 see Figure 2-10). The low number of AuI tasks that could be included in the analysis makes it particularly difficult to examine whether there are indeed two factors. Maybe even a third factor would emerge when including more tasks dealing with environmental sounds.

Further examination of the AuI structure was done with CFA. The complete structure (3 operations x 2 contents) could not be tested because after the exclusion of tasks for reasons of reliability, distribution, and technical problems the remaining number of tasks was not sufficient. Therefore, operational and content domains were tested separately. For the same reasons, some of the postulated factors are only indicated by two predictors. Although for a reliable finding we need three or more predictors, I decided to present these analyses since they are preliminary and should be used to improve the tasks and select appropriate subtests. Analysis confirms that three auditory operational domains cannot be justified. The factors of the well-fitting model (Chi²=24.27, df=17; p=.112; CFI=.97; RMSEA=.059 ; CI 90%: .000, .109; SRMR=.054) are corrrelated with .93 and .94. Thus, research question AuI-1 has to be answered negatively with regard to the operation facet. With regard to the content domains, we expected two factors, one speech-related factor and one nonverbal factor. The corresponding CFA model fitted the data in an excellent manner (Chi²=19.64, df=19; p=.417; CFI=1.00; RMSEA=.017; CI 90%: .000, .082; SRMR=.045). However, such as in the operational model one has to take into account that the model does not fulfil the criterion of the required three indicators that are needed for a reliable measurement (e.g. Bühner, 2006; Kenny, 1979; Urban & Mayerl, 2003). The speech and verbal tasks audiobook and disarranged sentences are better described by the two-factor model than by a one-factor model. The two factors are moderately correlated, pointing towards two separable domains that can be subsumed under a general auditory ability factor. An additional speech task is needed to get further information about the internal structure of auditory intelligence. Masked words seems to be a promising candidate regarding its reliability value for a limited sample. Although the content model needs further confirmation, the first results confirm the expectation of a content facet including two dimensions (nonverbal and speech).

Auditory Intelligence Related to Academic Intelligence

Research Questions:

AuI-2) Is AuI separable from AcI?

AuI-3) Do speech related auditory intelligence tasks show higher correlations with verbal AcI than nonverbal auditory tasks?

AuI-4) Are tonal auditory abilities correlated more highly with figural and numerical AcI contents than auditory speech tasks?

AuI-5) Can auditory intelligence be classified into the BIS model?

Next, I want to deal with the relationship between AuI and AcI, in particular whether they are separable constructs. The postulated BIS structure, was proved and confirmed by means of CFA. Since we do not have BIS data from three of our test takers and some data is missing with regard to the auditory tasks, analysis was performed with 120 cases. Figure 6-1 gives a first impression of the relationship between AuI and the BIS dimensions (cells).

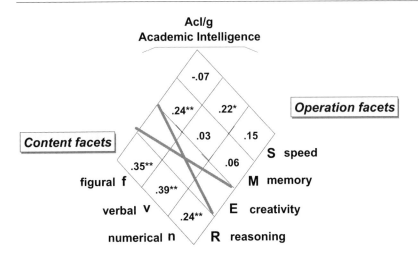

Figure 6-1. Correlations of Auditory Intelligence with the BIS Cells

It is apparent that correlations with the reasoning dimension are significant in all content domains. Therefore, the assumption arises that working memory may be involved in the cognitive operations of the auditory tasks. This assumption is in line with findings reported by Dun (2000), who applied some of the Stankov and Horn (1980) tasks and found a relationship between auditory tasks (particularly tonal tasks) and fluid intelligence (Gf). She interpreted this relationship as to be moderated by working memory and concluded that particularly tonal series, tonal memory, and detection of repeated tones rely strongly on reasoning abilities. These tasks require maintaining sounds, awareness, and processing of information simultaneously which reminds on the simultaneous storage and processing dimension of the working memory capacity (WM) model suggested by Oberauer et al. (2000). Surprenant and Watson (2001) expect a relationship between auditory discrimination and working memory as well. Thus, even detection/discrimination tasks seem to require reasoning or capacity processes as specified and reported in advance. In line with findings of Dun (2000), Stankov and Horn (1980; see also Horn & Stankov, 1982; Roberts & Stankov, 1999) assume that auditory abilities are related to fluid intelligence. However, that corresponds to results of Kyllonen and Christal (1990; see Süß et al., 2002) according to which WM and reasoning are strongly related. In the extended gf-gc theory (see chapter 2.1 and chapter 2.5) auditory processing is also expected to be closely related to STM (see also Danthiir et al., 2001). The shared variance with reasoning was particularly obvious for the auditory tonal marker task tonal series (which corresponds in its structure the number and letter series tasks of AcI) for rhythm reproduction and tonal figures. However, the auditory speech tasks show the strongest relationships to AcI. Audiobook correlates significantly with nearly every BIS cell (highest with memory as expected). Disarranged sentences is related strongest to reasoning verbal, also corresponding to the expectations (see test construction rationale, Table 4-11).

In EFA, general auditory abilities are clearly separable from AcI content domains and from AcI operations (research question AuI-2_1; Seidel, 2007). However, the unique variance of general auditory tasks seems to be disclosed by tonal/nonverbal tasks. The verbal tasks seem to measure rather AcI, in our example verbal memory and verbal reasoning.

Confirmatory analyses confirm EFA results in that the verbal component in the auditory speech tasks seems to be stronger than their auditory part. The best model fit is achieved, when only nonverbal auditory tasks are included in the analysis (Chi²=80.649; df=71; p=.203; CFI=.981; RMSEA=.034; CI 90% .000; .066; SRMR=.062). Interestingly, the auditory nonverbal factor does not correlate significantly with any of the BIS factors. It correlates highest with the verbal factor (.22). When relating the auditory tasks to the operation domains of the BIS, the task audiobook, besides its expected loading on the auditory factor also loads on the memory factor. In the same way, disarranged sentences besides its loading on the auditory factor is also assigned to the reasoning factor. The fit to data is satisfactory, although worse compared to the classification of the auditory tasks within the BIS content dimensions. The auditory-memory and the auditory-speed correlations are zero. That is why I did the calculation on a reverse model including a covariation of the auditory factor only with the reasoning factor. The fit improves slightly. Once again, it is apparent that the auditory abilities are rather different from AcI. The final model has an acceptable fit (Chi²=178.407; df= 127; p=.002; CFI=.921; RMSEA=.059; CI 90% .037; .078; SRMR=.070). Again, the task audiobook loads higher on the memory factor (.57) than on the auditory factor (.21), disarranged sentences shows a higher loading on the reasoning factor (.43) than on the auditory factor (.30). The variance of these auditory verbal tasks seems to be explained through factors of AcI rather than through a factor of AuI. WM tasks should be included in future investigations to make sure that the extra-variance that is explained through the auditory tasks is nothing else than pure working memory capacity. A contradiction to this assumption seems to be that in empirical investigations, WM correlated much more strongly with reasoning (e.g. Kyllonen & Christal, 1990; Süß et al., 2002), than the auditory ability factor within this investigation does.

When controlling for BIS variance the model fits the data even better (Chi²=178.488, df=129; p=.003; CFI=.924; RMSEA=.058, CI 90%=.035,.077; SRMR=.070). Compared to the model without controlling for academic intelligence loadings do not change much. The largest differences to the original model occur with regard to the speech tasks, because important (mainly verbal) parts of their variance are partialed out. However, even in speech tasks unique variance remains. Auditory speech tasks share parts with the auditory intelligence factor even if they are considerably smaller compared to auditory nonverbal tasks. Partialing out AcI variance of the two factor auditory model (including a speech and a tonal factor) we also find a considerable improvement of the model (Chi²=18.507, df=20; p=.554; CFI=1.00; RMSEA=.000; CI 90%: .000; .072; SRMR=.043).

Summary of findings

With respect to the relationship between AuI and AcI we can conclude the following: The three auditory operational domains could not be demonstrated; there are no separate discrimination, memory, and reasoning factors. In parts results met the assumption addressed in question AuI-2_1 that speech related auditory ability shows higher correlations with verbal AcI than the auditory tonal ability. Although the full model was not tested (need of an additional indicator for auditory speech abilities), the findings clearly indicate that the auditory speech tasks have loadings on the AcI domains (verbal content and operations memory and reasoning) that are even higher than their loadings on the corresponding auditory factor. Beyond the classification as an additional content dimension, the auditory tasks form a separate domain when related to the BIS operations. Research question AuI-4 (tonal auditory ability correlates with figural and numerical AcI contents) did not reveal an answer in the expected direction. The correlations of AcI with nonverbal auditory ability are all non-significant and highest with the verbal factor. Interpreting the results of this study, auditory nonverbal ability seems to compose a completely new ability. The findings are in line with Lohman (2003) who found in analyzing the WJ III test (see chapter 2.5.3) that the auditory tests have exceptional low loadings (incomplete words: .30 and sound blending:.42) on the general intelligence factor. Therefore, with respect to research question AuI-5 it does not make sense to classify nonverbal auditory intelligence into the BIS structure. Classification into the BIS can rather be considered for the speech auditory dimension.

The effort we put in the pilot studies paid off. Most of the tasks could be improved considerably with respect to their psychometric characteristics. However, there are still some modifications that have to be done for at least some of the tasks to enhance their reliability but also to save testing time by shortening the scales. The technical problems should be controlled for, so that the tasks masked words can complement the scale and serve as third indicator of speech related auditory ability. An additional speech task enables us to test the two-factor model (including a tonal and a speech auditory component) again with a higher reliability. This study revealed one general auditory factor but another study should be carried out to confirm this result checking whether there is more than one operational domain. The task chord decomposition should be excluded since its relationship with musical experience lets assume that this task is rather an indicator of musical ability than of an expected basic and underlying auditory intelligence. Besides confirming the results dealing with the relationship between AuI and AcI, the correlation between working memory and auditory intelligence has to be examined. The question of whether AuI exists even after controlling for both AcI and WM, should be subject of further investigation.

6.3.3 On the Impact of Musical Experience on Auditory Task Performance

A major objection that could be raised against treating auditory abilities as an intelligence is the influence by musical experience. In our study 36.2% (N=46) of our subjects indicated on a one-point rating scale to have musical experience. The auditory speech tasks showed zero correlations with musical experience (.07 - .08). Likewise did the environmental sounds task (-.02). However, the tonal tasks were significantly and moderately related to musical experience (.26 - .28.). It seems reasonable that the task chord decomposition is most strongly related to a person's musical experience (r=.44; p<.001). The AIT-P task also has a significant relationship to musical experience (.19). The results are in line with Kormann (1985), Shuter (1968), and Horn and Stankov (1982). Papenbrock (2005) contrasted musical experienced people and laypersons and examined gender differences. She reports that musically experienced people are significantly better with regard to tonal/nonverbal tasks (F= 9.94; df= 96; p=.02) and that there are gender differences in favor of men for general auditory abilities (F= 4.20; df=117; p=.04). These results correspond to the findings of Dun (2000). She concluded that musical ability is expected to aid performance in some of the auditory tasks, particularly chord decomposition and tonal discrimination, but that this experience is not necessary for task completion. The level of formal musical education showed a correlation of .21 with general auditory ability (Ga, Dun, 2000). According to Stankov (1983), experience with music is more strongly related to auditory abilities than knowledge about music. In future studies, it should be an objective to find out whether musical experience effects performance on AuI tasks or whether auditorily intelligent people are more engaged in gaining musical experience.

6.3.4 Results - Social and General Auditory Intellectual Abilities

Research questions:

SI-AuI-1: Are general and social auditory intellectual abilities correlated moderately because of the overlap with respect to auditory material?

SI-AuI-2: Do auditory speech tasks overlap more strongly with social auditory tasks than nonverbal auditory tasks since the former both make use of spoken language?

In order to answer the question of whether social auditory abilities can be differentiated from general auditory abilities, intercorrelations between the two ability domains were computed. Table 6-7 presents the result of the correlation analysis.

Table 6-7: Correlations Between General and Social Auditory Tasks

	SPa	SMa	SUa	MA1	AIT-P	MA3	RH	MA4	FES	AU
SPa	1.00									
SMa	.09	1.00								
SUa	.01	.18*	1.00							
MA1	-.09	-.01	-.14	1.00						
AIT-P	-.16	.00	-.08	.51**	1.00					
MA3	-.15	.13	-.13	.51**	.38**	1.00				
RH	.00	.08	-.06	.37**	.38**	.34**	1.00			
MA4	-.13	.08	-.12	.64**	.54**	.53**	.33**	1.00		
FES	-.15	.15	-.09	.17	.24**	.18*	.22*	.27**	1.00	
AU	-.05	.36**	.03	.05	.12	.08	.08	.17	.15	1.00
DS	.05	.18*	.14	.21*	.24**	.29**	.30**	.32**	.10	.23*

Note. Spearman correlations; listwise deletion, N=120; **Correlation is significant at p< 0.01 (2-sided); *Correlation is significant at p< 0.05 (2-sided); SPa=Social Perception-auditory; SMa=Social memory-auditory; SUa= Social understanding-auditory; MA1=Detection of repeated tones; MA3= Tonal figures; MA4=Tonal series; RH=Rhythm reproduction; AIT-P=Pitch discrimination; FES=Familiar environmental sounds; AU=Audiobook; DS=Disarranged sentences; Hypothesis relevant correlations are shaded in grey. The negative correlations with SPa are due to the reaction time measure that was applied. The lower the reaction time the better the result.

The correlations that are relevant to answer the question of the relationship between social and general auditory abilities, are shaded in grey. It is apparent, that most of the general auditory intelligence tasks do not correlate at all with the social auditory intelligence tasks. In some cases, the relationships are even negative. Thus, there is no general relationship between social and general auditory tasks because of the common use of auditory material (see SI-AuI-1 and chapter 3). The only significant correlations that point into a reliable relationship between the two subconstructs are the correlation between social auditory memory with audiobook (r_{SMa-AU}=.36) and with disarranged sentences (r_{SMa-DS}=.18). Additional correlations that do not reach the significance level but point into the expected direction are between social auditory perception (SPa) and AIT-P, MA3, MA4 and FES, between social auditory memory (SMa) and MA3 and FES, and between SUa and DS (Note, that the negative correlations with SPa are due to the reaction time measure that was applied). In summary, the correlations between social auditory intelligence and general auditory intelligence are rather low and do not point into a positive answer of question SI-AuI. However, there seem to exist some relationships between parts of the abilities. The highest and most frequent correlations can be discovered between memory tasks of both social auditory and general auditory intelligence tasks (see SMa with MA3, FES, AU). In addition, meeting my expectations, auditory speech tasks correlate higher with social auditory intelligence tasks than with tonal (nonverbal) tasks (seequestion SI-AuI-2 ad chapter 3). This is particularly true for the task SMa but also partly true for the SUa task. The nonverbal auditory tasks are related, even if not significantly, to the auditory perception factor. This is interesting against the background of Carroll (1993), who labelled the underlying latent variable for the auditory abilities "broad auditory perception factor".

The relationship of SMa with MA3 and FES may be attributed to the cognitive operation "memory", the tasks have in common. The reason that we have to search for relationships between the two subconstructs can be also explained by the missing correlations within the social auditory intelligence subconstruct. I mentioned earlier, that we could not identify a homogeneous social perception factor in this study. Neither social auditory memory nor social auditory understanding correlated with SPa. The only relationship existed between SMa and SUa, correspondent to the relationships within the other content dimensions. Therefore, it is doubtful that social auditory abilities emerge as a separate factor besides general speech and tonal auditory abilities. Factor analytic results support these assumptions. The social auditory tasks do not form a homogeneous social auditory ability factor and therefore cannot be contrasted against general auditory abilities. We also have to consider, that three of the general auditory intelligence tasks, namely AIT-P, RH, and FES have (minor) distribution problems. At this point, the results should be used for task selection and modification but it is worthwhile to address the question of the relationship between general auditory abilities and social auditory abilities again in the second study.

6.4 Modification and Completion of the Tests

6.4.1 General Modifications and Principles of Task Completion

The results of the first study were taken to modify the existing SI and AuI tasks. The following changes were implemented for all tasks: (1) Items that proved to be reliable and useful were selected. Items that did not meet the requirements of item-total correlation, did not reach chance level, and did not fit in with regard to difficulty were excluded. We tried to find theoretical reasons for the items that were excluded. (2) The items were re-ordered according to their difficulty values of the first study (AuI tasks). (3) We modified and shortened the instructions for all tasks to ensure a better understanding and to save time. In addition to the instruction that is presented on the computer screen, an additional instruction sheet was provided containing the most important information for each task. In the following chapters, the improved version of the language-based and the scenario SIM (Süß et al., 2008) tasks and their modifications compared to the first study that have been made beyond the mentioned general changes will be described.

In addition to the task modifications, new tasks were developed in order to represent each operation-content cell with two tasks, except for written social memory. Since written social memory already includes two parts (single person scripture and correspondence), we did it without developing a second task that would have taken too much testing time. Tasks were completed in order to represent either whole social situations (e.g., in social auditory perception, SPa1, subjects have to react during an ongoing conversation; in written social perception, subjects have to react on social/emotional terms in text extracts) or more specific aspects (e.g., perception of social/emotional words in single sentences, memory for couples, memory for voices). For each type of material both kinds of tasks (whole situation and specific aspects) should be represented.

6.4.2 Social Understanding Scenario Tasks

The scenario task is described in chapter 4.1.3. After the first study, the following modifications were implemented: (1) We focused on rating scales since they proved to be most reliable and economical. Some of the MC items and open-ended questions were converted into rating scales. (2) We altered the six-point rating scale to a seven-point rating scale, in order to allow the choice of a middle category. A seven-point rating scale instead of a five-point rating scale was chosen to cover the answer in finer gradation. We tried to keep information loss from visual scale as low as possible (Deviation measures were most reliable and exact.) at the same time striving for economy and not overtaxing our subjects with to many different gradations. (3) The task was practiced with an example scenario. (4) At the end, subjects are asked to rate their similarity to the target person as well as the sympathy they felt for that person. This information should be used as control variables. (5) Four additional scenarios were recorded in order to increase heterogeneity, reliability and validity. This time, we recorded comparably older target persons with different professions. (6) We professionalized our recordings and task development by generating more concrete situation specific questions and restricting our recordings to less material (as we did not need as much of the material we recorded in the first four scenarios). Table 6-8 presents an overview of our target persons including information about their age, gender and profession. In italics, you will find the scenarios that were newly developed for the second study.

Table 6-8: Overview of the Scenario Target Persons

Target person	Gender	Age	Profession	Education	Number of items
Rita (RF)	female	24	medical-technician	non-academic	73
Bertram (BS)	*male*	*43*	*internal medicine doctor*	*academic*	*73*
Carina (CK)	*female*	*41*	*owner of an billiard and dart café (gastronomy)*	*non-academic*	*75*
Christian (CP)	male	23	student (law)	academic	64
Kathrin (KL)	female	26	student (psychology)	academic	83
Friedhelm (FB)	*male*	*69*	*real estate salesman*	*non-academic*	*60*
Herma (HR)	*female*	*60*	*special education teacher*	*academic*	*75*
Martin (MM)	male	33	dancing teacher with an own dancing school	non-academic	73

The target persons live in different parts of Germany (Berlin, Bavaria, Palatinate, Rhineland, Saxony, Lower Saxony and Westphalia). That is why in some conversations, persons speak a dialect. We tried to select only conversations that could be understood by people who are not familiar with the specific dialect. Moreover, empirical results show that dialect has no predictive power for trait judgments when subjects are provided with cues to the social location of the speaker (Foon, 1986).

The personality profiles of the target persons are heterogeneous with respect to all Big Five personality dimensions (NEO-FFI). In the interpersonal circumplex dimensions (IIP-C), profiles are more similar. The target persons we chose were active rather than passive, and they were characterized by a middle level of closeness and cooperation. However, even in those rather similar dimensions, scores within the categories zero and four range between .38 to 2.13 (close), .38 to 2.13 (passive) and 1 to 3.13 (cooperative). The figures of both the NEO-FFI and the IIP-C profiles are illustrated in appendix A.2.

6.4.3 Language-based Social Memory Tasks

Task Modification

a)   Memory for correspondence (Social memory-written, SMw 1 & 2)

Within the correspondence memory task, subjects have to memorize social information in text extracts as accurately as possible in order to recognize/recall it afterwards. The recognition/recall part of the task consists of both MC questions (two thirds of the items) and open-ended questions (one third of the items). MC items have five answer alternatives. One of them is completely correct, the others either completely wrong or partly wrong (scored with half points). The task consists of six text extracts each followed by six to ten questions. The first three texts are one-sided correspondence and the next three texts are two-sided correspondence. The task material varies the setting (privat vs. public) and the content of the situation (interpersonal circumplex, see chapter 4.1.2) systematically.

These are the modifications that were implemented after the first study:

Two texts were added, one monologue in public context, one dialogue in private context. For the construction of MC alternatives, answers being given to the open-answer questions of the first study were used. Time to answer questions was raised to reduce the speed component. The task contains 25 items in three monologues (8/25 open-ended questions) and 23 items in three dialogues (8/23 open-ended questions).

b)   Memory for conversations (Social memory-auditory, SMa1)

Subjects have to memorize social information in sound sequences as accurately as possible. Each sound file is presented only once. The time to answer open-ended (one-third) and MC questions (two-thirds) after the sound presentation is limited. MC items include five answer alternatives, one of them being completely correct, the others either completely wrong or partly wrong (scored with half points). The task consists of six sound files with four to nine questions for each conversation. The number of people heard in the sound sequences (single others, dyads, small groups), the setting (private vs. public), and the content of the situations (interpersonal circumplex, see chapter 4.1.2) are varied systematically.

These are the modifications that were implemented after the first study:

Similar to social auditory perception, the most reliable three conversations were selected and modified for the second study. Three additional conversations were recorded. Again, answers to open-ended questions of the first study test version were used to develop MC items. The time to answer questions was extended in order to reduce the load on the Acl speed factor. The task contains 36 items (one-third are open-ended questions).

Test Completion

c)   Memory for voices (Social memory-auditory, SMa2)

In this task, subjects listen to conversations with two, three, or four persons and have to memorize their voices as accurately as possible. In the following, they hear five different voices; only one of them was presented in the conversation displayed before. This voice has to be identified. Subjects have about 20 seconds to choose one of five alternatives. The context differs between the conversations and the answer alternatives to ensure that a voice is not only chosen because of the context information that is provided. The number of persons (voices), the setting (privat vs. public) and the situation content (interpersonal circumplex) are varied systematically. The task is practiced with one item and contains 12 test items.

This is the idea behind the task:

This task deals with the more specific aspects whereas the other social auditory memory task refers to the whole social situation. Within the social auditory memory tasks both the verbal/speech auditory content and the paralinguistic/nonverbal part should be represented. Since SMa1 covers the content, I constructed this task (SMa2) as a measure for nonverbal aspects (voices discrimination and recognition).

Some important information in the context of voices recognition:

In order to understand the test principle, I will summarize some main findings and assumptions known in voice recognition research. The proportion of recognition of a voice can vary between 96% with a constant intonation (tone of voice) and chance level when tone of voice changes from emotional loaded tone of voice to a neutral conversation tone (Hammersly & Read, 1990). Performance of recognition improves significantly as a function of the number of words that are presented (one word: 14% recognition; eight words: 69%; 33 words: 90%). Recognition of voices is much harder than recognition of faces. This is an example: On the phone, we are used to saying our name even when we talk to familiar conversation partners. This behavior would be quite strange if we were in a face-to-face interaction. Voice is strongly associated with the context. Characteristics of gender and accent are not very helpful if a voice has to be identified outside the context in which it was heard. This is particularly true for people with whom we are not familiar (Hammersly & Read, 1990). The number of possible persons influences the recognition rate, a smaller number of persons resulting in a higher recognition rate (Goldstein & Chance, 1985). The voice of a person is remembered more often when it is relevant to the listener (e.g., when the listener has to judge the person's personality). The duration of the original presentation of a voice is not important for its recognition if the presentation of the voice exceeds the length of a sentence at least for two seconds (Clifford, 1980; Hollin & Clifford, 1983). However, the probability of right recognition rises when the listener hears the voice one minute or longer. Recognition performance is best, when the listener tries to remember the voice actively. Recognition rate decreases with an increasing number of voices in a conversation, such as from five to ten and from ten to twenty voices (Hammersly & Read, 1990). Consequently, in the voice memory task (SMa2) the conversations have a length of about half a minute (27-36 seconds). To guarantee that subjets identify the correct voice rather than the surrounding social context, the five voices (answer alternatives) including the target were recorded in a context different from the one in which the conversation took place. However, this is also expected to make the task difficult. Since the possibility of correct recognition decreases with an increasing number of people talking in a conversation, I limited the number of people in a conversation to two to four persons.

6.4.4 Language-based Social Perception Tasks

Task Modification

a)   Perception of social target stimuli in text extracts (Social perception-written, SPw1)
Socially relevant stimuli (i.e., names, expressions of feelings, person descriptions, and social events) have to be perceived as quickly and accurately as possible in text extracts. The stimuli subjects have to react on, are presented a short time before the relevant text extract appears. The task contains two parts differering in the level of difficulty, with 30 items each. Each part is divided into two equivalent blocks and contains 15 items. Between the two blocks within one part of the task, participants are allowed to make a short break to keep concentration on a high level. Each part is practiced with two example trials. The level of difficulty is varied through the number of aspects (one or two) subjects have to monitor at the same time. The right solution can be found word by word in the text extract. Subjects have 20 seconds maximum to complete an item. The task material varies according to the setting (privat vs. public) and according to the content (interpersonal circumplex, see chapter 4.1.2, Figure 4-1). "Yes" and "no" answers are equally distributed. An earlier version of this task was tested in the first study.

These are the modifications that were implemented after the first study:
The part of the task that dealt with questions worked better than the part dealing with statements. Therefore, in the second study, only questions were used as task material. Items were simplified to reduce the reasoning and memory load of the task. Ambiguous wordings of the items were made clearer. The task includes 4 (2 x 2) practice trials and 60 test trials (4 x 15).

b)   Perception of social facts in conversations (Social perception-auditory, SPa1)

In the conversation perception task, subjects have to react as quickly and accurately as possible to certain social facts in sound files (i.e., names of persons, the voice of a child, rejection, and laughter) by pressing a key on the keyboard. The task is practiced with two example conversations (16 reactions) and seven test conversations (82 reactions). Complexity varies according to the kind of stimulus (simple vs. complex), to the setting (private vs. public), to the amount of speakers (1-6), and to the number of stimuli (one or two) that have to be monitored. Speakers differ from one conversation to another. Females and males are represented in equal proportions.

These are the modifications that were implemented after the first study:

Two practice conversations and three test conversations of the task applied in first study were maintained and shortened. The stimuli "correction" and "answering" were excluded. Four new conversations were included containing more complex stimuli such as reactions to questions and reactions to different interaction partners. Additional job related conversations were included since in the first study most of the conversations dealt with private life. Simultaneous monitoring and reaction to three stimuli did not work well. Therefore, test takers only have to monitor and react to one or two stimuli in the modified task version. The task contains two practice conversations (including 16 reactions) and seven test conversations (including 82 reactions).

Test Completion

c)   Perception of social content in text extracts (Social perception-written, SPw2)

Test subjects have to judge sentences according to their social and emotional content. The task consists of two parts, containing 30 items each. The items of each part are split up into two comparable blocks with 15 items. In the first part, sentences with social/emotional content have to be distinguished from sentences without social/emotional content. In the second part, subjects have to decide whether positive social/emotional content is expressed or whether the expressions are negative. The subjects have 12 seconds to work on each of the sentences. Every part is introduced and practiced with four example trials. The task material is unambiguous and varies according to the setting (private vs. public) and the situation content (interpersonal circumplex). This task parallels the auditory social perception task (SPa2) described next.

d)   Perception of social cues/emotions in voices (Social perception-auditory, SPa2)

Subjects have to indicate as quickly as possible which of the two emotions/social paraverbal cues is presented in a short sound sequence (1 to 4 seconds) that was extracted from real-life conversations. Test takers are instructed to react as soon as the sequence starts. The time to answer is limited. The task consists of three blocks (positive vs. negative emotions, irony vs. anger; emotional vs. neutral), each containing ten sound sequences and two practice trials. Subjects are instructed to concentrate on the tone of voice (how things are said) and to ignore the content of the conversation (what is said).

This is the idea behind the task:

Since, in judging other people, both verbal and nonverbal cues are important (O'Sullivan et al., 1985), the task concerns nonverbal, paralinguistic aspects of social auditory perception, whereas SPa1 deals with both verbal (i.e., names) and paraverbal aspects (i.e, laughter, voices). In order to classify a sentence as objectively as possible, 68 sentences were rated by seven experienced people. I extracted only sentences all raters agreed upon. The remaining 30 sentences built the final task. The sentences were aligned with the easily measureable objective parameters (e.g., intensity, falling/rising contour, pitch; see chapter 2.6). Confusion patterns (see chapter 2.6.5) were used in order to group emotions that are comparatively easily discriminable. Scherer (1996) argues correctly that the ability of discriminating between emotions does not mean that the person actually recognizes them correctly (see also chapter 2.6.4). However, this task is a speed test rather than being a power measure of emotion identification (typically applied in emotion research). This task should measure the speed with which an emotion can be classified correctly in one of two categories. The use of natural rather than acted sentences does justice to Scherer's claim (1996) that it would be worthwhile to carry out studies with natural utterances and compare them to acted samples. The verbal content of the task is not masked which is also a difference compared to the tests commonly used in emotion research. Although problems may emerge concerning the interference of content and tone of voice, research has shown that possibly understanding the verbal content is a crucial precondition for the correct interpretation of prosodic features (see chapter 2.6.4).

Complementing Task Constructed of the GVEESS Material

The emotion perception in voices task (SPa2) was applied in combination with three blocks of emotional meaningless sentences taken from the Geneva Vocal Emotion Expression Stimulus Set (GVEESS). The stimulus set is based on research conducted by Scherer, K., Wallbott, H., Banse, R., and Ellgring, H. (for detailed information, please see Banse & Scherer, 1996). I tried to build pairs of emotions as objectively as possible. Test takers should be able to identify emotions easily so that the reaction time of recognizing an emotion is decisive for the performance instead of the recognition itself. In order to make recognition easy, I considered information available through confusion matrices (see Banse & Scherer, 1996) in grouping the emotions. Confusion matrices inform us about the likelihood with which an emotion will be confused with another one. Consequently, for example, pride was not grouped together with interest but with boredom. Emotions showing a similar parameter recognition pattern belong to the same emotion family and are more likely to get confused. Further selection criteria concern the representation of a wide spectrum of different speakers (several sentences in the GVEESS are spoken by the same speaker), intensity (sentences had to be naturally loud enough to be selected), and agreement upon six raters about the correct classification.

6.4.5 Auditory Intelligence Tasks

Task Selection

Time constraints allowed us to include only six of the AuI tasks in the second study. First, the six tasks were selected with the aim of maintaing both content domains (tonal and speech) and the operation domains (discrimination, memory and reasoning) although the latter could not be confirmed in our first study. Second, tasks were selected according to their reliability. Among tasks with similar reliability, those which required less time in duration were favored. Third, items with a middle degree of difficulty were chosen (see Table 6-6). Factor analysis and correlation matrices were used to analyze convergent and discriminant validity. The verbal domain was only represented by one task for the memory and the reasoning cell so that there were no possibilities to choose. Although the task audiobook has a rather low reliability value (.60), we included an improved version in the battery of the second study (see information later on). In the perceptual speech domain, there was the choice between Detection of repeated voices and masked words. I decided to include masked words because of its promising reliability value and short duration in a subsample of 57 students. Detection of repeated voices had not only a low reliability value but also a relationship to SI with regard to its content. With respect to the nonverbal/tonal domain, I chose detection of repeated tones representing perception/discrimination because the AIT-P took too much time, was not well accepted by our participants, and judged as being uncomfortable. In addition, usually many subjects have severe problems in making the pitch discrimination at any duration. In a study of Brand and Deary (1982), over 20% of the subjects could not meet the training criterion of the task. Only 42.4% of the subjects were able to make the pitch discrimination reliably enough for their data to be included in the analysis (Deary, Head, & Egan, 1989). In the memory domain, I decided to include rhythm reproduction because of its high reliability and short duration. This task contributes to representativeness since it covers an important aspect of auditory ability that is different from the other auditory tasks (manual reproduction of a rhythm). The task tonal series was chosen to represent the reasoning domain because of its similarity (correspondence) to the BIS tasks number series and letter series. Other reasons concern the low reliabilities of tonal analogies (.43) and chord decomposition (.54). The reduced matrix is represented in Table 7-1. The selection of

191

nonverbal auditory intelligence tasks includes two tasks identified as marker tests by Dun (2000). Detection of repeated tones serves as a marker of temporal tracking. Tonal series can be regarded as a marker of auditory cognition of relationships (see also Stankov & Horn, 1980).

Task Modification

In the following, the major modifications implemented in the selected tasks beyond the changes already mentioned in chapter 6.4.1. are listed.

a)   Masked words

The dimensions of the task were retained in 27 selected items. Each combination of the 3 x 3 x 3 matrix with the dimensions "loudness of the background noise" (quiet – middle – loud), loudness of the spoken word (quiet – middle – loud), and word frequency (one syllable – two syllables frequent – two syllables rare) was represented once.

b)   Audiobook

The spoken text of the audiobook was only presented once. Besides saving testing time, the single presentation of the text should increase the difficulty of the task. Open-ended questions were converted into MC items (five alternatives, one correct option). Answers to open-ended questions to the first study were used to develop wrong alternatives. Five additional items were developed so that the task contains 19 items.

6.4.6   Additional Modifications

Berlin Intelligence Structure Test

In the task *meaningful text* (memory verbal) of the BIS test, test takers have to remember characteristics of peoples' descriptions. After a limited amount of time, they are asked to recall the relevant information provided in the peoples' descriptions. This task is quite similar to the written social memory task (SMw1) and is assumed to require social memory instead of academic memory. In order to exclude social content, we developed a new task, equivalent in item number and length, that deals with different types of soil (see Seidel, 2007).

6.4.7   Questionnaires

In order to get more detailed information, in the second study, participants had to rate their musical experience on a five-point rating scale instead of using a one-point rating scale (first study). Participants had to judge their musical ability as being very low to very high compared to people of their age. In addition, subjects should specify their musical ability (school of music, kind of instrument, choir etc.) and indicate how long they have already been engaged in their musical activities.

7 Second Study

7.1 General Aims and Expectations

The second study aimed at evaluating the task modifications. I expect increased reliabilities with respect to almost all tasks that did not already show high reliability values (e.g., the task rhythm reproduction). Reliability and validity are expected to increase since we improved the instructions. In addition, the newly developed tasks have to undergo a first critical evaluation. This study should be confirmative with regard to the results that were obtained on the SI and on the AuI structure. Confirmation also concerns the investigation of a representative adult sample different to the student sample that was tested in the first study (aspect of generality across samples, see condition 3, chapter 1.2). For the following results it should be investigated whether they can be confirmed or not.

Internal structure of social and auditory intelligence

The following assumptions derived from the first study will be investigated:

- The factors social understanding and social memory emerge as uniutary and moderately intercorrelated subconstructs.
- The SI structure is valid for both target and consensus scoring.
- Auditory intelligence splits into two content factors, nonverbal and speech auditory intelligence.

Relationship to academic intelligence

I will examine whether the following results obtained in the first study can be confirmed in the second study.

- Social understanding is independent from academic intelligence.
- Social memory is related to all BIS factors, academic intelligence memory, reasoning and speed. Nevertheless, it has its unique parts.
- Nonverbal auditory ability is independent from academic intelligence.
- Speech auditory ability is strongly related to academic intelligence.

Relationship between auditory intelligence and musical experience

According to the results of the first study, I expect musically experienced people to perform better in nonverbal/tonal auditory tasks.

Relationship between social auditory and general auditory abilities

The following assumptions will be tested with respect to the interrelation of social and general auditory intellectual abilities:

- Social auditory abilities show only marginal relationships to auditory intelligence.
- Social auditory memory is related to auditory intelligence tasks that require memory.

Additional Questions

In addition, new questions that arise from the findings of the first study will be examined. The question of whether social perception can be measured as a homogeneous subconstruct will be addressed again with newly developed social perception tasks and the modified versions of the old tasks including items with higher complexity. Another aim is the investigation of auditory nonverbal intelligence controlled for working memory (WM). Since WM usually is strongly related to reasoning and the AuI factor remained stable when reasoning was partialed out (see chapter 6.3.2), I expect nonverbal auditory ability to be stable, when controlled for WM. Empirical results provided evidence for the independence of emotion perception from other social/emotional abilities (see Roberts et al., 2006). Moreover, I expect them to be independent from general auditory intelligence.

7.2 Description of the Study

7.2.1 Participants

In the second study, 191 subjects participated. After exclusion of participants with a lack of commitment, participants outside the age-range of 23 to 40 years, and drop-outs during the study, 182 complete data sets remained. The mean age of our participants was 28.69 years (SD=5.57); 58.8% of the test takers were female. With regard to education, 56.6% finished with a high school degree, 17% with a middle school degree, 6% with a subject specific high school degree (Fachhochschulreife), and 20.3% already finished their university studies. The participants covered a broad spectrum of different professions that can be classified in 21 different groups. The largest groups were clerical and commercial occupations (N=24, 13.19%); health care (N=14; 8%), occupations in engineering science (N=11; 6%); and social sciences (N=10; 5%). Seven participants indicated having severe hearing problems (partially hard of hearing, i.e., inner ear or deaf one ear, need of hearing aid, tinnitus). They were excluded from all analysis concerning the auditory tasks. The N for analysis including auditory tasks is therefore reduced to 175 persons. Only one person was not German native speaker but was very familiar with the German language. Concerning the self-assessment of musical abilities, compared with their age group, 6.6% indicated having very low musical abilities, 15.6% indicated having rather low musical abilities, 46.7% chose the middle category, 23.6% judged themselves to have rather good musical abilities and 7.1 indicated being musically very good compared to their age group.

7.2.2 Materials

Compared to the tasks of the first study, additional questionnaires, such as empathy and emotional intelligence, were administered. We applied three adaptive working memory tasks (Oberauer et al., 2003) to examine their influence on AuI. Furthermore, the Profile of Nonverbal Sensitivity (PONS, Rosenthal et. al., 1979) was applied. In the following, short descriptions of the remaining SI tasks (pictorial and video-based) and of the other instruments that have not already been described in the context of the first study or in the modification chapter 6.4 will be presented. Table 7-1 presents an overview of the tasks that were administered. This table includes only the performance-based tasks.

Table 7-1: Overview of the Task Material of the Second Study

	Subconstruct	Methods			
		written (w)	auditory (a)	pictorial (p)	video-based (film) (f)
SIM	Social understanding (SU)	Scenarios			
	Social memory (SM)	SMw1+2	SMa1 SMa2	SMp1 SMp2	SMf1+2
	Social perception (SP)	SPw1 SPw2	SPa1 SPa2	SPp1 SPp2	SPf1 SPf2
		verbal (v)		figural-spatial (f)	numerical (n)
BIS	Reasoning (R)	B_WS B_WA B_TM		B_AN B_CH B_AW	B_RD B_ZN B_SC
	Memory (M)	B_WM B_ST ("soils") B_PS		B_WE B_OG B_FM	B_ZZ B_ZP B_ZW
	Processing speed (S)	B_UW B_TG B_KW		B_ZS B_BD B_OE	B_SI B_XG B_RZ
WM tasks	Working memory	Word span (WM_WSp)		Dot span (WM_DSp)	Memory updating numerical (WM_MUn)

	Subconstruct	Methods			
		written (w)	auditory (a)	pictorial (p)	video-based (f)
AulT	Auditory Reasoning (AR)		Tonal series (MA4) Disarranged sentences (DS)		
	Auditory Memory (AM)		Rhythm repro - duction (RH) Audiobook (AU)		
	Auditory Perception (AP)		Repeated tones (MA1) Masked words (MW)		
Emotion Tests	Social/emotion perception/ understanding		GVEESS (see Banse & Scherer, 1996)		PONS (Rosenthal et al., 1979)

Nonverbal social intelligence tasks

a)   Memory for couples (SMp1, Weis & Süß, 2007)

Subjects regard pairs of heterosexual couples and pairs of colleagues. After the presentation occurring in blocks, subjects have to choose the correct partner of a presented target person (multiple choice).

b)   Memory for social situations-pictures (SMp2)

Subjects are asked to memorize social information about a situation that is presented through meaningful sequences of pictures. Afterwards, subjects have to answer questions given in MC and open-ended format.

c)   Memory for situations in videos (SMf1 & 2; Weis & Süß, 2007)

Subjects are instructed to memorize social information that is presented in videos as accurately as possible. Immediately afterwards, they have to answer questions that are presented in MC and open-ended format.

d)   Person perception in pictures (SPp1)

Subjects have to click on the head of a target person presented in pictures as quickly as the person has been identified. The target person is previously presented in close-up. In the test items, the target person is shown in different settings wearing different clothes.

e)   Interaction perception in pictures (SPp2)

Subjects have to perceive previously presented social facts that become obvious through observing the body language of the presented people (e.g. decide whether in several pictures, people have eye contact or not).

f)   Person perception in videos (SPf1)

Subjects are instructed to react by pressing the space bar as soon as they recognized a previously presented person in video sequences. Equal to SPp1, persons are shown in different settings and wearing different clothes.

g)   Interaction perception in videos (SPf2)

Subjects are instructed to react to certain social facts in body language as quickly and accurately as possible. The social fact (e.g. reacting on expressions of joy) is presented in advance of the test items.

Working Memory Tasks

We administered three working memory tasks (WM tasks) in order to answer the question of whether systematic variance that is explained with the Aul tasks is due to working memory or not. Three tasks representing different contents (verbal, numerical, figural) were adapted from the Oberauer et al. (2003) battery. Oberauer et al. (2000, 2003) base their model on facet theory and differentiate working memory theoretically along the dimensions content (kind of material: verbal, numerical, figural) and function (cognitive resources: simultaneous storage and transformation, coordination, monitoring). The verbal and numerical content and the functions *simultaneous storage and transformation* and *coordination* could not be differentiated empirically. The tasks we used in our study can be classified in the simultaneous storage and transformation domain applying the different kinds of material (see content facet). However, we did not administer all of the WMC tasks in the original version such as described in Oberauer et al. (2003; see also Süß et al., 2002) but instead used the two of the tasks, memory updating numerical (WM-MUn) and wordspan (WM_WSp), with the changes introduced by Sander (2005, see task description). Additional changes concern an adaptive version, which was programmed to save test time, since the standard version takes about 45 minutes for each task. We only had about this time available for three tasks. The algorithm we chose required subjects to answer three of five items correctly to proceed to the next level. In the case of failing, they went down to the next lower level. Successful completion (=answer at least three and at most five items correctly) promoted them to the next higher level. If they once went down, they did not have the possibility to get up again. The completion of each task took about 10 to 20 minutes depending on the best performing participant. The higher the level reached by the best person the longer the test took for the whole group since the tests were administered in groups. The three tasks are described in the following.

a)   Memory updating numerical (WM_MUn; Sander, 2005; adapted from Salthouse, Babcock, & Shaw, 1991)
A nine cell (3 x 3) matrix appears on the screen. Each item uses a certain number of active and inactive cells. The inactive cells in an item circle are shaded in grey. Task difficulty increases with the number of active cells. Within the active cells, numbers (1 to 9) appear successively. Following this initial number presentation, numerical operations are indicated by arrows appearing and disappearing in the cells where the numbers were presented previously. An arrow pointing upwards indicated that subjects have to add "+1" to the number that appeared previously, an arrow pointing downwards advises subjects to subtract "-1" from the previously presented number. The result has to be memorized and applied as a new value for the cell serving as the starting point for the next operation. After the end of a number-arrow sequence, a question mark appears in each of the previously active cells.

Subjects are instructed to type in the number representing the current value of the cell. Presentation time for initial elements and for numerical operations is fixed at 1000 ms. The interval between presentations of elements lasts for about 1500 ms. Level ranges from dealing with only two active cells (level 1) to up to seven active cells (level 6).

b)   Word span (WM_DSp; Sander, 2005; adapted from Craik, 1986, Alpha span)

Words were presented sequentially. One word was visible for 1800 ms. After the sequence of words had been completed, the first letters of the words had to be repeated in the order of their physical size. That differed from the original task (Craik, 1986), which required subjects to repeat letters of words in alphabetical order. Subjects had the possibility to correct the last letter when they recognized being wrong with their answer. After each letter they had to press the "return" bar. Correction of letters was then not possible. The task intended to measure simultaneous storage and processing (or coordination) with verbal material. Levels ranged from memorizing three words (level 1) up to nine words (level 7).

c)   Dot span (WM_DSp; Oberauer, 1993; see also Oberauer et al., 2000; Süß et al., 2002)

Dots appeared sequentially in cells of a 10 x 10 matrix for one second each. The inter-stimulus interval took 500 ms. Subjects were instructed to remember the position of the dots as accurately as possible. After the presentation of dots was completed, they were instructed to imagine the pattern of the dots that would appear as if they were all visible at the same time. They had to indicate whether that pattern was a) vertically symmetrical, b) horizontal symmetrical or neither of both. The second task was to click with the mouse in the cells of the matrix where the dots appeared previously. Levels ranged from memorizing two points (level 1) to six points (level 5).

Baseline Measures

As baseline measure for social perception tasks requiring the keyboard, Simple Reaction Time (SRT), described in chapter 6.2.3 was used. Mouse speed was used as a reference and baseline instrument for social perception tasks requiring the mouse (see chapter 6.2.3, first study). Since the readspeed measure we applied in the first study was problematic in terms of the combined score (reading comprehension measured through three questions at the end of the text combined with the speed of reading each word), and motoric speed played a major role (for each word a key had to be pressed), I decided to use an alternative readspeed task. This task should serve as a baseline measure for the social perception tasks dealing with written material (e.g. judgment whether the sentence is emotional/social or neutral or whether it contains specified socially relevant words). The new readspeed task leaned on WM tasks (see Daneman & Carpenter, 1980; Turner & Engle, 1989) and was also used in WM research (see Oberauer et al., 2000; Sander, 2005). Sixty sentences and an additional four example sentences from the reading span task (Daneman & Carpenter, 1980; Turner & Engle, 1989) were selected and simplified when they were judged as being too complex. They were shortened in case they were too long. The sentences contain 8 to 22 syllables. Subjects had to decide for each sentence whether it was true or false. However, in contrast to the task used in WM research, in this study, subjects had to judge the sentences only by pressing a key as soon as they identified the sentence as wrong or correct. In the WM task they had to write down the last words of the sentences in their presentation order. The reaction time for each judgment was recorded. The judgment should guarantee reading comprehension.

Complementary Materials

Questionnaire of Personal Data

The biographical questionnaire of the first study was improved and complemented through questions concerning the family background (e.g. number of children and their age), the sight abilities, and hearing abilities (selected questions of the questionnaire we applied in the first study). Questions with respect to hearing abilities concerned normal hearing ability vs. restricted hearing ability. If hearing ability was judged as restricted then detailed information should be provided. Subjects were instructed to rate their musical ability and to specify in which kind of music (singing, playing an instrument, musical school) they have been engaged in and for how long.

Self-report Questionnaires

We applied a number of self-report questionnaires. In addition to the instruments that were applied in the first study (Questionnaire of Computer Experience, see Süß, 1996; NEO-FFI, Borkenau & Ostendorf, 1993; and the SI self-report Prototypical Acts on SI, Amelang et al., 1989; see also chapter 2.2.3), in this study subjects also had to work on the Schutte Emotional Intelligence Scale (SEIS, Schutte et al., 1998), an empathy scale (see Enzmann, 1996), a depression questionnaire (Alter & Muff, 1979), and an altruism questionnaire (Fahrenberg et al., 2001). Four times during the study they had to complete a three-item strain questionnaire.

Long-term Memory

At the end of the second test session, a long-term memory test was administered with questions concerning information that was presented in each scenario, in either self-presentation or scenes. Questions were representative concerning method (written, auditory, pictorial, film) and contents of questions (cognition, emotion, relationship). Questions had to be answered in MC and open-ended format. In addition, we presented extracts of scenes of each modality, and subjects had to indicate of which scenario these were part. We provided help presenting the faces of the target scenario persons with the data projector.

7.2.3 Implementation

Equipment

The equipment was the same as in the first study (see chapter 6.2.4). This time we tested only in the computer pool of the Institute of Psychology, University of Magdeburg. With the exception of the questionnaires and the BIS test, for the presentation of all tasks the software program WMC (latest optimized version 0.18, using EWX 0.22). Again, reaction times were recorded by the program. The answers of the video-based and the written memory tasks were collected with answer sheets (paper-pencil), as were the SMa1 and the SMp2. The self-presentations of the target persons in our scenario tasks were shown with PowerPoint XP as the WMC program did not allow tone and video to be presented simultaneously. The data projector was used to make the target persons self-presentation available to all subjects without restrictions. The tone was boosted by speakers (Logitech Z3 M/N S-0085B; 50-60Hz).

Procedure

The application of all tests took about 12 hours. The time was split into two test sessions, each one lasting six hours including breaks. Session 1 always occurred before session 2. The test takers could choose between different possibilities (different days and times of day) of being tested. Subjects were tested in groups of up to 15 people each session. The sessions were conducted by different investigators (altogether six women). With the exception of sessions with only five participants or less, in every test session, two instructors were present. Instructors received a training on how the test was to be administered. They were all familiar with the test and the technical equipment. After having finished the second test session, each participant could choose a reward of either 60 Euro or 30 Euro together with a detailed written feedback of the test results. Again, psychology students had the possibility to record hours as test participant. Each session was subdivided into four blocks including three ten-minute breaks between the blocks. During the breaks, subjects had the possibility to recover, to refresh with some drinks and snacks, and to go outside the building to get some fresh air. To ensure motivation and change, the tasks of different types of material, different abilities, and the questionnaires were varied. Perception tasks, WM tasks, and parts of the Berlin Intelligence Structure Test that required the most focused attention were administered at the beginning of the blocks.

7.3 Results With Respect to Social Intelligence

7.3.1 Social Understanding Tasks (SU)

Table 7-2 addresses the psychometric properties for both target-scored and consensus-scored scenario scales. Psychometric properties are indicated for a selected number of items (see scale construction, chapter 6.4). The unreduced number of items is reported in parentheses, as is the reliability value for the complete unreduced scale.

Table 7-2: Psychometrics: Social Understanding

Scale	Item number[1]	Item mean (SD)	Skewness/ Curtosis[2]	Range (min.– max.)	r_{it}-range	Cronbach's Alpha 2nd study	1st study
Target scores							
written	37 (115)	-2.87 (.48)	-.08/-.37	-4.07 to -1.78	.14 - .48	.77 (.44)	.80
auditory	61 (152)	-2.26 (.42)	-.35/-.20	-3.40 to -1.33	.12 - .48	.80 (.61)	.73
pictorial	37 (113)	-2.26 (.50)	-.32/-.05	-3.53 to -1.08	.13 - .37	.73 (.47)	.69
video-based	74 (124)	-2.15 (.40)	-.57/1.19	-3.60 to -1.29	.12 - .42	.84 (.72)	.77
perso-nality	55 (72)	-2.35 (.51)	-.43/.26	-4.01 to -1.20	.15 - .45	.84 (.79)	.71
Consensus scores							
written	53 (115)	.23 (.03)	-.47/.42	.15 - .30	.10 - .35	.76 (.58)	.72
auditory	97 (152)	.24 (.02)	-.74/1.81	.14 - .29	.12 - .34	.83 (.74)	.69
pictorial	64 (113)	.23 (.03)	-.67/.71	.15 - .30	.12 - .36	.80 (.73)	.58
video-based	85 (124)	.23 (02)	-.82/.84	.15 - .28	.11 - .42	.83 (.79)	.60
perso-nality	67 (72)	.26 (.03)	-.61/.46	.16 - .33	.10 - .39	.83 (.82)	.69

Note. N=175; [1] In parentheses, unreduced item number (without selection); [2] Skewness is presented first; the second value represents curtosis, SE (Skewness): .18; SE (Curtosis): .37; r_{it} range= Item- total correlation range; SUpconsensus, SUfconsensus, SUpkconsensus and SUatarget are trimmed because of outliers.

On average, the written items are the most difficult (significant on p<.001 with respect to all other scales). The video-based items are the easiest for the subjects (significant on p<.01 with respect to all scales). These difficulty differences are not equally obvious for the consensus scores; the item mean is almost the same for all scales. In interpreting this result, one should not ignore that consensus scoring contributes to homogeneity. Reliability could be improved for all scales except for the target-scored written SU scale. All in all, the results prove evidence for a successful scale modification and confirm the choice of using only rating scales. However, the larger amount of items that were included in the scales may be a reason for the reliability differences. In the first study, the auditory SU scale using target scoring included only 21 items, the pictorial 15 items and the video-based 41 items. On the contrary, the written SU scale (weighted difference scores) with 19 items had a higher reliability than the same scale with 37 items in the second study. Thus, item number is not the only reason for better internal consistency values. Table 7-3 shows the correlations between the SU scales including both scoring methods.

Table 7-3: Correlations Between Social Understanding Scales

	1.	2.	3.	4.	5.	6.	7.	8.	9.
1. writt_t	1.00								
2. audi_t	**.27**	1.00							
3. pict_t	.34	.55	1.00						
4. film_t	.49	.43	.60	1.00					
5. pers_t	.62	.43	.46	.49	1.00				
6. writt_c	**.16***	.49	.44	.40	.37	1.00			
7. audi_c	.34	.69	.57	.59	.43	.60	1.00		
8. pict_c	.32	.45	.61	.60	.41	.53	.62	1.00	
9. film_c	.33	.50	.60	.78	.45	.53	.67	.66	1.00
10. pers_c	.20	.28	.39	.51	.36	.50	.48	.64	.65

Note. t=target scores; c=consensus scores; *The correlation is significant at the 0.05 level (2-tailed); All other correlations are significant at the 0.01 level (2-tailed); listwise deletion

Target- and consensus-scored scales correlate moderately to highly and thus confirm the findings obtained in the first study. These results are not in line with the correlations around chance level that have been reported in the literature (see chapter 2.2.3). An explanation for the results of this study may be yielded by the selection of task material and of the related questions. In order to avoid individual biases, we chose only material when a group of six to seven experienced people agreed. With this procedure, although involving only a small number of people, we relied on a consensus as well. This may be a reason for the moderate to high relationship of target and consensus scores. In addition, I want to direct the attention to two values (bold numbers). First, the written consensus score and the written target score correlate only with .16 (see Table 7-3, bold number). This means that the score built according to the target person's answers does not measure the same as the score reflecting the common opinion of the group does. A possible reason may be that written material does not provide as much information (socially relevant cues) as do the remaining materials. Therefore, the subjects may be more in danger to interpret something in a different way compared to the target person. Dynamic material, particularly video-based and auditory material, should yield more cues that can be interpreted much more clearly. On the one hand, this assumption confirmed by the difficulty values of the scores (the written scale is the most difficult, see Table 7-2) resulting in lower correlations between consensus and target scores. On the other hand, in the first study the written SU scores measured with different scoring methods correlated with .82. However, taking the same selection of items for each score reduces the correlation to .37 (orientated on the target score selection) and .28 (orientated on the consensus score selection). Second, the correlation between the auditory and the written scale, both target scores, is surprisingly low. Again, this may stem from differences in answering written items compared to the more social cues containing scores, including the auditory score. Another interesting result becomes apparent when comparing the correlations between the personality scale and the SU material scales. In the first study, we had zero correlations between these scales and wondered why. In this study, we find moderate to high correlations between the personality judgment and the SI material scales. The differences between the studies may be either due to the sample or to the selection of material being in agreement with the target persons' personality self-report.

The selected items (target scores) were also used to examine the content of the questions (cognition, emotion, and relationship to other people). Test takers found it easier to judge the relationship to others and most difficult to assess the cognition of the target persons. In all three content scales, judging written material was the most difficult. The intercorrelations between the material-specific content scales yield an explanantion for the low correlation between the auditory scale and the written scale. The low corrclation value seems to be due to the written emotion items. They show zero correlations with both the auditory cognition and the auditory relationship scale. In summary, people who are good at judging a target person's emotions were also good at judging his or her cognitions and relationships to other people, and were able to make a general judgment about their personality. These results including the intercorrelations between material scales indicate a homogeneous ability. For more information on these scales see Seidel (2007) and Weis (2008).

7.3.2 Social Memory Tasks (SM)

Memory for Conversations (Social Memory-Auditory, SMa1)

SMa1 was already administered in the first study; the descriptive statistics of the modified version are shown in Table 7-4. Neither the total scale nor the subscales are normally distributed. The following reasons for the distribution problem can be excluded: (1) This is not a perception task in which non-normality usually is more common; (2) There are no sample specific problems. (3) There are neither outliers that cause the skewed distribution. The distribution can be attributed to the fact that 43.5% of the test takers got a score between 60% and 70% correct, but there are also some participants who have rather low values in the task.

Table 7-4: Psychometrics of the Task Memory for Conversations (SMa1)

Conversations	Mean (SD)	Skewness/ Curtosis [1)	Range (min.-max.)	r_{it} range	Cronbach's Alpha
1. conversation	.70 (.20)	-.69/.16	.00 - 1.00	.19 - .31	.48 (6 items)
2. conversation	.71 (.22)	-.85/.22	.10 - 1.00	.23 - .46	.56 (5 items)
3. conversation	.58 (.25)	-.29/-.64	.00 - 1.00	.17 - .28	.39 (4 items)
4. conversation	.62 (.19)	-.32/-.41	.14 - 1.00	.13 - .31	.45 (7 items)
5. conversation	.49 (.17)	-.19/.43	.06 - 1.00	.12 - .43	.57 (9 items)
6. conversation	.59 (.21)	-.26/-.04	.00 - 1.00	-.01 - .17	.20 (5 items)
Total score	.61 (.13)	-.55/.07	.21 - .88	.11 - .45	.78 (36 items)
Reduced total score	.62 (.14)	-.58/.13	.20 - .91	.17 - .44	.79 (32 items)

Note.[1)]Skewness is presented first; the second value represents curtosis. SE (Skewness) is .18; SE (Curtosis) is .37

Although the task was rather easy (with the exception of the fifth conversation), the full range of scores is represented (see column "range"). The single conversations have rather low reliability values, which is not surprising because each contains only a few items. The total score of the memory task has a good reliability value (often in memory tasks we reach only reliabilities around .60). With half the items, we reached the same reliability score as in the first study and saved further test time through converting open-ended items into MC items.

Table 7-5 shows that most of the conversations intercorrelate moderately, indicating that they measure a common underlying ability. Higher correlations may not be reached because of the different contents of the conversations, which are expected to produce intra- and interindividual differences (for context effects see e.g. Fiedler, 1991).

Table 7-5: Correlations Between the Conversations of Memory for Conversations (SMa1)

	1. conv.	2. conv.	3. conv.	4. conv.	5. conv.
2. conv.	.33**	1.00			
3. conv.	.17*	.23**	1.00		
4. conv.	.27**	.34**	.19*	1.00	
5. conv.	.39**	.39**	.29**	.38**	1.00
6. conv.	.26**	.22**	.15	.12	.26**

Note. conv.=conversation; Spearman correlations, listwise deletion, N=175; ** Correlation is significant at the 0.01 level (2-tailed); *Correlation is significant at the 0.05 level (2-tailed)

Memory for Voices (Social Memory-Auditory, SMa2)

Psychometrics for the second social auditory memory task are displayed in Table 7-6. None of the scales are normally distributed but deviations are only minor. The test is not reliable enough, even when the least reliable items are excluded.

Table 7-6: Psychmetrics of the Task Memory for Voices (SMa2)

Scores	Mean (SD)	Skewness/ Curtosis [1]	Range (min.–max.)	r_{it} range	Cronbach's Alpha
Total score example included	.50 (.15)	.06/-.42	.17 - .83	-.02 - .13	.20 (13 items)
Total score without example	.52 (.14)	-.04/-.29	.15 - .85	.00 - .14	.20 (12 items)
Reduced score	.52 (.25)	-.11/-.70	.00 - 1.00	.09 - .19	.30 (5 items)

Note. The 13 items: example included,; r_{it} range=item-total correlation; [1] Skewness is presented first; the second value represents curtosis. SE (Skewness) is .18; SE (Curtosis) is .37

Reliability analysis was performed again involving only high performer on this task. This avoids error variance that may be caused by guessing the answer by low performers. However, reliability does not improve when splitting up the sample. The reason of the low reliability is not yet clear. The minutes we took during the investigations as well as my personal memories indicate that subjects were particularly attentive during their work on this task. The task difficulty does not seem to be the problem neither regarding the mean value (M=.50) nor the standard deviation (SD=.15); both are almost ideal. Conclusively, the items do not form a uniform scale but seem to measure something different. Some subjects seem to be better in recognizing voices in dyads, others in small groups, others in male, female or mixed groups. There is no logical pattern. According to Ambady and Rosenthal (1992, 1993), nonverbal behavior of half a minute duration allows observers to form an impression of a person's affective state and interpersonal attitudes that is highly correlated with objective criteria or long-term observation judgments. Thus, it should not have an effect giving more time to listen to the target voice in the conversation. A possible reason for the problem may be that the conversations are so interesting that test takers pay more attention to the content than to the voices. This hypothesis contradicts the good performance test takers showed in their reaction on paraverbal cues in the SPa1, which also applies to quite interesting conversations. However, whether or not the content of the interesting social conversation has an influence on the task performance could be examined using neutral (e.g., technical, science) topics. Another reason for the findings may be that several abilities get mixed up: First, subjects have to identify several voices presented in a conversation; Second, they have to keep them in mind; Third, they have to compare each of the presented voices with each of the five distractors. Thus, discrimination, encoding, working memory and comparison are required in one task. One could try to distinguish the mentioned abilities, break down the task in separate units, and investigate the performance of each step. Further suggestions concern the application of this task with more items of each type, and to test the effect complexity has (to many different voices that are displayed). The systematic testing with a reduced number of distractors seems to be worthwhile as well, accepting a higher chance level. Another interesting study concerns the introduction of a baseline measure, presenting only single voices of a length between 30 and 60 seconds and then different numbers of distractors. This procedure excludes the interference that is produced through hearing different voices in a conversation.

Memory for Correspondence (Social Memory-Written, SMw1 & SMw2)

The written social memory task is a combined task (see chapter 6.4.1): part one deals with one-sided correspondence, part two with two-sided correspondence. Table 7-7 gives an impression of the psychometric properties for each of the two parts, for a total score, and for each single correspondence.

Table 7-7: Psychometrics of the Written Social Memory Tasks (SMw1+2)

Scale	Mean (SD)	Skewness/ Curtosis [1]	Range (min.-max.)	r_{it} range	Cronbach's Alpha
Corres 1	.83 (.14)	-1.21/2.45	.17 - 1.00	.07 - .36	.46 (9 items)
Corres 2	.85 (.12)	-1.32/2.60	.30 - 1.00	.06 - .42	.44 (11 items)
Corres 3	.69 (.18)	-.34/-.28	.08 - 1.00	.14 - .23	.35 (6 Items)
Corres 4	.69 (.17)	-.19/-.47	.25 - 1.00	.02 - .36	.38 (6 Items)
Corres 5	.78 (.18)	-1.25/ 1.66	.07 - 1.00	.24 - .40	.58 (7 Items)
Corres 6	.67 (.16)	-.43/-.18	.15 - .95	.13 - .35	.51 (10 Items)
SMw1	.80 (.11)	-1.19/2.36	.32 - .98	.09 - .48	.67 (25 items)
SMw2	.71 (.14)	-.66/.07	.26 - .98	.04 - .40	.74 (23 items)
Total score SMw	.76 (.11)	-.86/1.20	.30 - .97	.02 - .43	.81 (48 items)
Reduced total score SMw	.74 (.12)	-.92/1.50	.23 - .96	.15 - .41	.81 (42 items)

Note. SMw1=part 1, one-sided correspondence; SMw2 = part 2, two-sided correspondence; N=175; [1] Skewness is presented first; the second value represents curtosis, SE (Skewness) is .18; SE (Curtosis) is .37; corres= correspondence; reduced score: exclusion of unreliable items

The total score (with and without reduction) is normally distributed whereas none of the single scales and excerpts follows normal distribution. Comparable to SMa1, this task is rather easy; in each conversation test taker's performance is above average. Single correspondence seems to be even easier than two-sided correspondence. In the first study, test taker's mean value was .49 (SD=.13, range: .17; .93). Conversion of two-thirds of the items to MC items and increasing the time subjects have to answer the questions, seem to have reduced the task difficulty. The worst result on average is around 25% correct. The reliability of the total score could be improved from .74 (selected items of first study scale) to .81 (see Table 7-7). Part 1 (one-sided correspondence) and part 2 (two-sided correspondence) correlate with .57 (N=175, Spearman correlations). The intercorrelations between the single correspondences are presented in Table 7-8. The six one-sided and two-sided correspondences correlate moderately to highly and indicate a common underlying factor. There are no differences in the strength of correlations within one-sided and two-sided correspondence and in correlations across different types of correspondence.

Table 7-8: Correlations of the Correspondences of Written Social Memory (SMw1+2)

	corres1	corres2	corres3	corres4	corres5
corres1	1.00				
corres2	.29	1.00			
corres3	.32	.32	1.00		
corres4	.33	.33	.36	1.00	
corres5	.24	.47	.26	.38	1.00
corres6	.28	.44	.37	.42	.55

Note. Spearman correlation; All correlation coefficients are significant at the 0.01 level (2-tailed); listwise deletion; N= 175; corres= correspondence

7.3.3 Social Perception Tasks (SP)

The psychometric properties of the language-based perception tasks will be presented for the original tasks and for the baseline corrected task scores. As I will show later, the baseline measures relevant for the language-based tasks (readspeed and simple reaction time) are correlated with AcI. Consequently, baseline correction eventually subtracts substantial variance. Therefore, analysis is done first without the use of corrected values. The relationship between baseline measures, SI and AcI will be addressed in chapter 7.3.4. Analysis was done for both reaction time measures and accuracy scores. Reaction time values were trimmed according to the steps described in chapter 5.2.3.

Perception of Social Facts in Conversations (Social Perception-Auditory, SPa1)

The trimmed values correlated at least .92 with the original mean values. Most of them correlated with more than .98 justifying the use of the trimmed values. Table 7-9 presents mean values and standard deviations of reaction time values for the scales and gives some information about the distribution, internal consistency, and item-total correlation. In some cases, practice items were included in the analysis after ensuring that they were not different in mean reaction time and proportion of mistakes.

Table 7-9: Psychometrics of Perception of Social Facts in Conversations (SPa1)

Scales	N	Number of items	Mean (SD)	Skewness/ Curtosis [1]	Range (min.-max)	r_{it} range	Cronb. Alpha
laughter	175	9	574.82 (91.74)	.48/-.21	404.33 - 835.00	.20 - .52	.72
names	175	12	615.13 (79.24)	.30/-.19	439.33 - 820.00	.25 - .58	.77
agreement	175	7	804.70 (160.98)	.36/.14	416.33 - 1230.00	.25 - .55	.72
voices	175	11	581.68 (118.86)	1.00/1.15	353.91 - 955.00	.46 - .71	.89
rejection	173	5	617.41 (108.53)	.53/.03	403.40 - 950.00	.25 - .48	.65
filling words	172	7	803.41 (226.34)	1.12/1.02	433.00 - 1550.00	.55 - .74	.86
change of gender	175	19	695.74 (85.75)	.01/-.23	493.88 - 905.00	.15 - .47	.70
questions	166	4[1]	1415.43 (259.40)	-.62/-.15	700.00 - 1912.00	.46 - .61	.72
different interaction partners	175	9	980.59 (192.49)	.27/.22	543.00 - 1550.00	.32 - .72	.78
Total scale	171	93	00 (.55)	.28/-.22	-1.24 - 1.59	.05 - .52	.89
Reduced total scale	163	85	00 (.60)	.36/-.04	-1.33 - 1.79	.17 - .52	.90

Note. [1] One item was excluded because of bad reliability (16_40); Cronb. Alpha=Cronbach's Alpha; [1]Skewness is presented first; the second value represents curtosis. SE (Skewness) is .18; SE (Curtosis) is .37

Reactions to questions took the longest time followed by stimuli of recognizing a person switching from one interaction partner to another. These two conversations were assumed to be the most complex as well. The easiest task was to react on laughter or on a single (baby) voice. This seems to indicate that reactions are fastest to easy paraverbal stimuli. However, in the first study results were quite different. Reaction to laughter took comparatively longer (see Table 6-5) whereas test takers reacted fastest to filling words (mean=555.44, SD=102.80) and agreement (mean=646.26, SD=74.23). Without including the two very complex conversations just mentioned reactions to these two scales, filling words and agreement took the longest. The differences may be due to the sample. All Cronbach's Alpha values are satisfactory, particularly with regard to the low number of items that is included in some of the scales. The total scale shows a high reliability value. High internal consistencies are common to speed tasks. However, reacting to complex auditory stimuli within conversations is different from reactions to easily discriminable, highly predictable stimuli we are used to with AcI tasks. The reduced total score excludes the *questions* scale and some other items that do not show sufficient reliability in the total scale. Total and reduced score correlate with .98. Data indicate that the question scale is different to all other scales. A reason may be that only in reacting to questions, anticipation is required (i.e., react as soon as they recognize a person asking a question). Whether the person actually rises a question is only clear when the question is finished. The non-normality of the *filling words* scale seem to be due to the long reaction times of some test takers which becomes evident in a positively skewed distribution. I decided to maintain these longer reaction times in the single scales because variance should not be reduced until summarized to a total score. As far as the subscale filling words will be included in analysis, we will take attention to the results concerning this scale. Table 7-10 shows the intercorrelations between the subscales of the auditory perception task.

Table 7-10: Correlations Between Subscales of the Task Perception of Social Facts in Conversations (SPa1)

	laughter	names	agree	voices	reject	filling	gender	quest
laughter	1.00							
names	.19*	1.00						
agree	.11	.31**	1.00					
voices	.22**	.50**	.34**	1.00				
reject	.20*	.45**	.29**	.41**	1.00			
filling	.13	.23**	.30**	.25**	.18*	1.00		
gender	.19*	.47**	.35**	.48**	.28**	.29**	1.00	
quest	.14	.01	-.02	.05	-.12	-.08	-.01	1.00
interact	.20**	.31**	.22**	.17*	.11	.10	.31**	.03

Note. *Correlation is significant at the 0.05 level (2-tailed); **Correlation is significant at the 0.01 level (2-tailed); listwise deletion, N=163; agree=agreement; reject=rejection; filling=filling words; gender=change of gender talking; quest=rising questions; interact=communication with different interaction partners

With the exception of the *question* scale and some single correlation values (interaction scale, filling words, and laughter), Table 7-10 shows a pattern of moderate to high intercorrelations, indicating common systematic variance. The correlations with the question scale confirm the findings being revealed through reliability analysis. Therefore, in the following analysis the reduced total score of SPa1 is used. In the future, further improved, accuracy scores of the tasks may provide additional interesting information, especially with respect to the scales which show sufficient reliability, namely dealing with names, agreement, and the reaction to different interaction partners.

Perception of Social Cues/Emotions in Voices (SPa2) and GVEESS Sentences

Table 7-11 presents the psychometric properties of the second social auditory perception task (SPa2) and the selection of sentences taken from the Swiss data bank of auditorily expressed emotions (GVEESS, see chapter 2.6.5). The descriptive statistics of SPa2 are presented on the top of the table, the GVEESS data below. The statistics concern the scales after item selection (see chapter 5).

Table 7-11: Psychometrics of the Task Perception of Paraverbal Social Cues/Emotions in Voices (SPa2) and the GVEESS Sentences

Scales	Number of items	Skewness/ Curtosis[1]	Range (min.–max.)	Mean (SD)	r_{it} range	Cronbach's Alpha
SPa2						
emotional vs. neutral	7	.06/-.69	579.25 – 2900.00	1800.91 (528.30)	.32 - .58	.74
positive vs. negative	9	.51/-.25	480.00 – 1910.00	1124.63 (329.95)	.58 - .74	.87
irony vs. anger	6	.31/.01	631.25 – 3042.00	1596.11 (450.43)	.46 - .66	.79
Total real	22	.29/.40	-2.07– 2.26	.00 (.74)	.33 - .73	.91
GVEESS						
joy vs. anger	9	.70/-.08	220.00 – 1235.00	633.58 (238.55)	.41 - .62	.79
boredom vs. pride	10	.96/.74	270.00 – 1580.00	776.29 (283.10)	.57 - .70	.88
contempt vs. interest	10	.62/.00	420.00 – 1900.00	984.47 (342.36)	.46 - .62	.82
Total fictitious	29	.75/.26	-1.53 – 2.42	.00 (.85)	.42 - .75	.92
Total scale	*51*	*.63/.51*	*-1.57 – 2.16*	*.00 (.70)*	*.32 - .71*	*.94*

Note. N=174, item-total correlations and alpha values belong to selected values (unreliable items excluded, see number of items), mean values concern total scales including all items; [1] Skewness is presented first; the second value represents curtosis. SE (Skewness) is .18; SE (Curtosis) is .37. Trimmed values correlate with original values at least with .96.

Interestingly, reactions to emotions displayed in realistic sentences (SPa2) take much longer than reactions to emotions presented in acted sentences (GVEESS sentences). This difference in time is probably due to the much clearer expressions that are made in acted situations (see e.g. chapter 2.6.4). The GVEESS sentences worked quite well; only one item had to be eliminated. With regard to the SPa2 task, the most difficult decision was between emotional and neutral sentences. This is in line with Noller (2001), who reports that neutral messages were more often incorrectly decoded compared to emotional messages. However, the relatively lower recognition rate may also be due to getting used to a new task as this was the first part. Reliability is sufficient for the subscales and very good for the total scales.

Some of the SPa2 items had to be excluded since they did not differentiate well between test takers and reactions were outside the allowed time interval (see chapter 6.4.4). Total RT scores of SPa2 and GVEESS correlate with .56. The SPa2 scales show accuracy values between 69% correct and 77% correct, the GVEESS scales proportion correct is between 82% and 89%. This confirms the results obtained in other studies that also led to focus more on acted than on natural sentences. Natural conversation extracts mainly include not only one distinct and clear emotion but contain several emotions in different proportions. Therefore, it should be much more difficult to identify or recognize a natural emotion than an acted one. However, what we need in our daily interactions with other people is the ability to deal appropriately with that emotion mixture. Table 7-12 addresses the intercorrelations of the scales. The GVEESS scales correlate stronger with one another than the SPa2 task (see shaded cells, Table 7-12). Reasons for the differences may be that the GVEESS acted emotions are comparably less ambiguous and thus produce less interference. The intercorrelations between SPa2 and GVEESS indicates that both tasks measure parts of the same underlying ability.

Table 7-12: Correlations Between Subscales of the Task Perception of Social Cues/Emotions in Voices and GVEESS Scales

	emotional vs. neutral	positive vs. negative	irony vs. anger	joy vs. anger	boredom vs. pride
emotional vs. neutral	1.00				
positive vs. negative	.37**	1.00			
irony vs. anger	.22**	.40**	1.00		
joy vs. anger	.31**	.47**	.47**	1.00	
boredom vs. pride	.19*	.39**	.35**	.60**	1.00
contempt vs. interest	.26**	.38**	.34**	.50**	.63**

Note. **Correlation is significant at the 0.01 level (2-tailed); *Correlation is significant at the 0.05 level (2-tailed); listwise deletion, N=174

Perception of Social Target Stimuli in Text Extracts (SPw1)

Table 7-13 presents an overview of the descriptive statistics of the reaction time scores. Subscales were formed with regard to the two levels of difficulty (reaction to one cue=level 1 vs. reaction to two cues=level 2). Paying attention to two aspects (reaction to two questions) takes more time on average. Therefore, a combined score was built of the mean value of the z-standardized scores of the two levels. Reliability values of the RT time scores indicate a successful scale modification, since, in the first study, the total mean of the statements part had an Alpha of .83, the questions part of .80. The reaction time level scores correlate with

.82 (p<.0001). The descriptives of the accuracy scores can be found in Seidel (2007). Total RT and accuracy scores correlate with zero (r=-.08). Being fast seems to have nothing to do with being accurate in the task. Thus, there does not seem to be a speed-accuracy trade-off.

Table 7-13: Psychometrics of the Task Perception of Social Target Stimuli in Text Extracts (SPw1)

Scales	Number of items	Skewness/ Curtosis [2]	Range (min.–max.)	Mean (SD)	r_{it} range	Cronbach's Alpha
Level 1	28	1.04/1.39	1694.08 - 8879.74	3971.91 (1303.39)	.38 - .76	.95
Level 2	30	.74/.80	2613.10 - 10606.31	5314.21 (1515.48)	.52 - .77	.96
Total	58	.76/.63	2178.65 - 9483.61	4670.40 (1341.03)	.39 - .77	.98
Total, combined score	58	.80/.72	-1.76 – 3.43	.00 (.95)	---	---

Note. N=182; rit range=item-total correlation; [1]Score after item selection. Original score and trimmed score correlate with .996. [2]Skewness is presented first; the second value represents curtosis. SE (Skewness) is .18; SE (Curtosis) is .36

Perception of Social Content in Text Extracts (Social Perception-Written, SPw 2)

The descriptives of the SPw2 reaction time scores are presented in Table 8-19. Accuracy scores can be found in Seidel (2007). On average, test takers need about the same time to decide whether a sentence is neutral or emotional and whether it expresses a positive or a negative emotion. The scores correlate with .82 (p< .001). Therefore, there is no need for building an aggregate of z-standardized values in order to get a total score. Reliabilities are all very high.

Table 7-14: Psychometrics of the Task Perception of Social Content in Text Extracts (SPw2)

Scales	Number of items	Skewness/ Curtosis [2]	Range (min.–max.)	Mean (SD)	r_{it} range	Cronbach's Alpha
Neutral- emotional	30	.48/.08	824.02 – 4058.83	2057.66 (522.20)	.53 - .80	.97
Positive– negative	30	.33/.19	869.55 – 3404.14	1995.10 (616.19)	.56 - .73	.96
Total	60	.29/.05	846.40 – 3689.65	2019.45 (496.73)	.55 - .78	.98

Note. [1]Score after item selection; [2]Skewness is presented first; the second value represents curtosis. SE (Skewness) is .18; SE (Curtosis) is .36; r_{it} range=item-total correlation; Original and trimmed values correlate with .98.

7.3.4 Baseline Correction of Social Perception Tasks

We used baseline measures to correct the social perception tasks for simple reactions that cover the actual performance. The written social perception tasks were controlled by a readspeed test. On the auditory SP tasks, the video-based SP tasks, and one of the pictorial SP, SPp2, the SRT task was applied as a control measure. Since the SPp1 makes use of the computer mouse, we administered a mouse speed test to control for dealing with a computer mouse (see chapter 6.2.3). Each score formed by the baseline measures was normally distributed and excelled by high alpha coefficients (mouse speed and SRT: alpha=.97; readspeed=.98). However, the use of the baseline measures in order to control for unwanted variance was problematic in this study since the tasks did not only measure simple reactions but were correlated with AcI (see Table 7-15).

Table 7-15: Correlations of Baseline Measures with BIS Scales and Social Perception Tasks

	SRT	Mouse speed	Readspeed
Academic Intelligence (AcI)			
speed	-.34**	-.13	-.49**
memory	-.13	-.11	-.28**
reasoning	-.18*	-.29**	-.40**
verbal	-.26**	-.15*	-.55**
figural	-.25**	-.27**	-.30**
numerical	-.19*	-.16ᴬ	-.41**
Social Perception (SP)			
SPw1	.28**	.13	.62**
SPw2	.32**	.22**	.79**
SPp1	.39**	.48**	.19**
SPp2	.19*	.18*	.18*
SPf1	.26**	.12	.17*
SPf2	.23**	.11	.15
SPa1	.43**	.14	.25**
SPa2	-.01	-.02	-.03
GVEESS	-.08	-.00	-.07

Note. Negative correlations are due to RT measures (baseline measures) and are in the expected direction.

The readspeed task is moderately to highly correlated with all of the BIS scales and thus appears to measure not only basic reading speed but intellectual performance that is related to each of the BIS scales. Probably, there is an underlying factor of both AcI and readspeed that might be working memory capacity (WM). Readspeed correlates with word span (WM_WSp) r=.37 (p<.00, N=175), with memory updating numerical (WM_MUn) r=.17 (p=.02, N=175), and with dot span (WM_DSp) with r=.17 (p=.03, N=175). Since the SPw2 and the readspeed task correlate r=.79, it does not seem to measure much additional specific (social) variance. SPw1 correlates strongly with readspeed, too (r=.62). Although we do not exactly know what the readspeed task measures (besides WM), it is obvious that it is not only simple speed of reading. Thus, it does not make sense to control for readspeed variance in analyzing the written SP tasks. Mouse speed shows low to moderate correlations with the BIS scales except for the memory and the speed scale. Although it can be considered as a speed task, it does not correlate strongly with speed but is rather related to reasoning. Süß (1999) used the mouse task as well and found it to be related to computer experience. We did not expect these relationships since these days most people are very used to the computer. The self-reported computer experience in comparison to peers correlates with r_{SP}=.26 (p=.001, N=175), and the time spent using the computer correlates with r_{SP}=.36 with mouse test performance. We can therefore expect that the mouse test measures the skill of dealing with the computer as well. Even the SRT task, which only requires the subjects to press the space bar as quickly as possible correlates with the BIS scales, except for memory. The problem touches on the hypothesis according to which individuals with faster information processing are more intelligent (see e.g. Deary, 2000; Jensen, 1982a; Neubauer, 2001). However, there are several indices that mental speed is not basic but rather includes various types of performance speed (motoric speed, decision time, perceptual speed, etc., see Stankov & Roberts, 1997). Besides the relationship to processing speed, simple cognitive speed tasks are substantially related to reasoning (gf, see Danthiir, Roberts, Schulze, & Wilhelm, 2005), and a little less to other factors of intelligence (i.e., memory and creativity) (see Neubauer & Bucik, 1996). Because of the mentioned difficulties, I decided to control only for the SRT variance in tasks that require simple or choice reactions. In contrast to mouse speed and read speed, the SRT correlation pattern with other constructs seems to be rather plausible and comprehensive. In addition, it correlates the least with WM (only with WM_WSp r=.16, p=.036). Thus, the danger of reducing important variance through the application of the SRT baseline correction is rather low. However, in some analyses, I controlled for readspeed and mouse speed as well, in order to investigate the effect these variables have on the new tests. In addition to any analysis applying baseline corrections, values without correction factor will be reported. With regard to content effects in speed task, different views and findings exist. Neubauer and Bucik (1996) report a general mental speed factor contradicting the hypothesis of Ceci (1990) who represents the specifity of mind view resulting in the expectation of higher correlations between tasks of the same content. I decided to control for the visual SRT task also in the auditory tasks. However, the content may have an effect since in visual perception tasks, task relevant variance may be partialed out.

7.3.5   Internal Construct Validity of the Social Intelligence Tasks

With respect to the inner structure of SI the following research questions will be addressed. The data analytic procedure was described in chapter 5.3.

SI-1_2: The factors social understanding and social memory emerge as unitary and moderately intercorrelated subconstructs.

SI-2_2: The SI structure is valid for both target and consensus scoring.

SI-3_2: Can social perception be measured as a unitary subconstruct using newly developed social perception tasks and the modified versions of the old tasks including items with higher complexity?

SI-4_2: Do emotions research measures and emotion perception measure the same?

Intercorrelations Between the Social Intelligence Tasks

The full correlation matrix of the SI tasks is presented in Table 7-16. It is apparent, that scale revision and the new task constructions for social perception were successful. Whereas social perception tasks did not correlate at all in the first study, they are now low to moderately related. Nevertheless, the pattern of correlations is still quite mixed. The written SP tasks both correlate with the auditory SPa1, and also with the pictorial SP tasks. They neither show correlations with the emotion perception task SPa2 nor with the GVEESS items nor with the video SP tasks. Besides its correlations with the written SP tasks, the auditory SPa1 correlates with SPp1 and with both SPf tasks. With the exception of the unreliable SMa2 task, the memory tasks intercorrelated moderately. Written social memory (SMw) and auditory social memory (SMa) even correlate highly (.61). Interestingly, the SU tasks are not at all correlated with the social perception tasks except for some single values with the SU personality scale. Written and auditory SM correlate with written SP. The pictorial SM tasks correlate with the auditory SP tasks as well. Note that the correlations of SP with SU and SM are expected to be negative because the SP scales rely on reaction times (the higher the value, the worse the result). SM and SU tasks correlate moderately, SU-pictorial and SM-written being related the strongest (.27). However, the pattern is mixed. There are also several zero correlations especially with regard to SMf. In the same way the voice memory task (SMa2) correlates zero with almost all of the other SI tasks. I will deal with it carefully in further analysis because of its insufficient reliability. Past studies have shown that comparatively unreliable tasks were criterion valid (see Bronfenbrenner, Harding, & Gallwey, 1958) since heterogeneous scores may be better in representing the criterion behavior.

Table 7-16: Intercorrelations Between the Social Intelligence Tasks

	SPw1	SPw2	SPa1	SPa2	GVE	SPp1	SPp2	SPf1	SPf2	SMw	SMa1	SMa2	SMp1	SMp2	SMf	SUw	SUa	SUp	SUf
SPw2	.66**																		
SPa1	.12	.21**																	
SPa2	.00	.04	-.01																
GVE	-.07	.01	-.08	.48**															
SPp1	.18*	.18*	.20*	.02	.02														
SPp2	.30**	.18*	.12	.03	.10	.36**													
SPf1	.12	.09	.23**	-.05	-.09	.44**	.24**												
SPf2	.13	.13	.46**	-.11	-.10	.09	.23**	.19*											
SMw	-.45**	-.46**	-.08	-.07	-.03	-.09	.02	-.02	-.06										
SMa1	-.27**	-.33**	.07	.01	-.14	.03	.10	.02	.01	.61**									
SMa2	-.15	-.10	-.05	-.09	-.04	-.13	.01	-.21**	.05	.09	.19*								
SMp1	-.15	-.16*	-.21**	.07	-.01	-.20*	-.12	-.24**	-.19*	.30**	.28**	.14							
SMp2	-.14	-.21**	-.16*	-.03	.11	-.22**	.04	-.16*	-.08	.44**	.39**	.08	.34**						
SMf	-.10	-.06	.06	-.03	-.02	-.17*	.01	-.13	-.05	.35**	.42**	.03	.14	.34**					
SUw	.01	-.02	.06	.03	.06	.09	.06	.10	.07	.12	.11	.12	.08	.04	-.03				
SUa	-.03	-.04	-.09	.01	.01	-.08	-.05	-.06	-.06	.13	.16*	.11	.15	.07	.00	.26**			
SUp	-.07	-.14	-.05	-.06	-.06	-.03	-.04	-.00	-.10	.27**	.20*	-.05	.19*	.22**	-.01	.34**	.53**		
SUf	-.02	-.06	-.01	-.04	-.06	.03	.01	.15	.05	.17*	.11	-.05	.14	.09	-.04	.46**	.40**	.57**	
SUpk	-.07	-.17*	.07	-.07	-.04	-.00	-.02	.04	.14	.18*	.15	.05	.10	.05	-.12	.60**	.40**	.44**	.42**

Note. Spearman correlations, listwise deletion, N=175; **Correlation is significant at the 0.01 level (2-tailed); *Correlation is significant at the 0.05 level (2-tailed); SPw1=Social perception-written 1; SPw2=Social perception-written 2; SPa1=Social perception-auditory 1; SPa2=Social perception-auditory 2; GVE=GVEESS; SPp1=Social perception-pictorial 1; SPp2=Social perception-pictorial 2; SPf1=Social perception-video-based1; SPf2=Social perception-video-based 2; SMw=Social memory-written1+2; SMa1=Social memory-auditory 1; SMa2=Social memory-auditory 2; SMp1=Social memory-pictorial 1; SMp2=Social memory-pictorial 2; SMf=Social memory-video-based1+2; SUw=Social understanding-written; SUa=Social understanding-auditory; SUp=Social understanding-pictorial; SUf=Social understanding-video-based; SUpk=Social understanding-personality; Expected correlations are shadowed.

Confirmatory Factor Analysis of the Internal Social Intelligence Structure

In EFA, SU and SM scales were found again to load on the correspondent factors whereas social perception, despite the positive manifold among the variables, split into three subfactors, namely social written, nonverbal and auditory perception (see Seidel, 2007). First, further investigations of the SI internal structure will be done by means of CFA, separately for the SM-SU structure and for the social perception structure. Then, the subcomponents will be combined into an overall SI model. The latter will, however, tap the limits of the data set (sample size, degrees of freedom).

1) Social understanding and social memory

I start with the confirmation analysis of the two-factor structure (see SI-1_2; and 6.2.1), hypothesizing a social understanding and social memory factor. Including all SU and all SM variables resulted in model SUSM1 (see Table 7-17). Doing without the relatively unreliable task SMa2 made the fit worse. A model that excludes SUPk and keeps all SM variables fitted the data (see model SUSM2, Figure 7-1). Although, in this study, the personality scale is positively correlated with the content SU variables, it seems to measure some other aspects. Additional elimination of variables, for example SMp1, does not improve the fit either. Compared to the correlations we obtained in the first study, the correlations between the two SI factors are stronger for the target-scored version (.31, this study compared to .29, first study). The same SU–SM models with the only difference that the SU variables are scored consensus-based are presented in Table 7-17 as model SUSM1C (full model) and model SUSM2C (reduced final model without SUPk). Both models fit the data even better than the target-scored models and thus confirm the findings presented in the first study (see chapter 6.3.1). Again, involving the SUPk in the model with the consensus-based SU scores decreases the fit to the data. Thus, we can confirm this structure doing without the SUPk scale as being the best independent from the scoring procedure that was applied. Both final models, SUSM2 (target-scored) and SUSM2C (consensus-scored, in italics) are illustrated in Figure 7-1.

Table 7-17: Models of Social Understanding/Social Memory

Model	Model description	Chi² (df)	Prob.	CFI	RMSEA (CI 90%)	SRMR
Target-scored						
SUSM1	Complete model including all SM and all SU variables	90.914 (43)	.000	.91	.080 (.057, .102)	.067
SUSM2	Excluding SUPk	46.250 (34)	.078	.97	.046 (.000, .076)	.056
Consensus-scored						
SUSM1C	same as model SUSM1	63.801 (43)	.021	.97	.053 (.021, .078)	.050
SUSM2C	same as model SUSM2	43.610 (34)	.125	.98	.040 (.000, .072)	.049

Note. CFI=Comparative fit index; RMSEA=Root mean square error of approximation; Prob.=Probability value; SRMR=Standardized root mean square residual; SU=Social understanding; SM=Social memory; SUPk=Social understanding-personality judgment; C=Consensus scored SU variables

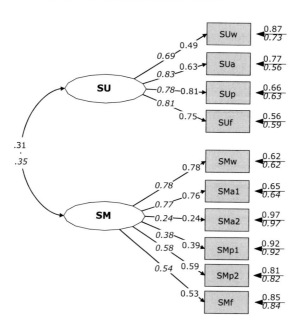

Figure 7-1: Model of Social Memory/Social Understanding Considering Different Scoring Methods

Note. Target Scores (SMSU2) and Consensus Scores (SUSM2C); Consensus-scored model in italics; SMw=Social memory-written1+2; SMa1=Social memory-auditory 1; SMa2=Social memory-auditory 2; SMp1=Social memory-pictorial 1; SMp2=Social memory-pictorial 2; SMf=Social memory-video-based1+2; SUw=Social understanding-written; SUa=Social understanding-auditory; SUp=Social understanding-pictorial; SUf=Social understanding-video-based

To sum up, the factors social understanding and social memory can be confirmed (see SI-1_2). They are moderately intercorrelated. Moreover, the SI structure is valid for both target and consensus scoring (see SI-2_2). The loadings are even higher and of greater stability compared to our first study.

2) Social perception

I begin my analysis with the nonverbal part of social perception forming the largest proportion according to the EFA results. SPa1 is excluded for theoretical reasons even if it was also part of this factor in EFA. The parameters of this model SP1 are presented in Table 7-18. Although the model fits the data very well, there are some shortcomings: The task SPf2 has a relatively low load (.35). This is the task which is most related to the auditory SPa1. Testing the other parts of social perception is not as easy as with the nonverbal SP factor. The written and the auditory perception factors consist of only two parts. In EFA the written SP tasks and the auditory emotion perception tasks, SPa2 and GVEESS, formed two separate factors, not correlating with any other of the SI variables. Both factors include only two indicators. Concerning the auditory social/emotional perception tasks, I decided to split both the GVEESS and the SPa2 in two parts. They are built of three scales each. All scales were normally distributed. Considering criteria of item number, intercorrelation and reliability, I aggregated the SPa2 scales 1 and 3 and the GVEESS 1 and 2 by means of z-transformation. Correlations of residuals were non-significant or on the border of being significant. The verbal perception tasks each consist of two parts (see Table 7-13 and Table 8-19; the SPw2 parts are assumed to be more similar than the SPw1 parts since they only differ with respect to the target to which subjects have to react (social/non social vs. positive/negative). This gets also evident through the combined score that was built for SPw1 using z-values but not necessary for SPw2. Therefore, I decided to split the SPw1 in two parts (SPw1_1 and SPw1_2). They have reliability values of .95 and .96, respectively. Model SP2 (see Table 7-18) includes the two language-based SP factors: emotion perception with two GVEESS and two SPa2 variables, and written SP being composed of two SPw1 scales and the SPw2 task. Although RMSEA and SRMR are slightly too high, the model has an acceptable fit. The two factors intercorrelate moderately with $r_{SPw-SPa}=.37$. Model SP3 combines the language-based factors (see model SP2) with the nonverbal factor model (SP1). The three factor model of social perception fits the data satisfactorily. Again, RMSEA and SRMS are slightly too high. Note that the loadings are boosted because of the task splitting. Including the remaining task SPa1 in factor 1 leads to a worse fit (see model SP4). However, the fit is still acceptable. The complete model, involving all social perception variables, is shown in Figure 7-2. All SP factors correlate moderately. It may be that there is an additional SP factor, composed of SPf2 and SPa1, which is more closely related to the nonverbal SP factor than to the language-based SP factors. This should be examined in a further study including more variables of this type.

Table 7-18: Models of Social Perception

Model	Model description	Chi² (df)	Prob.	CFI	RMSEA (CI 90%)	SRMR
SP1	*Nonverbal SP (1 F)* (SPp1, SPp2, SPf1, SPf2)	3.126 (2)	.210	.98	.057 (.000, .171)	.032
SP2	*Language-based SP (2 F)* F1: SPa2_1 & SPa2_2, GVE1& GVE2; F2: SPw1_1 & SPw1_2, SPw2	33.123 (13)	.002	.96	.095 (.055, .135)	.068
SP3	*3 factor model* F1: see model SP1; F2 & F3 see model SP2	67.871 (41)	.005	.96	.062 (.034, .087)	.065
SP4	see SP3 plus SPa1included in F1	109.384 (51)	.000	.91	.081 (.060, .102)	.074
SP3b	see SP3 with baseline SRT correctioned variables, SPp2, SPf1, SPf2, SPa2, GVE)	69.711 (41)	.003	.95	.069 (.036, .088)	.064
SP4b	see SP4 with baseline SRT correction (SPp2, SPf1, SPf2, SPa2, GVE, SPa1)	107.794 (51)	.000	.90	.080 (.059, .101)	.079

Note. SP=Social perception; F1...2...: Factor 1...2...; CFI=Comparative fit index; RMSEA=Root mean square error of approximation; Prob.=Probability value; SRMR=Standardized root mean square residual; SPw1=Social perception-written 1; SPw2=Social perception-written 2; SPa1=Social perception-auditory 1; SPa2=Social perception-auditory 2; GVE= GVEESS; SPp1=Social perception-pictorial 1; SPp2=Social perception-pictorial 2; SPf1=Social perception- video-based 1; SPf2=Social perception-video-based 2

The models SP3b and SP4b can be derived from models SP3 and SP4. Model SP4b corresponds exactly to model SP4 except for using baseline corrected variables. The fit of the model SP4b (see Figure 7-2; numbers in italics) gets slightly better. The model shows an improved fit when doing without the SPa1 score (see model SP3b, Figure 7-2; numbers are displayed in bold letters).

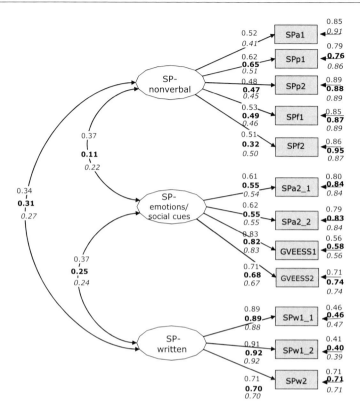

Figure 7-2: Models of Social Perception

Note. Basic model SP4; In addition, models SP4b (in italics) and SP3b (bold) are shown. SPw1=Social perception-written 1; SPw2= social perception- written 2; SPa1 = social perception- auditory 1; SPa2=Social perception-auditory 2; GVE=GVEESS; SPp1=Social perception-pictorial 1; SPp2=Social perception-pictorial 2; SPf1=Social perception- video-based 1; SPf2=Social perception-video-based 2

To sum up, common variance is explained through three social perception subfactors being moderately intercorrelated (see SI-3_2). Thus, there is a common reliable variance between -at least nonverbal- social perception tasks in this study. This may have several reasons: improved SP tasks yield more reliable and valid results; the comparatively higher degree of social complexity plays an important role in revealing the social information more clearly; the increased number of SP tasks makes a more reliable measurement possible; the different strategy of analysis (task splitting) favors the factor structure.

In the following, the combined structure of social memory, social understanding, and social perception will be tested. In a first model SIS2Int1 (see Table 7-19 and Figure 7-3) the baseline corrected social perception variables, SU target scores and SI memory scales were introduced. Factor intercorrelations were all allowed. The model fittet the data satisfactorily, in particular with respect to the number of degrees of freedom related to the Chi² value and the sample size. Some of the variables show relatively low loadings (e.g., SPp2; SPf2; Spw2; SMp1; SMa2). Obviously, the social understanding factor is not at all related to social perception. The moderate covariance with social memory remains. This is in line with the first study results: the SU variables were almost uncorrelated with both SP and AcI. The perception tasks share some common variance as already indicated by the SP model (see Figure 7-2). The written social perception factor (.26) is related more closely to SM than the nonverbal (.13) and auditory perception factor (.17). This may be due to the common use of written language since answers required in social memory tasks are often verbal. The more parsimonious model without the nonsignificant factor intercorrelations is presented in Table 7-19 and Figure 7-3 (continuous lines and numbers presented in normal style). Compared to the corresponding models without a basline correction (Models SIS2Int3 and SIS2Int3), the fit is only slightly better and some of the loasdings a little higher. However, in summary the baseline correction does not affect the complete model essentially. Although we do not exactly know what the baseline tasks measure, it does not seem to have anything to do with SI. The only task that is strongly affected is the task SPw2.

Table 7-19: Models Concerning the Internal Structure of Social Intelligence

Model	Model description	Chi² (df)	Prob.	CFI	RMSEA (CI 90%)	SRMR
SIS2Int1	Complete model, all factors intercorrelated; Mit baseline correction	294.267 (179)	.000	.87	.061 (.048, .073)	.076
SIS2Int2	Without nonsignificant correlations	302.109 (187)	.000	.87	.062 (.049, .074)	.086
SIS2Int3	Complete SI model; Without baseline correction, all factors intercorrelated	297.855 (179)	.000	.89	.062 (.049, .074)	.073
SIS2Int4	Without nonsignificant corrs; without baseline correction	305.217 (184)	.000	.89	.062 (.049, .074)	.086

Note. CFI=Comparative fit index; RMSEA=Root mean square error of approximation; Prob.=Probability value; SRMR=Standardized root mean square residual

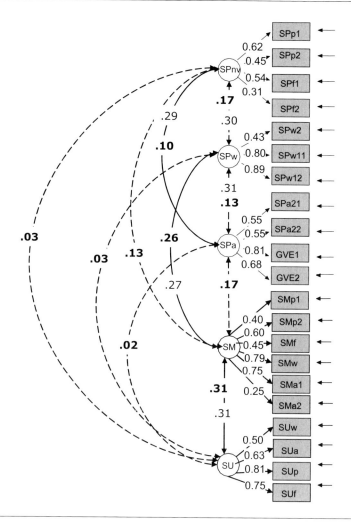

Figure 7-3: Complete Social Intelligence Model

Note. Model SIS2Int1: Dashed and continuous lines, bold numbers: With Baseline Correction, all factors intercorrelated; Model SIS2Int2: continuous lines only, numbers in normal style: Model without non-significant factor intercorrelations

Social Intelligence Contents

At least three social intelligence content factors were expected: a nonverbal factor, including video-based and pictorial tasks, an auditory factor, and a written factor. Neither of the factors emerged in CFA. Models assuming this factor structure do not fit the data. The same is true for a two-factor model, assuming a nonverbal factor (pictorial and video-based) and a language-based factor (written and auditory material). A four-factor structure separating all four contents does not fit either. These confirm results of the first study and EFA of this study. Once again, we can expect that the content variance is covered by the comparatively stronger SI operational variance (similar to the BIS; see chapter 2.1.5). Testing the full MTMM model did not result in meaningful findings if only because some methodological problems emerged (constraints at lower/upper bound; degrees of freedom, etc.). A parceling technique (see Jäger, 1982, 1984) cannot be applied to examine whether an underlying content structure becomes apparent since we still do not have enough tasks. However, a proof for the existence of content specific variance and thus an evidence of the correctness of the hypothesis of three content factors is indicated through the findings concerning social perception (SP). The SP factor splits into a nonverbal component (pictorial and video-based), an auditory component (GVEESS and SPa2), and a written component containing the social written perception tasks SPw1 and SPw2.

7.3.6 Relationship Between Social Intelligence and Academic Intelligence

The following questions will be addressed with respect to the relationship between AcI and SI.

SI-AcI-1_2: Social understanding is independent from academic intelligence.

SI-AcI-2_2: Social memory is related to all BIS factors, academic intelligence memory, reasoning and speed. Nevertheless, it has its unique parts.

The CFA will be done with the SRT baseline corrected SP tasks, SU target scores, and BIS parcels (For the confirmation of the BIS structure see appendix C). The PONS test is not analyzed as it does not belong to our test battery and did not show any meaningful relationship to the SI variables in EFA (see Seidel, 2007). The GVEESS will be included (loaded with SPa2 on one emotions/social cue perception factor).

The basic model SIAcIS2_1 (see Table 7-20) includes the BIS factors and the already established SI factors, SU and SM. This model serves the confirmation of first study results (see chapter 6.3.1). It is obvious, that the model did not show an excellent fit to the data. However, it is sufficient to confirm the first study results. The difference compared to the first study analysis is that the model presented here (see SIAcIS2_1) includes the BIS-S factor in addition to the BIS-R and BIS-M factor (see chapter 2.1.5 and 7.2.2). The introduction of the BIS-Speed factor has negative effects on the model fit compared to the model doing without BIS-S (Chi²=161.295, df=100, CFI=.94, RMSEA=.059; SRMR=.073).

Model SIAcIS2_2 involves the three social perception factors in addition. Considering the loadings (see Figure 7-4) and fit statistics (see Table 7-20) data can be evalauted to fit the model satisfactorily, in particular, taking into account the large number of degrees of freedom ralated to the Chi² value. The data set is clearly limited to such a model here. With respect to the assumption SI-Acl-1_2 (see also chapter 7.1) social understanding was again independent from Acl and only significantly related to SM. Social memory, however, was most highly correlated with Acl memory (.68). Additional moderate to high correlations of SM could be found with SPw (.45), Acl-R (.38), and Acl-S (.30), indicating that in this second study as well SM is more highly related to Acl than to SI. Nevertheless, SM explains some unique variance as it can be predicted by the BIS factor with the following equation (see SI-Acl-2_2 and chapter 7.1): SM=-.003*BIS-Speed+.675*BIS-Memory+.056*BIS-Reasoning +.710 D1 (R^2=.495). The regression model fits the data excellently (Chi²= 135.672, df=84; p<.000; CFI=.95; SRMR=.057; RMSEA=.059 (CI: .040; .077)). SM is mainly predicted through BIS-Memory. BIS–Speed and BIS–Reasoning contribute nearly anything to the explanation of SM. Written SP is related to all BIS factors. Probably the common written/verbal variance causes this relationship. SPw is also stronger correlated with BIS-S than with SPnv and SPa. Interstingly, SPa is only related to SPnv and SPw and has nothing in common with SU and SM and neither with the Acl factors. Thus, SPa seems to explain systematic valriance as well that was ot measured by the instruments introduced in the analyses.

Table 7-20: Models of Social Intelligence Related to Academic Intelligence

Model	Model description	Chi² (df)	Prob.	CFI	RMSEA (CI 90%)	SRMR
SIAcIS2_1	BIS-R, BIS-M, BIS-S, SU, SM, (reason: First study) without SP	239.050 (146)	.000	.92	.061 (.046, .074)	.091
SIAcIS2_2	Complete SI model related to the BIS factors	622.211 (389)	.000	.883	.059 (.050, .067)	.094

Note. CFI=Comparative fit index; RMSEA=Root mean square error of approximation; Prob.=Probability value; SRMR=Standardized root mean square residual; SP=Social perception; SM=Social memory; SU=Social understanding; BIS-R=BIS reasoning; BIS-S=BIS speed; BIS-M=BIS memory

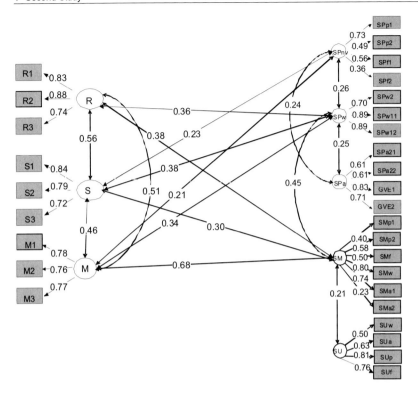

Figure 7-4: SI Model related to AcI Model (Model SIAcIS2_2)

Note. M=AcI memory; R= AcI reasoning; S= AcI speed; SPw1=Social perception-written 1; SPw2=Social perception-written 2; SPa1=Social perception-auditory 1; SPa2= Social perception auditory 2; GVE= Geneva Vocal Expression Stimulus Set; SPp1=Social perception-pictorial 1; SMp1=Social memory-pictorial 1; SM=Social memory; SU=Social understanding; SPnv= Social perception–nonverbal; SPa= Socail perception-auditory; SPw= Social perception-written; R1-R3 =BIS Parcel reasoning; S1-S3=BIS Parcel speed; M1-M3=BIS Parcel memory

2) Social intelligence without academic intelligence

The following models examine the structure of social intelligence when controlled for academic intelligence variance. The analysis will be performed for the SU-SM model and for the SP model separately and then together. Model SUSM-AcI controlling for BIS variance in the SU-SM model, has an excellent fit to the data (see SUSM-AcI, Table 7-21). The SI components SU and SM remain stable independent from partialing out AcI variance.

Table 7-21: Models of Social Intelligence Controlled for BIS Variance

Model	Model description	Chi² (df)	Prob.	CFI	RMSEA (CI 90%)	SRMR
SUSM-BIS	SU, SM without AcI	43.409 (34)	.129	.97	.04 (.000, .072)	.055
SP-AcI	Social perception without AcI	94.853 (51)	.000	.91	.071 (.048, .092)	.074
SIcomp-AcI_1	Complete SI model without AcI	281.790 (179)	.000	.88	.058 (.044, .070)	.075
SIcomp-AcI_2	See SIcomp-AcI_1without nonsignificant factor intercorrelations	282.566 (184)	.000	.88	.056 (.042, .068)	.076

Note. CFI=Comparative fit index; RMSEA=Root mean square error of approximation; Prob.=Probability value; SRMR=Standardized root mean square residual;SI=Social Intelligence; AcI=Academic Intelligence; SP=Social perception; SU=Social understanding; SM=Social memory

Concerning loadings and intercorrelations, the model remains stable and almost the same compared to the model without controlling for BIS variance and thus confirms the first study results with another sample. Again, the core factor, social understanding, is not at all affected by the BIS factors. For the corresponding figures see Seidel (2007). The social perception model without the BIS variance fits the data as well (Model SP-AcIsee Table 7-21), indicating that there is a social perceptual ability independent from AcI. SPw2 and SPp1 are the tasks that are most affected by partialing out BIS variance. Nevertheless, the model remains stable, including loadings and correlations. When partialing out AcI variance of the complete SI model (see model SIcomp-AcI_1, Table 7-21), the model remains stable as well compared to model SIAcIS2_2. Only the loadings of the tasks SPp1, SPw2, SMp1, SMp2, SMw and SMa1 are noticably reduced and thus seem to be affected most by AcI. The core dimension SU is not affected by AcI. When doing without the nonsignificant correlations between SU and the SP factors and without a SM –SPnv relationship, the model fit is comparable (see model SIcomp-AcI_1, Table 7-21); thus the model should be preferred as being the more parsimonious. It is presented in Figure 1-1.

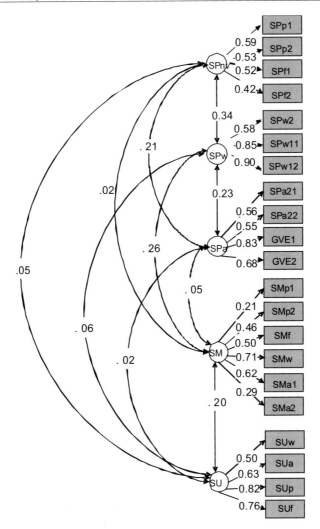

Figure 7-5: Complete SI Model without AcI variance (Model SIcomp-AcI_2)

Note. SPw1=Social perception-written 1; SPw2=Social perception-written 2; SPa1=Social perception-auditory 1; SPa2= Social perception auditory 2; GVE= Geneva Vocal Expression Stimulus Set; SPp1=Social perception-pictorial 1; SMp1=Social memory-pictorial 1; SM=Social memory; SU=Social understanding; SPnv= Social perception–nonverbal; SPa= Socail perception-auditory; SPw= Social perception-written

7.4 Results with Respect to Auditory Intelligence

7.4.1 Psychometric Properties of the Auditory Intelligence and the Working Memory Tasks

Psychometrics: Auditory Intelligence Tasks

I turn to the presentation of the psychometric properties of the AuI tasks (see Table 7-22). In the first three rows, the nonverbal tasks MA1, RH, and MA4 are presented. In the bottom part, the three speech tasks are shown.

Table 7-22: Psychometrics of the Auditory Intelligence Tasks (Second Study)

Task	Number of items [1]	Scale	Skewness/ Curtosis [2]	Difficulty mean (SD)	Range (min.–max.)	r_{it} -range [1]	Cronbach's Alpha [1]
MA1 N=175	15 (13)	8 point scale	.36/-.50	.43 (.19)	.00 - .91	.19 - .49 (.24 - .48)	.75 (.75)
RH N=175	19 (19)	repro-duction	.36/-.01	.42 (.18)	.05 - 1.00	.14 - .56 (.24 - .56)	.80 (.80)
MA4 N=173	15 (11)	4 point scale	-.04 (.19)/ -.51	.51 (.23)	.00 - 1.00	.10 - .49 (.31 - .50)	.74 (.76)
MW N=175	26^2 (14)	open	.15/-.38 Reduced: .08/-.43	.38 (.14) .44 (.20)	.05 - .73 (.00 - .93)	.07 - .47 (.22 - .44)	.68 (.70)
AU N=174	19 (16)	MC 5 alter-natives	-.63/.71 Reduced: -.75/.69	.69 (.15) .71 (.18)	.21 - 1.00 (.08 - 1.00)	.01 - .40 (.17 - .35)	.59 (.61)
DS N=175	16 (13)	open	-.47/.71 Reduced: -.36/.40	.70 (.14) .67 (.15)	.19 - .97 .15 - 1.00	.11 - .33 (.20 - .36)	.62 (.61)

Note. [1] in parentheses: reduced item number after item selection (items with rit <.20 are excluded); [2] Skewness is presented first; the second value represents curtosis. SE (Skewness) is .18; if not reported, SE (Curtosis) is .37; r_{it} -range=Item total correlation range; MA1=Detection of repeated tones; RH=Rhythm reproduction; MA4=Tonal series; MW=Masked words; AU=Audiobook; DS=Disarranged sentences

The tasks MA1 and AU are not normally distributed. However, the deviation is not severe for neither of the two tasks. There are problems neither concerning the sample nor concerning the calculation with reaction times. The task detection of repeated tones (MA1) had a gap in its distribution. There are no subjects reaching a value of .50. Moreover, the task does not differentiate well at values around .30. The distribution of the task audiobook (AU) was slightly skewed on the left hand side. There were few test takers who got a very low score on the task. As the deviations are not severe, the tasks will be used for further analysis.

Regarding the average difficulty of the AuI tasks, the values of the tonal tasks, MA1 and MA4, and the task masked words are rather low. On the contrary, the remaining speech tasks are comparably easy. Compared to the first study, the task disarranged sentences was easier in the second study, whereas rhythm reproduction, masked words and audiobook remained nearly unchanged. Performance in the tonal tasks was better in the first study, probably due to the well-educated student sample.

In summary, the modifications of the auditory tasks that were implemented after the first study were quite successful. Concerning rhythm reproduction, tonal series and detection of repeated tones, the reliability values were even better than anticipated (see Table 6-6). The selected items proved to work well, especially with regard to the tonal tasks detection of repeated tones (MA1) and tonal series (MA4). However, the result of the promising task masked words (MW) was a little disappointing. In the first study, with data of only 57 test takers, psychometric values were better compared to those values presented here. Possibly, the differences between the groups (students vs. mixed group of adults) are responsible for the findings. With respect to the task audiobook (AU), the conversion of open-ended questions into multiple choice items and the development of additional items did not lead to an improved reliability value. The disarranged sentences (DS) score with selected items did not reveal an improved reliability but shows correspondence to the anticipated value reported in Table 6-6. For further analysis reduced mean values of the tasks AU, MW and MA4 will be used. With regard to the remaining tasks, I will deal with the unreduced scores. Reduced and original values correlated at least with .96 except for the task audiobook (.85).

Psychometrics: Working Memory Tasks

In the first study, the hypothesis emerged that working memory (WM) may be the underlying component of the AuI factor (see chapter 6.3.2). Whether WM explains systematic variance on the AuI tasks, will be examined in the next section. Before the adaptive WM tasks will be related to the AuI tasks, their psychometric properties will be reported. Two performance scores were computed for each WM task. The first is described through the highest level that was completed successfully (Level score); the second combines this value with the percent of correctly answered items at the next higher level (Combined score). The following table displays the psychometric properties of both values for all three tasks.

Table 7-23: Psychometrics of the Working Memory Tasks

Task	Score	Mean (SD)	Skewness/ Curtosis	Range (min. – max.)
WM_WSp (max. level: 7)	Level	2.10 (.86)	.40/-.22	0 - 4
	Combined	2.65 (.85)	.31/-.14	0.16 – 4.76
		2.66 (.84)	*.41/-.34*	1.00 – 4.76
WM_MUn (max. level: 6)	Level	2.52 (.92)	.15/.16	0 – 5
	Combined	3.13 (.92)	.12/.17	0.44 – 5.71
		3.14 (.90)	*.30/-.17*	1.35 – 5.71
WM_DSp (max. level: 7)	Level	1.64 (1.22)	.24/-.87	0 – 5
	Combined	2.16 (1.25)	-.24/-.73	0.14 – 5.85
		2.15 (1.24)	*.18/-.92*	0.14 – 5.00

Note. N=182; scores corrected for outliers (trimmed distribution) are presented in italics. SE (Skewness) is .18; if not reported, SE (Curtosis) is .37; WM_WSp= Word span; WM_MUn=Memory updating numerical; WM_DSp=Dot span

Whereas in the task *dot span* (WM_DSp), some subjects achieved the final level, in the tasks "word span" (WM_WSp) and *memory updating numerical* (WM_MUn) test takers did not attain the final levels. As far as the task *wordspan* (WM_WSp) is concerned, subjects were able to deal with six words in remembering and ordering their first letters. This result is in line with findings reported by Anderson (1996) that a person is only seldom able to process more than seven units at the same time (see also Horn, 2006). In WM_DSp, participants succeeded in indicating symmetry and remembering the position of six dots. None of the working memory tasks follows a normal distribution no matter which score we take. Even so, a closer look shows that we can take the tasks for further analysis. The level score follows an even distribution, similar to the bell-shaped normal distribution curve. However, a closer look at the more precise combined value reveals the difficulties of the score. Several single distributions seem to form one complete, each with a different modal value. This becomes clear by considering the adaptive algorithm we applied (see chapter 7.2.2). The single "distributions" seem to be due to the different levels achieved by the participants. On each level, there are differences on how many extra percentage points subjects reach of the next higher level. This inevitably leads to this kind of distribution. This is equally true for the other two WM tasks, dot span (WM_DSp) and word span (WM_WSp). Since this seems to be the reason for the distribution, despite these problems, the combined scores, containing more detailed information compared to the level scores, will be taken for further analysis. Table 7-24 shows that the WM tasks are moderately intercorrelated, indicating that they share systematic common variance although operating with different kinds of material.

Table 7-24: Intercorrelations Between Working Memory Tasks

	WM_WSp	WM_MUn
WM_MUn	.32	
WM_DSp	.25	.37

Note. All correlations are significant at the 0.01 level (2-tailed). listwise deletion; N= 182

Since we developed an adaptive version of the working memory tasks described in Sander (2005), we can only determine a reliability value by means of Item Response Theory (IRT) that should be a future aim for item and test analysis. In this book, in order to indicate reliability in addition to the task intercorrelation, I will refer to data that was obtained with the standard version of the task in past investigations.

Sander (2005) reports internal consistency values (Cronbach's Alpha) of .76 (WM_WSp), .83 (WM_MUn), and .81 (WM_DSp). Each of the three standard version tasks contains 18 items. In his study, 182 students (68.69% male; mean age: 24.5 years, SD=5.3) participated. Compared to our study, the intercorrelations between the three tasks are lower but are in the same order, with WM_DSp and WM_MUn correlating highest and WM_WSp and WM_DSp lowest. Oberauer (2002) applied the tasks WM_DSp (Alpha=.70), WM_MUn (Alpha=.82), and "Reading span" (verbal indicator) in order to assess WM. The 135 participants were mainly students (56% were male; mean age: 25.8, SD=3.8). WM_DSp and WM_MUn correlated with r=.50. In an earlier study reported in Oberauer (2000), 128 students (mean age: 26.2, SD=5) worked on WM_MUn (Alpha=.81) and Dotspan (Alpha= .75) that correlated with r= .51.

To summarize, the reliability of the standard version of the WM tasks we applied was proved to be reliable in several studies. The correlations between the WM tasks are, although not as high as in the results obtained with the standard version, comparable. The relatively lower correlations may be due to the adaptive procedure, since every person works on different items, some work on only a few whereas others get nearly the whole battery. Individuals differ in their ability to deal with verbal, numerical and figural material. Therefore, we would even expect lower intercorrelations between the tasks.

7.4.2 Relationship Between Auditory Intelligence and Working Memory

Aul-1_2: Nonverbal auditory ability to be stable, when controlled for working memory.

One of the second study aims was to control systematic variance that is produced by Aul for the influence of WM (Seidel & Süß, 2007). Table 7-25 shows the correlations between the Aul tasks with and without controlling for working memory. First, as expected, the nonverbal tasks (MA1, MA4, RH) show significant correlations indicating a common underlying factor. The correlations between the speech tasks are not in the assumed strength. The task MW is only weakly related to the other speech tasks. With regard to the operational domains, only the reasoning tasks seem to share variance. Similar to the first study, the discrimination and memory domain lack significant correlations between the speech and the nonverbal tasks. Taking into account the working memory influence, it is apparent that the intercorrelations between the auditory nonverbal intelligence tasks decrease only marginally (confirmation of Aul-1_2). However, some correlations between speech (in particular AU and DS) and tonal tasks decrease remarkably. The task MW seems to be nearly completely uninfluenced by working memory, indicating that it measures something different that is neither explained by WM nor by the Aul tasks we applied.

Table 7-25: The Effect of Working Memory on the Intercorrelations Between the Auditory Intelligence Tasks

	MA1	RH	MA4	MW	AU
RH	.40** **.37***	1.00			
MA4	.47** **.43***	.28** **.20***	1.00		
MW	.11 **.12**	.04 **.01**	.01 **.02**	1.00	
AU	.13 **.05**	.08 **-.01**	.10 **-.02**	.08 **.10**	1.00
DS	.12 **.02**	.15 **.00**	.21** **.06**	.10 **.12**	.30** **.19***

Note. **Correlation is significant at the 0.01 level (2-tailed). *Correlation is significant at the 0.05 level (2-tailed); Significance starting with .16; listwise deletion N= 172; Bold: correlations controlled for working memory; Expected correlations within content variables (nonverbal vs. speech) are shaded in dark grey, within operation variables (discrimination, memory, and reasoning) in light grey.; MA1=Detection of repeated tones; RH=Rhythm reproduction; MA4=Tonal series; MW=Masked words; AU=Audiobook; DS=Disarranged sentences

7.4.3 Internal Construct Validity of the Auditory Intelligence Tasks

> AuI-2_2: Auditory intelligence splits into two content factors, nonverbal and speech auditory intelligence.

In EFA the two-factor structure is confirmative for the results of the first study (see chapter 6.3.2) could be confirmed (see also Seidel & Süß, 2007). By means of CFA, I will examine whether these results can be justified. First, I will test the two internal structure models of AuI I already examined in the first study in order to see whether the structure is stable using different samples. Therefore, a general auditory factor model (model AuInt1) and a model suggesting two content factors, speech and nonverbal auditory ability (model AuInt2), are tested. Since there are only two indicators for each cognitive operation, I will not be able to test the operational structure again. The two models are presented in Table 7-26.

Table 7-26: Models of Auditory Intelligence

Model	Model description	Chi² (df)	Prob.	CFI	RMSEA (CI 90%)	SRMR
AuInt1	One general auditory factor	21.080 (9)	.012	.88	.089 (.039, .138)	.066
AuInt2	Two content factors, speech and non-verbal auditory ability	6.693 (8)	.570	1.00	.000 (.000, .079)	.029
AuInt3	Two-factor model without WM	3.664 (8)	.886	1.00	.000 (.000, .042)	.026
AuInt4	Two-factor model without WM and BIS	6.173 (8)	.6279	1.00	.000 (.000, .075)	.036

Note. CFI=Comparative fit index; RMSEA=Root mean square error of approximation; Prob.=Probability value; SRMR=Standardized root mean square residual; BIS=Berlin Intelligence Structure; WM=Working memory capacity

The CFA results are another proof for the validity of the two content domains (Seidel & Süß, 2007). As hypothesized (AuI-2_2; see chapter 7.1), the two-factor model fits the data excellently and much better than the general factor model. The two factors correlate with $r_{nonv\text{-}speech}$=.39 (p<.01) which is a little lower than in the first study. The task MW does not really fit in well, as already indicated by correlational and exploratory factor analysis. Correlation analysis (see chapter 7.4.2) indicates that concerning nonverbal auditory ability, the correlations remain stable even when controlled for WM. In order to confirm this result, I controlled for working memory variance in the auditory tasks and examined the two-factor structure model again (see model AuInt3). The model remains stable and its fit even improves. The correlation between the two factors decreases. Controlling for AcI variance in addition to working memory decreases the fit slightly but the model remains still stable (see

AuInt4), the factors correlating with r=.14. This implies that AuI can be stably measured besides AcI and WM and again confirms AuI-2_2. All three models (AuInt2-4) are presented in Figure 7-6. Numbers in italics belong to the model controlled for WM (model AuInt3). The model controlled for WM and the BIS variance is shown in bold numbers (model AuInt4).

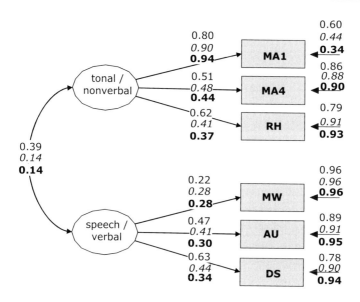

Figure 7-6: Internal Structure of Auditory Intelligence With and Without Controlling for Working Memory and Academic Intelligence

Note. Numbers controlling for working memory capacity are presented in italics. Bold letters represent the model, which is controlled for both WM and the BIS. MA1= Detection of repeated tones; MA4=Tonal series; RH=Rhythm reproduction; AU=Audiobook; DS= Disarranged sentences

7.4.4 Relationship between Auditory Intelligence and Academic Intelligence

AuI-AcI-1_2: Nonverbal auditory ability is independent from academic intelligence.

AuI-AcI-2_2: Speech auditory ability is strongly related to academic intelligence.

Table 7-27 addresses the correlations between the auditory intelligence tasks and the BIS cells, namely speed, memory and reasoning, each relying on figural-spatial, numerical and verbal material.

Table 7-27: Correlations Between the Auditory Intelligence Tasks and the BIS Cells

	B_Sf	B_Sv	B_Sn	B_Mf	B_Mv	B_Mn	B_Rf	B_Rv	B_Rn
MA1	.11	.17*	.09	.15	.03	.00	.16*	.22**	.14
RH	.11	.10	.04	.18*	.06	-.01	.21**	.22**	.06
MA4	.18*	.18*	.20**	.23**	.12	.12	.36**	.27**	.30**
MW	-.07	-.01	.10	-.02	.13	.11	.08	.08	.02
AU	.19*	.29**	.29**	.27**	.30**	.34**	.21**	.40**	.23**
DS	.07	.20**	.31**	.07	.29**	.14	.26**	.51**	.31**

Note. **Correlation is significant at the 0.01 level (2-tailed). *Correlation is significant at the 0.05 level (2-tailed); Significance starting with .16; listwise deletion; N=172; Expected correlations are shadowed; MA1=Detection of repeated tones; RH=Rhythm reproduction; MA4=Tonal series; MW=Masked words; AU=Audiobook; DS=Disarranged sentences; B=BIS; Sf=Speed figural; Sv=Speed verbal; Sn=Speed numerical; Mf=Memory figural; Mv=Memory verbal; Mn=Memory numerical; Rf=Reasoning figural; Rv=Reasoning verbal; Rn=Reasoning numerical

The AuI tasks correlate particularly with BIS reasoning. An exception is the task MW that correlates with none of the BIS cells. Note that this task neither shows correlations with the other auditory tasks nor with working memory. MA1 and RH also do not correlate significantly with reasoning numerical which indicates that these tasks do not require a cognitive numerical operation. This is a little surprising considering that rhythm involves counting and MA1 is expected to require some counting as well. Similar to the first study results, the task AU correlates with almost all of the BIS cells, indicating that it shares a great deal of variance with AcI. DS correlates with less of the BIS cells but consistent moderate to high with the reasoning cells. It is apparent that, even if we had applied three tasks for each operation, these domains would not have emerged with these tasks. There are two explanations for this result that stand to reason: First, with these AuI tasks it is not possible to measure AuI operations. Second, it may be that these kinds of operations indeed do not exist in AuI.

EFA confirmed the first study results of two auditory factors, verbal/speech and nonverbal/tonal, applying the six auditory tasks. In the following analysis, the two-factor AuI model is contrasted with BIS contents and operations in CFA. In both models, the auditory tasks are controlled for WM.

Table 7-28: Auditory Intelligence and Academic Intelligence Contents

Model	Model description	Chi² (df)	Prob.	CFI	RMSEA (CI 90%)	SRMR
Aul-Acl1	two Aul contents and three Acl contents, all factors correlated	126.189 (82)	.001	.94	.056 (.035, .075)	.064
Aul-Acl2	see Aul-Acl1; but double assignment of AU; no corr. between Aul-speech & Acl-fig and Aul-nv & Acl-num	120.382 (81)	.003	.97	.053 (.032, .072)	.059

Note. In all models, I controlled for WM variance. Aul=Auditory Intelligence; Acl=Academic Intelligence; fig=figural; num=numerical; nv=nonverbal; CFI=Comparative fit index; RMSEA=Root mean square error of approximation; Prob.=Probability value; SRMR=Standardized root mean square residual

The Aul factors can be clearly separated from the BIS content factors. The basic model allowing all factor intercorrelations fits the data satisfactorily (see Aul-Acl1; Table 7-28). The refined model excluded the correlations between the auditory speech factor and the figural BIS factor, as well as the relationship between the numerical BIS factor and the auditory nonverbal abilities. It also assumed a double assignment of the audiobook to the verbal BIS factor besides its loading on the auditory speech factor (see model Aul-Acl2, Table 7-28). This model showed an even better fit to the data. The model refinement was done in steps introducing each change separately thus improving the model continuously (for more information, see Seidel, 2007). In model Aul-Acl2, the task AU is closer related to verbal Acl than to Aul. MW again has a low loading on the auditory speech factor. The factor intercorrelations showed the auditory nonverbal factor not very related to any other factor of the model. As expected, the auditory speech factor had its strongest relationship with the verbal BIS factor. The BIS contents correlated strongly making their common variance apparent that is different from the Aul variance. Model Aul-Acl2 is illustrated in Figure 7-7.

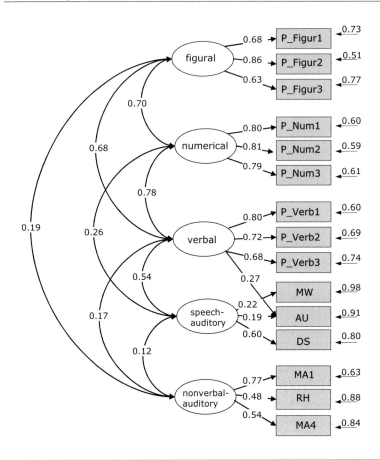

Figure 7-7: Model of Auditory Intelligence and BIS Contents

Note. P_verb=BIS Parcel verbal; P_num=BIS Parcel numerical; P_figur=BIS Parcel figural; MA1=Detection of repeated tones; MA4=Tonal series; RH=Rhythm reproduction; AU=Audiobook; DS=Disarranged sentences

Concerning the classification of the AuI tasks within the BIS operations, I first suggested a model allowing for all factor intercorrelations (see Model AuI-AcI3). Removing some of the zero correlations between the auditory nonverbal factor and BIS-M, BIS-R, BIS-S, and the auditory speech factor, resulted in a better fit and more parsimonious models (AuI-AcI4 and AuI-AcI5). An additional assignment between the audiobook and the memory factor of the BIS improved the fit again (see model AuI-AcI6). This model is presented in Figure 7-8.

Table 7-29: Models of Auditory and BIS Operations

Model	Model description	Chi² (df)	Prob.	CFI	RMSEA (CI 90%)	SRMR
Aul-Acl3	all intercorrelations allowed	108.888 (80)	.018	.96	.046 (.020, .066)	.052
Aul-Acl4	without correlations of: (BIS-M, AuNv); (AuNv, AuSp) and (AuNv, BIS-R)	111.101 (83)	.021	.97	.044 (.018, .065)	.056
Aul-Acl5	see Aul-Acl4 but without correlation between (BIS-S, AuNv)	112.163 (84)	.022	.97	.044 (.018, .064)	.058
Aul-Acl6	see Aul-Acl5, but double assignment of audiobook; AuSp uncorrelated with BIS-M	107.752 (84)	.041	.97	.041 (.009, .061)	.057

Note: I controlled for working memory variance in all models. CFI=Comparative fit index; RMSEA=Root mean square error of approximation; Prob.=Probability value; SRMR=Standardized root mean square residual; Aul=Auditory Intelligence; Acl=Academic Intelligence; BIS-S=BIS speed; BIS-M=BIS memory; BIS-R=BIS reasoning; AuSp=Auditory speech; AuNv=Auditory nonverbal

The model presented the auditory nonverbal factor as completely independent from Acl. Although the auditory speech factor was related to Acl, it also seemed to include a unique part of variance being unrelated to the auditory nonverbal ability. The task audiobook may be rather considered as an Acl task (memory, verbal) than an Aul task suggested by both the content model (Figure 7-7) and the operation model (Figure 7-8). This is in line with the remarks made in chapter 2.5, since audiobook contains larger speech units instead of single ones and thus requires verbal comprehension as a part of verbal Acl as well.

In summary, nonverbal auditory ability was proved to be independent from Acl operations (see Aul-Acl-1_2; chapter 7.1), whereas the auditory speech factor was related to the BIS contents and BIS operations (see Aul-Acl-2_2, see chapter 7.1) (see Seidel & Süß, 2007). With respect to the operation domains, auditory speech tasks correlated low to moderate with BIS-reasoning and with BIS-speed. Despite these relationships, they explain unique variance. However, this variance did not appear to be specific auditory since the auditory nonverbal factor was not related to the auditory speech factor. Concerning the relationship to the BIS contents, the auditory speech factor had its strongest correlation with the verbal BIS factor (.54). In addition, it was related to the numerical factor indicating that some crystallized ability (see chapter 2.1) was assessed. The auditory nonverbal factor showed a lower correlation with the verbal factor, a slightly stronger relationship with the BIS figural factor (.19), and no correlation at all with the numerical factor.

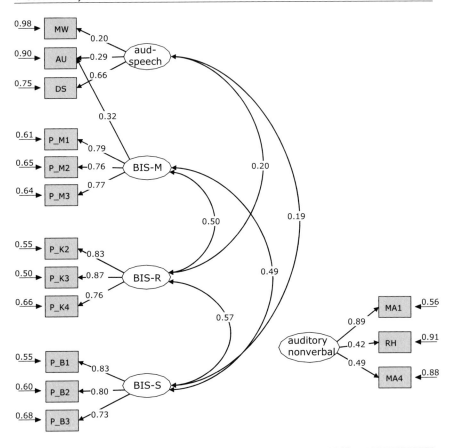

Figure 7-8: Auditory Intelligence Related to BIS Operations

Note. The auditory tasks are controlled for working memory. P_R=BIS parcel reasoning; P_S=BIS Parcel speed; P_M=BIS Parcel memory; MA1=Detection of repeated tones; MA4=Tonal series; RH=Rhythm reproduction; AU=Audiobook; DS=Disarranged sentences; MW=Masked words

7.4.5 Relationship Between Musical Experience and Auditory Intelligence

AuI-MUS1: Do musically experienced test takers perform better in the tonal auditory tasks?

Subjects had to judge their musical skills in comparison to peers on a five-point rating scale (1=extremly good; 5= extremely bad). 6.3% (N=11) indicated to have extremely well developed musical skills compared to their peers; 16.6% (N=29) rated their skills with a "2"; 45.7% (N=80) judged themselves as being in the middle; 24% (N=42) indicated to have rather poor and 7.4% (N=13) to have extremely poor musical skills when compared to their peers. This variable correlated significantly moderate to high with the nonverbal auditory intelligence tasks (correlations for MA1: r=.50; RH: r=.30; MA4: r=.28, for all p<.001) and thus confirmed AuI-MUS1 and the results of the first study (see chapter 6.3.3 above). The auditory speech tasks did not correlate at all with the musical skills self-assessment. Future studies should address the question of whether the nonverbal auditory tasks measure an auditory ability which serves as a precondition to acquire musical skills or whether it actually represents a musical ability that is unique for musically gifted people. There were no gender differences in the AuI tasks, indicating that the performance differences in favor of men that were found in the first study (see chapter 6.3.3) are due to a sample effect (high proportion of mathematicians). Empirical results support the positive relationship between mathematical abilities and musical giftedness (Bundesministerium für Bildung und Forschung, 2006).

7.5 *Results With Respect to the Relation Between Social Auditory and General Auditory Intellectual Abilities*

The following assumptions will be examined with respect to the relationship between social and general auditory abilities (see also Seidel, Weis, & Süß, 2007 for questions and results):

SI-AuI-1_2: Social auditory abilities show only marginal relationships to auditory intelligence.
SI-AuI-2_2: Auditory speech tasks correlate more highly with social auditory tasks than with nonverbal auditory tasks.
SI-AuI-3_2: Within the auditory domain, an emotion/social cues perception factor emerges that is clearly separable from both nonverbal and speech auditory and social memory and understanding tasks (see also Roberts et al., 2006).

The correlation matrix between social auditory and general auditory intelligence tasks is presented in Table 7-30. In italics, the correlations with baseline correction are shown.

Table 7-30: Corrrelations Between Social and General Auditory Abilities

	MA1	RH	MA4	MW	AU	DS
SPa1	.06	.13	.14	.04	.04	.01
	.01	*.06*	*.10*	*.07*	*.00*	*.03*
SPa2	.07	.08	.22**	.06	.21**	.17*
	.01	*.03*	*.17**	*.03*	*.18**	*.16**
GVEESS	.01	.09	.19*	.07	.13	.12
	.08	*.02*	*.15*	*.07*	*.10*	*.12*
SMa1	.07	.18*	.18*	.17*	.38**	.41**
	.07	*.18**	*.18**	*.17**	*.38***	*.41***
SMa2	.07	.08	.12	-.03	.11	.12
	.07	*.08*	*.12*	*-.03*	*.11*	*.12*
SUa	-.03	.08	.10	.02	.20**	.21**
	-.03	*.08*	*.10*	*.02*	*.20***	*.21***

Note. listwise N=171; in italics (correlations with baseline correction); MA1=Detection of repeated tones; MA4=Tonal series; RH=Rhythm reproduction; AU=Audiobook; DS=Disarranged sentences; MW=Masked words; SPa1=Social perception-auditory 1; SPa2=Social perception-auditory; GVEESS=Geneva Emotion Expression stimulus set; SMa1=Social memory-auditory1; SMa2=Social memory-auditory 2; SUa=Social understanding-auditory

The pattern of intercorrelations between social auditory and general auditory tasks is rather inconsistent: there are zero correlations, low correlations, and some moderate correlations. Although the correlation patterns appears inconsistent, correlations do exist, and social auditory abilities show more than only marginal relationships to general auditory abilities and thus disconfirm SI-AuI1_2 (see chapter 7.1). This is valid in particular with respect to auditory speech tasks. With the exception of MA1 (which is zero correlated with all of the social auditory tasks), all AuI tasks are significantly related to SMa1. This partly confirms H35SAu (Social auditory memory is related to general auditory intelligence tasks that require memory.). Relationships to SI are stronger for auditory speech tasks, probably because both use spoken language (see also chapter 6.3.4). However, when the AuI tasks are controlled for working memory, the correlations decrease. Only the relationships between SMa1 and audiobook and distracted sentences (speech tasks) remain significant (r=.34 and r=.31 respectively). Thus, common variance between auditory nonverbal and social auditory memory seems to be due to working memory whereas the relationship between the auditory speech tasks and social auditory memory does not seem to be affected by working memory. The task MA4 (auditory cognition of relationships/reasoning) is related to both social auditory perception (SPa2, GVEESS) and social auditory memory (SMa1). When working memory is partialed out these correlations also decrease (.11 to .13). The strongest relationship remains between MA4 and SMa2 (.13, p=.08). The task *masked words* is only significantly related to SMa1 (.17). Note that MW was neither related to AcI nor to the nonverbal auditory ability tasks. The two auditory speech tasks (AU and DS) are both related to auditory SP in realistic sentences, to SMa1 and to SUa. These are the tasks in which auditory communication by language is most important. In addition, the content may play an important role: The GVEESS task deals with meaningless sentences and the task SMa2 with voice recognition.

Both focus on the paraverbal features (tone of voice) rather than concentrating on the conversation content. However, when controlled for working memory in the general auditory tasks, correlations between the auditory speech tasks and social auditory tasks decrease as well. The relationships to SMa1 remain significant. Additional correlations close to reaching significance are between MW and SMa1 (.14, p=.07) and between distracted sentences and SMa2 (.13). The comparatively higher correlations between the auditory speech tasks and social auditory tasks are a first confirmation of assumption SI-AuI-2_2.

In performing CFA, analysis started with the two factors that were expected to be identified easiest according to the findings obtained in correlational analysis and EFA (see Seidel, 2007). Therefore, the first two models (model SAuI-GAuI1 and SAuI-GAuI2) presented in Table 7-31 contrast the general nonverbal auditory factor (GAuI-nv) including the tasks RH, MA1 and MA4 with the auditory SP factor (SPa) containing the GVEESS, the SPa2 and the SPa1. I used SRT baseline corrected social perception tasks. The model SAuI-GAuI1 fits the data very well. However, the two auditory factors are not significantly related (r=.04, p=.10). Model SAuI-GAuI2 excludes these intercorrelations and did not fit the data worse ($\Delta Chi^2=0.114$, $\Delta df=1 < Chi^2_{crit95\%}= 3.84$). The model is presented in Figure 7-9. The GVEESS and the SPa2 had to be included as splitted variables. Taking their aggregates led to constraints at the lower bound. Integrating the additonal auditory tasks in the model as an auditory spoken language based factor made the fit worse but fit was still attained (see SAuI-GAuI3). Doing without the zero correlation between the auditory nonverbal factor and the auditory perception factor again resulted in a better fit (model SAuI-Gaul4, see also Figure 7-9).

Table 7-31: Models of Social Auditory and General Auditory Intelligence

Model	Model description	Chi² (df)	Prob.	CFI	RMSEA (CI 90%)	SRMR
SAuI-GAuI1	two factors: GAuI-nv and SPa, intercorrelation: .04	26.895 (19)	.107	.97	.049 (.000, .089)	.056
SAuI-GAuI2	see SAuI-Gau1; but without factor intercorrelation	27.009 (20)	.135	.97	.045 (.000, .085)	.059
SAuI-GAuI3	three factors: GAuI_nv, SPa, and language-based auditory (Au_lang) intercor: F1,F2:-.06; F1,F3:.34; F2,F3:.18	103.067 (74)	.014	.92	.048 (.022, .069)	.064
SAuI-GAuI4	see SAuI-GAuI3; but without correlation between F1, F2	103.373 (75)	.017	.92	.047 (.021, .068)	.066
SAuI-GAuI5	see SAuI-GAuI4; but without the tasks SPa1, MW, SUa	60.408 (42)	.033	.94	.051 (.015, .078)	.063

Note. CFI=Comparative fit index; RMSEA=Root mean square error of approximation; Prob.=Probability value; SRMR=Standardized root mean square residual; Saul=Social auditory intelligence; Gaul=general auditory intelligence; nv=nonverbal; SPa=Social auditory perception; Au_lang=Auditory language-based; MW=Masked words; SUa=Social understanding-auditory

Figure 7-9 presents two models, the complete three-factor model SAuI-GauI4 including a spoken language factor besides a social/emotional perception factor and a nonverbal auditory factor. In addition, the two-factor model SAuI-GAuI2 is illustrated. It is evident in Figure 7-9, that SPa1 (factor auditory SP) and the tasks MW and SUa did not fit in the structure since they are not memory tasks. The model characteristics without the mentioned tasks are presented in Table 7-31 (see model SAuI-GauI5). This model provides a better fit to the data. The factors can be interpreted as (1) nonverbal auditory ability, (2) auditory emotion perception, and (3) auditory memory (social and general). Factor 1 and 3 correlate with .33, factor 2 and factor 3 are related with .21. This result also confirms SI-AuI-3_2 (see chapter 7.1) which formulates the expectation of an independent social/emotion auditory perception factor separable from both general (nonverbal) auditory intelligence and social intelligence factors (SU and SM) (see also Roberts et al., 2006). This factor however, unites perception tasks coming from emotions research tradition (GVEESS) and those that we developed from a psychometric perspective (SPa2, realistic sentences).

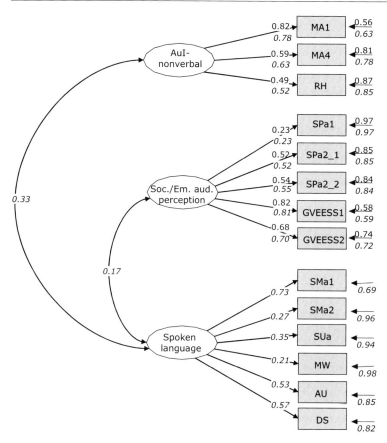

Figure 7-9: Model of General Auditory and Social Auditory Abilities

Note. Two-factor model (GAuI-SAuI2); three-factor model (GAuI-SAuI4): in italics, including a spoken language factor; MA1=Detection of repeated tones; MA4=Tonal series; RH=Rhythm reproduction; AU=Audiobook; DS=Disarranged sentences; SPa1=Social perception-auditory 1; SPa2=Social perception-auditory; GVEESS= Geneva Emotion Expression Stimulus Set; SMa1=Social memory-auditory1; SMa2=Social memory-auditory 2; SUa=Social understanding-auditory

8 Discussion

This chapter discusses the results of the two studies, focusing on the three aims of this book: assessing the usefulness of (1) social intelligence (SI), and (2) auditory intelligence (AuI), and (3) determining how the two hypothesized constructs are related. In addition, it addresses some special questions relevant for SI research, scoring and the nature of the material. In addition to some criticism, this chapter will provide some suggestions for further test improvement, give some information about the conditions of test application and make some remarks about possible test extensions. The chapter finishes with recommendations for future work on the topic and related research questions.

8.1 Are Auditory Intelligence and Social Intelligence Useful Constructs?

8.1.1 First Objective: Examination of the Internal Construct Validity

The first objective of this book is to examine aspects of validity in auditory and social intelligence (see chapter 1.2). Despite the difficulties we encounter when dealing with construct validity (e.g. no numerical index, results depend on the measurements and the conditions of data collection, see chapter 1), this book aims to approach this question using a framework of Süß (1996, 2001) which specifies conditions that have to be fulfilled in order to speak of a useful ability construct. The following discussion goes through each of these conditions that were examined in the context of the two studies.

Development of Performance Measures Requiring Only Basic Knowledge

Two tests, one assessing SI (Social Intelligence Test – Magdeburg, SIM (Süß et al., 2008)) the other AuI (Auditory Intelligence Test, AuIT) were developed, composed, and completed by more than 300 test takers in order to meet the first condition of the Süß (1996, 2001) framework (empirical foundation with test data, see chapter 1.2). The two tests are both performance measures, thus fulfilling the second condition (see chapter 1.2). Tasks of the SIM (Süß et al., 2008) and the AuIT were developed requiring the least possible knowledge and experience (see condition 3, chapter 1.2). This is constrictive with respect to the auditory test since musically experienced test takers showed better results in the nonverbal auditory tasks than subjects without this sort of experience. There are different possibilities of interpretation: First, the nonverbal auditory tasks depend on knowledge/experience; second, an underlying auditory ability predisposes musically experienced people to engage in musical activities and to acquire music knowledge. The relationship between auditory intellectual abilities and musical skills and abilities should be addressed in future investigations.

Generality

The fourth condition (generality/operationalizing the construct across different tasks) was supported for social memory (SM) and social understanding (SU) since these abilities were found to be independent of the kind of material (auditory, written, pictorial, video-based) that was applied. However, concerning SU, homogeneity may be overestimated because questions using different materials can be expected to influence one another. Social perception (SP) split into three minimally to moderately correlated parts: social written perception (SPw), social/emotional auditory perception (SPa), and social nonverbal perception (SPnv; pictorial and video-based) and thus appears to measure content-specific abilities. The findings let me assume that the three subfactors rely on different latent variables (e.g., abilities specific to the senses) instead of being part of one common social perception factor. As far as the content structure of social intelligence is concerned, further research working with a larger number of SI tasks is needed in order to be able to apply parceling technique. In this book the content structure of the four types of material was not identified, which corresponds to Noller (2001), who does not report relationships between the visual and auditory channels.

With respect to auditory intelligence a nonverbal auditory latent variable was indicated by different kinds of tasks (e.g., rhythm and tonal series). This is not unambiguous for the auditory speech factor, which will be discussed in further detail when dealing with the nomological network. In all the content domains, the operation structure (discrimination, memory, and reasoning) failed to emerge. It remains unclear whether the operation domains could not be justified in auditory intelligence because they do not exist or whether there are other reasons, such as the selection and development of task material.

Interrelations Between Subconstructs

This section deals with the interrelations of the subconstructs of both, social and auditory intelligence, and forms an important part of the construct validity evaluation (see condition 5). Concerning social intelligence, the SM and the SU factor were found to be moderately correlated. This correlation was higher using SU consensus-scores than applying target-scores. SU was not related to SP whereas SM was moderately to highly correlated with SPw (.48, see chapter 7.3.5), and minimally to SPa and SPnv. The relatively stronger relationship between SPw and SM may be due to the common written/verbal variance. The minimal correlations between SM and SPa and SPnv were also reflected in exploratory factor analysis (EFA) and confirmatory factor analysis (CFA). It is rather doubtful whether SPnv and SPa and the other social intelligence variables (SM and SU) are indicators of the same latent variable. The correlation among the nonverbal and auditory perception subfactor was also rather low. The result of perception factors different from other social intelligence variables is in line with Stankov's (2000) view, which regards emotion perception as separate from the other emotional/social intelligence variables. However, Stankov (2000) attributes this assumption to the different scoring modi (objective scoring criteria in case of perception), which cannot be applied to our test since SM and SP are both scored completely objectively and the SU variables are target-scored. Similar results have been obtained with scores on the facial expression subtest that did not correlate with other facial expression measures (O'Sullivan, 1982) or with other social skill tests such as the Interpersonal Perception Task-15 (see Hall, 2001). In a recent article Roberts et al. (2006) also found emotions measures (i.e., PONS) and EI measures (MSCEIT, emotion perception) loading on different factors. The authors attribute this to a validity problem with the MSCEIT, as its first branch intends to measure emotion perception. Like Stankov (2000), the authors see additional explanations for the missing correlations in different scoring methods (correct vs. incorrect in the emotions measures vs. consensus-based scoring in the MSCEIT); differences in the number and kind of stimuli (stimuli of emotion perception measures are more specific and contain more items); differences in instructions (EI research: rate of the emotional intensity of a series of emotions vs. emotion measures: select the primary emotion in a stimulus), quickness of emotion measures in contrast to EI measures; the duration of the stimulus presentation; spontaneous or acted emotions as stimuli; the relevant channel (face, body, voice); and in the criterion and chance level. Another reason could be the convergent validity problems that were often discovered with emotion measures (see Ambady, LaPlante, & Johnson, 2001; Hall, 2001; Scherer, 2003). The measures may tap different cognitive operations. The PONS, for example, requires the subjects to *judge* a short video scene whereas in other instruments subjects are instructed to *recognize* the appropriate emotion in social/emotional stimuli. Despite these divergent findings, Bänziger et al. (2005) recently gained some convergent validity proof and reported coefficients of about .50 (N=72) for correlations between the PONS, the JACFEE (Biehl, Matsumoto, Ekman, Hearn, Heider, Kudoh, 1997), the DANVA (Nowicki & Duke, 1994), and the MERT (see chapter 2.6.5). Scherer (in press) mentions common variance between emotion recognition measures using different modalities (r=.24 between Facial I and Vocal I). Austin (2004, 2005, Austin & Saklofske, 2006; see chapter 2.3.1) found a visual emotion perception factor that was correlated with the Faces Test (Ekman, 2004). Both were nonverbal perception tasks without the use of language. There seems to be a clear difference in judging audio and video cues (DePaulo & Rosenthal, 1979; Rosenthal et al., 1979). The effects produced by the auditory modality differ from those we know from dealing with vision. Additional differences between the sensory channels (hearing, sight, olfaction, gustation, touch) are reported in Danthiir et al. (2001), who found olfaction to be clearly distinguishable from auditory tasks. Similarly, Stankov (2001) found no relationship between factors of tactile and kinesthetic abilities. The view of social perceptual abilities as being rather basic and peripheral (see Radex, Marshalek et al., 1983) is similar to how "simple" sensory abilities are defined in inspection time research (e.g. Deary, 2000; Raz et al., 1987; see chapter 2.5.5). In a similar way, sensory abilities are described in the context of the psychology of aging (see Baltes & Lindenberger, 1997; Li, Jordanova, & Lindenberger, 1998; Lindenberger, Scherer, & Baltes, 2001).

Social memory takes a middle position in the SI structure. It correlates with both social perception abilities and social understanding. I can imagine that SP is a precondition for social memory, which itself has to exist to be able to judge a person's feelings, behaviors, cognitions, and relationships correctly. A good social memory also favors the acquisition of social knowledge, which is also expected to influence SU (see chapter 9.5.2).

Regarding the within structure of auditory intelligence, we found the auditory nonverbal factor to be moderately related to the auditory speech factor (r=.39). However, when controlled for WM variance the correlation dropped to r=.14. As in case of social perception, it is doubtful whether the two factors belong to the same construct. The two AuI factors seem to have less auditory variance in common than variance that distinguishes the factors. These findings are comprehensive against the background of the outcomes resulting from high auditory abilities or skills. Auditorily gifted people may have advantages in learning foreign languages since their discrimination and memory abilities in dealing with sounds are favourable for learning the correct pronunciation and wording. In addition, they may also develop musical skills because of their comparatively better ability to discriminate and memorize sounds and tones and their sense of how these tones or sounds may be related to build a "whole." Further research is needed in order to see whether and how auditory and musical abilities can be distinguished.

8.1.2 Second Objective: Examination of the Relationship to Other Constructs

The second objective is to contribute to the clarification of the position of auditory and social intelligence within the nomological network of human intellectual abilities (see Cronbach & Meehl, 1955). This corresponds to the sixth condition (see chapter 1.2) Süß (1996, 2001) demands for construct validity. The well-established academic intelligence (AcI) was chosen as a reference construct for SI and AuI in order to examine the degree of autonomy in the nomological network. AcI was measured by the Berlin Intelligence Structure Test (BIS, Jäger et al., 1997), which is based on the Berlin Intelligence Structure Model (see Jäger, 1982, 1984).

Social Understanding

Two studies with different groups of people found social understanding (SU) to be completely autonomous from academic intelligence. The results we obtained with the SI core dimension are in line with the findings of Lee et al. (2000), who did not find AcI and SI to be related.

251

There are several possibilities to explain the independence of SU from AcI, in particular from the corresponding reasoning operation: First, according to an audacious hypothesis of Tooby and Cosmides (1992), empirical findings indicate that reasoning is a product of a collection of functionally specified evolved mechanisms, most of which are content dependent. Thus, Tooby and Cosmides (1992) argue for specialized, domain-specific, and highly adapted mechanisms that are activated specifically and differently for threat, social exchange, etc., rather than assuming a general underlying mechanism for human reasoning activities. In their opinion, all content features of the human mind are socially constructed or environmentally developed. Thus, for the reasoning domain, Tooby and Cosmides (1992) argue in the opposite direction as compared to Willingham (2005), who assumes a general underlying latent variable for meaningful memory. An example of Tooby and Cosmides' view on reasoning is provided by the application of the well-known Wason selection task (see Wason, 1968). In this task, the subject gets four cards, each of which is labelled with a different number or letter. The subjects are asked to check an abstract rule (e.g. If one side of the card has a vowel, then the other side should show an even number) by turning as few cards as possible. Studies described in Cosmides and Tooby (2005) revealed that only about 20% of the test takers turned the correct cards. However, when the same task is embedded in a social context the performance of subjects increases to 76% (e.g., "Teenagers borrowing their parent's car have to fill up the tank with gas"; subjects have to find out whether this is true by turning only the cards that are absolutely necessary). The sceptical reader may argue that this result is affected by the concreteness (vs. abstractness) of the material. However, another concrete but not social example ("If you spray lacana tea on your flowers, deer will stay out of your yard.") also including a short introduction story is completed correctly by only 26% of subjects (see Cosmides & Tooby, 2005). Social material/social context appears to tap different cognitive processes (see also chapter 8.3.6). The effect of the social/emotional material is also mentioned by Blanchette and Richards (2004), who claim that reasoning about emotional statements is much more likely to be logically invalid than reasoning about neutral statements.

A second explanation for the findings lies in the type of scenario task that was used for the assessment of SU and the influencing variables in building an impression from the target person (see also issues of generality). How a person answers the items of the scenario task (e.g. about the emotion of the target person in a conversation) is based on the impression that is formed while working on former questions and materials. In addition, forming an impression may be strongly affected by a person's personality. However, in the first study none of the SU scales correlated with the NEO-FFI scales and in the second study correlations between the NEO-FFI and the SU variables were also rare. The SU language-based tasks correlated only with conscientiousness and agreeableness of the NEO-FFI ($r=.18$ - $.25$, $p=.01$ - $.00$) (The presentation of detailed results in this book was not possible because of the limited number of pages.). The relatively rare correlations between personality and SI may be due to the different kinds of measures (self-report vs. performance test). Although one may argue that there is no need to measure personality with an ability test since it is not an ability construct, the differences in the measurement procedure inevitably produce different kinds of variance. It would be interesting to invent a personality measure that is less susceptible to social desirability and dependence on own imaginative power required for the interpretation, for example, of one-sentence written statements used in the NEO-FFI. Such a personality assessment could be operationalized with a computer-based test applying video scenes with sound that deal with various situations. Instead of judging the behavior of other people presented in the scenes, the test taker's task could be to imagine himself in the presented situation. One of several possible answer alternatives (presented auditorily and video-based) has to be chosen, serving as an indicator of the degree to which a certain personality variable is present. Besides the personality, the similarity and the sympathy the test taker feels for the target person may affect the result. In the second study, we asked the subjects to indicate on a seven-point rating scale the degree of similarity and the sympathy they felt for the target person. Only in three of eight scenario tasks was the sympathy for the target person related to the performance in the corresponding scenario ($.18-.37$; $p<.05$); in one of eight scenario tasks the test takers estimated similarity with the target person affected the test result (scenario Friedhelm: $.30$, $p<.001$). The scenarios with the described effects on first sight only have in common that the target people are all males.

A third aspect that requires mention with respect to the zero correlations between SU and AcI is the level of complexity which is crucial for intelligence in that it may lead to different degrees of relationships between latent variables (see chapter 2.1.3). Dealing with complexity is itself a complex issue (see Suedfeld, 1994) and has several perspectives. At this point, I refer to the complexity of cognitive processes required for information processing. They may vary depending on 1) the task material and 2) personality characteristics such as knowledge, working memory, and academic intelligence. Literature indicates that SI involves more complex processing compared to AcI (e.g., Frederiksen et al., 1984; Kaiser, 1998). This may be due to the characteristics social situations have in common with problem-solving tasks. Often they do not have a clear starting point or goal, and they are often not transparent but integrated in a complex and dynamic network (Kaiser, 1998). Gigerenzer (1997) concludes that SI is special and cannot be subsumed under "general intelligence" together with AcI.

Social Memory (SM)

Although we found a partial independence of SM from AcI, the factor intercorrelations between SM and BIS-Memory are higher than the correlation of SM with SU (first study:

r(SM, SU)=.28; r(SM, BIS-M)=.38; second study: r(SM, SU)=.21; r(SM, BIS-M)=.69). Nevertheless, specific parts of SM could be shown in the regression model (see chapter 6.3.1 and 7.3.6). The question of whether SM can be justified as unique ability has to be further examined in a criterion validation study figuring out the incremental variance SM has beyond AcI and the remaining SI subfactors. Possible reasons for the difficulties in separating SM from the BIS factors may also lie in the type of SM tasks we used. Despite trying to include paraverbal aspects, most of our memory tasks required an answer sheet presented in written language. With the exception of SMa2 (second study), the social memory tasks correlated highly significantly with BIS-verbal (between r=.20 and r=.58). One should do a comparable study again, replacing the memory tasks with a high verbal part through nonverbal tasks (e.g., an improved version of the voice memory task; a social emotions task with movies and voices). A computer-based presentation of answer alternatives (auditorily or with video extracts) should help to minimize the verbal part. Another explanation for the particularly strong relationship between SM and BIS-M is a result known from the field of musical psychology. According to Bruhn (2003), areas of the cortex that are responsible for long-term memory are connected with all senses and interchange information with areas responsible for reasoning. Social (as well as auditory) memory according to his view should be related to other kinds of memory (Bruhn, 2003), too. In line with this statement, Willingham (2005) proclaims that most memories are stored in terms of meaning instead of being stored in a modality specific manner. This may yield an explanation for the relationships that were almost always highest between the memory domains of the different constructs. According to Willingham (2005), (modality) specific memory systems help to store the part of information that is independent from content meaning (e.g., what is said), such as the sound of voice in auditory memory (e.g., how something is said). This may explain the differences between the two auditory memory tasks, SMa1 (memory for conversations) as a content based task, and SMa2 (memory for voices). Their relationship should be investigated again with improved reliability of the voice memory task. A good voice memory also contributes to the acquisition of the sound of a foreign language (Willingham, 2005). This may connect paraverbal, social aspects to academic learning abilities that may be reflected in subjects dealing with different languages.

Social Perception-Component of Intelligence or Sensory Ability?

The relationships among the suggested social perception factors remained stable even when BIS variance was partialed out (see 7.3.6 and Figure 7-3 compared to Figure 7-5). The written social perception factor (SPw) was most closely related to academic intelligence. If we model it separately from the other perception factors, it cannot be distinguished from BIS-speed. In contrast, the social nonverbal perception (SPnv) and social auditory perception (SPa) factors could be clearly distinguished from AcI. A model relating the SPnv factor to the BIS variables showed a good fit to the data (Chi²=85.351, df=59; p=.014; CFI=.97;

SRMR=.057; RMSEA=.051; CI: 023, .073). SPn correlated with .29 with both BIS-speed and BIS-memory and did not show any relationship to BIS-reasoning. The auditory social perception factor (SPa) was not at all related to academic intelligence measured by the BIS. A model relating SPa to the BIS variables without allowing an intercorrelation fitted the data very well (Chi²=82.645, df=59, p=.023; CFI=. 973; SRMR=.054; RMSEA=.048, CI: .019, .071). Surprisingly, the SPa factor did not correlate with general auditory intelligence either (see Figure 7-9).

The special role perception abilities take was emphasized by Stankov (1999), who applied several emotion perception measures (for further information, see Davies et al., 1998) and found emotion perception not to be linked to personality or ability traits. It correlated only marginally with gf (r=.15) and showed zero correlation with gc (r= .05). Conclusively, Stankov considers emotion perception as the most likely candidate for pure EI measurement.

A possible explanation and approach for further examination may yield findings obtained in the psychology of aging (see Baltes & Lindenberger, 1997; Li et al., 1998; Lindenberger et al., 2001). Researchers of this branch found an increasing covariation between intelligence and sensory functioning depending on age. The source of the decline of intelligence together with a decline of sensory functioning in older participants appears to be due to either sensory speed or sensory discrimination or both (Li et al., 1998). On the contrary, the reduction of (auditory) acuity does not have an effect on standard cognitive performance (Lindenberger et al., 1998). These results may provide an explanation for our findings: In contrast to social written perception which shares common variance with AcI through both verbal crystallized components and sensory speed, social auditory perception tasks may have something in common with auditory acuity rather than affecting sensory discrimination or sensory speed. In this context again empirical findings discovered by Stankov (1999, 2000) may be useful. Stankov describes the appearance of a strong general intelligence factor as soon as sensory and psychomotor abilities are excluded from analysis. In contrast, the general intelligence factor is rather weak if sensory and psychomotor abilities are included in the analysis of intellectual ability tasks (see also Danthiir et al., 2001). Thus, the inclusion of a broad variety of tasks varying in terms of difficulty and complexity tends to produce a weaker general factor (first principal component not more than 20% of total variance) than studies that are based on a narrower sampling of tasks (see Roberts, Pallier, & Goff, 1998). In our studies, this assumption is confirmed. Including social perception tasks in the exploratory factor analysis together with SU and SM tasks as well as AcI tasks leads to a first component explaining not more than 20.84% of the total variance. With respect to the internal structure of SI (2nd study), the first component explains only 18.14% of the variance.

How can the results be explained? The differences that have been found between abilities that stem from the five senses and their relationship to AcI can be traced back to the early works of Galton (1883) who assumed individual differences in the five senses (visual, auditory, tactile, olfactory, and taste) to result in individual differences in the power of the mind. However, instead of the expected considerable relationship between sensory abilities and intelligence, elementary sensory processes relate only at a very low level to the reasoning, acquisition, and retention processes of human intellect (see Horn, 2006). Cattell (1998), in his triadic theory, speaks of provincial factors when mentioning the so-called "sensory centers" and differentiates them from the two classes, general capacities (e.g., fluid intelligence, gf) and agencies (narrow abilities in different areas of cultural content such as inductive reasoning or word fluency). Taking up Cattell's (1998) perspective, the low correlations between the SP-factors and their relationship to AcI can be attributed to discarding principles of symmetry (see Wittmann, 1988). Perceptual (sensory) abilities appear to be arranged on a lower hierarchical level compared to the remaining SI factors and compared to AcI factors. In terms of the facet theoretical radex approach suggested by Marshalek et al. (1983), the sensory specific social perception factors can be classified in the periphery. The more peripheral in a radex, the larger the distance between tests (see Marshalek at al., 1983). The lower the complexity level (=number of relatively simple ingredient steps; Stankov, 2000), the less the factors seem to be related to each other and load on a common "general factor".

Auditory Intelligence

Nonverbal auditory intelligence proved to be independent from academic intelligence. This was also true when controlled for working memory variance. We have to take a different perspective with respect to the auditory speech tasks. These appear to measure quite similar aspects to those assessed with AcI tasks (especially verbal AcI, reasoning and memory operations). Apparently, there are some relationships between the auditory general factor and AcI, particularly with reasoning. Therefore, another explanation for the failure to prove the operational structure of AuI is that the auditory intelligence tasks require a combination of AcI operations and specific auditory parts. Additional auditory ability tasks are needed to examine this question in further detail. An additional explanation comes up when considering that auditory intellectual abilities are comparatively basic perceptual/sensory and serve as a precondition for higher order processes (see remarks in the context of SP, this section). The perceptual nature of auditory intellectual abilities is emphasized by Carroll (1993) who talks of a "broad auditory perception factor". However, restricting auditory abilities to the perception domain does not seem correct, since undoubtedly some tasks such as tonal series should be related to reasoning rather than to perception. And this is what results confirm (see chapter 6.4.3 and 8.4.4).

Findings of our two studies show that the auditory modality has specific characteristics: It not only appears to be harder for auditory tasks to reach high reliability values, but also the tasks seem to measure something different compared to AcI and SI. The special role auditory abilities take was already discovered by Atkin et al. (1977), who found a listening test clearly standing apart from all other cognitive measures. However, individual differences in children on the listening comprehension test were causally related to later intellectual development, thus forming an important precondition for high AcI. Possibly, attention is a moderating variable between auditory processing and intellectual level, since learning and development is only possible with a sufficient amount of attention. The auditory tasks demand a lot of attention. In contrast to tests of AcI, it is impossible to look again at the test material after having listened to the relevant excerpts. In order to control for effects of attention, such a measure should be included in further investigations. Another difference between the auditory and AcI tasks is the proportion of speed and level measures. Whereas the indicators of all cognitive operation factors are strictly limited in time, the auditory tasks are not restricted in time. We asked subjects to work quickly, but also waited for the test takers who took longer. For the time restricted tasks (e.g. the audiobook) enough time was provided so that everyone could finish the task without hurrying. By contrast, BIS tasks are designed in a way that almost nobody will complete every item. This fact may lead to common speed variance between the BIS factors, whereas the auditory modality is not affected by speed to this extent.

8.1.3   Third Objective: Relating Social Auditory and General Auditory Intelligence

In a factor model including social and general auditory ability tasks, three factors emerged: an auditory language-based factor (speech auditory and social auditory SM and SU), an auditory nonverbal factor, and a social auditory perception factor. Whereas the social auditory perception factor was independent of the other two factors, the language-based and the auditory nonverbal factor co-varied with .33 (see Figure 7-9). Thus, general speech auditory abilities tasks and social auditory memory and understanding tasks could be subsumed under one factor. The close relationship between social and non-social language-based abilities fits with a statement of Ford (1994), in whose opinion in some contexts (e.g. involving teaching, public speaking or social persuasion) language production skills may account for a significant proportion of the variance in the assessment of SI. In addition, Zeidner, Matthews, Roberts, and MacCann (2003) point out that individual differences in emotional learning seem to be strongly linked to individual differences in verbal ability. I take the view that people who are able to deal effectively with other people train their language skills (e.g., talking more, talking to different people in different ways, etc.), which may also affect social knowledge (learning how to behave in certain situations, cultures, etc.; see chapter 8.5.2). These assumptions are similar neuropsychological results dealing with the relationship between auditory language-based and auditory nonverbal abilities (see Koelsch & Siebel, 2005; Patel, Peretz, Tramo, & Labreque, 1998). In several studies, language and music were found to be related since they are both means of communication and both use a certain syntax (e.g. music: tonic, subdominant, supertonic, dominant; German language: subject-verb-object). Even more they both serve social functions. Music is one of the oldest and most basic socio-cognitive domains of the human species. A review points into the direction that human musical abilities played a key phylogenetic role in the evolution of language and that music-making behavior covered important functions such as communication, cooperation, social cohesion, group coordination as well as social and emotional development (see Bundesministerium für Bildung und Forschung, 2006; Zatorre & Peretz, 2001). From a developmental perspective it is known that infants' first steps into language are based in large part on prosodic information (see Jusczyk, 1999) such as speech melody, metre, rhythm, timbre, and pitch relationships. Maternal music is thought to play an important role in the emotional, cognitive, and social development of children (see Trehub, 2003). Making music in a group affects the whole brain (perceptual, memory, social, emotional etc. processes, see Koelsch & Siebel, 2005). Even people without any musical training show sophisticated abilities to acquire knowledge about musical syntax and to understand music, which indicates the existence of an underlying natural ability (see Koelsch & Siebel, 2005), which may be auditory intelligence. The assumption of an intimate connection between music and speech is corroborated by the findings of overlapping and shared neural resources for music and language syntactic processing (e.g., Koelsch, Gunther, Wittfoth, & Sammler, 2005). The processing of both musical and linguistic syntax requires the activation of neural resources that mediate the processing of complex, regularity-based sequential information (Koelsch et al., 2005). ERP (Event-related potential) studies provide evidence for shared neural resources. In addition to syntax, semantics was found to be a basic dimension of language: The semantic processing of words can be influenced systematically by advance presentation of musical information. The human brain seems to process music and language similarly (see Koelsch, 2004). Both make use of the broca and wernicke regions of the brain (Magnet-Resonanz-Tomographie, MRT; functional magnetic resonance imaging, fMRI). This is true not only for musically experienced people but also for people without any prior knowledge of music (Koelsch, 2004). Jenschke, Koelsch, and Friederici (2005) showed that musical training can improve language abilities in children. Against this background, the link between language and musical abilities via syntax is especially relevant, assuming a common underlying auditory resource basic to both language and music (see Bundesministerium für Bildung and Forschung, 2006). A first confirmation of this assumption is obtained by Anvari, Trainor, Woodside, and Levy (2002) who examined the relationships between phonological awareness, music perception, and early reading in a sample of 100 four- and five-year-old children. Two moderately intercorrelated (.33 - .59) factors emerged, music perception and phonological awareness.

Music perception skill predicted reading even after the variance shared with phonemic awareness was removed. The findings are interpreted such that phonemic awareness and music perception ability have basic auditory abilities in common that are needed for reading but additionally tap unique processing skills (Anvari et al., 2002). The differences between language and music should not be ignored from the neuropsychological perspective: linguistic syntax is more lateralized to the left hemisphere, whereas processing of musical structure is more lateralized to the right hemisphere.

Interestingly, within the auditory domain, social perception was related neither to SM nor to SU, nor to language-based general auditory abilities. This is particularly surprising since all tasks worked with auditory material and used language. In order to obtain such a result, the auditory and social common variance has to be minor, whereas the different (maybe operational) variance has to be predominant. One of the differences between the social auditory tasks (SU and SM vs. SP) is the apparent focus on paraverbal aspects of language in social auditory perception tasks, whereas the SU and SM tasks contain both paraverbal and verbal aspects, or even completely focus on verbal aspects. The other difference is the focus on emotions in the social perception tasks, whereas the other social auditory tasks concentrate on the interactive components. Whether there is indeed an emotional intelligence component separable from social intelligence perception should be further investigated with additional indicators for both constructs. Measurement issues may be responsible for the results, too, since analysis in the perception tasks is done with reaction times, whereas in the SM and SU tasks accuracy scores are used. The social auditory perception tasks were clearly separable not only from other social and speech auditory abilities but also from nonverbal auditory abilities. Thus, the auditory common part of SPa and AuI-nv seems to be subordinate. Conclusively, auditory is not equal auditory. Paraverbal aspects (here emotions) seem to tap another underlying latent variable compared with abilities that focus on the content of language, even when using the same (auditory) material.

8.1.4 Interrelation Between the Examined Constructs: A Summary

Figure 8-1 presents the modified perspective I take with respect to the constructs that have been the subject of research in this book. Findings revealed four different constructs: the "old" academic intelligence, social intelligence, auditory intelligence, and social/emotional perception, the latter probably being sensual rather than intellectual. The four constructs overlap in important parts, particularly with respect to AcI and SI memory, with respect to AcI verbal and AuI speech, and with respect to SPw and AcI speed and memory. Taking AcI as a reference construct, the following subconstructs could be identified as reliable and useful candidates for different novel intelligences (on condition that additional proof, in particular incremental criterion validity, can be shown) in two studies with different subjects: social understanding, nonverbal auditory ability, and social/emotional auditory perception.

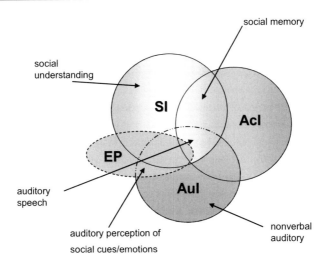

Figure 8-1: Relationship between Academic, Auditory, and Social Intelligence, and Perception of Nonverbal Social Cues/Emotions

8.1.5 A Comment on Validation Frameworks and General Questions Concerning "Intelligence"

In this book, I focused on the conditions for ability constructs suggested by Süß (1996, 2001). However, some researchers mention divergent conditions for the establishment of construct validity. Austin and Saklofske (2006) claim that three conditions have to be fulfilled in order to be able to speak of a valid ability construct: (1) convergent and discriminant construct validity, (2) criterion and predictive validity, and (3) genetic and biological foundations comparable to academic intelligence. In summary, the framework of Süß (1996, 2001) is much broader (see chapter 1.2) but does not explicitly include the third criterion mentioned by Austin and Saklofske (2006). However, the Süß conditions are based on a cognitive theory instead of a biological one. If the Süß conditions are completely fulfilled, high stability (retest reliability) included, one could infer genetic causes. Nevertheless, it is always worthwhile to get further support from other research disciplines. This may include neuropsychology and/or also social or developmental psychology (see e.g., neuropsychological links below).

I already mentioned that in almost all condition catalogues "positive manifold" is considered as an essential condition for a valid ability construct (see also Mayer, Caruso, & Salovey, 1999). Austin and Saklofske (2006) deal with the positive manifold in the context of their first criterion, the convergent and discriminant construct validity. According to their view, a new intelligence construct should be classified within the hierarchical structure of Carroll's (1993) Three-Stratum Model of intelligence and show correlations with corresponding group and specific factors. The positive correlations of the new construct with the already established constructs (the authors even speak of "existing") should be not too high in order to make a unique contribution to established intelligence constructs. Austin and Saklofske (2006) suggest classifying EI, SI and PI within the second stratum of Carroll's Three-Stratum Model. It is evident that Austin and Saklofske start from a very narrow perspective that assumes (1) that Carroll's model is "true", (2) that new intelligence constructs cannot exceed the scope of the already well-established academic intelligence (they can belong to the second stratum!), and (3) that every new intelligence construct, in order to deserve the label "intelligence", has to be positively correlated with academic intelligence. The latter perspective (see 3) is shared for example by Carroll (1993); Mayer et al. (1999); Schulze, Wilhelm, and Kyllonen (in press); and Wilhelm (2005) who all seem to assume that there is one underlying factor that relates the sub- or lower order factors to one another. In the same way, broad auditory perception ability in Carroll's model and in the CHC theory is subsumed under a general intelligence factor (see Carroll, 1995). However, we could show in two studies that auditory abilities formed a reliable but separate domain from AcI when related to both content domains and operation domains. The same happened with SU. Aren't these constructs ability/intelligence constructs because they are not related to the other already defined constructs of AcI? This would be the view most researchers (e.g., Austin & Saklofske, 2006; Carroll, 1993; Lee et al., 2000; Mayer et al., 1999; Schulze, in press; Wilhelm, 2005) would take since they regard a moderate correlation with the already established AcI as a precondition to be treated as an intelligence. But who limits the virtual space of constructs to the already investigated ones? Why should we exclude the possibility of discovering completely new variance? I take the position that a new intelligence construct can also be an intelligence if it is not correlated with AcI at all (see e.g., SU, SPa, AuI-nv) in the case that all of the mentioned conditions (see Süß, 1996, 2001) are fulfilled. One could argue whether a label different from the term "intelligence" then would be more appropriate for constructs being not related to the "old AcI." However, whatever label we chose, it seems to be evident that reliable and useful ability constructs do exist that are different from AcI. How we label them will not make a difference as to their existence. In the following, I will argue that in spite of being independent from AcI, SU is a promising candidate for a useful intelligence construct. First, the possible explanations for the SU results do not exclude the possibility that SU is a factor of intelligence. On the contrary, SU may just tap different reasoning processes, seems to be rather unrelated to personality variables, and may be characterized through a different degree of complexity. Second, the positive manifold is not sufficient (see Horn, 1998). Instruments that do not measure cognitive abilities nevertheless correlate with intelligence tests (e.g., assessments of ego-strength and law abidance). Third, the intercorrelations between measures often result in a general factor which cannot be generalized as soon as a different composition of measures was applied. The critical proof of whether SU indeed is a useful ability construct able to explain incremental variance compared to AcI has to be examined by means of a criterion validation study using relevant symmetrical criteria (see Wittmann, 1988; see chapter 8.6.1). Figure 9-2 summarizes my perspective on intelligence and the different (sub-) constructs that have been examined within this book. The figure illustrates that SU and AuI-nv are within the "circle of intelligences" despite being unrelated to AcI.

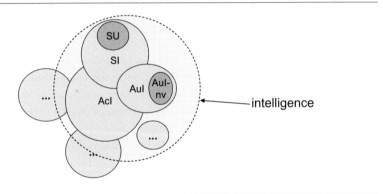

Figure 8-2: Model of Intelligences

Note. SU=Social understanding; AcI=Academic intelligence; AuI=Auditory intelligence; AuI-nv=Auditory nonverbal intelligence

8.2 Discussion of the Use of Social Material and Scoring Procedure

8.2.1 The "Concern" of Social Task Material

During the two studies, all examiners reported that test takers behaved differently working on the social intelligence tasks compared to the academic intelligence tasks. They not only gave the impression of better concentration while working on the SI tasks but also seemed to identify themselves with the characters (target persons) of our social understanding tasks. The material can be expected to have an intervening effect since the test takers have to argue with the target persons. They need to compare their own view and reflect their own perspective with that of the presented characters.

Not only in our social understanding tasks but also in the social memory and perception tasks, the social nature of the material affects performance. In both studies, we got the impression that our test takers performed better in the social memory tasks compared to the academic memory tasks. With the exception of recognition of numbers with M=100.94 (SD=.911), all academic memory tasks had a mean standard value below the average (91.34 to 99.68) (average is M=100). By contrast, in the tasks regarding social auditory memory for conversations (SMa1) and social written memory for correspondence subjects performed above average (SMa1: 61% correct; SD=.13; SMw1+2: 76%, SD=.11). These results have to be interpreted with caution since the absolute performance values are not directly comparable. For a more profound result a study with two parallel tasks, one applying social information, the other using academic information, should be carried out. Nevertheless, literature yields some confirmation for the presented assumption. Rummer and Engelkamp (2000) report a study wherein pleasant social/emotional content was remembered better than unpleasant content; both were better remembered than neutral content. Bower and Forgas (2001) also mention that emotional/social events remain in memory for a longer time. At the end of the test session (2nd study), we asked the test takers to complete a long-term memory test containing questions about the target scenario persons and their private and public life. We were impressed with the amount of information they remembered even after several weeks. Why do social tasks appear to be easier than academic tasks? Subjects may be better at remembering socially relevant details because these concern their own person. When we hear or read about other people we quickly form a picture, evaluate the information, and compare it to our own perspective and experience. Similarly, perception of social vs. academic content provokes differences in the speed of reaction. Rummer and Engelkamp (2000) found that emotionally unpleasant words were recognized more slowly than neutral words. Pleasant words were recognized the fastest.

8.2.2 Issues of Scoring

In the analysis of results I focused on target scoring. The scales formed with this technique proved to be reliable (see Table 7-2). Compared to consensus scores, the target scores were even more reliable in the first study. In the second study they showed slightly better reliability values with respect to the auditory and the pictorial scale. Compared to consensus-scored values, target scores have several advantages: The main pro is certainly independence from common sense and from the selected sample, since they rely on an external criterion. In addition, target scores are more similar to the scoring (one right answer) that is commonly applied in intelligence research. To score an ability measure according to common sense does not fit in the tradition of intelligence testing (see also Van Rooy, Viswesvaran, & Pluta, 2005). Moreover, people high on the crucial ability would be punished when the "empirically correct" score and their own answer diverge from common sense. Mac Cann et al. (2004)

could show, that various procedures of consensus-based scoring do not necessarily converge. In a reliable test, consensus scores result in highly negatively skewed scores (MacCann et al., 2004b) and in a lower score for a person with an exceptionally high ability who completed a task differently compared to the majority. "Consensus or stereotypic accuracy has gone from a bias to be avoided (Cronbach), to an error to be controlled or identified (Kenny), to a potential source of information about understanding people in the absence of specific information (Funder), to the criterion for accuracy (Sternberg), not only for items for which no veridical criterion is available, and therefore consensus is a stop-gap measure (Nowicki) or a desirable one (Mayer), to arguments that consensus scoring is actually superior to known truth as the criterion for accuracy test items (Legree). (see O'Sullivan, in press, p. 451).

Nevertheless, models using consensus scores fit the data better than those applying target scores (see Table 7-17). Another difference is the slightly higher correlation consensus-based models reveal between SU and SM in both studies (see Figure 7-1). The similarities we find between models making use of different scoring procedures indicate that consensus scores do not necessarily produce results completely different from those found when using an external criterion. The consensus and target score scales correlated between .69 and .82 in the first study (see table 2-7) and, except for the written score (.16), between .61 and .78 in the second study (see table 4-3). These findings provide some justification for the utilization of consensus scores since this way of scoring was often regarded as problematic (see Roberts et al., 2006, p. 667, see chapter 2.2.3 and 2.7.2). However, the strong relationships between the two scoring methods may also be due to item selection that was done by a small group of women, who only included items with which everyone in the small group agreed.

With respect to target scores, we discovered methodological and economical problems with the scaling. First, targets had the preference to select an extreme answer category (e.g. 1 or 7). The problem with these answers is that they have the possibility of deviance only in one direction. This deviance can cause a higher difference score than a target person's answers located in the middle of the scale (e.g. "3" which can deviate only 4 points). In item selection, we paid attention to select items representatively with regard to the distribution of deviation points. Moreover, target scores were weighted according to the maximum possible deviation in one item. Second, the simple problem of using rating scales also produces unsystematic variance with respect to the individual answer tendency: some of the subjects may have a preference for extreme answers (severity or leniency effect), whereas others may tend towards choosing the middle category. I standardized the items in order to reduce these influences. In addition, a successful but lavish way to avoid these problems may be to develop some reference questions applying the same scale to try to get an impression of individual preferences. Furthermore, the assessment of self-description ability (see Damarin, 1970) and the inclusion of context manipulation checks may be useful to control for systematic biases (e.g. with respect to frequencies) and context dependency in human judgment (for further information see Schwarz, 1999). Approaches in order to deal with social desirability are, for example, provided in Furnham (1986) and Paulhus (1991). Paulhus mentions factor-analytic and covariate techniques during test construction and recommends using a forced-choice format and control questionnaires (for an overview see Paulhus, 1991) in order to control for response biases such as careless, consistent, extreme, and social desirable responding. In reaction time tasks the RTs of wrongly answered items can also be used as indication for response styles. A MTMM design may be used in order to investigate whether answer tendencies (response biases) in subjects are due to method effects or to personality characteristics of the subjects. Third, the emotions that have to be judged in the scenario tasks were considered as independent items (e.g. test takers had to rate boredom and joy in one specific situation). One might argue, that certain emotions will probably not occur together (e.g. anger and joy) and thus, items should not be treated as independent. Future investigations should take confusion patterns into account such as mentioned in chapter 2.6.4. Fourth, compared to consensus scoring a target-oriented scoring procedure is very costly and time intensive and therefore only rarely applied. Besides our SIM (Süß et al., 2008) test, only the EARS (Emotional Accuracy Research Scale, Mayer & Geher, 1996), the CARAT (CARAT = Communication of Affect Receiving Ability Test, Buck, 1976), and the IPT-15 (see section 2.2.3) make use of target scoring. Future research should evaluate the criterion validity of both scoring methods.

Besides the two scoring procedures that have been applied in the two studies there are alternative ways of scoring. I already mentioned that we started to collect peer ratings to get some validation data for the target persons' answers. Moreover, the collection of expert ratings of the single scenes and items may yield interesting additional information. With respect to consensus-based scoring, future studies on the SIM (Süß et al., 2008) and the AuIT should take into account Mac Cann et al.'s (2004) advice. They suggest to use Euclidean distance scoring or Mahalanobis scoring in order to treat all responses based on one stem as one multi-part item. This technique was used in tacit knowledge research, for example by Hedlund et al., (2003), who computed a squared Euclidean distance of the incumbent's responses from the experts' answer means corrected by the variability of the experts' ratings.

8.3 Criticism of the Studies

There are several points that have to be criticized with regard to the studies that have been carried out in the context of this work. First, the conditions of testing have to be criticized. Our first study was split up in two sessions taking five hours each, the second study consisted of two sessions with a duration of six hours each. Although we took breaks and provided refreshments, testing time was too long. Concentration is expected to be reduced, which has an impact on the task performance, in particular with respect to the latter tests. This result is confirmed by the strain questionnaires that were applied at the beginning and at the end of each test session. Motivation decreased considerably and strain increased during test performance. It was difficult to reduce the test time since we wanted to gain as much information as possible to make reliable statements about the validity of the measures. Moreover, the new tests were in a preliminary form, implying that more items were needed for each task. For the second study we considered splitting the test time in three instead of two parts. However, the test takers preferred being tested in two sessions as this reduced the effort with regard to the journey and departure.

Another critical point concerns the choice of the general auditory intelligence tasks. The attentive reader may have wondered why I did not choose more specified tasks with respect to the preliminary model I suggested in Figure 2-10 (see chapter 2.5.6). That would have focused more on actual Auditory Intelligence part instead of including tasks from the transition areas to musical and spoken language abilities. To answer this question I cite Loevinger (1957), who recommended choosing items and test tasks from a broader area than the trait expected to be measured. When possible, the items of the pool should be chosen so as to sample all possible content which might comprise the putative trait according to all known alternative theories of the trait (p. 659). For this stage of test development and exploration I decided to use this strategy rather than focusing on specific tasks that I actually subsumed under "auditory intelligence."

The selection of target persons for the scenario task can be criticized with respect to representativeness. In order to ensure reliability of the target person's answers, we chose people whom we personally knew and who were open to tell us about their feelings, thoughts and relationships. Consequently, despite the fact that the target persons were selected representatively with respect to age, gender, and education/profession, they did not form a representative selection as far as self-disclosure and openness are concerned.

8.4   Some Suggestions for Test Improvement

8.4.1   Suggestions for the Magdeburg Social Intelligence Test (SIM)

This section will provide some suggestions for future modifications on the SIM (Süß et al., 2008). I will concentrate on some of the tasks that need most improvement or seem to be most important to discuss since the space in this book is limited.

Scenario Task

With respect to the scenario task there is a need to shorten the single scenarios, as without shortening the test would take too long to be an attractive measure for use in the practice. Shortening can be done in different ways. First, single items that did not prove to be reliable or valid with respect to the SU subconstruct can be deleted. That may include single emotion judgments. Second, one could exclude whole scenes. A third possibility is in doing without covering all cells of our taxonomy in one scenario but instead trying to represent the cells with items across scenarios. The latter approach has been used in a recent study in cooperation with the German Aerospace Center (Deutsches Zentrum für Luft- und Raumfahrt). The data of this study has not yet been analyzed.

In the long run, an English version of the scenario task is needed to open the test for the international public. The problem is more with the auditory than with the written, pictorial and video-based material, since the latter can either be translated or does not rely on spoken language. However, we can expect that cultural differences exist in general and affect the scenes, in both private and public contexts, so that it will be worthwhile to do the complete recordings again in another cultural context. This project would profit from a refinement and further improvement of the already existing rationale of the recordings. In the second study we used interviews in addition to the written information we collected with visual scales. These interviews proved to be successful in getting as much information about the target person's feelings, cognitions, and relationships as possible. The future rationale should keep this method of data collection including specifying questions in the actual situation as well as encouragement of the target persons to mention mixed feelings and very specific cognitions. In addition, other people involved in the recordings might be interviewed to maximize information gain.

It would be worthwhile to investigate the differences between the test taker's own judgment of the target person and the view the subjects take when evaluating emotions, cognitions, and relationships in light of the target person's view (which corresponds to the original scenario task). The latter includes the ability to take a distance from one's own view, which I assume to be a necessary component in order to make true social understanding possible. I tried to get an impression of the effect the perspective change has in making judgments from both the own and the target person's perspective with a small group of students in a seminar. The students reported to have had much difficulty distinguishing between the two perspectives. A detailed change of instructions could assist in a better differentiation between the two perspectives, for example with questions like: "Imagine, you are Rita, how do you think she would answer the question about her feelings in this situation?" versus "How would you think she feels in the situation?" In the first question the view of the target person is central, whereas in the second question the own perspective is decisive.

Another interesting question to deal with is the correlation between a judgment of the target person's personality after viewing a simple self-presentation and after completing the whole scenario (like we did in our studies). Several studies indicate that forming an opinion about a person takes only a few seconds (e.g. Ambady & Rosenthal, 1992, 1993; see also Borkenau, Mauer, Riemann, Spinath, & Angleitner, 2004). It would be worthwhile to study in how far this opinion can be modified through the acquisition of additional information during completion of the scenario task. There are some indications that the degree of acquaintance looms large in the correspondence of judgments between target and consensus as well as self- and other (Funder & Colvin, 1988; Paunonen, 1989; Stinson & Ickes, 1992). A systematic study could yield interesting results.

A related question concerns the self-awareness of the test takers. The more expert a person is in knowing him- or herself and being aware of his or her own reactions, feelings and thoughts, the easier it should be to evaluate the feelings, thoughts, and relationships of others and to differentiate between them and his or her own. An additional questionnaire may be applied to investigate this effect. The same is true for additional bias effects, such as the halo effect (forming a general impression of goodness or badness of a scenario person and judge the person globally instead of in detail) or logical errors (certain conceptions of judges what traits go with what other traits). For a detailed description of the effects see Obermann (1992). In addition, taking role behavior into account could also refine and improve the test. Possible questions may be how far carrying out certain roles affects the social understanding of a particular target person e. g., a mother with two children or a doctor), whether the number of roles a person holds is an important variable (e.g., father, husband, head of department, member of a sports club). Stereotypic views may also influence the subject's answers to the scenario task questions and may be controlled. Social knowledge is expected to play a major role and should be examined as far as possible (see section 8.5.2).

Voice memory

The voice memory task (SMa2) was not sufficiently reliable, although it correlated significantly with some of the social intelligence tasks (e.g., with SPf1: r=.21; see Table 7-16). There may be several reasons for these problems (see also chapter 7.3.2). First, the conversations may be so interesting for the test takers that they pay more attention to the content of the audiofiles than to the tone of voice. Contradicting this hypothesis is the good performance test takers showed in their reaction on paraverbal cues in the perception of auditory cues within conversations (SPa1). Whether the content of the social conversations has an influence on the task performance could be examined using neutral (e.g., technical, science) topics in a parallel test version. The comparison between the results of the two versions (social vs. non-social content) could indicate whether the subjects pay more attention to the social content than to the paraverbal voice aspects (superiority of language) or not. A second reason for the findings with SMa2 may be that in this task several abilities get mixed up: subjects have to identify different voices, presented in a conversation, which have to be remembered afterwards. In a next step, they have to compare each of the presented voices with five answer alternatives. Thus, discrimination, encoding, working memory, and comparison are needed. One could try to break down the task into separate units and investigate the performance for each step. Furthermore, the effect of complexity should be the subject of future research. More items of each type are needed to examine the effect the number of people in a conversation, the context, and the number of distractors have on the task performance. The effect of the number of distractors could, for example, be examined by introducing a baseline measure, presenting only single voices of 30 to 60 seconds followed by different numbers of distractors. That would exclude the interference that is produced through the different voices involved in a conversation. Additional information could be acquired by asking subjects, during the time they take the test for each item, how they decide and what makes them to decide in this way (thinking aloud protocols).

Auditory Social/Emotions Perception (SPa2)

Scherer (in press) notes that it is surprising that established tests of nonverbal emotion recognition ability based on performance accuracy (e.g., for the voice, Banse & Scherer, 1996; Scherer, Banse, Wallbott, & Goldbeck, 1991), are not used more frequently in the area of social and emotional intelligence. In our second study, we made use of sentences of the GVEESS that are also part of the VOCAL-I (see Scherer, Banse, & Wallbott, 2001). One of the aims was to relate fictitious content masked sentences to realistic sentences. Both tasks loaded on the same latent variable and correlated with .56.

Most of the so-called emotion recognition tasks require discrimination rather than recognition (Scherer, 1996). However, being able to discriminate between alternative emotions does not automatically mean that the person is able to recognize the particular emotion or social cue correctly. In the task I developed, subjects have to decide which of two previously mentioned emotions or social cues correspond better to the sound sequence in question. In the present work, social perception measures were operationalized as speed tasks correspondent to perceptual speed in AcI but recording reaction times. This guideline made it difficult to develop a task requiring recognition of the actual emotion or social cue. A recognition test is an open answer test or a test with much choice possibility which requires the subject to be quite sure about the right answer. This would have exceeded the effort of this book. An alternative task for the future would be an open answer test of emotional/social cue recognition including a concrete and critically evaluated rationale for scoring both target and expert answers. A different possibility is to use actors such as was done for the GVEESS and the VOCAL I. On the one hand, working with actors will certainly lead to clearer emotions. On the other hand, we do not know exactly how far these judgments can be taken as indicators for realistic situations.

Objective Measurement in Social/Emotional Auditory Tasks

In chapter 2.6.4 and 2.6.5, some information about the objective assessment of social cues/emotions in voices was provided. In the future, objective data about the emotion which was present in a certain sound sequence may reveal useful information and enhance validity in addition to the methods we applied (e.g. SPa2: rating in order to ensure that the classification of an item is unambiguous; SU: target person's answer to indicate the emotion that was present in a certain situation). Recently I had the opportunity to talk to an expert in voice analysis[3] who works with an objective and experience-driven approach in order to identify the voice of a person blackmailing, to attain proofs about the culprit of a crime situation, etc. The following recommendations for emotion identification stem from analysis with that criminal psychologist considering F_0 intensity, tempo, pitch, additional spectral parameters (analyzed with Adobe Audition 1.5.), the typical way of speaking of a person, and decades of experience in our sound sequences. (1) Sound sequences should last for at least seven seconds, recommended are 15 - 20 seconds minimum. (2) The stimulus sequences should involve the emotion eliciting event (particularly important to the short SPa2 excerpts). In addition to the actual stimulus material, an excerpt of monotonous talking should be taken in order to discover the individual standard excitation. (3) One has to be also cautious in misinterpreting accentuating (e.g. by increasing voice intensity) as the occurrence of an emotion. (4) Important information is revealed by (a) The use of phrases (e.g., meaningless confirming phrases such as "isn't it" are only possible with slight states of excitement not with strong agitation) (b) repetitions (e.g., if someone often gets stuck in a sentence and is not a stutterer, nervousness is indicated), (c) continuation of a conversation (e.g., after an angry outburst, naturally, conversations do not continue like nothing happened). (5) Recordings should take place in quiet and furnished rooms to avoid echo and disturbance. (6) The use of headsets is recommended. (7) Overlapping voices should be avoided. (8) Emotion identification is more reliable in statements and exclamations than in questions. (9) It should be ensured that speakers are not drunk since alcohol accentuates the characteristics of a voice that may lead to misinterpretations. (10) One should not use voices of persons speaking different dialects, since emotion expression may differ and lead to uncertainty when one is not familiar with the specific dialect. (11) Noise reduction filter should not be used as important information is reduced or modified. Despite that all these suggestions appear useful, some of them (e.g. overlapping) are almost impossible in natural settings.

8.4.2 Suggestions for the Auditory Intelligence Test (AuIT)

As for the SIM (Süß et al., 2008), further test developments and task improvements can be suggested for the AuIT.

Auditory Nonverbal Tasks

a) Auditory Inspection Time
The auditory pitch discrimination inspection time task (AIT-P) was only applied in the first study since it has an adverse impact on the test takers mood, took too long (about 20 minutes minimum), and had the problem that some of the subjects were not able to make the pitch discrimination at any duration (see also Brand & Deary, 1982; Deary, Head, & Egan, 1989; see also chapter 2.5.5). For the future, I would therefore recommend using an auditory inspection time task similar to the one developed by Parker, Crawford, and Stephen (1999). This AIT task deals with sound localization and thus is more similar to visual inspection time (VIT) tasks which also deal with localization and thus are expected to share common operation processes According to Parker et al. (1999), the task was easy enough for all participants and did not have the problems that were encountered with pitch and loudness discrimination.

b) Tonal tasks
Musically experienced subjects showed better results in the tonal tasks. This may be due to better auditory abilities of musically skilled people or, alternatively, to the task demands of the tonal tasks selected for this study that measure rather musical than auditory ability. Which of the two alternatives is true, or whether a third option is correct, should be examined on the basis of a detailed evaluation of the tonal tasks wherein characteristics of both auditory intelligence tasks and musical tasks, are specifically detailed. Then, the two concepts should be related. One of our musically skilled students looked again at the score of the tonal series task taken from Stankov and Horn (1980). She found three of the fifteen items have a diverging logical and musical solution to the corresponding task. The answers

---

[3] I gratefully acknowledge the help of Gerd Böttger, department of criminal psychology (Landeskriminalamt Brandenburg)

have to be unequivocally either musical or logical everything else may have confused the musically skilled test takers.

The auditory tasks were administered as power tests, whereas the academic intelligence tasks are pure speed tests or time-limited power tests concerning the reasoning and the memory tasks. Future studies should examine whether the conditions of testing have an effect on the relationship between auditory and academic intelligence. Therefore, an auditory test version that corresponds to the BIS test in that it also includes a time limitation would be worthwhile to develop. A subject should be able to hear one item as often as needed to find an answer. As in academic intelligence tests, subjects should be able to skip an item. After a specified amount of time, the right answers are scored.

Similarly to the voice memory tasks, further research is needed to determine the appropriate number of answer alternatives (we increased the number from 3 to 4 in some of the tasks described in Stankov & Horn, 1980). With two or three options, we have to deal with the problem of an increased chance level. If we offer too many options, we may measure working memory or something else instead of auditory nonverbal ability. Additional related questions concern the time distance with which the alternatives follow the target sequence of tones and the interval between the answer alternatives. If the interval is too long, the trace will get lost. If the sequence continues too quickly or if the tones are played quickly one after another, the rules of gestalt psychology will make subjects group the tones instead of distinguishing between them. Experimental studies are required in order to determine the optimal features of the tasks.

Auditory Speech Tasks

The tasks (particularly audiobook and dissected sentences) can be evaluated as being indicators of verbal intelligence rather than of auditory ability. Hithero, attempts to improve reliability (multiple choice items, reduction of ambiguity) have not been successful (see audiobook, Table 7-22, chapter 7.4.1). For future examinations of the task masked words it would be recommended to make use of results obtained by Li, Daneman, Qi and Schneider (2004) as well as by Li, Qi, He, Alain and Schneider (2005). These researchers worked with the perceived separation of stimuli from background masking noises and the precedence effect. Separating the perceived location (not the physical location) of the masker from the target speech sequence produced an improvement in performance. Applying this knowledge can be especially useful for the improvement of items that were difficult to recognize for most of the participants. Putting theory into practice, one should introduce a delay into the noise lasting not longer than 15 ms (longer delays cause an echo effect). This gap in the noise is perceived as occurring in the leading (target) stimulus and the lagging stimulus is heard as continuous noise without a gap.

8.5 Test Application and Test Extension

8.5.1 Applying the Social Inteligence Test and the Auditory Intelligence Test: Formal Questions and Further Research Need

Who Can Take the Test?

In addition to the mentioned modifications, it is important to specify exactly for which groups of people the tests can be applied. Two different samples worked on the SIM (Süß et al., 2008) and on the AuIT. The first group was a student sample, the second was a mixed sample including many different professions and differences in the education level. Despite its variety, the group can be considered as a selected sample, too, since the subjects participated voluntarily. Although people were educated differently, we lacked those with a very low education level. Future studies should include samples with less educated people. We can be quite sure that this will have an effect on the results of the test since during the second study, all examiners including myself noticed that it took much longer to explain the tasks to the mixed sample than to the homogeneous student sample. There were tremendous differences in the speed people worked on the tasks. However, the dispersion was much lower in the first students sample compared to the second heterogeneous group. In addition, the representativeness of the models and tests for different cultures have to be investigated. It is not evident whether a group of test takers of a different culture would answer the questions in a similar way. The validity of a test and model has to be proved before using them in countries other than Germany.

Calibration of the Test

Calibration concerns questions such as: How much of a difference is needed to say that a person is socially intelligent? How much of a difference is needed to make a noticeable difference, for example, in people's everyday social interactions? Since the validity coefficients of psychological measures are at best on the order of a difference of about one standard deviation (SD) on a measurement score, we can expect that more than one third of a SD is required to be reflected in a behavioral change (see Sechrest, McKnight, & McKnight, 1996). This is confirmed by Ozer (1993), who states that a very large difference is required between test scores in order to be observable. Calibration is not only relevant against external criteria but also against other measures intended to measure the same construct. Sechrest et al. (1996) recommend using standard measures serving as a reference for other measures. Many standards become so by convention, accident, availability or ease of use. New and creative developments should be related to these standard instruments. Linking measures via calibration should result in a database of methods to relate findings from disparate measures so that one does not only have to rely on statistical significance or effect size estimation to equate outcomes. However, neither in the field of social intelligence nor in the domain of auditory intelligence there are such standard measures as suggested by Sechrest et al. (1996). The authors' recommendation in these cases is to relate the newly developed tests to the existing non-standards (since they e.g. include only parts of the construct) and to wait for further calibration until new measures will be available (email correspondence with Patrick McKnight, April 3rd, 2007).

Who Can Administer the Test?

The test should only be administered by psychologists who have a special training. All our examiners received training on how to prepare the test session, handle the computer software, administer the tests, and react appropriately in difficult situations (for example a crash of the system or program).

How Short Should the Test Be?

Our social understanding test with eight scenario tasks took about three hours, an example task included. The language-based memory tasks (written and auditory) took about an hour, and the language-based perception tasks took 50 minutes. Another hour and 40 minutes were required for the pictorial and video-based tasks. The complete SIM (Süß et al., 2008) thus takes about six and a half hours, which is definitely too long. One of our future aims is to make testing more economical. However, a valid diagnosis of all domains will probably not be possible within one hour. Thus, people have to accept a longer testing time. Shortening is expected to be most difficult for the scenario tasks since the presentation of the material alone takes significant time (for suggestions see chapter 8.4.1). Despite several possibilities, the more the information about a target person is reduced, the more difficult it is to put oneself into that person and to provide a reliable personality estimation at the end.

8.5.2 Additional Social Intelligence (SI) Dimensions

The SI test was developed in order to cover social understanding, social memory and social perception. In addition, the model described in Süß et al. (2005; see also Weis and Süß, 2005) includes social knowledge and social flexibility. We did not include these suggested subconstructs, as this would have exceeded the scope of the project. However, for the future it would be worthwhile to develop measures of these subconstructs for the test. Some ideas and information will be provided below.

Social Knowledge

At first sight, the inclusion of social knowledge seems to contradict the nature of intelligence, since it is culturally dependent (see chapter 2.2) and can increase/develop through learning and experience. It appears to be incompatible with the Süß (1996, 2001) conditions of an ability construct (see chapter 1.2) and the conceptualizations that were made in chapter 1.3. The special status of social knowledge compared to the cognitive SI dimensions has already been emphasized in chapter 2.2. I take the perspective that social knowledge is not part of cognitive SI but immediately relevant and related to it and should be controlled in order to measure the SI potential of a person. I expect the SI potential to influence the acquisition of social knowledge: A person who is socially intelligent (i.e., has the potential to judge another person's behavior, relationship to others, cognitions, and emotions) with a sufficient motivation should be able to acquire a more elaborate social knowledge than a person without this potential. Thus, SI and social knowledge are confounded and it will be hard if not impossible to separate them adequately. Social knowledge is particularly important with respect to the SU scenario task. In some of the scenes, certain roles (e.g. the role of a doctor) have a major impact. It may be that subjects answer the questions according to their experiences (e.g., appointments with a doctor) or to their knowledge (e.g., of how a doctor typically behaves). Then, social knowledge instead of social understanding is measured. There have been some attempts to assess social knowledge (see chapter 2.2 and Table 2-6). The Tacit Knowledge Inventory for Managers (TKIM, Wagner & Sternberg, 1991) and the Social Etiquette Test (Wong et al., 1995) have already been mentioned. The problem of knowledge tests is that they are domain specific. Knowledge of how a doctor behaves is different from knowing how to deal with a five-year-old hyperactive child. In the same way, the mentioned tests are very specific: the TKIM is a specific situation questionnaire in the domain of management; the Social Etiquette Test measures the knowledge of specific rules of etiquette. The development of a reference instrument for our scenario task should include knowledge questions corresponding to the selected scenes. A more general approach would be to use the taxonomy of possible social situations described in chapter 4-1 (see Figure 4-1) taxonomy and develop situation descriptions dealing with single others, dyads, or groups (inter-)acting in private or public life in situations with different topics (see Wiggins, 1979). This corresponds to the perspective that is taken in social cognition research: social knowledge is regarded as knowledge of persons (including self) and groups. Social knowledge is assumed to have an associative structure (see e.g. Greenwald, Banaji, Rudman, Farnham, Nosek, & Rosier, 2001). In addition, Kang, Day and Meara (2006) suggest a differentiation between knowledge about oneself and knowledge about others. Social knowledge is not only expected to influence social understanding but also to affect social perception (e.g., Tagiuri, 1969). The sensitivity to certain social cues appears to depend on the knowledge and experiences available about a topic, situation, or person. For example, if a person has knowledge about certain nonverbal cues, this person will be more likely to perceive the cues when paying attention to them. In a similar way, preceding events with a certain valence (e.g., good or bad) are expected to increase sensitivity to certain cues. This should have implications for training and development issues as well (see also chapter 8.6.2). Whereas SI is assumed to be rather stable, social knowledge may be trained (e.g., through providing straight information or through experience within certain situations) and may influence performance in SI tests. In addition, social knowledge clearly depends on the culture, whereas SI is expected to be less affected by it.

Social Flexibility

Social flexibility is the analogue to creativity in the BIS, dealing with the flexible application of knowledge (see Jones & Day, 1997) or the ability for a flexible production of ideas that can be used for the interpretation, solution or management of social situations (see Weis et al., 2006 and chapter 2.2.2). The operationalization of social flexibility in addition to SU, SM, and SP would have required an immense effort, especially with respect to scoring. The answers to such a measure have to be evaluated with regard to the number of inventive ideas. Although the inclusion of social flexibility would have exceeded the scope of this work, for the future, integrating tasks of this dimension appears worthwhile. Possible tasks would present a short conversation or a short video scene. Afterwards, the test taker would be asked to generate possible outcomes. Another idea is to present an outcome and require the subjects to invent scenes that may have occurred before.

The issue of social knowledge and social flexibility is relevant in relationship to the theory of crystallized and fluid intelligence (see e.g. Cattell, 1963, 1987; Horn & Noll, 1997; see also chapter 2.1). Kang et al. (2006) distinguish between social and emotional knowledge as components of crystallized intelligence and regard social and emotional flexibility as components of fluid intelligence. Whether this classification is useful still has to be examined empirically. Figure 8-3 presents a revised conceptualization of social intelligence summarizing and integrating the results of the two studies and the expected arrangement of additional dimensions (social knowledge and flexibility) and the overlap and distinctiveness with respect to other constructs (e.g., AcI).

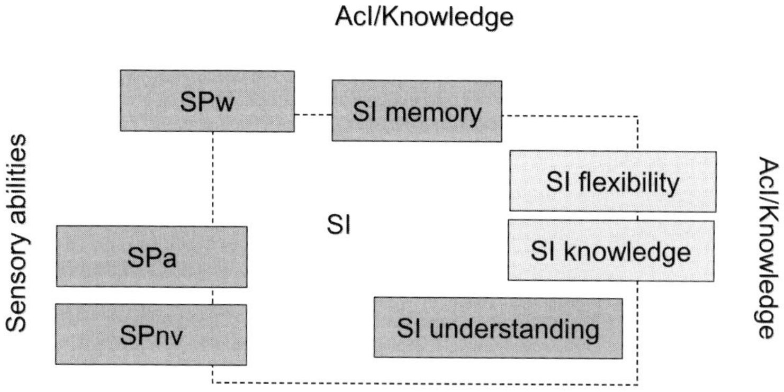

AcI/Knowledge

Figure 8-3: Revised Conceptualization of Social Intelligence and its Overlap with Related Constructs

Note. The frame marks the SI domain. The figure attempts to illustrate relationships rather than absolute proportions (of the framed field and also with respect to the boxes). Distances between boxes do not indicate the closeness of their relationships. The boxes with a lighter shadow represent hypotheses since SI knowledge and SI flexibility were not examined within this book. AcI and knowledge were not meant to be the same but were combined to make the figure more comprehensive. SPa=social perception-auditory; SPw=social perception–written; SPnv=social perception-nonverbal

Using Video and Audio Together

The combined use of video-based and auditory material would be interesting and realistic. We did not include this type of task in our research design since as a first step we wanted to examine the influences/effects the separate materials have. According to Ekman, O'Sullivan, Friesen, and Scherer (1991) deceit detection was much more accurate using body language, tone of voice, and facial expressions together than applying only one of the three methods. Borkenau and Liebler (1992) showed that self-stranger agreement is stronger if strangers view a sound film than if they view a silent film or a still picture of targets. Thus, we can expect that the judgment of a target person's feelings, thoughts, and relationships is more accurate when relying on combined video-based and auditory material (but see divergent findings reported by Archer & Akert, 1980; chapter 2.7.2). Moreover, this type of combined task serves as a more economic marker variable of social intelligence, since material- and channel-specific disadvantages may be reduced.

8.5.3 Additional Auditory Intelligence (AuI) Dimensions

Besides the already mentioned issue of clarifying the overlap and distinctiveness of auditory and musical intelligence, it would be worthwhile to add further tasks dealing with natural (e.g., birdcalls, animal voices, wind and water sounds) and artificial environmental sounds (appliance noise, noise produced by engines, telephones, and factories) to the test battery to complement the memory task "recognition of environmental sounds." A perceptual task relying on environmental sounds could use several similar sounds such as birdcalls, which have to be distinguished by the test takers (i.e., corresponding to the task detection of repeated tones, see chapter 4.2.1 and 0). Reasoning with environmental sounds could be assessed by tasks in which environmental sounds have to be sorted and arranged according to a logical sequence, for example in daily activities like teeth brushing (e.g. turn on the faucet to get some water for the tooth paste → brush teeth → rinse the mouth→ rinse the washbasin). Analogies (e.g., sounding one's horn is related to noise of engines such as the signal when the dryer is finished is related to the dryer's noise while working) and sound classification (e.g., identify the sound which does not belong to the others: e.g., three animal sounds and one sound produced by an appliance) can be operationalized with environmental sounds as well. In a second step, these tasks could be related to both auditory nonverbal and auditory speech tasks.

Figure 8-4 presents a revised conceptualization of AuI summarizing the results obtained in the two studies and the hypothesized structure, overlap, and distinctiveness with respect to related constructs.

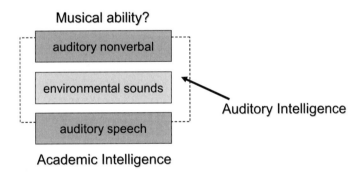

Figure 8-4: Revised Conceptualization of Auditory Intelligence and its Overlap with Related Constructs

Note. AuI=Auditory intelligence; AcI=Academic intelligence; AuI is indicated by the frame. The box with a lighter shadow presents a hypothesis that is not yet examined. The relationship/overlap/distinctiveness between musical and auditory intelligence still have to be explored.

8.6 Evidence That Needs to Be Furnished

In this book, with the exception of two, the conditions of the Süß (1996, 2001) framework (see chapter 1.2) were investigated successfully. Evidence of the fulfilment of the remaining conditions, namely, (6) the stability of the construct across time, and (7) the evidence of incremental criterion validity when compared to established constructs, still has to be furnished. Thus, future aims include a criterion validation and a retest study for the SIM (Süß et al., 2008) and the AuIT. Since there is not much to say with respect to a retest study, I focus on the criterion validation in the following section and provide some ideas with respect to stability, training, and change across lifespan in chapter 8.6.2.

8.6.1 Criterion Validation

Predicting Socially Intelligent Behavior

Investigating the criterion validity of social intelligence is not as easy as validation studies that have been carried out to provide predictive criterion evidence of AcI. Criteria in the evaluation of AcI have mainly been training and proficiency success evaluated by school grades, teachers' ratings, supervisors' ratings, work sample tests, etc. "G" measured by classical intelligence tests was sought to be sufficient for prediction of these criteria. Differences in the predictive validity were interpreted as a consequence of method effects such as restriction of range and reliability problems (see Schmidt & Hunter, 1998). I take a different position from researchers (e.g., Austin & Saklofske, 2006) who suggest validating new constructs against the criteria used with AcI. It does not appear appropriate to do the criterion validation for the SI construct with the same criteria used in validating AcI. In the past, the lack of correlation between social/emotional intelligence and training/proficiency success was considered to be a proof that the constructs are not incrementally valid with respect to AcI (see e.g. Van Rooy & Viswesvaran, 2004). Job success was often globally defined instead of classifying jobs as "social" vs. "nonsocial" (I know that transitions are smooth.). I plead for using appropriate social criteria (real-life criteria, see also Süß, 2006) for the criterion validation of social intelligence orientating on the principles of symmetry (see Wittmann, 1988). Immediate application (and criteria) of the SIM (Süß et al., 2008) may be the prediction of the effect of the company of nurses with patients measured by patients' ratings, or the prediction of a waiter's tip. The number of relevant criteria is unlimited. Every additional proof of validity supports the usefulness of a construct (see Süß, 2006). A test is never generally valid but only valid with respect to specified aims (see American Educational Research Association, American Psychological Association & National Council on Measurement in Education, 2000). Findings of Ford and Tisak (1983) support the importance of selecting appropriate symmetrical criteria. They found incremental validity of social intelligence compared to academic intelligence in the effectiveness of socially intelligent behavior in an interview. SI could explain 18% of the variance compared to 13% explained by AcI.

In the next few sections, I mention some challenges we encounter when dealing with criterion validation. First, in a criterion validation study it is important to define "success" in detail: Is it the assessment of the supervisor, the salary someone earns, or the healthy growing up of one's children? In the view of Mayer, Salovey, and Caruso (2000b) we have to define success, then carefully develop good criteria for success. However, I would query whether this is actually possible: success at one point of time may be turned into failure later on. A lying doctor my have immediate success after he is revealed to be a liar who did not take his proficiency seriously, he will be in trouble. Who evaluates success in the defined criterion of social behavior? Is there a "hard" evaluation criterion or do we have to deal with ratings?

Second, SI cannot be understood outside its cultural context (see also Sternberg & Grigorenko, 2006, p. 37). There are vast differences between cultures, such as the relatively higher emphasis on social aspects of intelligence in African and in Asian cultures contrary to Western cultures (Azuma & Kashiwagi, 1987; Lutz, 1985; White, 1985). Also, the problem of context specification can be encountered within one culture (e.g., different roles of a single person). Assume an employee works in computer programming (information technology, IT) and does not have much contact with colleagues and supervisors ("non-social" job). Carrying out a criterion validation study with different groups (e.g., social vs. non-social jobs), one might expect that employee to have a lower social intelligence value than the secretary who is in daily touch with supervisors and employees. Now imagine that the programming IT employee in his private life spends time with his wife, his children and a large network of friends, that he is engaged in social activities etc., whereas the secretary holds a single person household and prefers engaging in artwork to dealing with other people. It would be not surprising, if the test result did not match the predictions. Evaluating the test as a bad measure would be a premature mistake. Therefore, the private as well as the professional context has to be examined or at least controlled for, which is difficult if not impossible because of the many interacting variables which have to be considered.

What are possible methods and criteria for validation of the SIM (Süß et al., 2008)? In this book, I do not want to develop complete scenarios of criterion validation but instead provide some general ideas with respect to methods, criteria and context of application. A possible technique to be applied is the "peer nomination technique" suggested and described in Moreno (1934). An example is the nomination of a specified number of classmates according to certain social criteria (Whom do you like best? Whom would you trust most/tell your problems to, etc.?). This approach can be applied in a variety of settings, such as with teachers' evaluations, in the assessment of nurses (e.g., ask patients: Whom would you most like to look after you? With whom would you feel most comfortable?), or with colleagues (e.g., With whom would you start a new project? Whom would you like to have in your team?). Alternatively, one could borrow from approaches used in social psychology (e.g. the dyadic interaction paradigm, see Ickes, 2001; Snodgrass, 2001): While two people interact in various tasks, they complete questionnaires on which they rate their own thoughts and feelings, the other person's thoughts and feelings according to the own view, and the expected thoughts of the other person about the own thoughts and feelings. The ratings are correlated afterwards. With respect to criteria, objective criteria seem to be particularly useful, such as the tone of voice (e.g. firm, dominant, but also friendly language in convincing someone to buy the own products), the mimic and body language (e.g. a teacher dealing with a student who did not do his homework), and the content of what is said (e.g. number of encouraging words in an email or conversation dealing with cheering up a friend). It is important to keep in mind that the aims should be fixed in advance. Is the aim in a certain situation to assert oneself, to help a person, to acquire sympathy, etc.? Only with specified goals can a certain behavior be evaluated using predefined and appropriate criteria.

Predicting Auditorily Intelligent Behavior

The general issues of criterion validation remain the same concerning auditory intelligence; the circumstances, the context, and the criteria have to be adapted. One may imagine evaluating auditory discriminative abilities through the acquisition of pronunciation competence in foreign languages and in studies with speech therapists. Another field is that of musical ability (which has to be still differentiated from auditory ability). The combined abilities defined by the SI and the AuI construct may deal with call center agents who have to have good auditory but also good social intelligence, for example with respect to their tone of voice.

8.6.2 Issues of Training and Development

The question of whether social intelligence and auditory intelligence can be trained/improved will be discussed against the background of the conceptualization of intelligence (see chapter 1.3) and with respect to psychological intervention programs for the training of social perception, memory, and understanding. In the view of Mayer et al. (1999), a condition to apply the label "intelligence" is that development and increase with age in the crucial ability are possible. On the contrary, I regard intelligence as a stable precondition and underlying potential that can result in certain skills, competencies, and knowledge which in turn can be trained (see chapter 1.3 and chapter 8.5.2). The position I take is that if conditions of variables such as sufficient motivation and an appropriate context (e.g., possibility of getting in touch with different kinds of people) are fulfilled, a person with a high social intelligence potential may train communication skills to a very high expert level, whereas a person with minor SI will never reach that level. For the latter, improvement by training is also possible, but to a lesser extent. If training results in increased knowledge I assume performance to be increased, too. However, I do not expect the actual cognitive dimensions to be changeable by training.

Associated with the training and development of social skills is the relationship to wisdom and age. In academic intelligence research, changes in academic performance have been found across the lifespan (see Schaie, 1994). In the same way, Cattell and Horn (Horn, 1970; Horn & Cattell, 1966) as well as Baltes (1990) found different development processes across the life span for gf and gc and for mechanic and pragmatic respectively (see chapter 2.2 and references). Similarly, such changes are expected to occur with regard to the performance in SI and AuI tests. A person's knowledge in social situations and experience in dealing with different people increases with age, which is expected to have an impact on the modification of socially intelligent behavior (see Kaiser, 1998). This also indicates that in the mentioned boundaries an improvement in social skills is very likely since the knowledge about social situations and different people increases. On the other hand, when people get older changes of perspective are sometimes more difficult (e.g., putting oneself into a much younger person's place), which may be a consequence of both generation changes (e.g., different conditions of growing up) and age distance. It would be interesting to know whether the improvement of auditory or social skills influences the performance in an auditory or social intelligence test.

With respect to the training of SI-perception and SI-memory, I expect modifications to be minor as these two dimensions seem to be more basic. It could be shown that social memory is correlated with academic memory. Effects of age and training known in combination with academic memory should be related to so-called social memory as well. With respect to social perception, we can expect that reduced sensory functions in advanced age affect performance in perception tasks. However, stability may be high even against the background of reduced performance, since the ranking of persons may remain the same. Studies on social intelligence across the life span would be recommended since, in later life, social intelligence may be even more important than cognitive abilities (Sternberg & Grigorenko, 2006).

Similarly, I regard auditory intelligence as a potential, which cannot be modified. In particular, sensory abilities are hard to train since they are expected to be strongly linked with anatomical and physiological structure. I assume these abilities to be a necessary but not sufficient precondition to develop excellent language skills, musical skills, and skills in detection of changes in the voice (e.g., emotion changes). The existence of these preconditions determines the degree to which these skills can be trained. There is some hint in the literature that there are resources in dealing with auditory material common to all human beings since even people without any formal musical training and experience were able to process and understand musical syntax and semantics (Koelsch, 2004). However, similar to SI, musically skilled people with increased knowledge about tones and sounds and their relationship may perform better in auditory tests. This is expected to be due to increased knowledge rather than increased underlying cognitive abilities. As in the SI domain, perception and discrimination abilities, which rely on sensory functioning, are assumed to decrease across the lifespan and in turn do not affect the ranking of a person's performance within a reference group of the same age.

8.7 Concluding Comments

I started my book with a comment on the "inflation of intelligences" and mentioned some arguments why auditory and social intelligence are candidates for viable constructs instead of being illusory. It could be shown SI and AuI are indeed promising constructs that do not have to be subsumed under the label of inflationary constructs. However, the unique components of the constructs, social understanding, nonverbal auditory intelligence, and auditory social/ emotion perception are narrower than expected.

In this work, the often neglected auditory abilities have been included side by side with the visual abilities. For the future we should not ignore other senses such as the tactile, olfactory, and kinesthetic sensory modality (e.g. Danthiir et al., 2001; Li et al., 1998; Roberts, Stankov, Pallier, & Dolph, 1997; Stankov, 2001). It has been found that tactile sensory information processing is related to cognitive functioning (see, e.g. Stankov, 2000). The strength of the tactile-cognitive link is compatible to the strength of the auditory-cognitive and the visual-cognitive links. Researchers in the psychology of aging assume that neural functioning of the brain is an underlying variable of both sensory functioning and cognitive information processing (see Baltes & Lindenberger, 1997). On the basis of theoretical argumentation and empirical findings, we have to evaluate whether individual differences in perceptual abilities are rather due to sensory functioning than to factors of intelligence.

We started to relate measures of emotion research tradition to measures applied in differential and diagnostic psychology. I would strongly recommend continuing research in this direction in the future. The fact that several research traditions (e. g. emotion research, diagnostic psychology, social psychology, developmental psychology, and neuropsychology) examine SI without knowing and including findings from one another has to be changed.

Sharing findings, knowledge, and instruments could contribute to a deeper knowledge of the construct. The same is true with regard to AuI: the results obtained in the context of our research project should be combined with findings obtained in neuropsychology, musical psychology, and audition research.

In the past, there was a tendency to overemphasize the role of the general factor at the expense of broad and primary factors, leading to an impoverished view of human cognition and ignoring a large body of contrary evidence. If researchers want to predict and understand what happens with people in their lives, academic intelligence scores on their own are clearly inadequate, and as they grow older they become less important (Stankov, 1999). Assuming a simple "g-factor" underlying each kind of cognitive functioning although parsimonious, is too easy (see also Stankov, 2000). The variety of underlying abilities that seem to be partly dependent but also completely different from one another widens our horizon with respect to interindividual differences. Again, it becomes clear that in the same way as the underlying cognitive factors complement each other, we complement each other with our unique blend of capabilities. Constructs are our inventions; their structure and relationships are more complex than we would expect. In the laws of nature "such a superior reason is revealed that every meaningful human thinking and grouping/arrangement is only a void reflection." (Einstein, 1953, p. 21). God in heaven alone can presume to know which kind of ability constructs and processes determine our cognitive functioning. Most likely, we would be very surprised if we knew how our mind worked indeed.

> Now we see but a poor reflection as in a mirror; then we shall see face to face.
> Now I know in part; then I shall know fully, even as I am fully known.
> (1. Corinthians 13:12; Holy Bible, New International Version)

9 References

Abrams, D. & Hogg, M. A. (Eds.) (1999). *Social Identity and Social Cognition.* Oxford: Blackwell Publishers.

Ackerman, P. L. (1987). Individual differences in skill learning: an integration of psychometric and information processing perspectives. *Psychological Bulletin, 102,* 3-27.

Ackerman, P. L. (1989). Individual differences and skill acquisition. In P. L. Ackerman, R. J. Sternberg, & R. Glaser (Eds.), *Learning and individual differences. Advances in theory and research* (pp. 165-217). New York: W. H. Freeman & Co.

Adler, N. & Guttman, R. (1982). The radex structure of intelligence: a replication. *Educational and Psychological Measurement, 42,* 739-749.

Adolphs, R. (2001). The neurobiology of social cognition. *Current Opinion in Neurobiology,* 11, 231–239.

Adolphs, R. (2003). Cognitive neuroscience of human social behaviour. *Nature Reviews Neuroscience, 4,* 165–178.

Aftanas, M. S. & Royce, J. R. (1969). A factor analysis of brain damage tests administered to normal subjects with factor score comparisons across ages. *Multivariate Behavioral Research, 4* (4), 459-481.

Albrecht, A.-G. (2005). *Untangling the Laundry List - General Mental Ability, the Big Five, and context related variables as predictors for expatriate success.* University of Lüneburg, Germany: Unpublished diploma thesis.

Alden, L. E., Wiggins, J. S., & Pincus, A. L. (1990). Construction of circumplex scales for the Inventory of Interpersonal Problems. *Journal of Personality Assessment, 55,* 521–536.

Alter, U. & Muff, A. (1979). *Gewinnung von sozialen Indikatoren für depressives Verhalten mit Hilfe der Delphi-Methode.* Forschungsbericht des Psychologischen Instituts der Universität Zürich.

Ambady, N., LaPlante, D., & Johnson, E. (2001). Thin-slice judgements as a measure of interpersonal sensitivity. In J. A. Hall & F. J. Bernieri (Eds.), *Interpersonal Sensitivity.* Mahwah, NJ: LEA.

Ambady, N. & Rosenthal, R. (1992). Thin slices of expressive behavior as predictors of interpersonal consequences: A meta-analysis. *Psychological Bulletin, 111,* 256-274.

Ambady, N. & Rosenthal, R. (1993). Half a minute: Predicting teacher evaluations from thin slices of nonverbal behavior and physical attractiveness. *Journal of Personality and Social Psychology, 64,* 431–441.

Amelang, M. (1996). Intelligenz. In M. Amelang (Hrsg.), *Enzyklopädie der Psychologie, Differentielle Psychologie und Persönlichkeitsforschung,* Band 2: *Verhaltens- und Leistungsunterschiede* (S. 245-328). Göttingen: Hogrefe.

Amelang, M., Schwarz, G., & Wegemund, A. (1989). Soziale Intelligenz als Trait-Konstrukt und Test-Konzept bei der Analyse von Verhaltenshäufigkeiten. *Zeitschrift für Differentielle und Diagnostische Psychologie, 10,* 37-57.

Amelang, M. & Steinmayr, R. (2006). Is there a validity increment for tests of Emotional Intelligence in explaining the variance of performance criteria? *Intelligence, 34,* 459–468.

American Educational Research Association, American Psychological Association & National Council on Measurement in Education (2000). *Standards for educational and psychological testing.* Washington, D.C.: American Psychological Association.

Anastasi, A. (1954). *Psychological Testing.* MacMillan: New York.

Anastasi, A. (1986). Intelligence as a style of behavior. In R. J. Sternberg & D. K. Detterman (Eds.), *What is intelligence?* (pp. 19-21). Norwood, NJ: Ablex Publishing.

Anderson, J. R. (1996). *Kognitive Psychologie* (2. Aufl.). Heidelberg: Spektrum Akademischer Verlag.

Anvari, S. H., Trainor, L. J., Woodside, J., & Levy, B. A. (2002). Relations among musical skills, phonological processing, and early reading ability in preschool children. *Journal of Experimental Child Psychology, 83,* 111-130.

Apple, W. & Hecht, K. (1982). Speaking emotionally: The relation between verbal and vocal communication of affect. *Journal of Personality and Social Psychology, 42*, 864-875.

Archer, D. & Akert, R. M. (1980). The Encoding of Meaning: A Test of Three Theories of Social Interaction. *Sociological Inquiry, 50* (3-4), 393–419.

Archer, D., Costanzo, M., & Akert, R. (2001). The interpersonal perception task (IPT): Alternative approaches to problems of theory and design. In J. A. Hall & F. J. Bernieri (Eds), *Interpersonal sensitivity. Theory and measurement.* Mahwah, NJ: Lawrence Erlbaum Associates.

Aronson, E., Wilson, T. D., & Akert, R. M. (2004). *Sozialpsychologie.* München: Pearson Studium.

Asendorpf, J. B. (1996). *Psychologie der Persönlichkeit: Grundlagen.* Berlin: Springer.

Atkin, R., Bray, R., Davidson, M., Herzberger, S., Humphreys, L. G., & Selzer, V. (1977). Cross-lagged panel analysis of sixteen cognitive measures at four grade levels. *Child Development, 48* (3), 944-952.

Austin, E. J. (2004). An investigation of the relationship between trait Emotional Intelligence and emotional task performance. *Journal of Personality and Individual Differences, 36*, 1855–1864.

Austin, E. J. (2005). Emotional Intelligence and emotional information processing. *Personality and Individual Differences, 39*, 403–414.

Austin, E. J. & Saklofske, D. H. (2006). Viel zu viele Intelligenzen? Über die Gemeinsamkeiten und Unterschiede zwischen sozialer, praktischer und emotionaler Intelligenz. In P. A. Freund, R. D. Roberts, & R. Schulze (Eds.), *Emotionale Intelligenz. Ein internationales Handbuch.* Göttingen: Hogrefe.

Azuma, H. & Kashiwagi, K. (1987). Descriptors for an intelligent person: A Japanese study. *Japanese Psychological Research, 29*, 17-26.

Bachorowski, J.-A. & Owren, M. J. (1995). Vocal expression of emotion: Acoustic properties of speech are associated with emotional intensity and context. *Psychological Science, 6* (4), 219 - 224.

Baltes, P. B. (1990). Entwicklungspsychologie der Lebensspanne: Theoretische Leitsätze. *Psychologische Rundschau, 41*, 1-24.

Baltes, P. B. & Lindenberger, U. (1997). Emergence of a powerful connection between sensory and cognitive functions across the adult life span: a new window to the study of cognitive aging? *Psychology and Aging, 12* (1), 12-21.

Baltes, P. B. & Smith, J. (1990). Toward a psychology of wisdom and its ontogenesis. In R. J. Sternberg (Ed.), *Wisdom - Its nature, origins, and development.* Cambridge: Cambridge University Press.

Baltes, P. B., Smith, J. & Staudinger, U. M. (1992). Wisdom and successful aging. In T. Sonderegger (Hrsg.), *Nebraska symposium on motivation* (Bd. 39, S. 123-167). Lincoln, NB: University of Nebraska.

Baltes, P. B. & Staudinger, U. M. (1993). The search for a psychology of wisdom. *Current Directions in Psychological Science, 2*, 1-6.

Banse, R. (2000). Soziale Interaktion und Emotion. In J. H. Otto, H. A. Euler, & H. Mandl, *Emotionspsychologie. Ein Handbuch* (pp. 360-369). Weinheim: Psychologie Verlags Union.

Banse, R. & Scherer, K. R. (1996). Acoustic Profiles in vocal emotion expression. *Journal of Personality and Social Psychology, 70* (3), 614-636.

Bänziger, T. (2005). MERT. *Multimodal Emotion Recognition Test.* Presentation, Geneva Affective Science Week. Université de Geneve, Switzerland.

Bänziger, T., Grandjean, D., & Scherer, K. R. (2005). *Analyzing the multimodal perception of emotional expressions.* Poster presented at ISRE 2005, Bari, Italy.

Barchard, K. A. (2003). Does Emotional Intelligence assist in the prediction of academic success? *Educational and Psychological Measurement, 63* (5), 840–858.

Barnes, M. L. & Sternberg, R. J. (1989). Social Intelligence and decoding of nonverbal cues. *Intelligence, 13*, 263-287.

BarOn, R. (1997). *BarOn Emotional Quotient Inventory (EQ-i): Technical manual.* Toronto, Canada: Multi-Health Systems.

Bar-On, R. (1999). *BarOn Emotional Quotient Inventory (EQ-i): A measure of Emotional Intelligence. Technical Manual.* Toronto, ON: Multi-Health System.

BarOn, R. (2000). Emotional and Social Intelligence: Insights from the emotional quotient inventory. In R. BarOn & J. D. A. Parker (Eds.), *The handbook of Emotional Intelligence: Theory, development, assessment, and application at home, school, and in the workplace* (pp. 363-388). San Francisco: Jossey-Bass.

BarOn, R., Tranel, D., Denburg, N. L., & Bechara, A. (2003). Exploring the neurological substrate of emotional and Social Intelligence. *Brain, 126,* 1790-1800.

Baron-Cohen, S., Jolliffe, T., Mortimore, C., & Robertson, M. (1997). Another advanced test of theory of mind: Evidence from very high-functioning adults with autism or Asperger Syndrome. *Journal of Child Psychology and Psychiatry, 38,* 813 - 822.

Baron-Cohen, S., Ring, H. A., Bullmore, E. T., Wheelwright, S., Ashwin, C., & Williams, S. C. (2000). The amygdala theory of autism. *Neuroscience & Biobehavioral Reviews, 24,* 355–364.

Baron-Cohen, S., Wheelwright, S., Hill, J., Raste, Y., & Plumb, I. (2001). The "Reading the Mind in the Eyes" Test Revised Version: A Study with Normal Adults, and Adults with Asperger Syndrome or High-functioning Autism. *Journal of child psychology and psychiatry and applied disciplines (Oxford), 42* (2), 241–251.

Bastians, F. & Runde, B. (2002). Instrumente zur Messung sozialer Kompetenzen. *Zeitschrift für Psychologie, 210* (4), 186-196.

Baum, K. M. & Nowicki. Jr., S. (1998). Perception of emotion: measuring decoding accuracy of adult prosodic cues varying in intensity. *Journal of Nonverbal Behavior, 22*(2), 89-107.

Beauducel, A. (2001a). *Probleme und Perspektiven der psychometrischen Traitforschung. Zur Anzahl und Generalität von Persönlichkeitsdimensionen.* Unveröffentlichte Habilitationsschrift. TU Dresden.

Beauducel, A. (2001b). Problems with parallel analysis in data sets with oblique simple structure. *Methods of Psychological Research Online, 6,* 141-157.

Beauducel, A., Brocke, B., & Liepmann, D. (2001). Perspectives on fluid and crystallized intelligence: Facets for verbal, numerical, and figural intelligence. *Personality and Individual Differences, 30,* 977–994.

Beauducel, A. & Kersting, M. (2002). Fluid and crystallized intelligence in the Berlin Model of Intelligence Structure. *European Journal of Psychological Assessment, 18,* 97-112.

Beauducel, A. & Wittmann, W. W. (2005). Simulation Study on Fit Indexes in CFA Based on Data With Slightly Distorted Simple Structure. *Structural Equation Modeling, 12* (1), 41–75.

Bechtoldt, M. (2003). *Die Bedeutung sozialer Kompetenz für die Bewältigung interpersoneller Stresssituationen am Arbeitsplatz.* Frankfurt am Main: Wolfgang Goethe Universität.

Bentley, A. (1966). *Measures of musical abilities.* New York: October House. Inc.

Berg, C. A. (1986). The role of social competence in contextual theories of adult intellectual development. *Educational Gerontology, 12,* 313 - 325.

Bernieri, F. J. (2001). Judging Rapport: Employing Brunswik's lens model to study interpersonal sensitivity. In J. A. Hall & F. J. Bernieri (Eds.), *Interpersonal Sensitivity. Theory and measurement.* Mahwah, NJ: Lawrence Erlbaum.

Berry, J. W. & Irvine, S. H. (1986). Bricolage: Savages do it daily. In R. J. Sternberg & R. K. Wagner (Eds.), *Practical Intelligence: Nature and origins of competence in the everyday world.* (pp. 271-306). Cambridge: Cambridge University Press.

Berry, J. W., Irvine, S. H., & Hunt, E. B. (1987). *Indigenous cognition: Functioning in cultural context.* Dordrecht, Netherlands: Nijhoff.

Bezooijen, R. van (1984). *The characteristics and recognizability of vocal expression of emotions.* Drodrecht, NL: Foris.

Bickley, P. G., Keith, T. Z., & Wolfe, L. M. (1995). The three-stratum theory of cognitive abilities: Test of the structure of intelligence across the life span. *Intelligence, 20,* 309-328.

Biehl, M., Matsumoto, D., Ekman, P., Hearn, V., Heider, K., & Kudoh, T. (1997). Matsumoto´s and Ekman´s Japanese and Caucasian Facial Expressions of Emotion (JACFEE): Reliability data and cross-national differences. *Journal of Nonverbal Behavior, 21,* 3 – 21.

Birenbaum, M. & Tatsuoka, K. K. (1987). Open-ended versus multiple choice response formats-it does make a difference for diagnostic purposes. *Applied Psychological Measurement, 11* (4), 385–395.

Björkvist, K., Österman, K., & Kaukiainen, A. (2000). Social Intelligence - Empathy = Aggression? *Aggression and Violent Behavior, 5* (2), 191-200.

Blanchette, I. & Richards, A. (2004). Reasoning about emotional and neutral materials Is logic affected by emotion? *Psychological Science, 25*, 745–752.

Bohart, A. C. & Greenberg, L. S. (Eds.) (1997). *Empathy reconsidered: New directions in psychotherapy.* Washington, DC: American Psychological Association.

Boltz, M. (1991). Some structural determinants of melody recall. *Memory and Cognition, 19*, 239-251.

Borg, I. (1976). Facetten- und Radextheorie in der multidimensionalen Skalierung. *Zeitschrift für Sozialpsychologie, 7*, 231–247.

Borkenau, P. & Liebler, A. (1992). Trait inferences: Sources of validity at zero acquaintance. *Journal of Personality and Social Psychology,62*, 645-657.

Borkenau, P., Mauer, N., Riemann, R., Spinath, F. M., & Angleitner, A. (2004). Thin slices of behavior as cues of personality and intelligence. *Journal of Personality and Social Psychology, 86* (4), 599-614.

Borkenau, P. & Ostendorf, F. (1993). *NEO-Fünf-Faktoren Inventar (NEO-FFI) nach Costa und McCrae.* Göttingen: Hogrefe.

Bortz, J. (1999). *Statistik für Sozialwissenschaftler.* Berlin: Springer.

Bower, G. H. & Forgas, J. P. (2001). Mood and social memory. In J. P. Forgas, *Handbook of affect and social cognition.* Mahwah, NJ: Lawrence Erlbaum Associates.

Brackett, M. A. & Mayer, J. D. (2003). Convergent, discriminant, and incremental validity of competing measures of Emotional Intelligence. *Personality and Social Psychology Bulletin, 29*, 1147-1158.

Brand, C. R. & Deary, I. J. (1982). 'Intelligence and 'inspection time.' In H. J.Eysenck, *A Model for Intelligence* (pp. 133-148). Berlin and New York : Springer.

Brandtstätter, H. (1990). Emotionen im sozialen Verhalten (Chapt. 7). In K. R. Scherer, *Psychologie der Emotion, Enzyklopädie der Psychologie, Themenbereich C, Theorie und Forschung, Serie IV Motivation und Emotion, Band 3, Psychologie der Emotion.* Göttingen: Hogrefe.

Bretherton, I. & Beeghly, M. (1982). Talking about the internal states: The acquisition of an explicit theory of mind. *Developmental Psychology, 18*, 906-912.

Brody, L. R. & Hall, J. A. (2000). Gender, emotion, and expression. In M. Haviland-Jones & J. M. Lewis (Eds.), *Handbook of emotions* (2nd ed.). New York: The Guilford Press.

Brody, N. (1992). *Intelligence* (2nd ed.). London: Academic Press.

Brody, N. (2004). What cognitive intelligence is and what Emotional Intelligence is not. *Psychological Inquiry, 15*, 234-238.

Bronfenbrenner, U., Harding, J., & Gallwey, M. (1958). The measurement of skill in social perception. In D. C. McClelland, A. L. Baldwin, U. Bronfenbrenner, & F. L. Strodtbeck (Eds.), *Talent and Society* (pp. 29-111). Princeton: Van Nostrand.

Broom, M. E. (1928). A note on the validity of a test of Social Intelligence. *Journal of Applied Psychology, 12* (4), 426-428.

Brown, J. (1985). An introduction to the uses of facet theory. In D. Canter (Ed.), *Facet theory.* New York: Springer.

Brown, L. T., & Anthony, R. G. (1990). Continuing the search for Social Intelligence. *Personality and Individual Differences, 11*, 463-470.

Brüne, M. & Brüne-Cohrs, U. (2006). Review:Theory of mind-evolution, ontogeny, brain mechanisms and psychopathology. *Neuroscience and Biobehavioral Reviews, 30*, 437–455.

Brüne, M. & Bodenstein, L. (2005). Proverb comprehension reconsidered - 'theory of mind' and the pragmatic use of language in schizophrenia. *Schizophrenia Research (Amsterdam), 75*, 233–239.

Bruhn, H. (1993). Gedächtnis und Wissen. In H. Bruhn, R. Oerter, & H. Rösing, (Hrsg.) (1993). *Musik und Psychologie - Musikpsychologie. Ein Handbuch.* Reinbek: Rowohlt.

Bruhn, H., Oerter, R., Rösing, H. (Hrsg.) (1993). Musik und Psychologie- Musikpsychologie. *Musik und Psychologie - Musikpsychologie. Ein Handbuch.* Reinbek: Rowohlt.

Bucik, V. & Neubauer, A. (1996). Bimodality in the Berlin Model of Intelligence Structure (BIS): a replication study. *Personality and Individual Differences, 21,* 987-1005.

Buck, R. (1976). A test of nonverbal receiving ability: Preliminary studies. *Human Communication Research, 2,* 162–171.

Bühner, M. (2006). *Einführung in die Test- und Fragbogenkonstruktion.* München: Pearson Studium.

Bundesinstitut für Berufsbildung (1998). Stellenanzeigenanalyse. BIBB-Vorhaben 1/3/4.0009. Früherkennungssystem Qualifikationsentwicklung. Bonn: BIBB.

Bundesministerium für Bildung und Forschung (2006). *Macht Mozart schlau? Die Förderung kognitiver Kompetenzen durch Musik.* Bildungsforschung Band 18. Bonn, Berlin: BMBF.

Burns, N. R., Bastian, V. A., & Nettelbeck, T. (in press). Emotional Intelligence: More than personality and cognitive ability?. In G. Matthews, M. Zeidner, & R. D. Roberts (Eds.), *Science of Emotional Intelligence: Knowns and Unknowns.* New York: Oxford University Press.

Butsch, C. & Fischer, H. (Hrsg.) (1966). *Seashore-Test für musikalische Begabung.* Bern: Huber.

Buttsworth, L., Fogarty, G. & Rorke, P. (1993). Predicting aural performance in a tertiary music training programme. *Psychology of Music, 21* (2), 114-126.

Bye, L. & Jussim, L. (1993). A proposed model for the acquisition of social knowledge and social competence. *Psychology in the Schools, 30* (2), 143 -161.

Campbell, D. T. & Fiske, D. W. (1959). Convergent and discriminant validation by the multitrait-multimethod matrix. *Psychological Bulletin, 56* (2), 81–105.

Campbell, N. (2000): Databases of Emotional Speech. In R. Cowie, E. Douglas-Cowie, & M. Schröder (Eds.) *Proceedings of the ISCA Workshop on Speech and Emotion.* Belfast, Ireland.

Canter, D. (1985). Preface. In D. Canter, *Facet theory.* New York: Springer.

Cantor, N. & Kihlstrom, J. F. (1987). *Personality and Social Intelligence.* Englewood Cliffs, NJ: Prentice Hall.

Carroll, J. B. (1987). *Human cognitive abilities - A survey of factor analytic studies.* Cambridge: University Press.

Carroll, J. B. (1993). *Human cognitive abilities - A survey of factor-analytic studies.* Cambridge: University Press.

Carroll, J. B. (1995). On methodology in the study of cognitive abilities. *Multivariate Behavioural Research, 30,* 429-452.

Carson, R. C. (1969). *Interaction concepts of personality.* Chicago: Aldine.

Cattell, R. B. (1943). The measurement of adult intelligence. *Psychological Bulletin, 40,* 153-193.

Cattell, R. B. (1957). *Personality and motivation structure and measurement.* Yonker-on-Hudson, N.Y.: World Books Co.

Cattell, R. B. (1963). Theory of fluid and crystallized intelligence: A critical experiment. *Journal of Educational Psychology, 54,* 1-22.

Cattell, R. B. (1971). *Abilities: Their structure, growth, and action.* Boston: Houghton Mifflin.

Cattell, R. B. (1987). Intelligence: Its structure, growth, and action. Amsterdam: Elsevier.

Cattell, R. B. (1998). Where is intelligence? Some answers from the triadic theory. In J. J. McArdle & R. W. Woodcock (Eds.), *Human cognitive abilities in theory and practice (p. 29-38).* Mahwah, NJ: Lawrence Erlbaum.

Cattell, R. B. & Cattell, A. K. S. (1973). *Handbook for the Culture Fair Intelligence Test scale 2 forms A and B.* Campaign, IL: Institute for Personality and Ability Testing.

Ceci, S. J. (1990). *On intelligence… more or less – A bio-ecological treatise on intellectual development.* Englewood Cliffs, NJ: Prentice-Hall.

Ceci, S. J. (1996). *On intelligence: A bioethological treatise on intellectual development.* Cambridge, MA: Harvard University Press.

Ceci, S. J. & Roazzi, A. (1994). The effects of context on cognition: Postcards from Brazil. In R. J. Sternberg & R. K. Wagner (Ed.), *Minds in context: Interactionist perspectives on human intelligence* (pp. 74-101). New York: Cambridge University Press.

Chapin, F. S. (1942). Preliminary Standardization of a social insight scale. American Sociological Review, 7, 214-225.

Chapin, F. S. (1967). The Social Insight Test. Palo Alto, CA: Consulting Psychologists Press.

Christie, R. & Geis, F. L. (1970). Studies in Machiavellism. New York: Academic Press.

Christopherson, L. A., & Humes, L. E. (1992). Some psychometric properties of the Test of Basic Auditory Capabilities (TBAC). Journal of Speech and Hearing Research, 35 (4), 929-935.

Ciarrochi, J., Chan, A. Y. C., & Caputi, P. (2000). A critical evaluation of the Emotional Intelligence construct. Personality and Individual Differences, 28, 539-561.

Coren, S., & Hakstian, A. R. (1992). The Development and Cross-Validation of a Self-Report Inventory to Assess Pure-Tone Threshold Hearing Sensitivity. Journal of Speech and Hearing Research, 35, 921-928.

Cosmides, L. & Tooby, J. (2005). Social Exchange: The Evolutionary Design of a Neurocognitive System. In Michael S. Gazzaniga (Ed.), The New Cognitive Neurosciences, III. (pp. 1295-1 308). Cambridge, MA: MIT Press 2005.

Costanzo, M., & Archer, D. (1993). The Interpersonal Perception Task-15 (IPT-15) [Videotape]. Berkeley: University of California Extension Media Center.

Craik, F. I. M. (1986). A functional account of age differences in memory. In F. Klix & H. Hagendorf (Eds.), Human memory and cognitive capabilities (pp. 409-422). North-Holland: Elsevier.

Cronbach, L. J. (1960). Essentials of psychological testing (2nd ed.). New York: Harper & Row.

Cronbach, L. J. & Meehl, P. M. (1955). Construct validity in psychological tests. Psychological Bulletin, 52, 281-302.

Cudeck, R. (1989). Analysis of correlation matrices using covariance structure models. Psychological Bulletin, 105 (2), 317-327.

Damarin, F. (1970). A latent structure model for answering personal questions. Psychological Bulletin, 73 (1), 23-40.

Daneman, K. & Carpenter, P. A. (1980). Individual differences in working memory and reading. Journal of Verbal Learning and Behavior, 19, 450 - 466.

Danthiir, V., Roberts, R. D., Pallier, G., Stankov, L. (2001). What the nose knows. Olfaction and cognitive abilities. Intelligence, 29, 337 – 361.

Danthiir, V., Roberts, R. D., Schulze, R., & Wilhelm, O. (2005). Approaches to Mental Speed. In O. Wilhelm, & R. W. Engle (Eds.), Understanding and Measuring Intelligence (pp. 27-46). London: Sage.

Das, J. P. (1994). Eastern views of intelligence. In R. J. Sternberg (Ed.), Encyclopedia of human intelligence (pp. 387-391). New York Macmillan.

Davidson, J. E. & Downing, C. L. (2000). Contemporary models of intelligence. In R. J. Sternberg (Ed.), Handbook of intelligence (pp. 34-49). Cambridge: Cambridge University Press.

Davies, M., Stankov, L., & Roberts, R. D. (1998). Emotional Intelligence: In Search of an Elusive Construct. Journal of Personality and Social Psychology, 75, 4, 989-1015.

Davis, M. H. (1980). A multidimensional approach to individual differences in empathy. JSAS Catalog of selected documents in psychology, 10, 85.

Davis, M. H. (1983). Measuring individual differences in empathy: evidence for a multidimensional approach. Journal of Personality and Social Psychology, 44 (1), 113–126.

Davis, M. H. (1996). Empathy - A social psychological approach. Boulder, Colorado: Westerview Press

Davis, M. H. & Kraus, L. A. (1997). Empathic accuracy. In W. J. Ickes (Ed.), Empathic Accuracy. NeW York, NJ, US: Guilford Press.

Davison, L. & Torff, B. (1994). Musical intelligence. In R. J. Sternberg (Ed.), Encyclopedia of Human Intelligence (pp. 744-746). New York: Macmillan Publishing Company.

Dawda, D. & Hart, S. D. (2000). Assessing Emotional Intelligence: Reliability and validity of the BarOn Emotional Quotient Inventory (EQ-i) in university students. Personality and Individual Differences, 28, 797-812.

Deary, I. J. (1994). Intelligence and auditory discrimination: Separating processing speed and fidelity of stimulus representation. Intelligence, 18, 189-213.

Deary, I. J. (1995). Auditory Inspection Time and Intelligence: What Is the Direction of Causation? *Developmental Psychology, 31* (2), 237–250.

Deary, I. J. (2000). Simple information processing and intelligence. In R. J. Sternberg (Hrsg.), *Handbook of intelligence.* Cambridge: Cambridge University Press.

Deary, I. J., Bell, P. J., Bell, A. J., Campbell, M. L., & Fazal, N. D. (2004). Sensory discrimination and intelligence: Testing Spearman's other hypothesis. *The American Journal of Psychology, 117,* 1-18.

Deary, I. J., Head, B., & Egan, V. (1989). Auditory inspection time, intelligence and pitch discrimination. *Intelligence, 13,* 135-147.

Deary, I. J. & Stough, C. (1996). Intelligence and inspection time: Achievements, prospects, and problems. *American Psychologist, 51,* 599-608.

DePaulo, B. M. & Rosenthal, R. (1979). The structure of nonverbal decoding skills. *Journal of Personality, 47,* 506-517.

DePaulo, B. M., Rosenthal, R., Eisenstat, R. A., Rogers, P. L., & Finkelstein, S. (1978). Decoding discrepant nonverbal cues. *Journal of Personality and Social Psychology, 36,* 313–323.

Derksen, J., Kramer, I. & Katzko, M. (2002). Does a self-report measure for Emotional Intelligence assess something different than general intelligence? *Personality and Individual Differences, 32,* 37-48.

Dilchert, S. & Ones, D. S. (2004). *Meta-analysis of Practical Intelligence: Contender to the throne of g?* Paper presented at the Annual conference of the Society for Industrial and Organizational Psychology, Chicago, IL.

Domangue, B. B. (1978). Decoding effects of cognitive complexity, tolerance of ambiguity, and verbal nonverbal inconsistency. *Journal of Personality, 46,* 519–535.

Dörner, D. (1986). Diagnostik der operativen Intelligenz. *Diagnostica, 32* (4), 290-308.

Dörner, D. (1987). *Problemlösen als Informationsverarbeitung* (3rd ed.). Stuttgart: Kohlhammer.

Douay-Rheims (1899). (American Ed.). http://www.biblegateway.com/ (24.04.2007)

Drake, R. M. (1933a). The validity and reliability of tests of musical talent. *Journal of Applied Psychology, 17*(4), 447-458.

Drake, R. M. (1933b). Four new tests of musical talent. *Journal of Applied Psychology, Vol 17*(2), 136-147.

Drake, R. M. (1939). Psychology of music. *Journal of Applied Psychology, 23* (1), 215-217.

Dulewicz, V. & Higgs, M. (2000). Emotional Intelligence. *Journal of Managerial Psychology, 15,* 341-372.

Dun, K. (2000). *The Role of Binaural Processing in Spatial Localisation and Cognitive Abilities.* Unpublished Dissertation. University of Southern Queensland.

Dymond, R. F. (1949). A scale for the measurement of empathic ability. *Journal of Consulting Psychology, 13*(2), 127-133.

Dymond, R. F. (1950). Personality and empathy. *Journal of Consulting Psychology, 14* (5), 343-350.

Early, P. C. & Ang, S. (2003). *Cultural intelligence: Individual interactions across cultures.* Stanford, CA: Stanford University Press.

Educational Testing Service (1996). *Scholastic Aptitude Test (SAT).* Princeton, NJ: Educational Testing Service.

Einstein, A. (1953). *Mein Weltbild.* Zürich, Stuttgart, Wien: Europa-Verlag.

Ekman, P. (1973). Darwin and cross-cultural studies of facial expression. In P. Ekman (Ed.), *Darwin and facial expression: A century of research in review.* New York: Academic Press.

Ekman, P. (1984). Expression of the nature of emotion. In K. S. Scherer & P. Ekman (Ed.), *Approaches to emotion* (pp. 319-343). Hillsdale, NJ: Erlbaum.

Ekman, P. (2004). *Gefühle lesen.* Heidelberg: Spektrum Akademischer Verlag.

Ekrnan, P., & Friesen, W. (1975). *Pictures of facial affect.* Palo Alto, CA: Consulting Psychologists Press.

Ekman, P., Friesen, W. V., & Ellsworth, P. (1972). *Emotion in the human face.* New York: Pergamon.

Ekman, P., Friesen, W. V., & Hager, J. C. (2002). *Facial Action Coding System (FACS).* Salt Lake: A Human Face.

Ekman, P., Friesen, W. V., O'Sullivan, M., & Scherer, K. (1980). Relative importance of face, body, and speech in judgements of personality and affect. *Journal of Personality and Social Psychology, 38,* 270 - 277.

Ekman, P., Friesen, W. V., & Scherer, K. R. (1976). Body Movement and Voice Pitch in Deceptive Interaction. *Semiotica, 16,* 23–27.

Ekman, P., O'Sullivan, M., Friesen, W. V., & Scherer, K. R. (1991). Invited article: face, voice, and body in detecting deceit. *Journal of Nonverbal Behavior, 15,* 125–135.

Ekstrom, R. B., French, J. W., Harman, H. H. (1976). *Manual for Kit of factor-Referenced Cognitive Tests.* Educational Testing Service. Princeton, NJ: ETS.

Engelberg, E. & Sjöberg, L. (2004). Emotional Intelligence, affect intensity, and social adjustment. *Personality and Individual Differences, 37,* 533–542.

Enzmann, D. (1996). Gestreßt, erschöpft oder ausgebrannt? Einflüsse von Arbeitssituation, Empathie und Coping auf den Burnoutprozeß. *Prävention und psychosoziale Gesundheitsforschung: Forschungsberichte: Bd. 3.*

Enzmann, D. (1997). RanEigen: A program to determine the parallel analysis criterion for the number of principal components. *Applied Psychological Measurement, 21* (3), 232.

Epstein, S. (1984). Controversial issues in emotion theory. In P. Shaver (Ed.), *Review of personality and social psychology* (Vol. 5, pp. 64 - 88). Beverly Hills, CA: Sage.

Euler, D. (2004). *Sozialkompetenzen bestimmen, fördern und prüfen. Grundfragen und theoretische Fundierung.* Band 1 Sozialkompetenzen in Theorie und Praxis. St. Gallen: Institut für Wirtschaftspädagogik.

Eysenck, H. J. (1987). Speed of Information Processing, Reaction Time, and the Theory of Intelligence. In P. A. Vernon (Hrsg.), *Speed of Information-Processing and Intelligence (pp.* 21-67). Ablex Publishing Corporation: Norwood, NJ, 1987.

Fabrigar, L. R., Wegener, D. T., MacCallum, R. C., & Strahan, E. J. (1999). Evaluating the Use of Exploratory Factor Analysis in Psychological Research. *Psychological Methods, 4 (3),* 272-299.

Fahrenberg, J., Hampel, R., & Selg, H. (2001). Das Freiburger Persönlichkeitsinventar (FPI-R) (7., überarbeitete und neu normierte Auflage). Göttingen: Hogrefe.

Feffer, M. H. (1959). The cognitive implications of role-taking behavior. *Journal of Personality, 27,* 152-168.

Feffer, M. H., & Suchotliff, L. (1966). Decentering implications of social interactions. *Journal of Personality and Social Psychology, 4,* 415-422.

Feigenspan, J. (2005). *Computerversion des Berliner Intelligenzstruktur Tests.* Unpublished diploma thesis. University of Magdeburg, Germany.

Feldstein, S., Dohm, F.-A., & Crown, C. L. (2001). Gender and speed rate in the perception of competence and social attractiveness. *Journal of Social Psychology, 141* (6), 785 - 806.

Feshbach, N. D. & Feshbach, S. (1982). *Learning to care.* San Francisco: Scott, Foresman.

Feshbach, N. D. & Feshbach, S. (1987). Affective processes and academic achievement. *Child development, 58,* 1335-1347.

Fiedler, K. (1991). On the task, the measures and the mood in research on affect and social cognition. In J. P. Forgas (Ed.), *Emotion and social judgements.* Cambridge: Cambridge University Press.

Flavell, J. H., Botkin, P. T., Fry, C. L., Wright, J. W. & Jarvis, P. E. (1968), *The Development of Role-taking and Communication Skills in Children.* Wiley, New York, NY.

Fleishman, E. A. (1967). Individual differences in motor learning. In R. M. Gagné (Ed.), *Learning and individual differences.* Columbus, OH: Merrill.

Fleishman, E. A., Roberts, N. M., & Freidman, M. P. (1958). Factor analysis of aptitude and proficiency measures in radiotelegraphy. *Journal of Applied Psychology, 42,* 127–137.

Foa, U. G. (1961). Convergences in the analysis of the structure of interpersonal behavior. *Psychological Review, 68,* 341 – 353.

Foon, A. E. (1986). A social structural approach to speech evaluation. *Journal of Social Psychology, 126* (4), 521-530.

Ford, M. E. (1982). Social cognition and social competence in adolescence. *Developmental Psychology, 18,* 323-340.

Ford, M.E. (1986). For all practical purposes: Criteria for defining and evaluating Practical Intelligence. In R.J. Sternberg & R.K. Wagner (Eds.), *Practical Intelligence: Origins of competence in the everyday world* (pp. 183-200). Cambridge: Cambridge University Press.

Ford, M. E. (1994). A new conceptualization of Social Intelligence. In R. J. Sternberg (Ed.), *Encyclopedia of Human Intelligence* (pp. 974-978). New York: Macmillan Publishing Company.

Ford, M. E. & Tisak, M. (1983). A further search for Social Intelligence. *Journal of Educational Psychology, 75* (2), 196-206.

Forgas, J. P. (Ed.) (2000). *Handbook of affect and social cognition.* New Jersey: Lawrence Erlbaum Associates.

Formann, A. K., & Piswanger, K. (1979). *Wiener Matrizen-Test.* Weinheim: Beltz.

Franklin, E. (1956). *Tonality as a basis for the study of musical talent.* Goteberg: Gumpetus Forlag.

Frederiksen, N., Carlson, S., & Ward, W. C. (1984). The place of Social Intelligence in a taxonomy of cognitive abilities. *Intelligence, 8,* 315-337.

French, J. W. (1951). The description of aptitude and achievement tests in terms of rotated factors. *Psychometric Monographs, 5.*

Frey, A. & Balzer, L. (2003). Soziale und methodische Kompetenzen – der Beurteilungsbogen smk: Ein Messverfahren für die Diagnose von sozielen und methodischen Kompetenzen. *Empirische Pädagogik, 17* (2), 148-175.

Frick, R. W. (1985). Communicating emotion: the role of prosodic features. *Psychological Bulletin, 97* (3), 412-429.

Frijda, N. H. (1986). *The emotions.* Cambridge, UK: Cambridge University Press.

Funder, D. C. & Colvin, C. R. (1988). Friends and strangers. Acquaintanceship, agreement, and the accuracy of personality judgement. *Journal of Personality and Social Psychology, 55,* 149-158.

Funke, U. & Schuler, H. (1998). Validity of stimulus and response components in a video test of social competence. *International Journal of Selection and Assessment, 6,* 115-123.

Furnham, A. (1986). Response bias, social desirability, and dissimulation. *Personality and Individual Differences, 7* (3), 385–400.

Furnham, A. (2005). Gender and personality differences in self- and other ratings of business intelligence. *British Journal of Management, 16,* 91-103.

Furnham, A., & Chamorro-Premuzic, T. (2004). Estimating one's own personality and intelligence scores. *British Journal of Psychology, 95,* 149-160.

Gaab, N. & Schlaug, G. (2003). The effect of musicianship on pitch memory in performance matched groups. *Neuroreport, 14* (18), 2291-2295.

Galton, F. (1883). Inquiries into human faculty and its development. New York: Macmillan.

Gardner, H. (1983). *Frames of mind. The theory of multiple intelligences.* New York: Basic Books.

Gardner, H. (1998). Are there additional intelligences? The case for naturalist, spiritual, and existential intelligences. In J. Kane (Ed.), *Education, information, and transformation* (pp. 111-132). Englewood Cliffs, NJ: Prentice Hall.

Gardner, H. (2002). Intelligenzen – Die Vielfalt des menschlichen Geistes. Stuttgart: Klett-Cotta.

Gardner, H., & Hatch, T. (1989). Multiple intelligences go to school: Educational implications of the theory of multiple intelligences. *Educational Researcher, 18* (8), 4-9.

Gough, H. G. (1965). A validation study of the Chapin Social Insight Test. *Psychological Reports, 17,* 355-368.

Geher, G. (2004). *Measuring Emotional Intelligence: Common Ground and Controversy.* Nova Science Publishers.

Gigrenzer, G. (1997). The modularity of Social Intelligence. In A. Whiten & R. W. Byrne (Eds.), *Machiavellian Intelligence II – Extensions and Evaluations* (Chapt. 10; p.264-288). Cambridge: Cambridge University Press.

Giles, H., Mulac, A., Bradac, J. J., & Johnson, P. (1987). Speech accomodation theory: The first decade and beyond. In M. L. Laughlin (Ed.), *Communication Yearbook 10.* (pp. 13-48). Beverly Hills, CA: Sage.

Goldstein, A. G. & Chance, J. E. (1985). Effects of training on Japanese faces recognition: Reduction of the other-race effect. *Bulletin of the Psychonomic Society, 23,* 211-214.

Goleman, D. (1995). *Emotional Intelligence: Why it can matter more than IQ.* New York: Bantam Books.

Goleman, D. (1998). *Working with Emotional Intelligence.* London: Bloomsbury Publishing.

Goleman, D. (2006). *Social Intelligence: the new science of human relationships.* London: Hutchinson.

Gordon, E. E. (1961). A Study to Determine the Effects of Training and Practice on Drake Musical Aptitude Test Scores. *Journal of Research in Music Education, 9,* (1), 63-74.

Gordon, E. E. (1965). *Musical Aptitude Profile.* Boston: Houghton-Mifflin.

Gordon, E. E. (1989). *Advanced measures of music audiation.* Chicago. GIA publications.

Gordon, E. E. (1998). *Introduction to Research and the Psychology of Music.* Chicago: GIA Publications.

Gottfredson, L. S. (2003). On Sternberg´s "reply to Gottfredson". *Intelligence, 31,* 415-424.

Gough, H. G. (1968). *Manual for the Chapin Social Insight Test.* Palo Alto, CA: Consulting Psychologists Press.

Grady, C. L., & Keightley, M. L. (2002). Studies of altered social cognition in neuropsychiatric disorders using functional neuroimaging. *Canadian Journal of Psychiatry, 47,* 327–336.

Gratch, H. (1973). *Twenty five years of social research in Israel.* Jerusalem: Jerusalem Academic Press.

Greif, S. (1987). Soziale Kompetenzen. In D. Frey & S. Greif (Eds.), *Sozialpsychologie- Ein Handbuch in Schlüsselbegriffen* (pp. 312–320). München: Urban & Schwarzenberg.

Green, K. D., Forehand, R., Beck, S. J., & Vosk, B. (1980). An assessment of the relationships among measures of children's social competence and children's academic achievement. *Child Development, 51,* 1149-1156.

Greenwald, A. G., Banaji, M. R., Rudman, L. A., Farnham, S. D., Nosek, B. A., & Rosier, M. (2001). Prologue to a unified theory of attitudes, stereotypes, and self-concept. In J. P. Forgas (Ed.), *Feeling and thinking. The role of affect in social cognition* (Chapt. 13). Cambridge: Cambridge University Press.

Gregory, C., Lough, S., Stone, V. E., Erzinclioglu, S., Martin, L., Baron-Cohen, S., & Hodges, J. (2002). Theory of mind in frontotemporal dementia and Alzheimer's disease: Theoretical and practical implications. *Brain, 125,* 752-764.

Greig, T. C., Bryson, G. J., & Bell, M. D. (2004). Theory of mind performance in schizophrenia: Diagnostic, symptom, and neuropsychological correlates. *Journal of Nervous and Mental Disease, 192,* 12–18.

Groffmann, K. J. (1964). Die Entwicklung der Intelligenzmessung. In R. Heiss (Hrsg.), *Handbuch der Psychologie in 12 Bänden: Bd. 6. Psychologische Diagnostik* (pp. 148-199). Göttingen: Hogrefe.

Guilford, J. P. (1934). Introversion-extroversion. *Psychological Bulletin, 31* (5), 331-354.

Guilford, J. P. (1967). *The nature of human intelligence.* New York: MacGraw Hill.

Guthke, J. (1972). Zur Diagnostik der intellektuellen Lernfähigkeit. Berlin: Deutscher Verlag der Wissenschaften.

Guttman, L. (1954). An outline of some new methodology for social research. *Public Opinion Quarterly, 18,* 395-404.

Guttman, L. (1958). What lies ahead for factor analysis? *Educational and Psychological Measurement, 18,* 497-515.

Guttman, L. (1965). Tests and measurement. A faceted definition of intelligence (pp. 166-181. In R. Eiferman (Ed.), *Studies in psychology.* Jerusalem: Scripta hierosolymitana, 14.

Guttman, L. & Levy, S. (1991). Two structural laws for intelligence tests. *Intelligence, 15,* 79 - 103.

Gygi, B., Kidd, G. R., & Watson, C. S. (2004). Spectral-temporal factors in the identification of environmental sounds. *Journal of the Acoustical Society of America, 115* (3), 1252 - 1265.

Haier, R. J., Siegel, B. V. Jr., Nuechterlein, K. H., Hazlet, E., Wu, J. C., Paek, J., Browning, H. L., & Buchsbaum, M. S. (1988). Cortical glucose metabolic rate correlates of abstract reasoning and attention studied with positron emission tomography. *Intelligence, 12*, 199-217.

Halberstadt, A. G. (1986). Family socialization of emotional expression and nonverbal communication styles and skills. *Journal of Personality and Social Psychology, 51*, 827-836.

Hall, J. A. (1978). Gender effects in decoding nonverbal cues. *Psychological Bulletin, 82*, 1-20.

Hall, J. A. (1984). *Nonverbal sex differences: Communication accuracy and expressive style.* Baltimore, MD: John Hopkins University Press.

Hall, J. A. (2001). The PONS Test and the Psychometric approach to measuring interpersonal sensitivity. In J. A. Hall & F. J. Bernieri (Eds.), *Interpersonal Sensitivity.* Mahwah, NJ: LEA.

Hammersly, R. & Read, J.D. (1990). Das Wiedererkennen von Stimmen. In G. Köhnken & S. L. Sporer (Eds.), *Identifizierung von Tatverdächtigen durch Augenzeugen. Psychologische Erkenntnisse, Probleme und Perspektiven* (Kap. 6). Stuttgart: Verlag für Angewandte Psychologie.

Hanley, C. M. (1956). Factor analysis of speech perception. *Journal of Speech and Hearing Disorders, 21*, 76–81.

Hargreaves, W. A., Starkweather, J. A., & Blacker, K. H.(1965): Voice quality in depression. *Journal of Abnormal Psychology, 70* (3), 218-220.

Harris, J.D. (Ed.) (1969). *Forty germinal papers in hearing.* Groton, CT: Journal of Auditory Research.

Harris, P.L. (2000). Understanding emotion. In M. Lewis & J. Haviland-Jones (Eds.), *Handbook of emotions* (2nd edition). New York: Guildford Pres

Harter, S., Waters, P. L., Whitesell, N. R., & Kastelic, D. (1998). Level of voice among female and male high school students: relational context, support and gender orientation. *Developmental Psychology, 34* (5), 892-901.

Hathaway S., McKinley, J., & Engel, R. (2000). *Minnesota Multiphasic Personality Inventory 2: MMPI 2.* Bern: Huber.

Hedlund, J., Forsythe, G. B., Horvath, J. A., Williams, W. M., Snook, S., & Sternberg, R. J. (2003). Identifying and assessing tacit knowledge: Understanding the Practical Intelligence of military leaders. *Leadership Quarterly, 14*, 117-140.

Helmbold, N. & Rammsayer, T. (2006). Timing Performance as a Predictor of Psychometric Intelligence as Measured by Speed and Power Tests. *Journal of Individual Differences, 27* (1), 20-37.

Hendrickson, A. E. (1982). The biological basis of intelligence. Part I: Theory. In H. J. Eysenck (Ed.), *A model for intelligence* (pp. 151-196). Berlin: Springer.

Hess, U., Kappas, A. & Scherer, K. R. (1988). Multichannel communication of emotion: Synthetic signal production. In K. R. Scherer (Ed.), *Facets of Emotion: Recent research* (pp. 161-182). Hillsdale, NJ: Erlbaum.

Hinsch, R. & Pfingsten, U. (2007). *Gruppentraining sozialer Kompetenzen (GSK). Grundlagen, Durchführung, Anwendungsbeispiele.* (5. Auflage). Weinheim: PVU.

Hoepfner, R. & O'Sullivan, M. (1968). Social Intelligence and IQ. *Educational and Psychological Measurement, 28*, 339-344.

Hoffman, M. L. (2000), *Empathy and Moral Development* (Cambridge: Cambridge University Press).

Hofstätter, P. R. (1957). *Psychologie.* Frankfurt a. M.: Fischer-Lexikon.

Hogan, R. (1969). Development of an empathy scale. *Journal of Consulting and Clinical Psychology, 33*, 307-316.

Holliday, S. G. & Chandler, M.J. (1986). *Wisdom: explorations in adult competence.* Basel: Karger.

Holmstrom, L. G. (1969). Intelligence v. Progress in Music Education. *Journal of Research in Music Education, 17* (1), 76-81.

Holy Bible (New International Version). http://www.biblegateway.com/ (21.04.2007)

Holz-Ebeling, F. (1991) Das Unbehagen an der Facettenanalyse: Zeit für eine Neubestimmung, *Archives of Psychology, 2*, 265-292.

Holz-Ebeling, F. (1995). Faktorenanalysen und was dann? Zur Frage der Validität von Dimensionsinterpretationen. *Psychologische Rundschau, 46*, 18-35.

Horn, J. L. (1967). Intelligence: Why it grows, why it declines, *Transaction, 5*, 23-31.

Horn, J. L. (1970). Organization of data on life-span development of human abilities. In L. R. Goulet & P. B. Baltes (Hrsg.), *Life-span developmental psychology: Research and theory* (pp. 423-466). New York: Academic Press.

Horn, J. L. (1994). Theory of fluid and crystallized intelligence. In R. J. Sternberg (Eds.), Encyclopedia of human intelligence. New York, NY: Macmillan Publishing.

Horn, J. L. (1998). A basis for research on age-differences in cognitive capabilities. In J. J. McArdle & R. W. Woodcock (Eds.), *Human cognitive abilities in theory and practice*. Mahwah, NJ: Lawrence Erlbaum.

Horn, J. L. (2006). *Understanding human intelligence: Where have we come since Spearman?* In R. Cudeck & R. MacCallum (Eds.), Factor analysis at 100. Mahwah, NJ: Lawrence Erlbaum.

Horn, J. L. & Cattell, R. B. (1966). Refinement and test of the theory of fluid and crystallized intelligence. *Journal of Educational Psychology, 57*, 253-270.

Horn, J. L. & Noll, J. (1997). Human cognitive capabilities: Gf-Gc-Theory. In D. P. Flanagan, J. L. Genshaft & P. L. Harrison (Hrsg.), *Contemporary intellectual assessment. Theories, tests, and issues* (pp. 53-91). New York: The Guilford Press.

Horn, J. L. & Stankov, L. (1982). Auditory and visual factors of intelligence. *Intelligence, 6*, 165-185.

Hornstein, M. G. (1967). Accuracy of emotional communication and interpersonal compatibility. *Journal of Personality, 35* (1), 20–30.

Horowitz, L. M., Strauß, B., & Kordy, H. (2000). *Inventar zur Erfassung interpersonaler Probleme (IIP-D)* (Deutsche Version) (2., überarbeitete und neu normierte Auflage). Göttingen: Hogrefe.

Hough, L. M. & Ones, D. S. (Eds.) (2001). The structure, measurement, validity, and use of personality variables in industrial, work and organizational psychology, *Handbook of Industrial, Work and Organizational Psychology*.

Huffcutt, A. I., Conway, J. M., & Roth, P. L. (2001). Identification and meta-analytic assessment of psychological constructs measured in employment interviews. *Journal of Applied Psychology, 86* (5), 897-913.

Humphreys, L. (1962). The organization of human abilities. *American Psychologist, 17*, 475-483.

Hunt, E. B. (1980). Intelligence as an information processing concept. *British Journal of Psychology, 71*, 449–474.

Hunt, T. (1928). The measurement of Social Intelligence. *Journal of Applied Psychology, 12* (3), 317-334.

Huttar, G. L. (1968). Relations between prosodic variables and emotions in normal American English utterances. *J. Speech Hear. Res. 11*, 481-487.

Ickes, W. (2001). Measuring empathic accuracy. In J. A. Hall & F. J. Bernieri (Eds), *Interpersonal sensitivity. Theory and measurement*. Mahwah, NJ: Lawrence Erlbaum Associates.

Ickes, W., Stinson, L., Bissonette, V. & Garcia, S. (1990). Naturalistic social cognition: Empathic accuracy in mixed sex dyads. *Journal of Personality and Social Psychology, 54*, 730-742.

Irwin, R. J. (1984). Inspection Time and Its Relation to Intelligence. *Intelligence, 8* (1), 47-65.

Izard, C. E. (1977) *Human Emotions*. New York: Plenum.

Jacoby, R. (1968). BTMB Bentley-Test für musikalische Begabung [Measures of musical abilities]. Übertragen und für die Anwendung im deutschsprachigen Raum. Musikalische Begabung bei Kindern und ihre Messbarkeit. Frankfurt am Main: Diesterweg.

Jäger, A. O. (1967). *Dimensionen der Intelligenz*. Göttingen: Hogrefe.

Jäger, A. O. (1982). Mehrmodale Klassifikation von Intelligenzleistungen: Experimentell kontrollierte Weiterentwicklung eines deskriptiven Intelligenzstrukturmodells. *Diagnostica, x8*(3), 195-225.

Jäger, A. O. (1984). Intelligenzstrukturforschung: Konkurrierende Modelle, neue Entwicklungen, Perspektiven. *Psychologische Rundschau, 35*, 21-35.

Jäger, A. O., Süß, H.-M., & Beauducel, A. (1997). *Berliner Intelligenzstruktur Test. Handbuch.* Göttingen: Hogrefe.

Jäger, A. O. & Tesch-Römer, C. (1988). Replikation des Berliner Intelligenzstrukturmodells (BIS) in den "Kit of Reference Tests for Cognitive Factors" nach French, Ekstrom & Price (1963). *Zeitschrift für Differentielle und Diagnostische Psychologie, 9* (2), 77-96.

Jenschke, S., Koelsch, S., & Friederici, A. D. (2005). Investigating the relationship of music and language in children. *Ann. New York Academy of Science, 1060,* 231-242.

Jensen, A. R. (1982a). Reaction time and psychometric g. In H. J. Eysenck (Ed.), A model for intelligence (pp. 93 – 132). Heidelberg: Springer.

Jensen, A. R. (1982b). The chronometry of intelligence. In R. J. Sternberg (Hrsg.), *Advances in the psychology of human intelligence* (Bd. 1). Hillsdale, NJ: Lawrence Erlbaum Associates.

Jensen, A. R. (1986). g: Artifact or reality? *Journal of Vocational Behavior, 29,* 301-331.

Jensen, A. R. (1993). Test validity: g versus "tacit knowledge." *Current Directions in Psychological Science: A Journal of the American Psychological Society, 2* (1), 9.

Jensen, A. R. (2000). TESTING - The Dilemma of Group Differences. *Psychology, Public Policy, and Law, 6* (1), 121-127.

Johnson, J. A., Cheek, J. M., & Smither, R. (1983). The structure of empathy. *Journal of Personality and Social Psychology, 45* (6), 1299-1312.

Johnson, W. & Bouchard Jr., T. J. (2005). The structure of human intelligence: it is verbal, perceptual, and image rotation (VPR), not fluid and crystallized. *Intelligence, 33,* 393-416.

Johnson-Laird, P. N., & Oatley, K. (1989). The language of emotions: An analysis of a semantic field. *Cognition and Emotion, 3,* 81–123.

Johnstone, T. & Scherer, K. R. (2004). Vocal Communication of Emotion. In M. Lewis & J. M. Haviland-Jones, *Handbook of Emotions* (2nd edition) (Chapt. 14). New York: The Guilford Press.

Jones, K. & Day, J. D. (1997). Discrimination of two aspects of cognitive-Social Intelligence from Academic Intelligence. *Journal of Educational Psychology, 89* (3), 486-497.

Jusczyk, P. W. (1999). How infants begin to extract words from speech. *Trends Cogn. Sci., 3,* 323-328.

Kail, R. & Pellegrino, J. W. (1988). *Menschliche Intelligenz.* Heidelberg: Spektrum der Wissenschaft.

Kail, R. & Salthouse, T. A. (1994). Processing speed and a mental capacity. *Acta Psychologica, 86,* 199-225.

Kaiser, H. J. (1998). Soziale Intelligenz. In E. Roth (Ed.), *Intelligenz. Grundlagen und neuere Forschung.* Stuttgart: Kohlhammer.

Kallinen, K. & Ravaja, N. (2004). Emotion-related effects of speech rate and rising vs. falling background music melody during audio news: the moderating influence of personality. *Personality and Individual Differences, 37,* 275 – 288.

Kang, S., Day, J. D., & Meara, N. M. (2005). Social and Emotional Intelligence: Starting a Conversation about Their Similarities and Differences. In R. Schulze & R. D. Roberts (Eds), *International Handbook of Emotional Intelligence* (pp. 91-105). Göttingen: Hogrefe.

Kang, S., Day, J. D., & Meara, N. M. (2006). Soziale und emotionale Intelligenz: Gemeinsamkeiten und Unterschiede (Chap 5). In R. Schulze, P. A. Freund, & R. D. Roberts (Eds.), *Emotionale Intelligenz. Ein internationales Handbuch.* Göttingen: Hogrefe.

Kang, S. & Shaver, P. R. (2004). Individual differences in emotional complexity: Their psychological implications. *Journal of Personality, 72,* 687–726.

Kanning, U. P. (2002). Soziale Kompetenz - Definition, Strukturen und Prozesse. *Zeitschrift für Psychologie, 210* (4), 154-163.

Kanning, U. P. (2003). *Diagnostik sozialer Kompetenzen.* Kompendien Psychologische Diagnostik, Band 4. Göttingen: Hogrefe

Kappas, A., Hess, U. & Scherer, K. R. (1991). *Voice and emotion.* In R.S. Feldman & B. Rimé (Eds.), *Fundamentals of nonverbal behavior.* Cambridge University Press, 200-237.

Karlin, J. E. (1941). Music ability. *Psychometrika, 6,* 61-65.

Karlin, J. E. (1942). A factorial study of auditory function. *Psychometrika, 7*(4), 251-279.
Kaukiainen, A., Björkqvist, K., Lagerspetz, K., Österman, K., Salmivalli, C., Rothberg, S., & Ahlbom, A. (1999). The relationships between Social Intelligence, empathy, and three types of aggression. *Aggressive Behavior, 25*, 81 - 89.
Keating, D. P. (1978). A search for Social Intelligence. *Journal of Educational Psychology, 70*, 218-223.
Keightley, M. L., Winocur, G., Burianova, H., Hongwanishkul, D., & Grady, C. L. (2006). Age Effects on Social Cognition: Faces Tell a Different Story. *Psychology and Aging, 21* (3), 558–572.
Kelley, H. H., Holmes, J. G., Kerr, N. L., Reiss, H. T., Rusbult, C. E., & Van Lange, P. A. M. (2002). *An atlas of interpersonal situations.* Cambridge: University Press.
Kelley, H. P. (1964). Memory abilities: A factor analysis. *Psychometric Monographs*, 11.
Kemper, T. D. (2000). Social models in the explanation of emotions. In J. M Lewis & M. Haviland-Jones (Eds.), *Handbook of emotions* (2nd ed., pp. 45-58). New York: The Guilford Press.
Kenny, D. A. (1979). Correlation and causality. New York: Wiley.
Kidd, G. R., Watson, C. S., & Gygi, B. (2000). Individual diferences in auditory abilities among normal-hearing listeners. *Journal of the Acoustical Society of America, 108* (2), 2641.
Kiesler, D. J. (1983). The 1982 interpersonal cycle: A taxonomy for complementarity in human transactions. *Psychological Review, 90*, 185-214.
Kihlstrom, J. F. & Cantor, N. (2000). Social Intelligence. In R. J. Sternberg (Ed.), *Handbook of Intelligence.* Cambridge: Cambridge University Press.
Koelsch, S. (2004). *Das Verstehen der Bedeutung von Musik.* Tätigkeitsbericht 2004. Leipzig: Max Planck Institut für neuropsychologische Forschung.
Koelsch, S., Gunther, T. C., Wittfoth, M., & Sammler, D. (2005). Interaction between syntax processing in language and music: an ERP study. *Journal of Cognitive Neuroscience, 17* (10), 1565-1577.
Koelsch, S. & Siebel, W. A. (2005). Towards a neural basis of music perception. *Trends in cognitive Sciences, 9* (12), 578-584.
Kormann, A. (1971). *Der Zusammenhang zwischen Intelligenz und Musikalität unter entwicklungs- und kreativitätspsychologischem Aspekt (Dissertation).* Salzburg: Universität Salzburg.
Kormann, A. (1985). Tests in der Musikpsychologie. In H. Bruhn, R. Oerter, & H. Rösing (Hrsg.), *Musikpsychologie* (pp. 502-509). München: Urban & Schwarzenberg.
Kormann, A. (2005). Tests in der Musikpsychologie. In R. Oerter & T. H. Stoffer, *Spezielle Musikpsychologie. Enzyklopädie der Psychologie, Themenbereich D: Praxisgebiete, Serie 7: Musikpsychologie, Bd. 2.* Göttingen: Hogrefe.
Kosmitzki, C. & John, O. P. (1993). The implicit use of explicit conceptions of Social Intelligence. *Personality and Individual Differences, 15*(1), 11 - 23.
Kramer, E. (1963). Judgement of personal characteristics and emotions from nonverbal properties of speech. *Psychological Bulletin, 60* (4), 408-420.
Krauss, R. M., Freyberg, R. & Morsella, E. (2002). Inferring speakers' physical attributes from their voices. *Journal of Experimental Social Psychology, 38*, 618-625.
Krebs, D. (1975). Empathy and altruism. *Journal of Personality and Social Psychology, 32*, 1134-1146.
Kuncel, N. R., Credé, M., & Thomas, L. L. (2005). The validity of self-reported grade point averages, class ranks, and test scores: A meta-analysis and review of the literature. *Review of Educational Research, 75*, 63-82.
Kurth, E. (1931). *Musikpsychologie.* Berlin. Reprint 1969, Hildesheim: G. Olms.
Kyllonen, P. C. (1994). Aptitude testing inspired by information processing: a test of the four-sources model. *Journal of General Psychology, 120*, 375-405.
Kyllonen, P. C. & Christal, R. E. (1990). Reasoning ability is (little more than) working-memory capacity?! *Intelligence, 14*, 389–433.
Landy, F. J. (2006). The Long, Frustrating, and Fruitless Search for Social Intelligence: A cautionary tale. In K. R. Murphy (Ed.), *A Critique of Emotional Intelligence: What are the problems and how can they be fixed?* Mahwah, NJ: Lawrence Erlbaum Associates.

Lass, N. J. & Davis, M. (1976). An investigation of speaker height and weight identification. *Journal of the Acoustical Society of America, 60* (3), 700-703.

Lautenschläger, G. J. (1989). A comparison of alternatives to conducting Monte Carlo analyses for determining parallel analysis criteria. *Multivariate Behavioral Research, 24*, 365-395.

Lazarus, R. S. (1991). *Emotion and adaptation.* New York: Oxford University Press.

Leary, T. (1957). *Interpersonal diagnosis of personality.* New York: Ronald Press.

Lee, J.-E., Day, J. D., Meara, N. M., & Maxwell, S. E. (2002). Discrimination of social knowledge and its flexible application from creativity: a multitrait-multimethod approach. *Personality and Individual Differences, 32*, 913-928.

Lee, J.-E., Wong, C.-M. T., Day, J. D., Maxwell, S. E., & Thorpe, P. (2000). Social and Academic Intelligences: a multitrait-multimethod study of their crystallized and fluid characteristics. *Personality and Individual Differences, 29*, 539-553.

Legree, P. J., Psotka, J., Tremble, T., & Bourne, D. R. (2005). Using consensus based measurement to assess Emotional Intelligence. In R. Schulze & R.D. Roberts (Eds), *International Handbook of Emotional Intelligence* (pp. 155 -179). Göttingen: Hogrefe.

Levenson, R. W., & Gottman, J. M. (1978). Toward the assessment of competence. *Journal of Consulting and Clinical Psychology, 45,* 453-462.

Levenson, R. W. & Ruef, A. M. (1992). Empathy: A physiological substrate. *Journal of Personality and Social Psychology, 63*, 234-246.

Li, L., Daneman, M., Qi, J. G., & Schneider, B. A. (2004). Does the information content of an irrelevant source differentially affect spoken word recognition in younger and older adults? *Journal of Experimental Psychology: Human Perception and Performance, 30* (6), 1077–1091.

Li, L., Qi, J. G., He, Y., Alain, C., & Schneider, B. A. (2005). Attribute capture in the precedence effect for long-duration noise sounds. *Hearing Research, 202*, 235–247.

Li, S.-C., Jordaniova, M., & Lindenberger, U. (1998). From good senses to good sense: a link between tactile information processing and intelligence. *Intelligence, 26* (2), 99-122.

Lindenberger, U., Scherer, H., & Baltes, P. B. (2001). The strong connection between sensory and cognitive performance in old age: not due to sensory acuity reductions operating during cognitive assessment. *Psychology and Aging, 16* (2), 196-205.

Lindgren, H. C. & Robinson, J. (1953). An evaluation of Dymond's Test of Insight and Empathy. *Journal of Consulting Psychology, 17* (3), 172-176.

Loehlin, J. C. (2004). Latent variable models. An introduction to factor, path, and structural equation analysis) Hillsdale, NJ: Lawrence Erlbaum Publishers.

Loevinger, J. (1957). Objective tests as instruments of psychological theory. *Psychological Reports, 3*, 635-694.

Lohman, D. F. (2003). *The Woodcock-Johnson III and the Cognitive Abilities Test (Form 6). A concurrent validity study.* University of Iowa.

Lutz, C. 1985 Ethnopsychology compared to what? Explaining behaviour and consciousness among the Ifaluk. In G. M. White & J. Kirkpatrick (Eds.), *Person, self, and experience: exploring Pacific ethnopsychologies* (pp. 35–79). Berkeley, CA: University of California Press.

Lynn, R., Wilson, R. G., & Gault, A. (1989). Simple musical tests as measures od Spearman's g. *Journal of Personality and Individual Differences, 10*, 25-28.

MacCann, C. E. (2006). *New Approaches to Measuring Emotional Intelligence: Exploring Methodological Issues with Two New Assessment Tools.* Doctoral thesis. University of Sydney.

MacCann, C. E., Matthews, G., Zeidner, M., & Roberts, R. (2003). Psychological assessment of Emotional Intelligence: A review of self-report and performance-based testing. *International Journal of Organizational Analysis, 11* (3), 247-274.

MacCann, C. E., Matthews, G., Zeidner, M., & Roberts, R. D. (2004). The Assessment of Emotional Intelligence: On Frameworks, Fissures, and the Future. In G. Geher, *Measuring Emotional Intelligence: Common Ground and Controversy* (Chapt. 2). New York, NJ: Nova Science Publishers.

MacCann, C., Roberts, R. D., Matthews, G., & Zeidner, M. (2004). Consensus scoring and empirical option weighting of performance-based Emotional Intelligence (EI) tests. *Personality and Individual Differences, 36*, 645–662.

Maier, N. R. F. & Thurber, J. A. (1968). Accuracy of judgments of deception when an interview is watched, heard, and read. *Personnel Psychology, 21,* 23-30.

Mariacher, H. & Neubauer, A. (2005). *PAI30 Test zur Praktischen Alltagsintelligenz.* Göttingen, Hogrefe.

Marlowe Jr, H. R. (1985). Competence: A Social Intelligence approach. In H. A. Marlowe & R. B. Weinberg (Eds.), *Competence development: Theory and practice in special populations* (pp. 50-52).

Marlowe Jr, H. R. (1986). Social Intelligence: Evidence for multidimensionality and construct independence. *Journal of Educational Psychology, 78* (1), 52-58.

Marshalek, B., Lohman, D. F., & Snow, R. E. (1983). The complexity continuum in the radex and hierarchical models of intelligence. *Intelligence, 7,* 107-127.

Matsumoto, D., LeRoux, J., Wilson-Cohn, C., Raroque, J., Kooken, K., & Ekman, P. (2000). A new test to measure emotion recognition ability: Matsumoto and Ekman's Japanese and Caucasian Brief Affect Recognition Test (JACBART). *Journal of Nonverbal Behavior, 24,* 179–209.

Matthews, G., Zeidner, M., & Roberts, R. D. (Eds.) (in press), *Science of Emotional Intelligence: Knowns and Unknowns.* New York: Oxford University Press.

Mayer, J. D. (2001). A field guide to Emotional Intelligence. In J. Ciarrochi, J. P. Forgas, & J. D. Mayer (Eds.), *Emotional Intelligence and everyday life* (pp. 3-24). New York: Psychology Press.

Mayer, J. D., Caruso, D. R., & Salovey, P. (1999). Emotional Intelligence meets traditional standards for an intelligence. *Intelligence, 27,* 267-298.

Mayer, J. D., DiPaolo, M., & Salovey, P. (1990). Perceiving affective content in ambiguous visual stimuli: a component of Emotional Intelligence. *Journal of Personality Assessment, 54,* 772-781.

Mayer, J. D. & Geher, G. (1996). Emotional Intelligence and the identification of emotion. *Intelligence, 22,* 89-113.

Mayer, J. D. & Salovey, P. (1993). The intelligence of Emotional Intelligence. *Intelligence, 17 (4),* 433-442.

Mayer, J. D. & Salovey, P. (1997). What is Emotional Intelligence? In P. Salovey & D. Sluyter (Eds). *Emotional Development and Emotional Intelligence: Implications for Educators* (pp. 3-31). New York: Basic Books.

Mayer, J. D., Salovey, P., & Caruso, D. R. (2000a). Emotional Intelligence as zeitgeist, as personality and as mental ability. In R. BarOn & J. D. A. Parker (Eds.), *The handbook of Emotional Intelligence: Theory, development, assessment, and application at home, school, and in the workplace* (pp. 92-117). San Francisco: Jossey-Bass.

Mayer, J. D., Salovey, P., & Caruso, D. R. (2000b). Models of Emotional Intelligence. In R. J. Sternberg (Ed.), *Handbook of intelligence* (pp. 396-420). Cambridge: Cambridge University Press.

Mayer, J. D., Salovey, P., & Caruso, D. R. (2002). *The Mayer-Salovey-Caruso Emotional Intelligence Test (MSCEIT): User's manual.* Toronto, Canada: Multi-Health Systems.

Mayer, J. D., Salovey, P., Caruso, D. R., & Sitenarios, G. (2001). Emotional Intelligence as a standard intelligence. *Emotion, 1,* 232-242.

Mayer, J. D., Salovey, P., Caruso, D. R., & Sitenarios, G. (2003). Measuring Emotional Intelligence with the MSCEIT V2.0. *Emotion, 3,* 97-105.

McDougall, W. (1908, 1960). *An introduction to social psychology* (31st ed). London: Methuen.

McFall, R. M. & Marston, A. R. (1970). An experimental investigation of behavior rehearsal in assertive training. *Journal of Abnormal Psychology, 76,* 295-303.

McFarland, L. A. (2003). Warning against faking on a personality test: Effects on applicant reactions and personality test scores. *International Journal of Selection and Assessment, 11,* 265-276.

McGrew, K. S (1994). Woodcock-Johnson Tests of cognitive ability-revised. In R. J. Sternberg (Ed.), *Encyclopedia of human intelligence* (pp. 1152-1158). New York Macmillan.

McGrew, K. S. & Evans, J. J. (2004). Internal and External factorial extensions to the Cattell-Horn-Carroll (CHC) theory of cognitive abilities: a review of factor analytic research since Carroll's Seminal 1993 Treatise. *Carroll Human Cognitive Abilities (HCA) Project research Report # 2*. Evans Consulting: Institute of Applied Psychometrics.

McGrew, K. S. & Murphy, S.(1995). Uniqueness and general factor characteristics of the Woodcock-Johnson Tests of cognitive abilities-revised. *Journal of School Psychology, 33* (3), 235-245.

McKenna, F. P. & Sharma, D. (1995). Intrusive Cognitions: An Investigation of the Emotional Stroop Task. *Journal of Experimental Psychology: Learning, Memory, and Cognition,* 21 (6), 1595-1607.

McKenna, F. P. & Sharma, D. (2004). Reversing the Emotional Stroop Effect Reveals That It Is Not What It Seems: The Role of Fast and Slow Components. *Journal .of Experimental Psychology: Learning, Memory, and Cognition, 30,* 2, 382–392.

McLeish, J. (1950). The validation of Seashore's measures of musical talent by factorial methods. *British Journal of Psychology, 3,* 129–140.

Mehrabian, A. (1972). *Nonverbal communication.* Aldine-Atherton, Chicago, Illinois.

Mehrabian, A. & Epstein, N. (1972). A Measure of Emotional Empathy. *Journal of Personality, 40,* 525-543.

Merriam-Webster Online Dictionary. http://www.m-w.com/ (24.04.2007)

Meyer, W.-U., Schützwohl, A., & Reisenzein, R. (1997). *Einführung in die Emotionspsychologie (Band 2): Evolutionspsychologische Emotionstheorien.* Bern: Huber.

Michell, R. L. C., Elliot, R. , Barry, M., Cruttenden, A., & Woodruff, P. W. R. (2003). The neural response to emotional prosody, as revealed by functional magnetic resonance imaging. *Neuropsychologia, 41,* 1410-1421.

Minter, M., Hobson, R. P., & Pring, L. (1991). Recognition of vocally expressed emotion by congenitally blind children. *Journal of Visual Impairment & Blindness, 85,* 411-415.

Moreno, J. L. (1934). *Who shall survive? A new approach to the problem of human interrelations.* Washington, DC: Nervous and Mental Disease.

Morton, J., Frith, U., & Leslie, A. (1991). The cognitive basis of a biological disorder: Autism. *Trends in Neurosciences, 14,* 434-438.

Moskowitz, D. S. (1994). Cross-situational generality and the interpersonal-circumplex. *Journal of Personality and Social Psychology, 66,* 921–933.

Moss, F. A., & Hunt, T. (1927). Are you socially intelligent? *Scientific American, 137,* 108-110.

Moss, F. A., Hunt, T., Omwake, K. T. & Woodward, L. G. (1955). *Manual for the George Washington University Series Social Intelligence Test.* Washington, DC: The Center for Psychological Services.

Murphy, K. R. (2006). Four conclusions about Emotional Intelligence. In K. R. Murphy (Ed.), *A Critique of Emotional Intelligence: What are the problems and how can they be fixed?* Mahwah, NJ: Lawrence Erlbaum Associates.

Nass, C. & Lee, K. M. (2001). Does computer-synthesized speech manifest personality? Experimental tests of recognition, similarity attraction, and consistency attraction. *Journal of Experimental Psychology: Applied, 7,* 171-181.

Neisser, V. (1976). General, academic and artifical intelligence. In L. Resnick (Ed.), *The Nature of* Intelligence (pp. 135-144). Hillsdale, N.J.: Erlbaum.

Neisser, U., Boodoo, G., Bouchard, T. J., Boykin, A. W., Brody, N., Ceci, S. J., Halpern, D. F., Loehlin, J. C., Perloff, R., Sternberg, R. J., & Urbina, S. (1996). Intelligence: Knowns and unknowns. *American Psychologist, 51,* 77-101.

Neubauer, A. C. (1995). *Intelligenz und Geschwindigkeit der Informationsverarbeitung.* New York: Springer.

Neubauer, A. C. (2001). Elementar-kognitive und physiologische Korrelate der Intelligenz. In E. Stern & J. Guthke (Hrsg.), *Perspektiven der Intelligenzforschung* (S. 13-42). Lengerich: Pabst.

Neubauer, A. C. & Bucik, V. (1996). The mental speed-IQ relationship: unitary or modular? *Intelligence, 22,* 23–48.

Neubauer, A. C. & Freudenthaler, H. H. (2005). Models of Emotional Intelligence. In R. Schulze & R. D. Roberts (Eds.), *Emotional Intelligence - An international handbook*. Göttingen: Hogrefe & Huber.

Newsome, S., Day, A. L., & Catano, V. M. (2000). Assessing the predictive validity of Emotional Intelligence. *Personality and Individual Differences, 29*, 1005-1016.

Nigsch, O. (1999). Was ist Sozialkompetenz? *Österreichische Zeitschrift für Soziologie, 24* (1), 3-31.

Noller, P. (2001). Using standard content methodology to assess nonverbal sensitivity in dyads. In J. A. Hall & F. J. Bernieri (Eds). *Interpersonal sensitivity. Theory and measurement*. Mahwah, NJ: Lawrence Erlbaum Associates.

Nowicki, S. Jr. & Carton, J. (1993). The measurement of emotional intensity from facial expressions: The DANVA FACES 2. *Journal of Social Psychology, 133*, 749-750

Nowicki, S. Jr., & Duke, M. P. (1989). *A measure of nonverbal social processing ability in children between the ages of 6 and 10*. Paper presented as part of a symposium at the American Psychological Society, Alexandria, VA.

Nowicki, S. & Duke, M. P. (1994). Individual differences in the nonverbal communication of affect, The diagnostic analysis of nonverbal accuracy scale. *Journal of Nonverbal Behavior, 18*, 9-35.

Nowicki, S. Jr. & Duke, M. P. (2001). Nonverbal Receptivity: The diagnostic analysis of nonverbal accuracy (DANVA). In J. A. Hall & F. J. Bernieri (*Eds), Interpersonal sensitivity. Theory and measurement*. Mahwah, NJ: Lawrence Erlbaum Associates.

Nowicki, S. & Duke, M. P. (2007). *Manual for the receptive tests of the diagnostic analysis of nonverbal accuracy 2 (DANVA 2)*. Unpublished test manual.

Oberauer, K. (1993). Die Koordination kognitiver Operationen—eine Studie über die Beziehung zwischen Intelligenz und „working memory." *Zeitschrift für Psychologie, 201 (1)*, 57-84.

Oberauer, K. (2002). Access to information in working memory: Exploring the focus of attention. *Journal of Experimental Psychology: Learning, Memory, & Cognition, 28* (3), 411-421.

Oberauer, K., Süß, H.-M., Schulze, R., Wilhelm, O., & Wittmann, W. W. (2000). Working memory capacity - facets of a cognitive ability construct. *Personality and Individual Differences, 29*, 1017-1045.

Oberauer, K., Süß, H.-M., Wilhelm, O., & Wittmann, W. W. (2003). The multiple faces of working memory: storage, processing, supervision, and coordination. *Intelligence, 31*, 167-193.

Obermann, C. (1992). *Assessment Center*. Wiesbaden: Gabler.

Olea, M. M. & Ree, M. J. (1994). Predicting pilot and navigator criteria: Not much more than g. *Journal of Applied Psychology, 79*, 845-851.

Olsson, H., Björkman, C., Haag, K., & Juslin, P. (1998). Auditory inspection time: on the importance of selecting the appropriate sensory continuum. *Personality and Individual Differences, 25*, 627-634

Ones, D. S., Viswesvaran, C., & Dilchert, S. (2005). Personality at work: Rasing awareness and correcting misconceptions. *Human Performance, 18* (4), 389-404.

Orlik, P. (1978). Soziale Intelligenz. In K. J. Klauer (Ed.), *Handbuch der pädagogischen Diagnostik* (pp. 341-354). Düsseldorf, Germany: Schwann.

Ostendorf, F. & Angleitner, A. (2004). *NEO-Persönlichkeitsinventar nach Costa und McCrae, Revidierte Fassung*. Göttingen: Hogrefe.

O'Sullivan, M. (1982). Measuring the ability to recognize facial expressions of emotion. P. Ekman (Ed.), *Emotion in the human face (2nd* edition, pp. 281-317). Cambridge: Cambridge University Press.

O'Sullivan, M. (in press). Trolling for trout, trawling for tuna: The methodological morass in measuring Emotional Intelligence. In G. Matthews, M. Zeidner, & R. D. Roberts (Eds.), *The Science of Emotional Intelligence: Knowns and Unknowns*. New York: Oxford University Press.

O'Sullivan, M., Ekman, P., Friesen, W., Scherer, K. (1985). What you say and how you say it: The contribution of speech content and voice quality to judgements of others. *Journal of Personality and Social Psychology, 48* (1), 54-62.

O'Sullivan, M. & Guilford, J. P. (1966). *Six Factor Test of Social Intelligence, manual of instructions and interpretations.* Beverly Hills, CA: Sheridan Psychological Services.

O'Sullivan, M. & Guilford, J. P. (1975). Six factors of behavioral cognition: Understanding other people. *Journal of Educational Measurement, 12,* 255-271.

O'Sullivan, M., & Guilford, J. P. (1976). *Four Factor Tests of Social Intelligence: Manual of instructions and interpretations.* Orange, CA: Sheridan Psychological Services.

O'Sullivan, M., Guilford, J. P., & deMille, R. (1965). *The measurement of Social Intelligence. Report from the psychological laboratory.* (34). Los Angeles: University of Southern California.

Oswald, W. D. & Roth, E. (1987). *Der Zahlen-Verbindungs-Test (ZVT)* [Number connection test]. Göttingen: Hogrefe.

Ozer, D. J. (1993). Classical psychophysics and the assessment of agreement and accuracy in judgements of personality. *Journal of Personality, 61,* 739-767.

Panksepp, J. (1998). *Affective Neuroscience.* New York: Oxford University Press.

Papenbrock, J. (2005). *Geschlechtsunterschiede im Bereich der auditiven Fähigkeiten.* Unpublished diploma thesis. Otto-von-Guericke University of Magdeburg.

Parker, D. M., Crawford, J. R., & Stephen, E. (1999). Auditory inspection time and intelligence: a new spatial localization task. *Intelligence, 27 (2),* 131–139.

Parker, J. D. A., Summerfeldt, L. J., Hogan, M. J., & Majeski, S. A. (2004). Emotional Intelligence and academic success: examining the transition from high school to university. *Personality and Individual Differences, 36,* 163–172.

Patel, A. D., Peretz, I., Tramo, M., & Labreque, R. (1998). Processing prosodic and music patterns: A neuropsychological investigation. *Brain and Language, 61,* 123-144.

Paunonen, S. V. (1989). Consensus in personality judgements: Moderating effects of target-rater acquaintanceship and behaviour observability. *Journal of Personality and Social Psychology, 63,* 816–824.

Pérez, J. C. (2003). Adaptación y validación española del «Trait Emotional Intelligence Questionnaire» (TEIQue) en población universitaria. *Encuentros en Psicología Social, 5,* 278-283.

Pérez, J. C., Petrides, K. V., & Furnham, A. (2005). Measuring trait Emotional Intelligence. In R. Schulze & R. D. Roberts (Eds.), *International Handbook of Emotional Intelligence.* Cambridge, MA: Hogrefe & Huber.

Petrides, K. V. & Furnham, A. (2000). On the dimensional structure of Emotional Intelligence. *Personality and Individual Differences, 29,* 313-320.

Petrides, K V. & Furnham, A. (2001). Trait Emotional Intelligence: Psychometric investigation with reference to established trait taxonomies. *European Journal of Personality, 15,* 425-448.

Petrides, K. V. & Furnham, A. (2003). Trait Emotional Intelligence: Behavioural validation in two studies of emotion recognition and reactivity to mood induction. *European Journal of Personality, 17,* 39-57.

Pfister, H.-R. & Beauducel, A. (1993, August, 29 - September, 1). *Stability of operation and content facets: a facet analysis of the Berlin Model of Intelligence Structure (BIS).* Paper presented at the Proceedings of the 4th International Facet Theory Conference Prague, Czech Republic.

Plutchik, R. (1994). Measuring emotions and their derivates. In H. R. Plutchik & Kellerman (Ed.), *Emotion. Theory, Research, and Experience.* San Diego: Academic Press, Inc.

Porath, C. L., & Bateman, T. S. (2006). Self-Regulation: From Goal Orientation to Job Performance. *Journal of Applied Psychology, 91* (1), 185-192.

Prechtl, E. (2005). ISIS-Interaktives System zur Identifikation sozialer Kompetenzen. *Zeitschrift für Personalpsychologie, 4* (4), 195-199.

Premack, D., & Woodruff, G. (1978). Does the chimpanzee have a "theory of mind"? *Behaviour and Brain Sciences, 4,* 515-526.

Probst, P. (1975). Eine empirische Untersuchung zum Konstrukt der sozialen Intelligenz. *Diagnostica, 21,* 24-75.

Probst, P. (1982). Empirische Untersuchung zum Konstrukt der „sozialen" Intelligenz. In K. Pawlik (Ed.), *Multivariate Persönlichkeitsforschung* (pp. 201-226). Bern: Hans Huber.

Probst, P. (1998). Child Health Related Cognitions of Parents with Autistic Children: A Cross-National Exploratory Study. In U. P. Gielen & A. L.Communian (Eds.), *Family and Family Therapy in International Perspective* (pp. 461-483). Trieste: Edizioni LINT (Italy).

Rammsayer, T. H. & Brandler, S. (2002). On the relationship between general fluid intelligence and psychophysical indicators of temporal resolution in the brain. *Journal of Research in Personality, 36*, 507-530.

Raven, J. C., Raven, J., & Court, J. H. (1982). *Mill Hill Vocabulary Test*. London: Lewis.

Raz, N., Willerman, L., & Yama, M. (1987). On sense and senses: intelligence and auditory information. *Personality and Individual Differences, 8* (2), 201-210.

Reed, T. E. & Jensen, A. R. (1991). Arm nerve conduction velocity (NCV), brain NCV, reaction time, and intelligence. *Intelligence, 15*, 33-47.

Reilly, J. S., McIntire, M. L., & Seago, H. (1992). Affective prosody in American Sign Language. *Sign Language Studies, 75*, 113-128.

Reilly, J. & Seibert, L. (2003). Language and emotion. In R. Davidson, K. Scherer, & H. Goldsmith (Eds.), *Handbook of Affective Sciences (*pp. 535-559). Academic Press.

Reisenzein, R. & Hofmann, T. (1993). Discriminating emotions from appraisal- relevant situational information: baseline data for structural models of cognitive appraisals. *Cognition and Emotion, 7*, 271 - 293.

Ridgway. (1980). Construct validity through facet analysis: Scheduling tests do not necessarily measure scheduling ability. *Journal of Occupational Psychology, 53*, 253-263.

Riemann, R. & Allgöwer, A. (1993). Eine deutschsprachige Fassung des "Interpersonal Competence Questionnaire" (ICQ). *Zeitschrift für Differentielle und Diagnostische Psychologie, 14*, 153-163.

Riggio, R. E. (1989). *Manual for the Social Skills Inventory*. Palo Alto, CA: Consulting Psychologists Press.

Riggio, R. E., Messamer, J., & Throckmorton, B. (1991). Social and Academic Intelligence: conceptually distinct but overlapping constructs. *Personality and Individual Differences, 12*, 695-702.

Riggio, R. E. & Riggio, H. R. (2001). Self-report measurement of interpersonal sensitivity. In J. A. Hall & F. J. Bernieri (Eds), *Interpersonal sensitivity. Theory and measurement*. Mahwah, NJ: Lawrence Erlbaum Associates.

Riggio, R. E., Tucker, J. S., & Coffaro, D. (1989). Social skills and empathy. *Personality and Individual Differences, 10*, 93-99.

Roberts, R. D., Pallier, G., & Goff, G. N. (1998). Sensory Processes within the structure of human cognitive abilities. In P. L. Ackerman, P. C. Kyllonen, & R. D. Roberts, *Learning and individual differences. Process, trait, and content determinants* (Chapt. 12). Washington, DC: American Psychological Association.

Roberts, R. D., Schulze, R., O'Brien, K., MacCann, C., Reid, J., & Maul, A. (2006). Exploring the Validity of the Mayer-Salovey-Caruso Emotional Intelligence Test (MSCEIT) with Established Emotions Measures. *Emotion, 6* (4), 663–669.

Roberts, R. D. & Stankov, L. (1999). Individual differences in speed of mental processing and human cognitive abilities: Toward a taxonomic model. *Learning & Individual Differences, 11*, 1–120.

Roberts, R. D., Stankov, L., Pallier, G., & Dolph, B. (1997). Charting the cognitive sphere: Tactile-kinesthetic performance within the structure of intelligence. *Intelligence, 25* (2), 111-148.

Roberts, R., Zeidner, M., & Matthews, G. (2001). Does Emotional Intelligence meet traditional standards for an intelligence? Some new data and conclusions. *Emotion, 1*, 196-231.

Roberts, R., Zeidner, M., & Matthews, G. (in press). Emotional Intelligence: Knowns and Unknowns. In G. Matthews, M. Zeidner, & R. D. Roberts (Eds.), *The Science of Emotional Intelligence*. Oxford: University Press.

Roessler, R. & Lester, J. W. (1976). Voice predicts affect during psychotherapy. *Journal of nervous and mental disease, 163*, 166–176.

Rogers, P. L., Scherer, K. R., & Rosenthal, R. (1971). Content-filtering human speech: A simple electronic system.*Behavior Research Methods and Instrumentation, 3*, 16–18.

Rohracher, H. (1965). *Einführung in die Psychologie* (Vol. 9). Wien: Urban & Schwarzenberg.

Rosenstiel, L. von (2001). Führung. In H. Schuler (Hrsg.), *Lehrbuch der Personalpsychologie*. Göttingen: Hogrefe.

Rosenthal, R., Hall, J. A., DiMatteo, M. R., Rogers, P. L., & Archer, D. (1979). *Sensitivity to Nonverbal Communication: The PONS Test*. Baltimore, MD: Johns Hopkins University Press.

Roth, P. L. & Switzer III, F. S. (2002). Outliers and Influential Cases: Handling those Discordant Contaminated Maverick Rogues. In S. G. Rogelberg (Ed.), *Handbook of Research Methods in Industrial and Organizational Psychology*. (pp. 297-309). Oxford: Blackwell Publishers.

Rummer, R. & Engelkamp, J. (2000). Sprache und Emotion. In H. A. Euler, J. H. Otto, & H. Mandl (Ed.), *Emotionspsychologie. Ein Handbuch* (pp. 325 - 333). Weinheim: Psychologie Verlags Union.

Runde, B. (2001). *Multimodales Assessment sozialer Kompetenzen. Validierung eines computergestützten Tests*. Osnabrück: Methodos.

Runde, B., Bastians, F., Kluge, S., & Wübbelmann, K. (2001). *ISIS – Interaktives* System zur Identifikation Sozialer Kompetenz. In W. Sarges & H. Wottawa (Hrsg.), *Handbuch wirtschaftspsychologischer Testverfahren* (S. 313-318). Lengerich: Papst.

Runde, B. & Etzel, S. (2005). Vision (Videobasierte Identifikation Sozialer Intelligenz-Online). In W. Sarges & H. Wottawa (Hrsg.), *Handbuch wirtschaftspsychologischer Testverfahren* (2., überarbeitete und erweiterte Auflage). Lengerich: Papst.

Rüsseler, J. & Münte, T. F. (2001). Test Readspeed. University of Magdeburg. Unpublished.

Russell, J. A. (1980). A Circumplex Model of Affect. *Journal of Personality and Social Psychology, 39*, 1161-1178.

Russell J. A. & Fernández-Dols, J. M. (Eds.) (1997). *The Psychology of Facial Expression*. New York: Cambridge University Press.

Sackett, P. R., Zedeck, S., & Fogli, L. (1988). Relations between measures of typical and maximum job performance. *Journal of Applied Psychology, 73* (3), 482-486.

Salovey, P. & Mayer, J. D. (1990). Emotional Intelligence. *Inmagination, Cognition and Personality, 9*, 185-211.

Salovey, P., Mayer, J. D. Goldman, S. L., Turvey, C., & Palfai, T. P. (1995). Emotional attention, clarity, and repair: Exploring Emotional Intelligence using the Trait Meta-Mood Scale. In J. W. Pennebaker (Ed.), *Emotion, disclosure, and health* (pp. 125-154). Washington, DC: American Psychological Association.

Salthouse, T., Babcock, R., & Shaw, R. (1991). Effects of adult age on structural and operational capacities in working memory. *Psychology and Aging, 6*, 118–127.

Sander, N. (2005). *Inhibitory and executive functions in cognitive psychology: an individual differences approach examining structure and overlap with working memory capacity and intelligence*. Doctoral thesis. University of Magdeburg.

Schaie, K. W. (1994). The course of adult intellectual development. *American Psychologist, 49*, 304–313.

Scherer, K. R. (1971). Randomized splicing: A note on a simple technique for masking speech content. *Journal of Experimental Research in Personality, 5*, 155–159.

Scherer, K.R. (1974). Acoustic concomitants of e emotional dimensions: Judging affect from synthesized tone sequences. In S. Weitz (Ed.), *Nonverbal Communication* (pp. 249-253). New York: Oxford University Press.

Scherer, K. R. (1979). Personality markers in speech. In K. R. Scherer & H. Giles (Eds.), *Social markers in speech* (pp. 147-209). Cambridge: Cambridge University Press.

Scherer, K. R. (1986). Vocal affect expression: A review and a model for future research. *Psychological Bulletin, 99* (2), 143-165.

Scherer, K. R. (1989). Vocal correlates of emotion. In H. Wagner & A. Manstead (Eds.), *Handbook of Psychophysiology: Emotion and Social Behavior* (pp. 165–197). Wiley, London.

Scherer, K. R. (1990). Theorien und aktuelle Probleme der Emotionspsychologie. *Enzyklopädie der Psychologie. Band C/IV/3 Psychologie der Emotion* (pp. 2-38).

Scherer, K. R. (1996). Vocal affect expression. A review and model for future research. *Psychological Bulletin, 99*, 143-165.

Scherer, K. R. (1999). Universality of emotional expression. In D. Levinson, J. Ponzetti, & P. Jorgenson (Eds.), *Encyclopedia of human emotions* (Vol. 2, pp. 669–674). New York: Macmillan.

Scherer, J. (2000). Vocal communication of emotion. In M. Haviland-Jones & J.M. Lewis (Eds.), *Handbook of emotions* (2nd ed., pp. 220-235). New York: The Guilford Press.

Scherer, K. R. (2003). Vocal communication of emotion: A review of research paradigms. *Speech Communication, 40*, 227–256.

Scherer, K. R. (in press). Componential Emotion Theory Can Inform Models of Emotional Competence. In G. Matthews, M. Zeidner, & R. D. Roberts (Eds.), *The Science of Emotional Intelligence: Knowns and Unknowns* (pp. 167-212). New York: Oxford University Press.

Scherer, K. R., Banse, R., & Wallbott, H. G. (2001). Emotion Inferences from Vocal Expression Correlate across Languages and Cultures. *Journal of Cross-Cultural Psychology, 32* (1), 76-92.

Scherer, K. R., Banse, R., Wallbott, H. G., & Goldbeck, T. (1991). Vocal cues in emotion encoding and decoding. *Motivation and Emotion, 15*, 123–148.

Scherer, K. R., Ladd, D. R., Silverman, K. (1984). Vocal cues to speaker affect: Testing two models. *Journal of the Acoustical Society of America, 76*, 1346-1356.

Scherer, K. R., London, H., & Wolf, J. J. (1973). The voice of confidence-Paralinguistic cues and audience evaluation. *Journal of Research in Personality, 7*, 31-44.

Scherer, K. R. & Wallbott, H. G. (1990). Ausdruck von Emotionen (Chapt. 6). In K. R. Scherer, *Psychologie der Emotion, Enzyklopädie der Psychologie, Themenbereich C, Theorie und Forschung, Serie IV Motivation und Emotion, Band 3, Psychologie der Emotion.* Göttingen: Hogrefe.

Scherer, K. R. & Wallbott, H. G. (1994). Evidence for the universality and culture variation of differential emotion response patterning. *Journal of Personality and Social Psychology, 66* (2), 310-328.

Scherer, K. R., Wallbott, H. G., Matsumoto, D., & Kuhdo, T. (1988). Emotional experience in cultural context: A comparison between Europe, Japan, and the USA. In K. R. Scherer (Ed.), *Facets of Emotion: Recent research.* Hillsale, NJ: Erlbaum.

Schlesinger, I. M. & Guttman, L. (1969). Smallest space analysis of intelligence and achievement tests. *Psychological Bulletin, 71*, 95-100.

Schmidt, F. L. (2002). The role of general cognitive ability and job performance: Why there cannot be a debate. *Human Performance, 15 (1/2)*, 187-210.

Schmidt, F. L. & Hunter, J. E. (1993). Tacit knowledge, Practical Intelligence, general mental ability, and job knowledge. *Current Directions in Psychological Science: A Journal of the American Psychological Society 2 (1)*, 8-9.

Schmidt, F. L. & Hunter, J. E. (1998). The validity and utility of selection methods in personnel psychology: practical and theoretical implications of 85 years of research findings. *Psychological Bulletin, 124*, 262-274.

Schmidt, F. L., Ones, D. S., & Hunter, J. E. (1992). Personnel selection. *Annual Review of Psychology, 43*, 627-670.

Schmidt-Atzert, L. (2000). Struktur der Emotionen. In H. A. Euler, J. H. Otto, & H. Mandl (Ed.), *Emotionspsychologie. Ein Handbuch.* Weinheim: Psychologie Verlags nion.

Schmidt-Atzert, L. & Bühner, M. (2002, September). *Entwicklung eines Leistungstests zur emotionalen Intelligenz.* 43. Kongress der deutschen Gesellschaft für Psychologie. Humboldt-Universität Berlin.

Schneider, R. J., Ackerman, P. L., & Kanfer, R. (1996). To "act wisely in human relations": Exploring the dimensions of social competence. *Personality and Individual Differences, 21* (4), 469-481.

Schneider, R. J., Roberts, R. D., & Heggestad, E. D. (2002). Exploring the structure and construct validity of a self-report social competence inventory. In L. M. Hough (Chair), *Compound Traits: The Next Frontier of I/O Personality Research.* Symposium conducted at the 17th Annual Conference of the Society for Industrial and Organizational Psychology, Inc., Toronto, Ontario: Canada.

Schrank, F. A. (2006). *Specification of the cognitive process involved in performance on the Woodcock-Johnson III* (Assessment Service Bulletin No. 7). Itasca, IL: Riverside Publishing.

Schuler, H., Diemand, A., & Moser, K. (1993). Filmszenen. Entwicklung und Konstruktvalidierung eines neuen eignungsdiagnostischen Verfahrens. *Zeitschrift für Arbeits-undOrganisationspsychologie, 37*, 2-10.

Schuler. H. & Funke, U. (1995). Diagnose beruflicher Eignung und Leistung. In H. Schuler (Ed.), Lehrbuch Organisationspsychologie (2. ed.) (pp. 235-283). Bern: Huber.

Schulte, M. J., Ree, M. J., Carretta, T. R. (2004). Emotional Intelligence: not much more than g and personality. *Personality and Individual Differences, 37*, 1059–1068.

Schulze, R., Freund, P. A., & Roberts, R. D. (Hrsg.) (2006). *Emotionale Intelligenz: Ein internationales Handbuch.* Göttingen: Hogrefe.

Schulze, R. & Roberts, R. D. (Eds.) (2005). *International Handbook of Emotional Intelligence.* Göttingen: Hogrefe.

Schulze, R., Wilhelm, O., & Kyllonen, P. C. (in press). Approaches to the assessment of Emotional Intelligence. In G. Matthews, M. Zeidner, & R. D. Roberts (Eds.), *The Science of Emotional Intelligence: Knowns and Unknowns.* New York: Oxford University Press.

Schumacker, R. E. & Lomax, R. G. (1996). A beginner's guide to structural equation modeling. Mahwah, NJ: Lawrence Erlbaum.

Schutte, N. S., Malouff, J. M., Hall, L. E., Haggerty, D. J., Cooper, J. T., Golden, C. J., & Dornheim, L. (1998). Development and validation of a measure of Emotional Intelligence. *Personality and Individual Differences, 25*, 167–177.

Schwarz, N. (1999). Self-reports. How the questions shape the answers. *American Psychologist, 54* (2), 53–92.

Schweinberger, S. R. & Sommer, W. (1997). Recognizing famous voices: Influence of stimulus duration and different types of retrieval cues. *Journal of Speech, Language, and Hearing Research, 40*, 453-463.

Seashore, C. E. (1919). *The Psychology of Musical Talent.* New York: Silver Burdett.

Seashore, C. E., Lewis, D., & Saetveit, J. C. (1960). Manual of instruction and interpretations for the Seashore Measures of Musical Talents (2nd revision). New York: The Psychological Cooperation.

Sechrest, L. (2005). Validity of measures is not simple matter. *Health research and educational trust, 40* (5), 1584-1604.

Sechrest, L., McKnight, P., & McKnight, K. (1996). Calibration of measures for psychotherapy. Outcome studies. *American Psychologist, 51* (10), 1065–1071.

Seidel, K. (2007). *Social intelligence and auditory intelligence – useful constructs?* Doctoral dissertation, Otto von Guericke University of Magdeburg, Germany.

Seidel, K., & Süß, H.-M. (2007). *Can you hear it? – New findings about the inner structure of auditory abilities and their relationship to other ability constructs.* Magdeburg: Otto-von-Guericke University Magdeburg, Department of Psychology, Division of Psychological Methods, Psychological Assessment and Evaluation Research.

Seidel, K., Weis, S., & Süß, H.-M. (2004, July). *Overlap and distinctiveness of social and Emotional Intelligence as specified in personality-like models and self-report inventories.* Paper presented at the 12th European Conference on Personality. University of Groningen, The Netherlands.

Seidel, K., Weis, S., & Süß, H.-M. (2007). *How are social intelligence and auditory intelligence related?* Magdeburg: Otto-von-Guericke University Magdeburg, Department of Psychology, Division of Psychological Methods, Psychological Assessment and Evaluation Research.

Seyfried, B. (1995) (Hrsg.). *"Stolperstein" Sozialkompetenz. Was macht es so schwierig, sie zu erfassen, zu fördern und zu beurteilen?* Berlin: Bundesinstitut für Berufsbildung.

Shanley, L. A., Walker, R. E., & Foley, J. M. (1971). Social Intelligence: A concept in search of data. *Psychological Reports, 29*, 1123-1132.

Shaver, P., Schwartz, J., Kirson, D., & O'Connor, C. (1987). Emotion knowledge: Further exploration of a prototype approach. *Journal of Personality and Social Psychology, 52*, 1061–1086.

Shintel, H., Nusbaum, H. C., & Okrent, A. (2006). Analog acoustic expression in speech communication. *Journal of Memory and Language, 55*, 167 - 177.

Shuter, R. (1968). *The psychology of musical ability.* London: Methuem.

Shuter-Dyson, R. (1982). Psychologie musikalischen Verhaltens: angloamerikanische Forschungsbeiträge. Mainz: Schott.

Shuter-Dyson, R. & Gabriel, C. (1981). *The psychology of musical ability* (2nd ed.). London: Methuen.

Siegel, L. (1958). Drake Musical Aptitude Tests. *Journal of Counseling Psychology, 5* (2), 154-155.

Snodgrass, S. E. (2001). Correlation method for assessing interpersonal sensitivity within dyadic interaction. In J. A. Hall & F. J. Bernieri (Eds). *Interpersonal sensitivity. Theory and measurement*. Mahwah, NJ: Lawrence Erlbaum Associates.

Snow, R. E. (1986). Individual Differences and the Design of Educational Programs. *American Psychologist, 41 (10)*, 1029-1039.

Snow, R. E. (1996). Aptitude development and education. *Psychology, Public Policy, and Law, 2 (3/4)*, 536-560.

Snow, R. E., Kyllonen, P. C., & Marshalek, B. (1984). The topography of ability and learning correlations. In R. J. Sternberg (Ed.), *Advances in psychology of human intelligence*. Hillsdale, NJ: Lawrence Erlbaum Associates.

Solomon, L. M., Webster, J. C., & Curtis, J. F. (1960). A factorial study of speech perception. *Journal of Speech and Hearing Research, 2*, 101-107.

Sowarka, D. (1989). Weisheit und weise Personen: Common-sense-Konzepte älterer Menschen. *Zeitschrift für Entwicklungspsychologie und Pädagogische Psychologie, 21*, 87-109.

Spearman, C. (1904). "General intelligence" objectively determined and measured. *American Journal of Psychology, 15*, 201-293.

Spearman, C. (1914). The theory of two factors. *Psychological Review, 21* (2), 101-115.

Spearman, C. (1927). *The Abilities of Men*. London: Macmillan.

Spearritt, D. (1962). *Listening comprehension – A factorial analysis*. Melbourne: Australian Council for Educational Research.

Sperber, W. (1995). *Was ist praktische Intelligenz? Theoretische und empirische Untersuchung eines Fähigkeitsbereiches als impliziter Theorie psychologischer Experten* (Vol. Reihe VI, Vol. 469). Frankfurt am Main: Peter Lang.

Sperber, D. & Wilson, D. (2002). Pragmatics, modularity and mind-reading. *Mind & Language* (Special Issue on Pragmatics and Cognitive Science), *17*, 3-23.

Stankov, L. (1971). *The Hierarchical Structure of Auditory Abilities and the Relationship between Auditory and Visual Modalities*. Unpublished PhD thesis, University of Denver.

Stankov, L. (1980). Ear differences and implied cerebral lateralization on some intellective auditory factors. *Applied Psychological Measurement 4* (1), 21-38.

Stankov, L. (1983). *The role of competition in human abilities revealed through auditory tests*. Sydney, Australia: Society of Multivariate Experimental Psychology.

Stankov, L. (1986). Age-Related Changes in Auditory Abilities and in a Competing Task. *Multivariate Behavioral Research, 21* (1), 65-76.

Stankov, L. (1994). Auditory abilities. In R. J. Sternberg (Ed.), *Encyclopedia of Human Intelligence* (pp. 157-162). New York Macmillan.

Stankov, L. (1999). Mining on the no man's land between intelligence and personality. In P. L. Ackerman, P. C. Kyllonen, & R. D. Roberts (Eds.). *Learning and Individual Differences: Process trait, and content determinants* (pp. 315-338). Washington, DC: American Psychological Association.

Stankov, L. (2000). Structural extensions of a hierarchical view on human cognitive abilities. *Learning and Individual Differences, 12*, 35-51.

Stankov, L. (2001). Tactile and kinesthetic perceptual processes within the taxonomy of human cognitive abilities. *Intelligence, 29*, 1-29.

Stankov, L. & Horn, J. L. (1980). Human abilities revealed through auditory tests. *Journal of Educational Psychology, 75* (4), 471-490.

Stankov, L., & Roberts, R. D: (1997). Mental speed is not the 'basic process' of intelligence. *Personality and Individual Differences, 22* (1), 69-84.

Stankov, L., & Spilsbury, G. (1978). The measurement of auditory abilities of blind, partially sighted and sighted children. *Applied Psychological Measurement, 2* (4), 491-503.

Stern, W. (1911). The supernormal child. *Journal of Educational Psychology, 2* (3), 143-148.

Sternberg, R. J. (1985). *Beyond IQ: A triarchic theory of human intelligence.* New York: Cambridge University Press.

Sternberg, R. J. (1986). Intelligence is mental self-government. In R. J. Sternberg & D. K. Detterman (Eds.), *Human intelligence.* Norwood, NJ: Ablex Publishing.

Sternberg. R. J. (1990). Wisdom and ist relations to intelligence and creativity. In R. J. Sternberg, *Wisdom, its nature, origins and development. Wisdom and its relation to intelligence and creativity.* New York: Cambridge University Press

Sternberg, R. J. (1997a). Successful intelligence. New York: Plume.

Sternberg, R. J. (1997b).The triarchic theory of intelligence. In D. P. Flanagan, J. L. Genshaft, & P. L. Harrison (Eds.), *Contemporary intellectual assessment: Theories, tests, an issues* (pp. 92-104). New York: Guilford Press.

Sternberg, R. J. (2000). Intelligence and Wisdom. In R. J. Sternberg (Ed.), *Handbook of Intelligence* (pp. 631-649). Cambridge: Cambridge University Press.

Sternberg, R. J. (Ed.). (2005). *The triarchic theory of successful intelligence* (2nd ed.). New York, NJ: Guilford Press.

Sternberg, R. J., Conway, B., Bernstein, M. & Ketron, J.C. (1981). Peoples Conceptualisations of Intelligence. *Journal of Personality and Social Psychology, 41,* 37-55.

Sternberg, R. J., Forsythe, G. B., Hedlund, J., Horvath, J. A., Wagner, R. K., Williams, W. M., Snook, S. A., & Grigorenko, E. L. (2000). *Practical Intelligence in everyday life.* New York: Cambridge University Press.

Sternberg, R. J. & Grigorenko, E. L. (2006). Cultural intelligence and successful intelligence. *Group and Organization Management, 31* (1), 27-39.

Sternberg, R. J. & Powell, J. S. (1982). Theories of intelligence. In R. J. Sternberg (Ed.) *Handbook of human intelligence* (pp. 975-1005). Cambridge: University Press.

Sternberg, R. J. & Smith, C. (1985). Social Intelligence and decoding skills in nonverbal communication. *Social Cognition, 3,* 168-192.

Sternberg, R. J. & Wagner, R. K. (Eds.) (1986). Practical Intelligence: nature and origins of competence in the everyday world. Cambridge, MA: Cambridge University Press.

Sticht, T. G. (1972). Learning by listening. In J. B. Carroll & R. O. Freedle (Eds.), *Language comprehension and the acquisition of knowledge.* New York: Halsted Press.

Stinson, L. & Ickes, W. (1992). Empathic accuracy in interactions of male friends vs. male strangers. *Journal of Personality and Social Psychology, 62* (5), 787-797.

Stoffer, T H. & Oertcr, R. (2005). Gegenstand der Musikpsychologie und ihrer theoretischen und methodischen Ansätze. In T. H. Stoffer & R. Oerter (Hrsg.), *Allgemeine Musik-psychologie. Enzyklopädie der Psychologie, Themenbereich D, Serie VII, Band 1* (S. 1-69). Göttingen: Hogrefe.

Stone, V. E., Baron-Cohen, S., & Knight, R. T. (1998). Frontal lobe contributions to theory of mind. *Journal of Cognitive Neuroscience, 10,* 640-656.

Stricker, L. J. & Rock, D. A. (1990). Interpersonal competence, Social Intelligence, and general ability. *Personality and Individual Differences, 11* (8), 833-839.

Suedfeld, P. (1994). Cognitive complexity. In R. J. Sternberg (Ed.), *Encyclopedia of human intelligence* (pp. 286-291). New York Macmillan.

Sundberg, N. (1966). A method for studying sensitivity to implied meanings. Gawein *Tijdschrift voor Psychologie, 15* (1), 1-8.

Surprenant, A. M., & Watson, C. S. (2001). Individual differences in the processing of speech and nonspeech sounds by normal-hearing listeners. *The Journal of the Acoustical Society of America, 110* (4), 2085-2095.

Süß, H.-M. (1996). *Intelligenz, Wissen und Problemlösen. Kognitive Voraussetzungen für erfolgreiches Handeln bei computersimulierten Problemen.* Schriftenreihe Lehr- und Forschungstexte Psychologie (Folge 5). Göttingen: Hogrefe.

Süß, H.-M. (1999). *Kognitive Entwicklung im Alter.* Vortragsmanuskript zum Habilitation-Colloquium am 6. Dezember 1995 vor dem gemeinsamen Ausschuß der Fakultät für Philosophie, Psychologie und Erziehungswissenschaften unter der Fakultät für Sozialwissenschaften der Universität Mannheim.

Süß, H.-M. (2001). Prädiktive Validität der Intelligenz im schulischen und außerschulischen Bereich. In E. Stern & J. Guthke (Eds.), *Perspektiven der Intelligenzforschung* (pp. 109-135). Lengerich: Pabst Science Publishers.

Süß, H.-M. (2006). Eine Intelligenz; viele Intelligenzen? Neuere Intelligenztheorien im Widerstreit. In H. Wagner, *Intellektuelle Hochbegabung. Aspekte der Diagnostik und Beratung*. Tagungsband. Bad Honnef: K. H. Bock.

Süß, H.-M. & Beauducel, A. (2005). Faceted models of intelligence. In O. Wilhelm & R. Engle, *Understanding and measuring intelligence* (pp. 313-332). Thousand Oaks, CA: Sage.

Süß, H.-M., Oberauer, K., Wittmann, W. W., Wilhelm, O., & Schulze, R. (2002). Working-memory capacity explains reasoning ability - and a little bit more. *Personality and Individual Differences, 30*, 261-288.

Süß, H.-M., Seidel, K., & Weis, S. (2007). *The Social Intelligence Test Magdeburg (SIM) – An New Multidimensional, Persormance-based Measure of Sicoal Intelligence*. Magdeburg: Otto-von-Guericke University Magdeburg, Department of Psychology, Division of Psychological Methods, Psychological Assessment and Evluation Research.

Süß, H.-M., Seidel, K., & Weis, S. (2008). *The Magdeburg Test of Social Intelligence (MTSI)*. Otto-von-Guericke University Magdeburg, Germany, Department of Psychology, Division of Psychological Methods, Psychological Assessment and Evaluation Research.

Süß, H.-M., Weis, S., & Seidel, K. (2005). Soziale Kompetenzen. In H. Weber & T. Rammsayer (Hrsg.), *Handbuch der Persönlichkeitspsychologie und Differentiellen Psychologie, (Reihe Handbuch der Psychologie)* (S. 350-362). Göttingen: Hogrefe.

Tagiuri, R. (1969). Person perception. In G. Lindzey & E. Aronson, *The handbook of social psychology* (Vol. 3). Menlo Park, CA: Addison-Wesley Publishing Company.

Tanaka, J. S. (1993). Multifaceted conceptions of fit in structural equation models. In K. A. Bollen & J. S. Long (Eds.), *Testing structural equation models* (pp. 10–39). Newbury Park, CA: Sage.

Tangney, J. P., Miller, R. S., Flicker, L., & Barlow, D. H. (1996). Are shame, guilt, and embarrassment distinct emotions? *Journal of Personality and Social Psychology, 70*, 1256–1269.

Tartter, V. C. (1980). Happy talk: Perceptual and acoustic effects of smiling on speech. *Percept. Psychophys., 27*, 24–27.

Tenopyr, M. L. (1967). Symbolic tests as predictors of high-school grades. *Educational and Psychological Measurement, 27*, 385-391.

Thomson, G. H. (1939). *The factor analysis of human ability*. London: University of London Press.

Thorndike, E. L. (1920). Intelligence and its use. *Harper's Magazine, 140*, 227-235.

Thorndike, R. L. (1936). Factor analysis of social and abstract intelligence. *Journal of Educational Psychology, 27*, 231-233.

Thorndike, R. L. & Stein, S. (1937). An evaluation of the attempts to measure Social Intelligence. *Psychological Bulletin, 34*(5), 275-285.

Thurstone, L. L. (1938). *Primary mental abilities*. Chicago: University of Chicago Press.

Thurstone, L. L. (1947). *Multiple factor analysis*. Chicago: University of Chicago.

Tomkins, S. S. (1962). Affect, Imagery. Consciousness (Vol. 1). New York: Springer Publishing.

Tooby, J. & Cosmides, L. (1992). Cognitive adaptations for social exchange (Chapt. 3). In J. H. Barkow, L. Cosmides, & J. Tooby (Eds.). *The adapted mind. Evolutionary Psychology and the generation of culture*. New York: Oxford University Press.

Trehub, S. (2003). The developmental origins of musicality. *Nat. Neurosci. 6*, 669-673.

Turner, M. L. & Engle, R. W. (1989). Is working memory capacity task dependent? *Journal of Memory and Language, 28*, 127-154.

Urban, D. & Mayerl, J. (2003). Wie viele Fälle werden gebraucht? Ein Monte-Carlo-Verfahren zur Bestimmung ausreichender Stichprobengrößen und Teststärken (power) bei Strukturgleichungsanalysen mit kategorialen Indikatorvariablen. *ZA-Information, 53*, 41-69.

Van Rooy, D. L., Dilchert, S., Viswesvaran, C., & Ones, D. S. (2006). Multiplying Intelligences: Are general, emotional, and Practical Intelligences equal? In K. R. Murphy (Ed.), *A Critique of Emotional Intelligence: What are the problems and how can they be fixed?* Mahwah, NJ: Lawrence Erlbaum Associates.

Van Rooy, D. L. & Viswesvaran, C. (2004). Emotional Intelligence: A meta-analytic investigation of predictive validity and nomological net. *Journal of Vocational Behavior, 65,* 71-95.

Van Rooy, D. L., Viswesvaran, C., & Pluta, P. (2005). An evaluation of construct validity: What is this thing called Emotional Intelligence? *Human Performance, 18* (4), 445-162.

Vernon, P. E. (1933). Some characteristics of the good judge of personality. *Journal of Social Psychology, 4,* 42-57.

Vernon, P. E. (1950). The structure of human abilities. London: Methuen.

Vernon, P. A. (1983). Speed of information processing and general intelligence. *Intelligence, 7,* 53-70.

Viswesvaran, C. & Ones, D. S. (1999). Meta-analyses of fakability estimates: Implications for personality assessment. *Educational and Psychological Measurement, 59,* 197-210.

Wagner, R. J. (1986). The search for intraterrestrial intelligence. In R. J. Sternberg & R. K. Wagner (Eds.), *Practical Intelligence: Nature and origins of competence in the everyday world* (pp. 361-378). New York: Cambridge University Press.

Wagner, R. K. (1987). Tacit knowledge in everyday intelligent behavior. *Journal of Personality and Social Psychology, 52,* 1236-1247.

Wagner, R. J. (1994). Practical Intelligence. *European Journal of Psychological Assessment, 10* (2), 162-169.

Wagner, R. K. & Sternberg R. J. (1985): Practical Intelligence in real-world pursuits: The role of tacit knowledge. Journal of Personality and Social Psychology, 48, 436-458

Wagner, R. K. & Sternberg, R. J. (1991). *Tacit Knowledge Inventory for Managers.* San Antonio: The Psychological Corporation Harcourt Brace & Company.

Walker, R. E. & Foley, J. M. (1973). Social Intelligence: its history and measurement. *Psychological Reports, 33,* 839-864.

Wallbott, H. (1986). Person und Kontext: Zur relativen Bedeutung von mimischem Verhalten und Situationsinformationen im Erkennen von Emotionen. *Archiv für Psychologie, 138,* 211-231.

Wallbott, H. G. (1995). Kommunikation von Emotionen-Zur Bedeutung der Sprechstimme. *Wege zum Menschen, 47,* 201-214.

Wallbott, H. G. (1998). Bodily expression of emotion. *European Journal of Social Psychology, 28,* 879-896.

Wallbott, H. (Ed.). (2003). *Recognition of emotion in specific populations: Compensation, deficit or specific (dis)abilities?* Boston: Kluwer Academy Publishers.

Wallbott, H. G. & Scherer, K. R. (1986). Cues and channels in emotion recognition. *Journal of Personality and Social Psychology, 51,* 690-699.

Wallbott, H. G. & Scherer, K. R. (1988). *How universal and specific is emotional experience? - Evidence from 27 countries on five continents.* Hillsdale, NJ: Lawrence Erlbaum.

Wallbott, H. & Scherer, K. R. (1989). Assessing emotion by questionnaire. In R. Plutchik & H. Kellerman (Eds.), *Emotion: Theory, research, and experience. The measurement of emotion* (Vol. 4, pp. 55-82). New York: Academic Press.

Warwick, J. & Nettelbeck, T. (2004). Emotional Intelligence is. . .? *Personality and Individual Differences, 37,* 1091–1100.

Wason, P. C. (1968). Reasoning about a rule. *Quarterly Journal of Experimental Psychology, 20,* 273–281.

Waters, E. & Sroufe, L.A. (1983). Social competence as a developmental construct. *Developmental Review, 3,* 79-97.

Watson, B. U. (1991). Some relationships between intelligence and auditory processing. *Journal of Speech and Hearing Research, 34,* 621-627.

Watson, B. U. & Miller, T. K. (1993). Auditory perception, phonological processing, and reading ability / disability. *Journal of Speech and Hearing Research, 36,* 850-863.

Watson, C. S., Johnson, D. M., Lehman, J. R., Kelly, W. J., & Jensen, J. K. (1982). An auditory discrimination test battery. *The Journal of the Acoustical Society of America, Suppl., 171*, 73.

Watson, C. S. & Kidd, G. R. (2005). *Searching for sources of variance in speech recognition: Young adults with normal hearing.* Paper presented at the 149th Meeting of the Acoustical Society of America. Vancouver, Canada.

Weber, H. & Westmeyer, H. (1997). Emotionale Intelligenz: Kritische Analyse eines populären Konstrukts. Vortrag auf der 4. Arbeitstagung der Fachgruppe *Differentielle Psychologie, Persönlichkeitspsychologie und Psychologische Diagnostik* in Bamberg am 30.10.1997.

Weber, H. & Westmeyer, H. (1999). Emotionale Intelligenz: Kritische Analyse eines populären Konstrukts. *www.literaturkritik.de*, Nr. 2/99.

Weber, H. & Westmeyer, H. (2001). Die Inflation der Intelligenzen. In E. Stern & J. Guthke (Hrsg.), *Perspektiven der Intelligenzforschung* (pp. 251-266). Lengerich: Pabst.

Wechsler, D. (1958).*The Measurement and Appraisal of Adult Intelligence*. Williams and Wilkins, Baltimore.

Wechsler, D. (1964). *Die Messung der Intelligenz Erwachsener* (3rd ed.). Bern: Huber.

Wechsler, D. (1981). *Manual of the Wechsler Adult Intelligence Scale - Revised*. New York: Psychological Corporation.

Wedeck, J. (1947). The relationship between personality and 'psychological ability.' *British Journal of Psychology, 37*, 133-151.

Weiner, B. (1986). *A attributional theory of motivation and emotion*. New York: Springer.

Weis, S. (2002). Facets of Social Intelligence - Cognitive performance measures in a multitrait-multimethod design study. Universität Mannheim.

Weis, S. (2008). *Theory and Measurement of Social Intelligence as a Cognitive Performance Construct*. Doctoral dissertation. Otto von GuerickeUniversität Magdeburg, Germany.

Weis, S., Seidel, K., & Süß, H.-M. (2006). Messkonzepte sozialer Intelligenz – Literaturübersicht und Ausblick. In R. Schulze & R. D. Roberts (Hrsg.), *Emotionale Intelligenz. Ein internationales Handbuch* (S. 213-234). Göttingen: Hogrefe.

Weis, S. & Süß, H.-M. (2007). Reviving the search for Social Intelligence. *Personality and Individual Differences, 42*, 3-14.

White, G. M. (1985). Premises and purposes in a Solomon Islands ethnopsychology. In G. M. White & J. Kirkpatrick, *Person, self, and experience: exploring Pacific ethnopsychologies* (pp. 328–366). Berkeley, CA: University of California Press.

White, G. M. (2000). Representing emotional meaning: Category, metaphor, schema, discourse. In M. Lewis & J. M. Haviland-Jones (Eds.), *Handbook of emotions* (2nd ed., pp. 30-44). New York: The Guilford Press.

White, W. B. (1954). Visual and auditory closure. *Journal of Experimental Psychology, 48*, 234-240.

Whiten, A. (1991). *Natural theories of mind*. Oxford: Basil Blackwell.

Widaman, K. F. (1993). Common factor analysis versus principal component analysis: Differential bias in representing model parameters? *Multivariate Behavioral Research, 28*, 263-311.

Wiggins, J. S. (1979). A psychological taxonomy of trait-descriptive terms: The interpersonal domain. *Journal of Personality and Social Psychology, 37*, 395–412.

Wiggins, J. S. (1991). Agency and communion as conceptual coordinates for the understanding and measurement of interpersonal behavior. In W. M. Grove & D. Ciccetti (Eds.), *Thinking clearly about psychology: Vol. 2. Personality and psychopathology* (pp. 89-113). Minneapolis, MN: University of Minnesota Press.

Wiggins, J. S. (1996). An informal history of the international circumplex tradition. *Journal of Personality Assessment, 66*, 217-233.

Wiggins, J. S. & Trobst, K. K. (1997). When is a circumplex an "interpersonal circumplex"? The case of supportive actions. In R. Plutchik & H. R. Conte (Eds.), *Circumplex models of personality and emotions (Chapt. 3)*. Washington, DC: American Psychological Association.

Wilhelm, O. (2005). Measures of Emotional Intelligence: practice and standards. In R. Schulze & R. D. Roberts (Eds.), *Emotional Intelligence. An international Handbook*. Göttingen: Hogrefe.

Willingham, D. T. (2005). Visual auditory, and kinesthetic learners need visual, auditory, and koinesthetic instruction? *American Educator, Summer, 31-35,* 44.

Wing, H. D. (1948). Tests of musical ability and appreciation. *British Journal of Psychology Monograph Supplement, 27,* 88.

Witte, E. H. (2005). *Soziale Beziehungen, Gruppen- und Intergruppenprozesse.* Hamburg: Universität Hamburg, Arbeitsbereich Sozialpsychologie.

Wittmann, W. W. (1988). Multivariate reliability theory. Principles of symmetry and successful validation strategies. In J. R. Nesselroade & R. B. Cattell (Eds.), *Handbook of multivariate experimental psychology* (pp. 505-560). New York: Plenum.

Wittmann, W. W. & Süß, H.-M. (1999). Investigating the paths between working memory, intelligence, knowledge, and complex problem solving performances via Brunswik-symmetry. In P. L. Ackerman, P. C. Kyllonen & R. D. Roberts (Eds.), *Learning and individual Differences: Process, Trait, and Content Determinants* (pp 77-108). Washington, D.C.: American Psychological Association.

Wong, C. - M. T., Day, J. D., Maxwell, S. E., & Meara, N. M. (1995). A multitrait-multimethod study of academic and Social Intelligence in college students. *Journal of Educational Psychology, 87* (1), 117-133.

Woodcock, R. W. (1998). Extending Gf-Gc theory into practice. In J. J. McArdle & R. W. Woodcock (Eds.), *Human cognitive abilities in theory and practice.* Mahwah, NJ: Lawrence Erlbaum.

Woodcock, R. W., McGrew, K. S., & Mather, N. (2001). Woodcock-Johnson III Tests of Cognitive Abilities. Itasca, IL: Riverside Publishing.

Woodrow, H. (1939). The common factors in fifty-two mental tests. *Psychometrika, 4,* 99-108.

Young, A. W., Perrett, D. I., Calder, A. J., Sprengelmeyer, R., & Ekman, P. (2002). *Facial expressions of emotion: stimuli and tests (FEEST).* Bury St. Edmunds: Thames Valley Test Company.

Zatorre, R. J. & Peretz, I. (Eds.). (2001). The biological foundations of music. *Ann. New York Acad. Sci, 930* (Special Issue).

Zeidner, M., Matthews, G., & Roberts, R. D. (2001). Slow down, you move too fast: Emotional Intelligence remains an "elusive" intelligence. *Emotion, 1,* 265-275.

Zeidner, M., Matthews, G., Roberts, R. D., & MacCann, C. (2003). Development of Emotional Intelligence: Towards a multi-level investment model. *Human Development, 46,* 69-96.

Zuckerman, M. & Larrance, D. T. (1979). Individual differences in perceived encoding and decoding abilities. In R. Rosenthal (Ed.), *Skill in nonverbal communication: Individual differences* (pp. 170-195). Cambridge, MA: Oelschlaeger, Gunn & Hain, Publishers, Inc.

Zwick, W. R. & Velicer, W. F. (1986). Comparison of five rules for determining the number of components to retain. *Psychological Bulletin, 99,* 432-442.

Appendices

A Preparation and Implementation of Studies

A.1 Computer Settings

- Deactivate anti-virus programs; without deactivation, the software will be susceptible to interruptions
- Additional audio settings required for the task "masked words": deactivate 1 sterical; set ups and downs to second line on the right
- Mouse speed: set to middle speed
- Screen: set to 16 Bit

A.2 Personality Profiles of the Target Persons

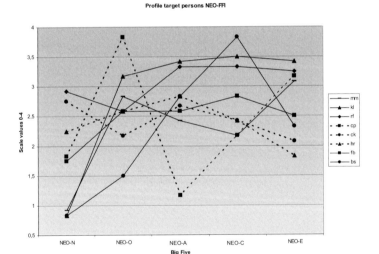

Profile target persons NEO-FFI

Note. N=Neuroticism; O=Openness; A= Agreeableness; C=Conscienciousness; E=Extraversion

Profile target persons IIP-C

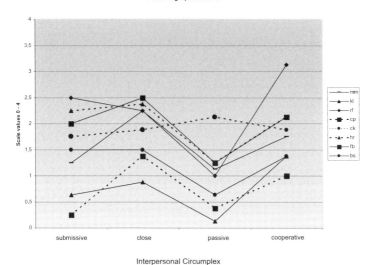

Interpersonal Circumplex

Note. IIP-C: Inventory of interpersonal problems- Circumplex scales

B   Additional Results and References – First Study

B.1   Social Intelligence

B.1.1   Psychometrics of different scoring modi in the sopcial understanding tasks

	Item number	Item mean (range)	r_{it}-range	Cronbach's Alpha
Weighted difference scores, all types of items				
written	19	.18 [-.26; .72] 1.24 [-3.11; 0]; SD=0.57	.20 - .61	.80
auditory	21	.12 [-.22; .71] -1.25 [-2.88; -.29]; SD=.47	.15 - .52	.73
pictorial	15	.10 [-.19; .83] -.83 [-2.17; -.20]; SD=.40	.05 - .51	.65
video-based	41	.08 [-.23; .85] -1.47 [-2.46; -.93]; SD=.35	.09 - .43	.77
Weighted difference scores, only rating scales				
written	18	.19 [-26; .72] -1.35[-3.31; 0]; SD=0.59	.21 - .61	.80
auditory	20	.12 [-.22; .71] -1.33 [-3.05; -.33]; SD=.49	.09 - .54	.73

	Item number	Item mean (range)	r_{it}-range	Cronbach's Alpha
pictorial	6	. 27 [.03; .74] -.91 [-4.00; 0]; SD=.63	.17 - .74	.69
video-based	40	.08 [-.23; .85] -1.52 [-2.52; -.96]; SD=.36	.09 - .43	.77
Deviation points				
written	18	.14 [-.17; .45]	.08 - .54	.75
auditory	14	.14 [-.15 - .49]	.03 - .61	.71
pictorial	7	.14 [-.07; .50]	.11 - .54	.52
video-based	21	.11 [-.19; .50]	.06 - .48	.73
Right–wrong scores				
written	16	.10 [-.14; .40]	.06 - .50	.65
auditory	14	.13 [-.18; .52]	.06 - .54	.67
pictorial	6	.14 [-.12; .44]	.06 - .45	.49
video-based	19	.10 [-.18; .41]	.07 - .41	.69
Proportion-based consensus scoring				
written	16	.15 [-.14; .48]	.11 - .58	.72
auditory	14	.15 [-.15; .47]	.03 - .51	.69
pictorial	6	.16 [-.07; .49]	.05 - .55	.58
video-based	17	.08 [-.15; - .41]	.07 - .39	.60

Note. In order to make the scores comparable to the alternative scoring procedures, the items were z-standardized before summarizing them to a score. In addition, with z-transformation, individual answer tendencies (e.g. preference for extreme answers) are balanced. The scores presented in the following table therefore diverge from their original deviation scale (zero to -5 or -6 respectively). A comparison score with the original metric to the original score is provided for the weighted target scores below the standardized values. r_{it}-range= Item-total correlation range; right–wrong scores and deviation scores: item number was kept as large as possible to have a valid comparison to deviation scores; target scores: exact deviation from the target's answer, weighted by the deviation that was possible in each item; deviation points: right answer is scored with 2 points, deviation of 1 with 1 point, all other 0 points; right – wrong scores: only the exact correspondence with the targets answer is scored as 1 point, all other zero; Two persons were excluded because of lacking commitment (large deviations from mean score).

B.1.2 Selected Items in Social Understanding Scenario Tasks

Percent selected (number)	Rating	Open		Multiple choice
written	35.29 % (18/51)	50 %	(2/4)	0 % (0/9)
auditory	26.79 % (15/56)	45.45 %	(5/11)	0 % (0/1)
picture	46.67 % (7/15)	0 %	(0/3)	22.22 % (2/9)
video	32.86 % (23/70)	20 %	(1/5)	9 % (1/11)

	Cognition	Emotion		Relationship /Behavior
written	25 % (1/4)	48.39 %	(15/31)	13.79 % (4/29)
auditory	50 % (5/10)	32.5 %	(13/40)	11.11 % (2/18)
picture	0 % (0/4)	50 %	(4/8)	33.33 % (5/15)
video	50 % (1/2)	46.15 %	(12/26)	20.69 % (12/58)

Note. The numbers represent proportions of selected items; the total number of ratings is listed in parentheses. The higher the proportion of selected items, the better this type of item construction worked.

B.1.3 Intercorrelations Between the Social Intelligence Tasks

	SPw	SPw (corr.)	SPa	SPa (corr)	SPp	SFp	SMw	SMa	SMp	SMf	SUw	SUa	SUp	SUf
SPw corr	.94**	1.00												
SPa	.00	.02	1.00											
SPa corr	-.02	.04	.92**	1.00										
SPp	.19	.18	.06	.05	1.00									
SFp	-.03	-.05	.18	.08	.41**	1.00								
SMw	-.25*	-.17	-.07	.06	.0	-.09	1.00							
SMa	-.05	-.05	.04	.14	.05	-.01	.51**	1.00						
SMp	-.11	-.11	.10	.11	-.05	.05	.19	.09	1.00					
SMf	-.18	-.15	.06	.10	-.25*	-.16	.34**	.33**	.22*	1.00				
SUw	-.02 / *-.06*	.04 / *-.01*	-.05 / *-.06*	-.01 / *.00*	-.14 / *-.13*	.02 / *-.03*	.28** / *.33***	.23* / *.26***	.03 / *-.02*	-.08 / *-.11*	1.00			
SUa	-.09 / *-.16*	-.11 / *-.17*	-.02 / *-.05*	.01 / *-.02*	-.12 / *-.09*	.03 / *.09*	.17 / *.23**	.16 / *.27***	.17 / *.10*	-.04 / *-.14*	.59**	1.00		
SUp	.04 / *.11*	.01 / *.07*	.23* / *.02*	.16 / *-.02*	.06 / *.09*	.01 / *-.04*	.05 / *.09*	.41** / *.36***	.02 / *.06*	-.04 / *-.08*	.25*	.18	1.00	
SUf	-.07 / *-.10*	-.03 / *-.07*	.13 / *.05*	.20* / *.16*	-.09 / *-.12*	-.08 / *-.10*	.23* / *.27***	.22* / *.23**	.06 / *.10*	-.07 / *.10*	.53**	.60**	.32**	1.00
SUPk	-.11 / *-.05*	-.09 / *-.07*	-.11 / *-.07*	-.02 / *-.05*	.07 / *-.18*	-.12 / *-.03*	-.03 / *.27***	-.07 / *.27***	-.07 / *.08*	-.27** / *.10*	.06	-.02	.00	-.08

Note. In italics: consensus-scored variables; SPw=Social perception- written; SPw corr=Social perception-written, baseline corrected (readspeed); SPa=Social perception-auditory; SPa corr=Social perception-auditory, baseline corrected (simple reaction time); SPp= Social perception-pictorial; SPf=Social perception-video-based; SMw=Social memory-written; SMa=Social memory-auditory; SMp=Social memory-pictorial; SMf=Social memory-video-based; SUw=Social understanding-written; SUa=Social understanding-auditory; SUp=Social understanding-pictorial; SUf=Social understanding-video-based (videos); SUPk=Social understanding-personality

B.1.4 Correlations Between the Social Intelligence Variables and the BIS Cells

	B_Sf	B_Sv	B_Sn	B_Mf	B_Mv	B_Mn	B_Rf	B_Rv	B_Rn
SP written	.03	-.35**	-.20*	-.06	-.30**	-.07	-.22*	-.19	-.08
SP audio	-.13	-.01	-.01	-.02	-.15	.09	.09	.13	.13
SP pictures	-.14	-.33**	-.09	-.04	-.09	.03	.01	-.17	-.03
SP film	-.22*	-.11	-.04	-.14	-.04	-.13	-.04	-.17	.03
SM written	-.02	.27**	.11	.00	.46**	.14	.12	.40**	.15
SM audio	-.05	.36**	.10	.10	.30**	.15	-.05	.31**	.08
SM pictures	-.05	.03	.04	.11	.26**	.22*	-.14	-.03	.08
SM film	.14	.28**	-.04	.03	.18	.10	-.08	.12	-.12
SU written	-.04	.13	.00	-.02	.05	-.10	-.05	.18	.02
SU audio	-.14	.10	-.10	.12	.16	-.17	-.10	.02	-.01
SU pictures	-.07	.01	-.06	-.01	.06	.02	-.14	-.05	-.09
SU film	-.07	.07	-.08	.11	.04	.02	.05	.10	.02

Note. Spearman correlations; ** Correlation is significant at p< 0.01 (2-sided); * Correlation is significant at p< 0.05 (2-sided); listwise deletion; N= 101; SP=Social perception; SM=Social memory; SU=Social understanding; B_ =Berlin Intelligence Structure Test; Sf=BIS speed-figural; Sv=BIS speed-verbal; Sn=BIS speed-numerical; Mf=BIS memory-figural; Mv=BIS memory-verbal; Mn=BIS memory-numerical; Rf=BIS reasoning-figural; Rv=BIS reasoning-verbal; Rn=BIS reasoning-numerical

B.2 Auditory Intelligence

B.2.1 Intercorrelations between the Auditory Intelligence Tasks

	MA1	AIT-P	MA3	RH	FES	MA2	MA4	MA5	RV	AU
Detection of repeated tones (MA1)	1									
Pitch discrimination (AIT-P)	.51**	1								
Tonal figures (MA3)	.51**	.37**	1							
Rhythm reproduction (RH)	.36**	.39**	.34**	1						
Familiar environmental sounds (FES)	.15	.22*	.17	.20*	1					
Tonal analogies (MA2)	.18*	.07	.19*	.14	-.01	1				
Tonal series (MA4)	.64**	.54**	.53**	.33**	.25**	.26**	1			
Chord decomposition (MA5)	.44**	.28**	.36**	.33**	.03	.07	.38**	1		
Detection of repeated voices (RV)	.00	.02	.19*	.12	.03	-.11	-.03	.04	1	
Audiobook (AU)	.06	.12	.09	.08	.15	.06	.17	.08	.01	1
Disarranged sentences (DS)	.20*	.22*	.28**	.29**	.08	.10	.30**	.16	.08	.23**

Note. Spearman correlations, listwise deletion, N=121; **Correlation is significant at p< 0.01 (2-sided); *Correlation is significant at p< 0.05 (2-sided)

C Additional Results and References - Second Study

C.1 BIS Model Second Study (S2)

C.1.1 Operation Structure

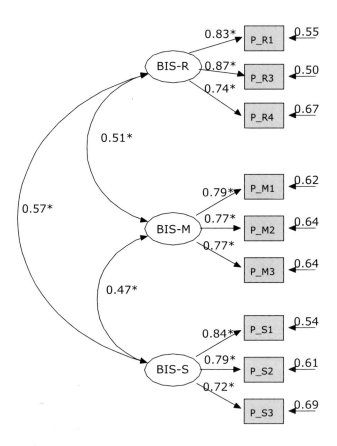

Note. Model characteristics: Chi²= 37.66; df= 24; p= .038; CFI= .98; SRMR=.041;
RMSEA= .057; CI (90%)= (.014, .091)

C.1.2 Content Structure

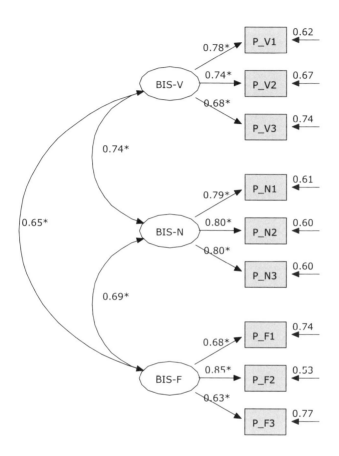

Note. ML estimation; Model characteristics: Chi²= 63.171; df= 24; p= .000; CFI= .94; SRMR=.059; RMSEA= .097; CI (90%)= (.068; .126)

Tanja Rabl

Private Corruption and its Actors
Insights into the Subjective Decision Making Processes

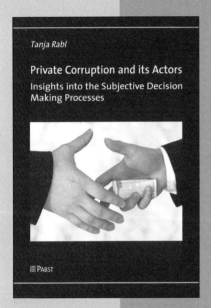

The present book deals with private corruption, that is, corruption in and between companies. It focuses on the subjective decision making processes of corrupt actors.

Based on a thorough literature review on the corruption phenomenon focusing on private corruption, a perspective neglected up to now, the author derives the central research questions: What makes decision makers in companies act corruptly? Which motivational, volitional, emotional, and cognitive components do play a role? How does their interplay finally lead to corrupt action? To answer these questions, the author develops a model of corrupt action. It is empirically validated using an experimental simulation design that includes a business game. Moreover, the work examines the influence of a number of important personal and situational factors on the model of corrupt action. It gives a picture of the frequently used reasons for corrupt and non-corrupt behavior and outlines the most frequently used rationalization strategies of corrupt actors.

The study does not only make a contribution to existing research, but also has important practical implications. The empirically validated model of corrupt action offers a useful tool for companies to derive suitable measures for the prevention and deterrence of corruption. The author gives recommendations for (human resource) management and some hints as to which measures may be used to influence the critical person-based determinants of corruption.

PABST SCIENCE PUBLISHERS
Eichengrund 28
D-49525 Lengerich
Tel. ++ 49 (0) 5484-308
Fax ++ 49 (0) 5484-550
pabst.publishers@t-online.de
www.pabst-publishers.de
www.psychologie-aktuell.com

308 pages, Price: 20,- Euro
ISBN 978-3-89967-525-2